THE LIFE OF LIVES

THE LIFE OF LIVES

FURTHER STUDIES IN THE LIFE OF CHRIST

BY

F. W. FARRAR, D.D., F.R.S.

DEAN OF CANTERBURY AND DEPUTY
CLERK OF THE CLOSET TO THE QUEEN

"O æterna Veritas, et vera Caritas, et cara Æternitas, tu es Deus meus." St. Aug.

> "Yea through life, death, through sorrow, and through sinning
> Christ shall suffice me, for He hath sufficed ;
> Christ is the end, for Christ was the beginning,
> Christ the beginning, for the end is Christ."—F. W. H. Myers.

"The longer I live the more I feel that Christianity does not consist in any particular system of Church Government, or in any credal statement, but that Christianity is Christ."—Rt. Hon. W. E. Gladstone.

NEW YORK

DODD, MEAD & COMPANY

1915

2000 - 838

CONJUGI

DILECTISSIMÆ ET FIDELISSIMÆ,

LABORUM, FELICITATIS, DOLORUM,

PER XL ANNOS PARTICIPI,

HUNC LIBRUM

D. D. D.

FREDERICUS GULIELMUS FARRAR

III Non. Apr. MDCCCC.

PREFACE.

TWENTY-SIX years ago I was led by "God's unseen Providence, which men nickname 'Chance,'" to write and publish a "Life of Christ." It was based on long study, primarily of the Four Gospels and the Old and New Testaments, and, next, of all the sources of knowledge open to me, from the most ancient to the most modern. Manifold as were the imperfections of my work—of which no one is more conscious than I am myself—the book was found useful, and has not only been read in all parts of the English-speaking world, but has also been translated into many languages—even into Japanese. It has been most widely disseminated in two translations throughout the whole of the Russian Empire, and has brought me many expressions of gratitude alike from English-speaking readers and from foreigners of every rank. I desire to record my humble thankfulness to God for permitting me to render this service—however small—to what I believe from my heart to be the cause of Righteousness and Truth.

Since my "Life of Christ" was published, much criticism, alike favourable and adverse, has been written upon it. But with perfect readiness to modify any statement which can be disproved, and to alter any error which can be demonstrated, I have seen no reason to correct a single conclusion of the smallest vital importance. It is therefore needless for me, and it would be superfluous, to attempt to re-narrate the external incidents in the mortal days of the Saviour of Mankind. In some pages, however, the subject has obliged me to revert to considerations on which I have already dwelt.

The object of the present book is different. It deals with questions of high importance, which the Gospels suggest, and aims at deepening the faith and brightening the hope in Christ of all who read it honestly. "*Sis sus, sis Divus, sum Caltha, et non tibi spiro.*"

And so I send it forth with the humble petition, offered " with bent head and beseeching hand," that He who deigned to bless my former efforts will bless this effort also, to the furtherance of His Kingdom, and the good of His Church.

He came to " holy and humble men of heart "; and those who believe in Him, and would fain go to Him —and to Him only—for knowledge and for wisdom, will say with St. Paul: " To me it is a very small thing to be judged by man's brief day." * They desire no approval, save that of Him whose "*Ite*" and " *Venite* " shall settle all questions and controversies for ever.

* 1 Cor. iv. 3. Ἐμοὶ δὲ εἰς ἐλάχιστόν ἐστιν ἵνα ὑφ' ὑμῶν ἀνακριθῶ ἢ ὑπὸ ἀνθρωπίνης ἡμέρας.

CONTENTS.

CHAPTER VI.

THE CLAIMS OF JESUS AND THE SPELL HE EXERCISED.

PAGE

CHAPTER VII.

THE HUMAN EDUCATION OF JESUS.

CHAPTER VIII.

THE FIRST ANECDOTE.

CHAPTER IX.

LESSONS OF THE UNRECORDED YEARS.

CHAPTER X.

THE HOME AT NAZARETH.

CHAPTER XI.

THE FAMILY AT NAZARETH.

CHAPTER XII.

THE CONDITION OF THE WORLD.

CHAPTER XIII.

THE STATE OF RELIGION IN PALESTINE.

CHAPTER XIV.

THE MESSIANIC HOPE.

CHAPTER XV.

JOHN THE BAPTIST.

CHAPTER XVI.

THE BAPTISM OF JESUS.

CHAPTER XVII.

THE TEMPTATION.

CHAPTER XVIII.

SCENES OF CHRIST'S MINISTRY.

CHAPTER XIX.

CHRIST'S METHODS OF EVANGELISATION.

CHAPTER XX.

THE FORM OF CHRIST'S TEACHING.

CHAPTER XXI.

THE FORM OF CHRIST'S TEACHING (*continued*).

CHAPTER XXII.

THE SUBSTANCE OF CHRIST'S TEACHING.

CHAPTER XXIX.

THE APOSTLES.

CHAPTER XXX.

ST. PETER, ST. JOHN, AND JUDAS.

CHAPTER XXXI.

THE APOSTOLIC COMMISSION.

CHAPTER XXXII.

ORDER OF EVENTS IN OUR LORD'S LIFE.

CHAPTER XXXIII.

THE CLOSING DAYS.

CHAPTER XXXIV.

THE LAST SUPPER.

CHAPTER XXXV.

GETHSEMANE.

CHAPTER XXXVI.

THE TRIALS BEFORE THE JEWS.

CHAPTER XXXVII.

THE TRIAL BEFORE PILATE.

CHAPTER XXXVIII.

THE SUFFERINGS OF JESUS.

CHAPTER XXXIX.

THE RIGHT VIEW OF CHRIST'S SUFFERINGS.

CHAPTER XL.

THE ATONEMENT.

CHAPTER XLI.

THE RESURRECTION.

CHAPTER XLII.

THE ASCENSION.

CHAPTER XLIII.

THE FINAL ISSUES.

THE LIFE OF LIVES.

CHAPTER 1.

THE DIVINE BIRTH.

"Who . . . emptied Himself, taking the form of a slave, being made in the likeness of man."—Phil. ii. 7.

"The unfathomable depths of the divine counsels were moved; the fountains of the great deep were broken up; the healing of the nations was issuing forth; but nothing was seen on the surface of human society but this slight rippling of the water."—ISAAC WILLIAMS, *The Nativity*.

To the vast majority of true Christians the unalterable belief that Jesus Christ was the Son of God, the Saviour of the World, comes from the witness of the Spirit in their hearts. It is not mainly derived from any one process of argument, or even from the convergence of many different lines of demonstration. Confluent streams of probability may have helped to swell the current of their conviction, but the main reason why their faith remains unshaken by any doubt is because they *know* Christ and are known of Him. The light which lighteth every man that is born into the world came from Him, and was concentrated upon Him in the fulness of its illuminating splendour. There are many whose whole life is lived by faith in the Son of God. They would say with St. Paul: "With me to live is Christ." We may indeed lose this blessed certainty—

> "For when we in our viciousness grow hard,
> O misery on't, the wise gods seal our eyes,
> In our own filth drop our clear judgments, make us
> Adore our errors, laugh at us while we strut
> To our confusion."

But "Belief lives in us through Conduct," [*] and while an immoral Deism produces men like Aretino and Marat, the faith in Christ has produced thousands of such saints as Francis of Assisi and Vincent de Paul. To all whose daily experience is that Christ is with them, and within them, belief has become part of their inmost being. With a power which transcends all earthly knowledge, the Spirit beareth witness with their spirits that they are "sons of God," because they have been admitted into the Brotherhood of Him who was *the* Son of God. To them He is not only "*Verax*" and "*Verus*," but "*ipsa Veritas.*"

To those who abound in this beautitude of certainty—and they are, thank God, "a great multitude whom no man can number"—argument has become needless. We may modify the words of the Poet and say that—

> "In such high hours
> Of inspiration from the living God,
> Thought is not, in devotion it expires."

But there are millions who have never attained to this experience. To us it seems as though man lived in the very midst of miracles—miracles stupendous, innumerable, incessant. To us "the starry heavens above," and still more "the moral law within," are a perpetual miracle; nor would the supernaturalness of those miracles be to us diminished, even though every phenomenon of the material, moral, and spiritual Universe could be directly explained by what are called "natural" laws. To us the outer Universe is but an atom in God's infinitude, or, as the Rabbis expressed it, "God (who in Talmudic literature is often called Maqôm or 'Space') is not the Universe (Ha-Maqôm), but all the Universe is in God." [†] To us the natural is itself a supernatural phenomenon. Nature is but a name to express the laws which God has impressed upon His Universe.

[*] Schleiermacher.
[†] See Hershon, *Genesis acc. to the Talmud*, p. 170.

Those who hold these views—those who think not only that God *is* but that He "worketh hitherto"; those who believe in God's perpetual Providence, and do not reduce Him to the Blind Fate of the Stoics, or the Supernal Indifference of the Epicureans; those who accept the words of Scripture that "He careth for us," and "is about our path, and about our bed, and spieth out all our ways"—constitute the immense majority of mankind, to whatever religion they may belong. We do not observe that such are, in any respect, less wise, less learned, or less intellectually clear-sighted, nor have they rendered fewer services to mankind, than the minority who take upon them to set aside such views as childish and obsolete superstitions. In this majority are numbered all the most supremely great of those who, compared with their brethren, have been "among the molehills as mountains, and among the thistles as forest trees." In all the histories of the nations you can scarcely find one man of epoch-making eminence who has not believed in the God who is not far from every one of us, since in Him we live, and move, and have our being. Are we not, then, entitled to say with confidence, as all the best, greatest, and wisest of men have believed, that God has *not* resigned His care for the creatures of His hand to the exclusive working of what are called "natural laws"? *Securus judicat orbis terrarum.*

Again, may we not urge a second argument upon those who, because of the supposed invariableness of natural laws, cannot conceive that God ever works, or has worked, in the affairs of man except in exact accordance with the observed order? May we not ask them to consider that miracles themselves are nothing but an outcome of that Natural Law which, after all, is but a partial synonym for the will of God? If it be perfectly within the power of man to make a machine which should, in unvarying sequence, push out, one by one, every number, from a unit to (say) ten millions, and then—simply by the pre-arranged construction of the machine itself—should skip a number, and go from ten million to ten million and *two*, how absurd is it to suppose that even the *apparent* violation, or supersession, of laws may not be due to the very laws themselves—just, for instance, as a balloon, very heavy and laden with human beings, mounts upwards by the very law of gravitation which seems to draw all objects downwards? To start, as sceptics have often done, with the dogma that "Miracles *do not*"—or even that "miracles *cannot*—happen" is surely short-sighted and unphilosophical; to say nothing of the fact that such an axiom sets aside masses of evidence—accumulated in age after age and still accumulating—that miracles (*i. e.*, events which apparently supersede or transcend the every-day order) *have* happened, and *do* happen continually. "Nature" is but a name for God's normal and continuous government; and "chance" is but a nickname for His unseen Providence. "What is disturbed by a miracle," said Professor Mozley, "is the mechanical expectation of a recurrence."* "Law I know; but what is this *necessity* but an empty shadow of my own mind's throwing?"†

Why, then, should the supernatural birth of the Saviour of the World appear to sceptics to be a difficulty so stupendous, and so insuperable, that it is only fit to be contemptuously set aside?‡ Is it wise to feel such confidence in arguments which, after all, convince very few, and which have *not* shaken the belief of men whose transcendent intellectual powers could be questioned by none? Are myriads of the most brilliant men of action and men of genius whom the world has ever seen, such utter fools that a sceptic, because of his own peculiar idiosyncrasy, may

---

* Mozley, *Bampton Lects.*, p. 56.   † Huxley, *Lay Sermons*, p. 158.

‡ It should be observed that, as Weber points out, the story of a Virgin-birth was not likely to have been invented by Jewish Christians, for it formed no part of the current Messianic expectation (*Die Lehren des Talmuds*, 339–342); and, even among the Jews, Is. vii. 14, was not understood in this sense.

sweep away, as though it were a mere contemptible nullity, the initial fact in the faith of Christians? If the Virgin-birth of the Saviour of Mankind had stood alone—if nothing had led up to it; if nothing had sprung from it; if the witnesses to it were untrustworthy liars, who were morally capable of having palmed off upon the world a conscious fiction—*then* doubt would have been natural. But when the event stands, as it does,—quite apart from religion,—as the central point of the destinies of mankind; when we see that all the history of the past led up to it, and that all the illimitable future was, and must still be, dominated by it; when we see how it fulfilled the prophecies and yearnings of Humanity among the heathen as well as among the Jewish race, and how it has been the germ of all that was best and greatest in the progress of the ages which have followed—the fact ceases to stand alone. Had "the man Christ Jesus" been but one of the millions—if He had been merely distinguished above His fellows by ordinary human greatness—doubt might have been excusable. But when we see in that Babe lying in the cradle One of whom all the Prophets had spoken, and One to whom ever since that Nativity—amid the intensification of all Light, and all Knowledge, and amid the undreamed-of splendour of immeasurable Progress—alike the humblest and the greatest of human intellects have looked;—when we see that (to use the words of the German historian whom a study of history converted to Christianity from unbelief) "Christ lifted the gate of the centuries off its hinges with His bleeding hand"—the case becomes far different. The greatness of Jesus, even if we regard Him simply as a man among men, not only transcends, but transcends inconceivably and immeasurably, the combination of all the forms and varieties of human greatness. The ages which have followed have all looked to

"Him first, Him last, Him midst, and without end."

As they have contemplated Him, in the Unity of the Father and the Holy Spirit, they have exclaimed, "Whom have we in heaven but Thee?" and as they have felt the penetrative, all-absorbing influence of His human personality, they have exclaimed, "There is none upon earth that I desire beside Thee." *

1. HISTORY has borne its witness to Him. The Jews, who in their decadence no longer listened to Moses and the Prophets, but to Sadducean Priests and posing Pharisees, fell into utter and immediate ruin in accordance with His prophecy. The grandeur of the Roman Empire was humbled to the dust, and vanished before Him. The Northern nations, abandoning their ignorance and savagery, knelt humbly before "The White Christ," and, conquerors though they were, accepted the religion of the Christians whom they had conquered. "In all my study of the ancient times," wrote the German historian Johann von Müller, "I have always felt the want of something, and it was not till I knew our Lord that all was clear to me; with Him there is nothing that I am not able to solve."

The great rulers have claimed their authority from Him alone, and have confessed His absolute pre-eminence. The first Christian Emperor wove upon the labarum of his armies His cross of shame; and it is set in jewels on the diadems of many kings. The oldest crown of Europe—the famous iron crown of Lombardy—was venerated most because it was believed to be made of an iron nail from the cross on Golgotha. "Bow thy head, Sicambrian," said St. Remigius to Clovis after the victory of Tolbiac; "burn what thou hast adored, adore what thou hast burned!" Godfrey of Bouillon, when crowned King of Jerusalem, would not wear a crown of gold where his Saviour had worn a crown of thorns. Rudolph of Hapsburg, founder of the great Empire of Germany, when no sceptre could be found amid the tumult of his coronation, grasped a crucifix and swore that *that* should be his sceptre. Napoleon, the last

* Ps. lxxiii. 25.

great conqueror of modern days, said in his exile, "I know men, and Jesus Christ is not a man. Superficial minds see a resemblance between Christ and the founders of empires and the gods of other religions. That resemblance does not exist. There is between Christ and all other religions whatsoever the distance of infinity : from the first day to the last He is the same—always the same, majestic, simple, infinitely firm and infinitely gentle. Between Him and whoever else in the world there is no possible term of comparison." *

2. POETRY is the choicest flower of all human thought ; and just as the greatest poets of the ancient world who *knew* God—like Isaiah, and Amos, and the Psalmists—had sung of the coming Christ, so, since He was born, all the supremest poets without exception—Dante, Shakespeare, Milton, Goethe, Wordsworth, Browning, Tennyson—have come to Him with their singing robes about them, and laid their garlands most humbly at His feet. Truly

> " Piety hath found
> Friends in the friends of Science, and true prayer
> Has flowed from lips wet with Castalian dews."

Nay, even in the ancient heathen world, supreme poets have stretched blind hands of faith and prayer to the Unknown Deliverer. Æschylus, sublimest of the Athenian tragedians, in his greatest drama, makes Hermes say to Prometheus : " Expect not at all any termination of this thy anguish till some one of the gods appear as a successor to thy toils, and be willing to go down into the unlighted Hades, and around the gloomy depths of Tartarus."† And Virgil, sweetest of all the Roman singers, wrote in his Fourth Eclogue a prophecy of the Golden Age which was at hand, and the Child whose manhood would inaugurate a reign of peace in a world of

---

* In a conversation with Genl. Bertrand, Comte de Montholon, *Récit de la Captiv. de l'Empereur Napoléon.*

† Æsch. *Prom.* v. 1026–1029.

beauty ; and this he wrote in such strains as almost elevated him to the rank of an inspired Seer.

3. PHILOSOPHY has occupied the minds of some of the loftiest of the human race, and it has been the lifelong pursuit of many a

> " Grey spirit, yearning in desire
> To follow knowledge, like a guiding star,
> Beyond the utmost bounds of human thought."

But these grave and earnest students of the problem of the world have often either sunk into despondency, like Zeno and Marcus Aurelius, for lack of the hope which Christ has inspired into the hearts of men ; or, like Plato, they have looked yearningly forward to some Unseen Deliverer whom as yet they knew not, though they were convinced of the awful necessity for His Advent. Kant used indignantly to repel every word spoken against the historic Saviour, and regarded himself as a mere bungler, interpreting Him as best he could.* "Philosophy," said Pico della Mirandola, " *seeks* truth. . . Religion *possesses* it." †

4. ART reveals to us the Unseen. It teaches us to see, and what to see, and to see *more* than we see with our bodily eyes; and since Christ was born, all the greatest Art in the world, without exception, has been consecrated to His glory. To Him have been reared those " Epic poems in stone," those glorious Churches and Cathedrals, shadowy with immortal memories, which make us exclaim,

> " They dreamt not of a perishable home
> Who thus could build ";

and under whose hallowed shade we feel that

> " Bubbles burst, and folly's dancing foam
> Melts if it cross the threshold."

To His glory the greatest of sculptors set free the impris- oned angels which, to his imagination, seemed to be strug-

---

* Vorowski, *Life of Kant*, p. 86.   † Pic. Mirand., *Opp.* 359.

gling in the blocks of unhewn marble; to His glory Giotto and Leonardo, Raphael and Luini, Vittore Pisano and Lorenzo di Credi, Giovanni Bellini and Carpaccio, Albrecht Dürer and Holbein—and with them the greatest of all the painters, down to our own Millais, and Burne-Jones, and Holman Hunt—have devoted the strongest and purest of their powers. For love of Him, and with no thought of gain, Fra Angelico and Sandro Botticelli painted their soft and silent pictures, even as, long centuries earlier, the poor and persecuted Christians of the Catacombs had made the walls of those dark corpse-crowded galleries bright with their emblems of Orpheus, the Dove, the Fish, the Vine, and the Fair Shepherd with the lamb or kid upon His shoulder. From the earliest dawn of the Gospel down to the present day, no pictures have been comparable in greatness to those in which the supremest artists have consecrated to the memory of Christ the glory of the fair colours, and the inspiration of hallowed thoughts.

5. And to take one other all-embracing sphere of human intellect, the sphere of SCIENCE, in that region, too, the most eminent human souls—men like Copernicus, Bacon, Leibnitz, Descartes, Haller, Pascal, Ray, Franklin, Herschell, Agassiz, Faraday, and many others—not losing sight of the Creator in the multitudinous marvels of His creatures, have looked to Christ as their Lord and their God. " A little Philosophie," as Bacon said, " inclineth a man's mind to Atheism, but depth in Philosophie bringeth men's minds about to religion." * Among the Coryphaei of Science two names stand supreme—Kepler and Newton. Kepler wrote of Christ with the profoundest reverence, and Newton—" the whitest of human souls " as well as one of the most richly endowed—raised his adoring eyes to heaven in uttermost simplicity, and sincerely believed in the Lord Jesus Christ with all his heart. The first mortal eyes which ever observed the transit of Venus were those of

* Bacon, *Essay* 16. *Of Atheisme.*

Jeremiah Horrocks, then a humble curate at Hoole. He hurried to his telescope in the intervals between three Sunday services, and, though his observation was of such consummate astronomical importance, he recorded in his diary—and the sentence is carved upon the tablet placed to his memory two centuries later in Westminster Abbey— that he broke off his work to go to the humble service in the little village church—"*ad majora avocatus quae ob haec parerga negligi non decuit.*"

On one occasion a friend, Sir Henry Acland, found Michael Faraday in tears; with his head bent over an open Bible. "I fear you are feeling worse," he said. "No," answered Faraday, "it is not that; but why, oh, why will not men believe the blessed truths here revealed to them?" A humble and reverent study of the laws which God has impressed upon the Universe has made

> "The pale-featured sage's trembling hand
> Strong as a host of armed deities,
> Such as the blind Ionian fabled erst:"

and yet of those sages, from Copernicus to Faraday, and down to the most eminent of our living students of Science, the foremost have not only had faith in God, but also have believed rightly in the Incarnation of our Lord Jesus Christ.

6. So, then, for Earth's loftiest intellects—as one of the foremost and most learned poets of our own generation has sung—

> "The acknowledgment of God in Christ,
> Accepted by the reason, solves for thee
> All problems in the world, and out of it."

And the same is true of those who have evinced a yet diviner greatness by scaling the loftiest moral heights and showing the utmost glories of self-sacrifice. If the men of loftiest *genius* in the world have acknowledged Christ, this was if possible even *more* the case with those who have conferred on the human race the highest and most deep-reaching services of pity and goodness. What was it but the Divine trembling pity which he had learned from Christ, and the commission which he had received from Him, that sent forth St. Paul to preach the Gospel amid his daily death of hatreds, miseries, and cruel persecutions, till, like the blaze of beacon fires kindled from hill to hill, its glory flashed from Jerusalem to Antioch, to Ephesus, and to Troas, and thence leapt over the sea to Athens, to Corinth, to Imperial Rome, and even to our Britain, the *Ultima Thule* of the World? What made the Roman lady Fabiola spend her fortune in founding hospitals at Rome, and in distant lands? Why did St. Jerome bury himself in the Cave of the Nativity at Bethlehem to translate the Bible from the Hebrew into Latin? What made the boy St. Benedict fly from the allurements of Rome to the Rocks of Subiaco and found the order to which learning owes so deep a debt? Why did St. Bonaventura, when asked the source of his great learning, point in silence to his Crucifix? Why did St. Thomas Aquinas, when asked by Christ in vision, *Bene scripsisti de me, Thoma. Quam mercedem recipies?* reply immediately "*Non aliam nisi Te, Domine?*" Why did sweet St. Francis of Assisi strip himself of everything, and, by living as a pauper and a beggar, infuse new life and holiness into an apostatising and luxurious world? What led St. Francis Xavier to lay aside his rank and his pleasures, and become a wandering missionary, gaining by his sacrifice a happiness so intense that he even prayed God not to pour upon him such a flood-tide of rapturous beatitude? What sent the Baptist cobbler, William Carey, with his first collection of £13 2s. 6d., to evangelise the mighty Continent of Hindostan? Every one of these, and thousands more of all those whose lives have been a blessing to the world, would have answered "CHRIST."

What but the love of Christ constraining him led John

Howard to toil among plague-stricken prisoners, until his
death at Cherson, on the Black Sea, " clothed a nation in
spontaneous mourning," and " he went down to his grave
amid the benedictions of the poor " ? What made
Elizabeth Fry go unaccompanied among the wild, degraded, brutalised women of Newgate, and take them by
the hand, and raise them from the depths of their fallen
humanity ? Why did men like Thomas Clarkson, Granville
Sharpe, Zachary Macaulay, and William Wilberforce, with
an energy which nothing could daunt, with a persistence
nothing could interrupt, use their time, their talents, their
fortunes, and every energy of their minds and bodies—and
that in spite of ridicule, hatred, peril, and reproach—" to
save England from the guilt of using the arm of freedom
to forge the fetters of the slave " ? * What sent Father
Damien to wretched and squalor-stricken Molokai, to live,
and catch the leprosy, and die a leper among the lepers in
the dismal isle ? What made Lord Shaftesbury vow himself, while yet he was a Harrow boy, to works of mercy
which added the brightest jewel to the glory of Queen
Victoria's reign ? What enabled him—amid the venomous
attacks of the Press and the world, and the chill aloofness
of the clergy—to toil on until he had inaugurated the
Ragged School movement, and passed the Ten Hours and
the Factory Bills ? Why should the poor Portsmouth
cobbler, John Pounds, have troubled himself, day after
day, to gather the ragged waifs into his stall, and teach
them with letters torn down from the advertisements upon
the walls, and so—poor and ignorant as he was—to give an
impulse to our great national system of education ? What
influenced Robert Raikes, the Gloucester printer, to begin
the work which established Sunday Schools throughout
the length and breadth of the world? " I thought, Can I
do nothing for all these wandering little ones ? A voice said
to me ' Try.' I did try, and lo ! What hath God wrought ! "

* From the epitaph on Granville Sharpe in Westminster Abbey.

Or take the best and most widely known of the effective workers of to-day amid the slums of unutterable squalor and degradation. Ask them what is the hidden force which sustains them in the long and thankless self-sacrifice of their lives, amid the scorn of worldlings and formalists, who look down upon them from the lordly altitudes of their own utter inferiority. What made General Sir Henry Havelock face so many sneers for holding Bible classes among his soldiers, and winning them to Total Abstinence? What made General Gordon so kind to the poor, ragged, homeless boys of Greenwich?

One and all, they would give the same answer, "The Love of Christ constraineth us." They would be ready to say with St. Ignatius, "Come fire, and the cross, and crowds of wild beasts; come tearings, breakings, and crunching of my bones; come the mutilation of my members, and shatterings of my whole body, and all the dreadful torments of the Devil, so I may but attain to Jesus Christ." * He felt that " he who is near to the sword, he who is among the wild beasts, is near to God." †

We are trying, they would say, to walk in the footsteps, we are trying to continue the work, of Him who was the Good Physician, of Him who went about doing good. We would fain be imitators of our Lord and Saviour Jesus Christ—of Him who taught that Love is the fulfilling of the Law; of Him who summed up the Law of God in Love to Him and to our neighbour. Has any unbeliever rendered to mankind the millionth part of such immortal services? I am not aware of a single supreme effort for the amelioration of the manifold miseries of mankind which has not been due to the inspiration of Christian enthusiasm. " There is nothing fruitful but sacrifice "—and the noblest and most continuous self-sacrifice which the world has seen has sprung simply from the belief in, and the imitation of, Jesus Christ.

* Ignat. *Ep. ad Rom.* **v.**   † Id. *ad Smyrn.* iv.

Christianity, then, is the highest, the most divine, the most eternal blessing in the world. It has been so in all these nineteen centuries; it is so in all the best conditions of our existence, and not to believers only, but even to those who deny, even to those who blaspheme Christ. But Christianity, had it only been a dead creed, or a purified ideal, or an organised society, would have been powerless. As a system of doctrine, or a code of loftier morals, it would have achieved but little. The permanent life, the regenerative force, the irresistible inspiration of Christianity is Christ.

It will be seen, then, that the reason why we believe in the records of that miraculous birth, of those angel melodies, of those bending Magi, is not only because they stand recorded by those who were far too feeble to have invented them, and of whom every one would have said, "I would rather die than lie"—but because, being so recorded, they have received the attestation of God Himself, seeing that the whole subsequent history of the world seems to us to have set its seal to the belief that they are true.

To us the records of Christ in the Gospels seem the reverse of non-natural or needless. If any man can really believe that Humanity is the result of the working of mechanical laws, deaf, and dead, and dumb, "blind as Fate, inexorable as tyranny, merciless as death—which have no ear to hear, no heart to pity, and no arm to save"; if any man can really persuade himself, not that "God formed man out of the dust of the earth, and breathed into his nostrils the breath of life," but that man is only the accident of accidents—the casual outcome of unconscious material forces—then with such a man it is simply impossible to argue at all. His mental peculiarities must be wholly different in kind from those of the human race in general. And deep below the surface of an avowed infidelity there often lurks an instinctive conviction that, after all, we *are* the creatures of God's hand. Even the reckless and depraved conspirator, who made an arrogant boast of his shallow scepticism, cried out on the scaffold, "O God, if there be a God, save my soul, if I have a soul!"

But if we believe even so elementary a truth as that God made man, then if God created the *first* Adam—if God created him who, whether literally or in an allegory, fell by eating that forbidden fruit

> " Whose moral taste
> Brought sin into the world, and all our woe "—

we cannot see the least difficulty in the belief that God also clothed with human existence, by the exercise of His supernatural power, His own Son, the *second* Adam, who came to redeem and save the fallen race. If indeed, God were some ruthless Moloch, to be appeased by

> " Blood
> Of children's sacrifice, and parents' tears ";

if He were like the Ahriman of the Persians, or the Typhon of the Egyptians, or the Sheeva of the Hindoos, or the Atua of the New Zealanders we might suppose that He would care nothing whether men perished in utter misery and corruption or not. But to all who believe that God is Love, and that, in spite of the insoluble problem of the existence of evil, "love is creation's primal law," to them a Divine interposition for the redemption and deliverance of mankind seems even *more* in accordance with Eternal Power than man's original creation. The instinct of mercy in our own nature forbids us to accept the Epicurean dream of gods who lie beside their nectar and

> " Smile in secret, looking over wasted lands,
> Blight and famine, plague and earthquake, stormy deeps and fiery sands,
> Clanging fights, and flaming towns, and sinking ships, and praying hands."

If Creation be but an ordinary exercise of the Divine power, why should *Re*-creation be less so? If God made man, and "breathed into his nostrils the breath of life and man became a living soul," why was it impossible or unlikely that Christ should be "born of a pure Virgin"? What seems impossible to man is always possible to God. And when God saw His children—and "we are all His offspring," as even the heathen recognised *—wandering and lost in the wilderness of shame and death—since God is God, and God is Love, it would have seemed to us infinitely *less* believable that He would leave the creatures of His hand to perish in their wickedness, than that His mercy should provide for them a way of salvation. There is no other name under heaven whereby we can be saved, *except* the name of Christ; and this seems to us a sufficient reason for, a sufficient explanation of, the truth that for us men and for our salvation, Christ took our nature upon Him, and was made in the likeness of sinful flesh.

And the more we study and learn what Christ was, and how He lived, and what He has done, the deeper will be this our conviction that He whom we worship, He whom we acknowledge as the Lord of Glory, came not into the world by the ordinary processes of human birth, but that when the fulness of the time was come, "God sent forth His Son, born of a woman, born under the Law, that we might receive the adoption of sons." †

But after all, the strongest part of the evidence to us is that we have "the witness *in ourselves*." ‡ We know that God is He "who also stamped us as with a seal for Himself, and gave us the earnest"—the *arrhabo*, at once pledge and part payment—"of the Spirit in our hearts." It is "*with the heart* that man believeth unto righteousness." §
If we would see Christ, we must, as Origen said, leave the

---

* Acts xvii. 28.　τοῦ γὰρ καὶ γένος ἐσμέν (St. Paul, quoting from Aratus and Cleanthes. *Cf.* Virgil *Georg.*, iv. 221–25).

† Gal. iv. 4.　　　　‡ 1 John v. 10.　　　　§ Rom. x. 10.

crowd of faithless disciples with the demoniac whom they
cannot cure, and must ascend the mountain top.* Of
every true Christian it may be said that " His seed is in
him ! " † and if " the *natural* man receiveth not the things of
the Spirit of God because " they are foolishness unto him," ‡
yet spiritual things are spiritually discerned. They who
are spiritually-minded recognise the truth not only by the
reason, but by the heart.§ " Christian faith is a grand
cathedral, with divinely-pictured windows. Standing *without* you see no glory, nor can possibly imagine any ;
standing *within*, each ray of light reveals a harmony of
unspeakable splendour." ‖

This is a demonstration stronger than any criticism can
take away, though to *all* such criticism, even on its own
chosen ground, we can offer what to us—as to the vast
majority of God's most gifted as well as of His humblest
sons—seems to be a decisive refutation.

* Orig. *c. Cels.* vi. 77.   † 1 John iii. 9.   ‡ 1 Cor. ii. 14.
§ Pascal, *Pensées*, iii. 208.   ‖ Nath. Hawthorne, *Transformation*, p. 262.

CHAPTER II.

THE UNIQUE SUPREMACY OF JESUS.

"To whom will ye liken Me, and make Me equal, and compare Me, that we may be like?"—Is. xlvi. 5.

Αὐτὸς ἐνηνθρώπησεν, ἵνα ἡμεῖς θεοποιηθῶμεν.—ATHANASIUS, *De Incarn.*, p. 51.

"*Dicimur et filii Dei; sed Ille aliter Filius Dei.*"—AUGUSTINE, *in* Ps. ii.

"Try all the ways of righteousness you can think of, and you will find no way brings you to it except the way of Jesus."—MATTHEW ARNOLD.

WE believe, then, in the Miraculous Birth of our Saviour Christ; and our belief is confirmed when we examine the records of all history through and through, and find that the Babe, at whose birth the heavens burst open to disclose their radiant minstrelsies, stood ALONE, UNIQUE, SUPREME among all the million millions of every age of all the sons of men. It would be more amazing that such an one— "holy, harmless, undefiled, separate from sinners," and, even in His human humiliation, but "a little lower than the angels";—that One who has thus visibly been made "the heir of all things";—that One who was foremost in the love and adoration of countless brethren, and to them a motive force of incomparable and inexhaustible vitality,— should have been born not otherwise than the mass of ordinary men. An infinite catastrophe required an infinite interference. God had created men sinless; it required a new man, even the Lord from Heaven, to uplift him from that gulf of sin into which he had been plunged by choosing the evil, and refusing the good, until his whole nature

18

had become perverted, the whole head sick, and the whole heart faint.

And here is a point which may be tested. The records of the ages are open to us. History unfolds to our eyes her ample page, "rich with the spoils of time." We know enough of tens of thousands of human beings to enable us to judge of them; and we know enough at least of all the greatest of mankind to enable us to compare them with Him whom we worship as the Son of God.

The unique supremacy of Jesus is especially illustrated by His sinlessness. By confession of all Scripture, and of all humanity, from the beginning until now, there never has been any other man who, being in human flesh, was not a sinner. There is no man that sinneth not, no, not one.* Our Lord Himself said to His disciples, "When ye have done all that is commanded you, say, We are unprofitable servants." † A thousand years earlier the Psalmist had said, Enter not into judgment with Thy servant, O Lord, for in Thy sight shall no man living be justified." ‡ Seven and a half centuries before the Incarnation, Isaiah had said, "We are all as an unclean thing, and all our righteousnesses are as filthy rags." § But those who knew, and day by day had lived with the Lord Jesus, and had watched His least actions, and shared His inmost thoughts, bear witness with one voice that "He did no sin." ‖ And He, in whose mouth there was no guile, and who was "meek and lowly of heart," yet spoke of Himself, as did all His Apostles, as of one who *could* not sin,¶ and as always doing the things that pleased God. **

Other human beings have become the founders of forms

---

* 1 Kings viii. 46 ; Rom. iii. 10. † Luke xvii. 10.

‡ Ps. cxliii. 2. § Is. lxiv. 6. R. V. " A polluted garment."

‖ 1 John iii. 5 ; 1 Pet. ii. 22.

¶ Heb. vii. 26. Comp. iv. 15 ; 2 Cor. v. 21 ; 1 Pet. i. 19, ii. 22, iii. 18 ; Rev. iii. 7.

** John viii. 29.

of religion adopted by whole peoples and generations, and
have been surrounded by legends with a blaze of miracles.
Yet enough has been recorded of their lives and teaching
to enable us to contrast them with the Saviour of the
World, and to show that they lie as far beneath Him as the
earth is beneath the highest heaven.

Let us take three such—the founders of the three religions to which, with Christianity, the great majority of the
human race belong.

1. Buddhism is said to number among its votaries many
millions of mankind, or nearly one-third of the human race.
"THE BUDDHA" is not the name, but the *title* of the
founder; his name was Gotama, and he was often spoken
of as Sakya Muni, or "Sakya the Sage." He was born
about B. C. 624. Nearly every fact and detail of his life is
lost in the dim mist of extravagant traditions. He lived
in prehistoric times, and the sacred book—the Tripitaka, or
" Three Baskets "—which professes to record his doctrine,
was not given to the world till centuries after his death.
Of Sakya Muni therefore we can only judge by the religion
which he taught—by the ideal which he set before himself
and his followers, and the results which that religion has
produced in the world.

Though in a certain sense Sakya Muni may be called
" The Light of Asia," and though Buddhism numbers more
adherents than any other religion in the world, yet, tried
by any standard whatever, Buddha cannot for a moment
be placed in the most distant comparison with Christ.

His ideal was in some essential particulars radically false,
and even pernicious. There is an uncleanly abjectness in
some of his precepts, a narrow selfishness in his morality.
His religion is a dreary atheism which tends to merge into
idolatry * ; his heaven an extinction of individual existence ; his piety a perverted bodily service. He taught

* " Il n'y a pas trace de l'idée de Dieu dans le Boudhisme entier." Barth.
St. Hilaire, *Le Buddha*, p. iv.

that there was "no God, no creation, no Creator—nothing but Mind minding itself."* "Insufficient for Time, and rejecting Eternity, the triumph of his religion is to live without fear, and to die without hope." † Its ideal is the life of its Bhikshahs, who, besides professing faith in Buddha, engaged to lead a life of self-denial, celibacy, and mendicancy, *and to enstrange themselves from all domestic and social obligations.* ‡

Buddhism, among many other glaring deficiencies and errors, involves a practical denial of the doctrine of man's immortality. It is a religion of despair, for it only offers a possibility of weary and endless metamorphoses, to be crowned at last by that obliteration of personal existence—that final loss of individuality—to which he gave the name of *Nirvâna.* Barthélemy St. Hilaire, who made a special study of the subject, says, "his religion is a spiritualism without soul, a virtue without duty, a morality without liberty, a world without nature and without God."

And what have been the religious results of Buddhism? There are men of excellent character and holy life among Buddhists as in all other religious communities, for God doth not leave Himself without witness among those whom He has made, and "in every nation he that feareth God and doeth righteousness is accepted of Him." § But Buddhism as a religion leaves the multitude with little but a false ideal and an unilluminated despair. "Vice had no intrinsic hideousness, and virtue was another name for calculating prudence; love was little more than animal sym-

---

* Max Müller, *Chips*, p. 269.

† Sir J. Em. Tennant, *Christianity in Ceylon*, p. 227.

‡ Prof. Wilson says: "Belief in a supreme God is *unquestionably* a modern graft upon the *unqualified atheism* of Sakya Muni" (*Journal of Asiat. Soc.*, xvi. 255). Wilson, *Essay*, i. 360. "Sin is, in the view of the Buddhist, a necessary thing: it is a cosmical and not a personal evil." Hardwick, *Christ and Other Masters*, i. 226.

§ Acts x. 35.

pathy; duty was devoid of moral motive. The Buddhist's principle of action was 'I *must*'; he could not say 'I *ought*.'" *

And the *national* outcome of Buddhism is utterly uninspiring. It wholly fails to create great nations or heroic deeds. The nations which profess it wither into unprogressive uselessness, adding little or nothing to the literature, the art, the science, the political wisdom, or the moral enthusiasm of the human race.† "Its inherent principles were such as left it well-nigh powerless in the training of society, and therefore it has left the countries which it over-ran the prey of superstition and of demonworship, of political misrule and spiritual lethargy."

2. Take another religious founder, CONFUCIUS, or Kungfoo-tsze. He was born B. C. 551, a few years after the death of the Buddha. The personal life of Confucius was highly respectable and correct, but his religion, if religion it can be called, does not furnish us with a single inspiring element. It was all lived on the dead level of conventional commonplace. It was an ideal of cold propriety and artificial respectability. It laid great stress on etiquette. He was narrow, cautious, and conservative. In Confucianism there is hardly any worship except the worship of ancestors, and yet it is very doubtful whether Kung-foo-tsze even believed in the actual continuance of life after death. When closely questioned on the subject he only gave hesitating and uncertain answers. All that he could say was that " he sacrificed to the dead *as if* they were present,"‡ and he said to his disciple Ke Lob, "While you do not know about life, how can you know about death?" "He threw no new light," says Dr. Legge, "on any of the questions that have a world-wide interest. He gave no impulse to religion. He had no sympathy with progress." § "The

---

* Hardwick, i. 239.   † Barthélemy St. Hilaire, *Le Bouddha.*
‡ *Li-ki*, p. 121 (Ed. Callery).
§ Legge, *Life and Teaching of Confucius*, p. 115.

last words he uttered savour not of hope and exultation, but of bitter disappointment."

The religion of Confucius can hardly be called a religion at all. It might be described as conventional polytheism, merging into atheism. * He deliberately avoided the subjects of God and Immortality. It is true that, in the arid desert of his writings, one may find here and there a tiny oasis. Once, when his disciple Tsze Kung asked him to sum up all religion in one word, he answered, "Is not *reciprocity* such a word?"†; and by "reciprocity" he meant something distantly akin, though immeasurably inferior to "altruism"—a faint and far analogy of our duty to our neighbour. Again, I find in his writings the sentence, "Heaven means principle." I am informed by a Chinese scholar of the highest authority that it is extremely doubtful whether this translation is correct, for it is taken from the maxims professedly drawn from the works of Kung-foo-tsze by the Jesuit Régis, the genuineness and exactitude of whose Confucian aphorisms has been seriously questioned. But here again we must, in any case, interpret the maxim by the illustration of it in the sage's life ; and, put to this test, it shrivels into very small dimensions.

And what result has Confucius produced in the empire in which his teaching prevails? It is an empire of stagnant decadence, full of corruption and cruelty. The Chinese are like a clever boy, who has grown to manhood, but whose mental development has been arrested at fifteen. Their religion has ended in deplorable morals, contented futility, and unprogressive stagnation. Its meagre formalism has never attracted the least respect from the inquirers of the world.

3. We know much more of MOHAMMED, the founder of the fourth great religion of the world, than we do of Sakya Muni or Kung-Foo-Tsze. But to compare him with the

---

* Neumann, in Ilgen *Zeitschr.*, vii. 19.
† *Doctrine of the Mean*, xx. *Analects*, xv.

Lord Christ would be a falsity too glaring for the most fanatical unbeliever. In his own Qu'ran he stands condemned. He has to defend his sensual irregularities by the fraud, or the self-deception, of pretended revelations.* He knew himself too well to make any claim of moral perfection. In one Sura (48) God says to him, "We have granted thee a decisive victory, that Allah may forgive thee thy sins, both past and future"; and in another (40) he is bidden to pray for the forgiveness of his sins. His last broken words were: "O God, pardon my sins—yes—I come."

Looking at Islam as a religion—its fanatical intolerance, its savage ruthlessness, its demoralising polygamy, its ever-deepening rottenness—who would dream of comparing it even for a moment with the religion of Christ?

And what has been the destiny of Mohammedan nations? Theoretically, both Mohammed and his followers recognised the holiness and the prophetic mission of Jesus—whom they nominally venerate as the prophet Issa—though in many countries they spit in execration when a Christian passes them. The strength of Mohammedanism in Arabia, and in the countries which were conquered by its votaries, lay in its proclamation of one great forgotten truth—the Unity of God. All that is of eternal validity in Islam its prophet learned directly from Jews and from Christians. Beyond this, it contains hardly a single element of the smallest value. Mohammed did indeed render one service to his adherents by the rigorous prohibition of strong drink. To this is due the fact that a Turk will, in a fortnight, recover from wounds which would send an ordinary English soldier to a certain grave. But when the first *élan* of splendid fanaticism ceased, one Mohammedan nation after another sank into effete corruption. Nothing can be lower, more squalid, more wretched, more depraved than the condition

---

* See his conduct towards Zeinab, the wife of his faithful servant Zeyd. Qu'ran xxxiii. 36. His ideal of Paradise is purely sensual. *Id.* lvi. 22.

of entire Mohammedan populations in Asia ; and in Europe the heart of humanity is sickened by the debasement, the brutality, and the many atrocities of "the unspeakable Turk."

By comparison, then, with the founders of the main religions of the world, Jesus stands not only supreme, but absolutely incomparable. He is elevated above them as high as the heaven is above the earth. He is separated from their human imperfections by an interspace as wide as the East is from the West.

Perhaps, however, it will be said that Sakya Muni, Kung-foo-tsze, and Mohammed were Easterns and Asiatics ; and that *Europe* has ever been the continent of energy, of progress, of the supremacy of human thought.

Well, the annals of the human race lie open before us. We know intimately all that can be known of "the glory that was Greece, and the grandeur that was Rome." The Greeks and Romans were the dominant progressive races of the ancient world. They belonged to the noblest branch of the human family, and spoke languages memorable for strength, beauty, and perfectness. They have expressed their thoughts and aspirations in literature which can never die. Surely, if anywhere in the wide world, we might look among these great and glorious nations for some men—if such have ever existed—who can be put in comparison with the man Christ Jesus.

Is even one such to be found ?

i. The GREEKS—and especially the Athenians—in the culmination of their national development, were a truly splendid race. Physically they could boast of specimens of beauty, and of perfection in the development of "the human form divine," such as the world has never seen surpassed. Intellectually they produced, in the course of little more than one brief century, a galaxy of brilliant stars. Their average intellect was far above the average intellect of Englishmen. They had philosophers like Heraclitus,

Thales, Socrates, Plato, Zeno, Epicurus, and Aristotle, "the master of those who know." They had poets like Pindar, Æschylus, Euripides, Sophocles, Aristophanes, and many more. They had historians like Herodotus, Thucydides, and Xenophon; orators like Demosthenes; statesmen like Pericles; men of science like Archimedes and Euclid; sculptors like Phidias and Praxiteles; painters like Zeuxis and Parrhasius; soldiers like Miltiades, Themistocles, Alexander. Did a race so gifted produce in its zenith one man who can for a moment be placed in comparison with Christ?

The name of SOCRATES might occur to some, but not to any who have most deeply studied what is recorded of him. That no Greek known to us was more outwardly blameless than he, may at once be conceded; yet *both* of his revering disciples, Xenophon and Plato, represent items of behaviour, and describe incidents in his biography, which, had they been narrated of Christ, would instantly shatter every fragment of belief that He was "God manifest in the flesh." The family life of Socrates, his views about ordinary moral questions, his estimate of women, who constitute one-half of the human race, rose in no particular above the ordinary Greek ideal. He could make himself intentionally and intolerably irritating. His attitude towards sin was dangerously, even ruinously, tolerant and familiar. Can we conceive of the humblest of Christ's followers talking as Socrates talked with Theodota* or with Agathon,† or making the coarse remark which he made about Critias? or dismissing his wife and children in the hour of death with the cold remark, "Let some one lead her away home." ‡ Even taking the word "sinless" ($ἀναμαρτητὸς$) in its lowest and most externally legal aspect, Xenophon himself says in so many words, "I see no single human being continuing in a sinless course,"—and that, be it remembered, though sins of sensuality were regarded by most Greeks—

* Xen. *Mem.* II. II.　　† Plat. *Sympos.* p. 4.　　‡ Plato. *Phaed.* 9.

even by the most eminent philosophers, and apparently by Socrates himself—as hardly sins at all, but as ἀδιάφορα, matters of indifference either way. Cicero was a deep student of philosophy, and he tells us that all the philosophers were at variance as to what should be the ideal of a man perfect in wisdom, " if ever he might be expected to exist." Even from a purely pagan standard he could not have regarded the life of Socrates as spotless, for he says, speaking merely of the victory over pain, " Never yet have we seen any man of perfect wisdom." * Never has the whole world seen any man—save Christ alone—in whom there has been either perfect wisdom or perfect holiness. He at once created and fulfilled that divine ideal.

PLATO—amid the exotic perfumes of many of his dialogues, and the dry dialectics of others—has indeed written for us one of the most remarkable of " the unconscious prophecies of Heathendom." He has even been called " a plank from the wreck of Paradise, cast upon the shores of idolatrous Greece." † Yet what chance would Christianity have had if its Apostles and Evangelists had written in the tone of the *Phaedrus* or the *Symposium*, or devised such a Republic as Plato's, with its tolerated and worse than tolerated crimes, including the degradation of the multitude, the exposition of children, and the community of women? Well might Plato yearn for the Deliverer for whose coming he, like many of the wisest of the heathen, felt there was an awful necessity, and who (as he believed) would come at last.

But, as far as ethics are concerned, the ideal drawn by Plato is the purely negative one of *outward* integrity, with no reference to the inner life or to the heart, out of which proceed evil thoughts ; nor does he furnish any hint of the *means* whereby alone this ideal can be attained. He seems only to have regarded it as a picture hanging in the air,

* Cic. *Tusc. Disp.* ii. 22. See Ullmann, *The Sinlessness of Jesus*, p. 97. G. T.
† Coleridge.

and neither says that it has been, nor expresses the belief that it ever will be, realised in human life.*

ii. When we turn from the Greeks to THE ROMANS, we find an imperial race which, strong in patriotism and courage, conquered the choicest part of the habitable world in its purer and better days. But its philosophy was in great measure second-hand, and Roman civilisation grew corrupt to the heart's core under the triple curses of imperialism, slavery, and sensuality. Conquered Greece terribly and effectually avenged herself on her conquerors by infecting them through and through with her worst vices, till

> "She whom mightiest kingdoms curtsied to,
> Like a forlorn and desperate castaway
> Did shameful execution on herself."

Few indeed of the great Roman poets—neither Catullus, nor Virgil, nor Horace—are free from the deadly taint of the worst impurity. "All things," says Seneca, "are crammed with wickedness and vices . . . there is a competition of worthlessness. . . Sins are no longer furtive— but openly parade themselves ; and so publicly has worthlessness prevailed in all bosoms that innocence is not only rare, but non-existent." † As they reprobated God, He had given them over to a reprobate mind. They became fools in their reasonings, and their senseless heart was darkened. Professing themselves wise, they were befooled.‡ The most striking comment on the paraded infamies of the decadent empire may be seen in the hateful sludge of Sodom and Gomorrha which bestrewed every street in Herculaneum and Pompeii. And as a consequence,

> " On that hard Roman world, disgust
> And utter loathing fell.
> Deep weariness and sated lust
> Made human life a hell."

---

* See Dem. *de Cor.* p. 322.
† Sen. *De Ira*, ii. 8. Comp. Juvenal *Sat.* xiii. 26–30
‡ See Rom. i. 22.

Not a few of the Romans, and Cicero among them, regarded the elder CATO as an ideal, yet Cato, in the affairs of private life, was guilty of a callousness and greed which would have stamped with infamy the humblest Christian. What sort of ideal is presented by the virtue of a man who, when his slaves became old and useless, ruthlessly turned them out to starve? or of a man who, meeting a young nobleman coming out of a haunt of vice, congratulated him on his *virtue—Macte virtute esto!* because he chose only such channels for the gratification of his animal desires?

There are, however, two men in later Roman history— the one a great and brave emperor, the other " poor and a slave, and lame, yet dear to the immortals"—who *did* attain to a very high degree of virtue, and may be regarded as "the bright consummate flowers of pagan morality."

EPICTETUS,

> " The halting slave who in Nicopolis
> Taught Arrian, when Vespasian's brutal son
> Cleared Rome of what most shamed him,"

wrote in Greek, and can hardly be counted as a Roman, though he was a subject of Rome and a slave in Roman households. It must be remembered that when he and Marcus Aurelius wrote, Christianity had long been in the air. Some breath of its divine teachings had been wafted into the miasma which was ever reeking upwards from the pestilential marshes of heathen corruption. Much pure, though imperfect, morality may be found in the pages of Epictetus. Yet his lofty Stoicism is a flower which has no root on which to live and thrive. His teachings never have been, or could be, a guide to the multitude, or a light to them which sit in darkness; and as for moral perfection, he frankly declares it to be unattainable. " What then?" he asks, " is it possible here and now to be faultless? Impossible! But this is possible—to have ever been straining every energy towards the avoidance of sin." *

* Epict. iv. 12.

I look on the "little golden passional" of the Emperor MARCUS AURELIUS as the most perfect moral book which heathen antiquity produced. It is Stoicism, touched—however unconsciously—with something of the Christian truth which the Emperor ignored, though by it he had been indirectly influenced. To ordinary ears it sounded like the despairing cry of an impossible virtue, and it was powerless to produce any effect upon the world. It did not for a moment stem—it was not even meant to stem—the awful tide of putrescence which rushed and swelled around him. It was but the salt of his own inner life preserved in his private diary, but it wholly failed to have any effect on his wife, or his son, or the nearest members of his own family. The personal morality did not reach beyond himself, and it is tinged with an unspeakable sadness. We see him standing, in noble despair, upon the bank of the River of Life, pure as crystal, proceeding out of the throne of God and the Lamb :

"Tendentemque manus ripae ulterioris amore."

Of other pagans it is hardly worth while to speak. No one would hold up SENECA as offering an effective moral example. His ideal is very imperfect, and his life fell immeasurably below even that imperfect ideal.

Philostratus drew a highly coloured picture of the Cappadocian thaumaturge, APOLLONIUS OF TYANA, who flourished in the reign of Nero. It was probably intended to represent him as a loftier being than Christ. But on the showing of his own panegyrist—who evidently drew very largely on his imagination—Apollonius, if he was not a gross impostor, was not a man who commands any deep admiration. He was guilty of glaring faults, and the "cloudy romance of the pagan sophist" who pretended to delineate his individuality has attracted very little notice, and has not exercised the very faintest influence upon the moral progress of the world.

In truth the pagan philosophers and poets disclaimed altogether the very possibility of sinlessness. Horace says:

" Nam vitiis nemo sine nascitur ; optimus ille est
   Qui minimis urgetur ; " *

and centuries before, Simonides had said: " To be a good man is impossible and not human ; God only has this high prerogative." " We have never yet seen any born," says Cicero, " in whom there has been perfect wisdom." † And Plato warns us that it is futile to exonerate ourselves by casting the blame on fortune, or demons, or anything rather than ourselves. ‡

And what was the total issue of Paganism in its utmost splendour, and most unquestioned dominance ? Did the teaching of any of the great Greek philosophers or Roman moralists produce the slightest appreciable effect in uplifting the world in general into loftier aspirations or a purer atmosphere ? It must be sadly confessed that, among the noble and heroic figures of Greek and Roman life, we can scarcely select one who distantly approached the Christian standard of holiness, or even of pure morality. The final culmination of Greek and Roman development in the days of the Empire was an unspeakable corruption. Nothing can be darker than the picture presented so unblushingly by Aristophanes in his day, and by the writers of the Anthologia in theirs. In Juvenal, and Suetonius, and Petronius Arbiter, and Apuleius, we have unbared to us the very depths of Satan.

Other writers are like a troubled sea foaming out their own shame with filth unspeakable. Over the history of Tacitus there seems to hang an atmosphere of the deepest gloom. In page after page he reveals the horror of times which, amid all their external gorgeousness, bore on them a truly infernal stamp. But it required the inspired eloquence of a St. Paul effectually to brand the harlot brow

* Hor. *Sat.* i. 3, 68.   † Cic. *Tusc. Disp.* ii. 22.   ‡ Plat. *Rep.* x. 16.

of Paganism with the stigma of her abominations; and it
is well that, in the first chapter of the Epistle to the
Romans, he should have torn the painted mask from that
leprous forehead, and should have shown what a heart of
agony—rank with hatred, and burnt out with vilest self-
indulgence—lay throbbing under the purple robe.

I ask, in passing, whether it does not show the *unique*
exaltation of Christ—whether it does not throw a reflected
light of antecedent probability on His miraculous birth—
that whereas, in all the Pagan world, alike in the East and
in the West, we cannot point to so much as one human
being to whom we could apply the epithet " *holy* "—that,
while, in all Pagan literature, during so many centuries, the
very conception of " holiness " has no existence—*now*,
because of Christ's teaching, and the force of His divine
indwelling life, there is no town, no village, scarcely even a
family, in which we cannot find holy women and holy men ?

" Why should it be thought a thing incredible with you,"
asked St. Paul of Festus and King Agrippa, " that God
doth raise the dead ! " * Even then he could say in the
presence of his enemies and accusers that " this thing was
not done in a corner." But he was speaking in the earliest
dawn of Christianity, before the facts to which he bore
witness had been tested by nineteen centuries of human
study and human progress; before the Gospel had proved
itself to be a divine regenerative force in all the world ;
before it had been found by millions of every race and age
—from philosophers in their studies to cannibals in the
Pacific, and Indians in their wigwams on the frozen shores
of Hudson's Bay—to be the power of God unto salvation
to all them that believe. The transcendence, the sinlessness of the Lord of Glory have been searched as with
candles by men of the most consummate intellect in many
epochs, and not one of them has been able to question His
unique superiority or to convince Him of sin. After these
nineteen centuries of sanctification, of victory, of wisdom and

* Acts xxvi. 8, 26.

enlightenment, may we not ask with tenfold force of every sceptic, " Why should it be thought a thing incredible with you that God should have granted to our fallen race the most priceless of all blessing by sending forth His Son into the world, and that He should have done this, not to condemn the world, but that the world through Him might be saved ? "

CHAPTER III.

THE UNIQUE SUPREMACY OF JESUS (*continued*).

" Even in the Prophets, after they had been anointed by the Holy Spirit, was there found mention of sin."—" *Unwritten Saying* " *in the Gospel of the Hebrews.*

" His beauty is eternal, his Kingdom shall have no end."--RENAN, *Vie de Jésus*, p. 457.

" The ideal representation and guide of Humanity."—J. S. MILL.

No sceptic, I think, will be able to dispute that—in the ancient world of Heathendom, and through all the æons during which it existed—neither among the founders of world-wide religions, nor among the greatest philosophers, the brightest poets, and the best men whom all former history records, can so much as *one* be found who can be offered as a distant parallel to Jesus Christ. The best and greatest of them all do not approach Him within any measurable distance, either in holiness of life, or perfect-ness of teaching, or in the ever advancing grandeur of the permanent results effected by His influence. But some might expect that, as THE JEWS were the recipients of a special inspiration, and since to them were entrusted " the oracles of God," we should be able to find among the twelve Tribes of Israel during the twenty centuries of the Older Dispensation, at least one or two Saints or Prophets whose lives and teaching might place them on the same level with the Son of Man. Yet it needs but little search to prove decisively that such is not the case.

What need is there to speak of NOAH ? Little as we are told of that preacher of righteousness, we think of that shameful scene when he lay drunken and uncovered in his tent, and laid his curse upon his son and grandson.

JOB, if he were a real person, and not created by the poetic imagination of the Jewish Haggadah, was in a lower sense "a blameless man and an upright, who feared God and eschewed evil." Yet he incurred the rebuke of the young Elihu for justifying himself rather than God, and when he is made to apprehend God's majesty, he can only cry—

> " Therefore I abhor myself,
> And repent in dust and ashes."

ABRAHAM was " the father of the faithful " and " the friend of God "; yet Abraham could twice be guilty of deception, and in other respects also shows the limitations of the nomad Sheykh. Other Patriarchs were still more imperfect. Isaac was guilty of deceit; Jacob of fraud, meanness, and partiality.

MOSES, the mighty law-giver of Sinai, was God's chosen mediator to deliver to Israel " the Ten words," in which are summed up our duties to God and man; yet Moses claims no exemption from human weakness, and records alike how he murdered the Egyptian and hid him in the sand, and how an outburst of unchastened anger forfeited for him the entrance into the Promised Possession.

Of DAVID and his terrible falls and manifold failures, though he was " the sweet Psalmist of Israel," there is no need to speak, for he does not conceal his own terrible guilt, and cries, " Behold I was shapen in wickedness, and in sin did my mother conceive me."

ELIJAH shewed the imperfection of an angry temper, and his wrathful spirit was far different from the spirit of Christ.

JEREMIAH, though some have fancied that his character had suggested to the later Isaiah the ideal of the Sinless Sufferer, yielded to passionate despair, and cursed the day of his birth. Not one of these, nor any of the Prophets or deliverers of Israel, made the slightest claim to perfectness. The plain testimony of their experience invariably is that all alike have gone astray, and that there is not one that sinneth not.*

The Jews themselves, deep—almost unbounded—as was their veneration for these Patriarchs and Prophets of their race, never pretend that they were faultless. In one of the apologues of the Talmud, God is represented as demanding from the Jews some surety for their future obedience. They offer Abraham, and Isaac, and Moses. God's answer is, "No! Abraham has sinned, and Isaac has sinned, and even Moses has sinned; *they* cannot be your sureties." As they can find *no sinless man in all their annals*, they offer to God their innocent little ones. And God accepted these, saying, "Yes, your little ones shall be your sureties," even as it is written, "Out of the mouth of children and little ones hast Thou built a bulwark, that Thou mightest still the enemy and the avenger."

As for later Judaism, its ideals shrank and shrivelled into utter pettiness.

The two Rabbis whom the Talmud most admires and exalts are HILLEL and AKIBA.

HILLEL had sweet and noble elements in his character, but they were accompanied by very unpraiseworthy deficiencies. His highest teaching is defective from its one-sidedness and incompleteness. Anything more ludicrously absurd than the notion—maintained by some Jewish writers, like Geiger and Grätz—that HILLEL was in any sense whatever "the master of Jesus," cannot be imagined! HILLEL belonged, in all essential particulars, to the Pharisees, who of all others were most repugnant to the soul of Jesus. His mind and life were occupied in the elaborate discussion of infinitesimal puerilities of ritual, such as whether one might or might not eat an egg which a hen had laid on a feast day, if the feast day was coincident with a Sabbath,† whether,

---

* See 1 Kings viii. 46 ; Prov. xx. 9 ; Eccl. vii. 20 ; 1 John i. 8–10.

†This is the question which occupies the 7th section of the second Book of the Mishnah, under the title *Bitsah*—" the egg." It is also called *Yom tob*.

when you are carrying myrtles and perfumed oil, you ought first to bless the myrtles and then the oil, or first the oil and then the myrtles ; whether you ought or ought not to take off your phylacteries during the performance of certain natural functions ; whether you ought first to wash your hands and then fill the glass, or *vice versa.* Can we imagine how full of holy scorn Jesus would have been at the discussion of these nullities, many of which are even more wearisomely repulsive than those I have mentioned, and some of which are absolutely nauseous ? Again, with what holy indignation would Jesus have regarded the application of some of HILLEL'S seven *middoth*, or rules of exegesis, which were used to turn Scripture into any purpose which Rabbinism might demand ! * We need not conjecture with what pity and anger the Son of God would have treated HILLEL'S decision that the words " *ervath dabhar,*" in Deut. xxiv. 1, † imply that a man may divorce his wife " even if she cooked his dinner badly "; ‡ and the thoroughly disingenuous shuffling by which he managed to set free his countrymen from the onerous Mosaic ordinance of letting property revert to its original owner in the Sabbatic year. He was cramped by the stagnation, the prejudice, the rigidity of party doctrine ; he lived and moved and had his being in the confined, heavy, turbid air of the Jewish Schools. §

Of Rabbi AKIBA in this connection it is not worth while to speak. He too was not only a Pharisee of the straitest sect of later Judaism, but his methods disgusted the more moderate even of his Pharisaic contemporaries.‖ He

---

* See my paper on " Rabbinic Exegesis." *Expositor* v. 366 (1877). Subsequent Rabbis expanded these rules, first to 13, then to 32, then to 49) Hamburger *Talm. Wörterb.*, ii. 36). R. Ishmael said (*Sanhedrin.* f. 34, 1) that exegesis is like the hammer which breaketh the rock into pieces (Jer. xxiii. 29).

† A. V. " matter of nakedness."

‡ Gittin, 90.

§ See Lightfoot, *Hor. Hebr.*, p. 256. Geiger, *Pharis. u. Sadd.*, 36. Jost. *Gesch.*, iii., p. 111. Delitzsch, *Jesus und Hillel*, 1866.

‖ For instance R. Jose the Galilean, R. Eliezer Ben Azarai, R. Tarphon, and

ostentatiously glorified, and was exclusively absorbed in,
the very methods and minutiæ of externalism which
Christ most emphatically repudiated and denounced. His
ideal of righteousness was inconceivably paltry and
shrunken. The Messiah of this coryphæus of particularism
in its latest and least sensible views was not the Son of
Man, but the False Messiah to whom he gave the name of
Bar Cochba, " son of a star," but whom, after his deadly
failure, the Jews characterised as Bar Coziba, the "son of
a lie."

But if it be granted that, in all the previous centuries,
moral perfectness was an unattained and even unimagined
ideal, some may ask whether the same is true of the centuries which followed the birth of Christ. May not men
have lived since the dawn of the Christian era, who, aided
by the inspiration of the Gospel, not only surpassed in
holiness the men of all previous ages, but may have even
attained to the same moral perfectness as was manifested
by their Lord? Again the answer is a demonstrable and
emphatic negative. The records of the Apostles and Evangelists themselves show proofs of the spiritual failures
which they humbly acknowledge. The confession of ST.
PETER—" Depart from me, for I am a sinful man, O,
Lord "—is amply confirmed by subsequent records of
faithlessness, of misunderstanding, of cowardice, of dissimulation. ST. PAUL, after his conversion, evidently speaks
in his own person when, after describing the struggles of
" a disintegrated individuality," he cries, " Wretched man
that I am, who shall deliver me out of the body of this
death?"; and he says with frank humility, " Not that I
have already attained, or am already perfected, but this one
thing I do, forgetting those things which are behind, and

others. R. Jose Haglili was called "the horned ram," because he rebutted so
often the reasonings of Akiba. See the references to the Lifras and Josephus
in which these passages of arms occurred in Hamburger's *Talm. Wörterb.*, ii. 36.

reaching forth to those things which are before, I press on
to the mark of the prize of the high calling of God in Christ
Jesus." * Yet, in spite of these efforts, he not only calls
himself " less than the least of the Apostles, who am not
meet to be called an Apostle," † but even characterises
himself as " the chief of sinners." ‡

The faults of the Sons of Thunder—ST. JAMES and ST.
JOHN, the disciples whom Jesus loved—are not concealed
in the Gospels; and, if the later legends of St. John be true,
they still exhibit traces of human passion and impetuosity.

Nor is there one of all the later saints of Christendom—
whether it be St. Ambrose, St. Augustine, St. Jerome, St.
Chrysostom, St. Gregory of Nazianzus, St. Basil, or the
saints of the later days, sweet St. Francis of Assisi, ardent
St. Bernard, St. Bonaventura the Seraphic, St. Thomas of
Aquino the Angelic Doctor, St. Francis Xavier, or St. Vincent de Paul—whose ideals were not more or less one-sided
or mistaken. Every one of them would, with indignant
humility, have repudiated the faintest attempt to represent
him as perfect. Every saint of Christendom, kneeling
humbly, on his knees, would have said to the Lord of his
life, that

> " Every virtue we possess,
> And every triumph won,
> And every thought of holiness
> Are thine alone."

" The young and unspotted, the aged and most mature,
he who had sinned least, he who had repented most, the
fresh innocent brow and the hoary head, they unite in this
one litany, ' God, be merciful to me, a sinner!' So was it
with St. Ignatius; with St. Aloysius; with St. Rose, the
youngest of the saints; with St. Philip Neri, one of the
most aged, who, when some one praised him, cried out,
' Begone! I am a devil, and not a saint!'" §

---

* Phil. iii. 12–14.   † Eph. iii. 8; 1 Cor. xv. 9.   ‡ 1 Tim. i. 15.
§ Newman, Sermon on *The Religion of the Pharisee.*

"What are the saints," asked Luther, "compared with Christ ? They are but as dewdrops scattered upon the head of the Bridegroom, lost in the glory of His hair." As regards all varieties and combinations of virtue and excellence—all things which are true, pure, honest, lovely, and of good report, which have ever been manifested in the character of the children of God—all Christians would express the conviction that

> "They are but broken lights of Thee,
> And Thou, O Lord, art more than they."

So far, then, we have seen enough to leave us with the secure certainty that of all the multitudes of mankind without number, under every condition, and in every age and clime, not one can be compared to Him who revealed Himself as the Son of Man and the Son of God. And this demonstrable uniqueness and unapproachable superiority— even if it stood alone—would not only go far to remove every shadow of difficulty from the record of His miraculous birth, but would lead us to suppose, were there no such testimony, that Jesus *must* have come into the world by the special intervention of an Omnipotent Love. The infinite supremacy of Christ Jesus in character and influence—the manner in which He is separated by an untraversable distance from all who have ever lived on earth—would naturally lead us to believe that He could not have been born as other men are, and that the Son of Man, the Second Adam, was, in a far deeper sense than the first Adam, the Son of God.

CHAPTER IV.

THE TESTIMONY OF SCEPTICS AND FREE ENQUIRERS.

"Christ stands alone, and unapproached in the world's history."— STRAUSS.

"The Incomparable Man to whom the universal conscience has decreed the title of Son of God—and that with justice, since He has advanced religion as none other has done."—RENAN.

"He stood in the first rank of the grand family of the true Sons of God."—IBID.

"The Chosen of God, His image, His darling, His world-guide, and world-shaper in the history of mankind."—KEIM.

"The Well-spring of whatever is best and purest in human life."— LESSING.

HITHERTO we have been led to the conclusion that Christ is "the vital centre of Christianity, the pulsating heart from which it all proceeds, to which it all returns";—that, without the force of His inspiring and ever-present Personality, Christianity itself would sink into nothing more than a system of morals and scheme of revelation. We have seen also that, demonstrably and by universal admission, Christ stands a Unique Being in the long annals of the world. There have been sceptics who have insinuated a faint and timid disapproval of some of His actions, and many have questioned the truth of the Gospels, and denied the divinity of Him whom they set before us. But it is worth while to pause and show that even over the most unfettered enquirers He has cast a spell which makes them hardly venture to hint at the most distant disparagement of Him. The beauty of His holiness compels them, almost in spite of themselves, to fall upon their knees, and to admit His unapproachable supremacy even when they speak of Him as nothing more than Man.

1. SPINOZA (Ep. 23) said: "This is the highest thing which Christ said of Himself, namely, that He is the Temple of God, since God chiefly manifested Himself in Christ; which St. John, that he might express it more efficaciously, clothed in the expression that 'the Word was made flesh.'"

2. LESSING called Christ "the first trustworthy and practical Teacher of the Immortality of the Soul."

3. ROUSSEAU concludes a famous passage with the words, "If the life and death of Socrates are those of a sage, the life and death of Jesus are those of a God."

4. The awful transcendency of the life of Jesus overawed even the flippant soul of VOLTAIRE, as we see in the account of his remarkable vision.*

5. KANT was indignant when a critic compared his teaching with that of Jesus. "One of those names," he said, "before which the heavens bow, is sacred; the other is only that of a poor scholar, endeavouring to explain to the best of his abilities the teachings of his Master."

6. SCHELLING spoke of Christ as "the turning-point of the world's history."

7. STRAUSS was the foremost champion of modern scepticism respecting Him, yet Strauss wrote that Jesus "stands foremost among those who have given a higher ideal to humanity"; and that "it is impossible to refrain from admiring and loving Him." "Never at any time will it be possible to rise above Him, nor to imagine any one who shall be even equal with Him." "He is the highest object we can possibly imagine in respect of religion: the Being without whose presence in the mind perfect piety is impossible." †

8. GOETHE calls Him "the Divine Man, the Holy One, the type and model of all men."

---

* See *Dict. Philosophique, s.v. "Religion."*
† Strauss, *Vergängl. u. Bleibende*, p. 132.

9. CHANNING was a Unitarian, yet he wrote: "I believe Jesus Christ to be more than a human being. The combination of the spirit of Humanity in its loveliest and tenderest form with the consciousness of unrivalled and Divine glories, is the most wonderful distinction of this wonderful character."

10. RENAN says: "Between Thee and God there is no longer any distinction." "His beauty is eternal, His Kingdom shall have no end." "This Christ of the Gospels is the most beautiful incarnation of God in the most beautiful of forms." *

11. J. S. MILL wrote that "there is no better rule than so to live that Christ would approve our life."

12. The views of KEIM diverge very widely from those of Churchmen in many points, yet he ends his *Jesu von Nazara* by saying that "Christianity is the crown of all the creations of God, and Jesus is the chosen of God, God's image, and best-beloved, and master-workman, and world-shaper in the history of mankind. He and no other is and remains the appointed standard-bearer of the world's progress, who shall triumph over the quagmires and the spirits of darkness of the nether Kosmos."

13. THEODORE PARKER testifies that "Christ unites in Himself the sublimest precepts and divinest practices. He pours out a doctrine beautiful as the light, sublime as heaven, and true as God."

14. DR. CONGREVE, the head of the English Positivists, wrote: "The more truly you serve Christ, the more thoroughly you mould yourself into His image, the more keen will be your sympathy and admiration."

15. DR. MARTINEAU was a Unitarian, yet he speaks of Christ as "the commissioned Prophet, the merciful Redeemer, the inspired Teacher, the perfect Model, the heavenly Guide."

16. MATTHEW ARNOLD differed widely from views re-

* Renan, *Ét. d'Hist. Rel.*, pp. 175, 213.

garded as orthodox, yet, after describing the True God as "the Eternal who makes for righteousness," he adds, "from whom Jesus came forth, and whose Spirit governs the course of humanity."

17. I will only add the testimony of the anonymous author of *Supernatural Religion*. He—surely an unprejudiced witness—spoke of Christ as "surpassing in His sublime simplicity the moral grandeur of Sakya Mouni, and putting to the blush the teaching of Socrates and Plato, and presenting the rare spectacle of a life, so far as we can estimate it, uniformly noble and consistent with His own lofty principles."

From the first, Jesus was "set for a sign which should be spoken against." * His cross was "to the Jews a stumbling-block, to the Gentiles foolishness." † His earliest Apostles were denounced as "pestilent fellows and ringleaders of sedition." ‡ His Gospel was stigmatised by the haughty Roman historians as a deadly and contemptible folly, to be classed with all monstrous and shameful things ; § and Christians as "creatures of a deplorable, illegal, and desperate faction," devoted to "a depraved and measureless superstition." ‖ His followers were everywhere spoken against ¶ as hated for their enormities, as "characterised by their hatred for the human race " ; ** as " atheists "—so that the cry against one of the poor Martyrs, St. Polycarp, as against Christians in general, was "Away with the godless one !" †† Is it no proof of the Divine blessing and approval that, in spite of all this hatred and execration, which united all pagan society, philosophy, and

---

* Luke ii. 34.   † 1 Cor. i. 23.   ‡ Acts xxiv. 5.

§ Tacitus *Ann.* xv. 44.   Suetonius *Ner.* 16; *Claud.* 25.

‖ Caecilius in Min. Fel. *Oct.* viii.   Comp. Dion Cassius lxvii. 14, and my *Witness of History to Christ*, p. 7; Lightfoot, *Apostolic Fathers* II. i. p. 260.

¶ Acts xxviii. 22.

** Tacitus l. c. Hist. v. 5.   See *Ep. Smyrn.* ap. Euseb. *H. E.* iv. 15. *Mart. Polyc.* 9.

†† *Ep. Smyrn.* ix.; Lucian, *Alex. Pseud.* xxxviii.

literature in a conspiracy of common detestation, the faith of Christ "in the unresistible might of weakness shook the world," over which, in spite of its being in flagrant disaccord with all that men naturally admire, it has since then maintained the unquestioned dominance? Many who more or less reject Christ's divinity—such as Hase, Weisse, Schenkel, and others—still describe Christ as "*ein Unicum*," "*ein Mysterium*." Thus sceptics (as Mr. Browning so admirably points out)

> " Bid us, when we least expect it,
> Take back our faith."

They say:

> " Go home, and venerate the myth
> I thus have experimented with ;
> This Man, continue to adore Him
> Rather than all who went before Him,
> And all who ever followed after."

> " Surely for this I praise you, my brother!
> Will you take praise in tears or laughter ? "*

* Browning, *Christmas Eve and Easter Day.*

CHAPTER V.

THE GOSPELS.

"Quousque mens tua humi defixa erit ? Sacrilegii enim vel maximi instar est, humi quaerere quod in sublimi debeas invenire."—CICERO, *Somn. Scip. Ad init.*

IN the desire to disprove the Divinity of Christ, every possible ground of objection has been urged; and it may now perhaps be said, "Your argument depends ultimately on the genuineness and authenticity of the Gospels, and against the Gospels the spirit of hostile criticism has concentrated its most powerful light."

Yes; but I say unhesitatingly that the result of that close and hostile criticism has not only left the substantial truth and accuracy of the Gospels untouched, but has, by its very failure and weakness, shown them to be of unassailable veracity. The Gospels exhibit on every page the *simplex veri sigillum.* They have no magnificent eloquence, no thundering denunciations, no high-wrought artificiality, no excited eulogies. They bear on the face of them the stamp of being unadorned and artless narratives of simple faith.

We may compare the Gospels with the greatest books of other religions, and they stand out in magnificent superiority, though the Evangelists may have been far inferior in earthly gifts and philosophic genius to the great sages of the East. "I confess," says a most competent witness, Professor Max Müller, "it has been many years a problem to me, how the great books of the East should, by the side of so much that is fresh, natural, simple, beautiful, and true, contain so much that is not only unmeaning, artificial, and silly, but even hideous and repellant. This is a fact, and

it must be accounted for in some way or other." But no
one could say this of our Christian Gospels; they do not
contain one silly or one repellent word; and what can
account for their absolute supremacy, except that their
writers bore witness to the simple truth?

The Evangelists simply *could* not have invented the history which they record. Standing as they do immeasurably below the grandeur of their Master, we feel almost
inclined to say that their *invention* of His teaching and
character would have constituted a less believable miracle
than any which they narrate. As Rousseau said, " L'inven-
teur en seroit plus étonnant que le héros." These Galileans could never have subjectively elaborated ideals so
inimitable, or morality so divine. They—even the greatest
of the Apostles, even a Peter and a John—possessed no
particle of what was regarded as learning in their own day.
Their words are, as Origen described them, ἰδιωτικοὶ λόγοι.
When they stood before the Sanhedrin, the High Priests—
the Kamhits, and Phabis, and Boethusim and Annanites,
and the Rabbis—the Shammaites, the Hillelites, the Gama-
liels, who were regarded with such reverence—looked down
on these Galileans as ἄγράμματοι καὶ ἰδιῶται—mere commonplace nobodies, who had never had a learned education.* They spoke a coarse provincial dialect; they
possessed none of the exegetic lore of the Scribes; they
knew nothing of the *Middoth* or the *Erubhin*, nothing of
Halacha or the *Haggadah;* they belonged to the common
amharatzim—the multitude who "knew not the law and
were accursed." † Such men could not even be pious, and
a Pharisee felt polluted (so Hillel declared) if he so much
as touched them with the hem of his garment. In the
Gospels themselves the Evangelists constantly record incidents which show that they were " dull and slow of heart

* Acts iv. 13.
† John vii. 49, ἐπικατάρατοι. The name *dmai*, from δῆμος, was also given
to these " Men of the People." See Hamburger, *s. v. Amhaaretz.*

to believe"; that they ignorantly misunderstood Christ's allusions; that without the aid of His tender condescension, they could not grasp the significance of His parables; that they were entirely unprepared for His line of action in many cases; that they would fain have hindered His divine purposes; that His plainest prophecies failed to impress their understandings; that they were liable to petty jealousies and ambitions among themselves; and that, even after His resurrection, He had to upbraid them for their unbelief and hardness of heart.* *Inferiority* is far too weak a word to express the depth at which they stood below their Master. How could these Galilean peasants and fishermen, " fresh from their nets, and with their clothes wringing wet"—how could tax gatherers and zealots, and men of individuality so unmarked that their fellows had little or nothing special to record about them, except their imperfections—how could they have *invented* a story, and *imagined* a character, which transcended them as infinitely as the heaven is higher than the earth, and which, when it was shining before them in heaven's own light, they could but very dimly understand? Who will believe that St. Paul, the learned Pharisee, who began with the most furious rage against Christianity, was so credulous that—in defiance of all his predilections, and all his past training— he suddenly accepted as true a mass of *myths*, freshly invented by unknown Galileans? Is there any one whose capacity for appreciating evidence is so paralysed as to believe " that the Holiest of Men was a deceiver, His disciples either deluded or liars, and that deceivers would have preached a holy religion of which self-denial is the chief duty?"† Whatever else the early Apostles, Disciples, and Evangelists may have been, they were undeniably holy men;—would they have invented falsities, and then, in preaching them, have poured out their lives like water, and sacrificed everything which life holds most dear?

* Mark xvi. 14.   † Niebuhr, *Lebensnachr.*, i. 470

The presence and the work of Jesus in Palestine in the days of the Herods are matters of ordinary history, as certain as any recorded in Tacitus or Dion Cassius. It would be the wildest of hypotheses that the poor Evangelists could have evolved out of their own consciousness a story so entrancing that, nineteen centuries later, it should be read with awe and ecstasy alike by emperors in their palaces and peasants in their hovels. Maories and Fijians, Kaffirs and Negroes, Esquimaux and Tahitians, can delight in the Gospels with no less intensity than men of the finest genius and the most consummate learning.

The Synoptists exhibit no special skill, or power, or insight. Their main function is simply to narrate. They do not enter into theological disquisitions. The technical scholasticism of theologians leaves no trace on their pages. There is no learning in their allusions, no brilliance or profundity in their style. Their records are fragmentary and unchronological. St. Matthew, accustomed to the use of the stylus from his trade as a despised toll-collector, was probably the first to commit to writing a collection of Christ's "sayings" (*Logia*); and he and the others, though guided by divine inspiration, yet in other respects followed the bent of their own individuality, and wrote as St. Augustine said, "*ut quisque meminerat, vel ut cuique cordi erat.*" It must also be borne in mind that they do not profess to offer complete or exhaustive records. Our Lord uttered His prophetic woe on Chorazin and Bethsaida as cities which had witnessed His mighty works; yet we do not know of a single miracle performed at Chorazin, and only one is recorded to have been performed at Bethsaida.*

St. Matthew belonged to the social class which was, of all others, regarded with the greatest contempt, and beyond this we know scarcely a single fact about him. He wrote mainly for the converts from Judaism.† It used

* Mark viii. 22.

† Hence in St. Matthew there are *eleven* quotations made by the Evangelist

to be thought that his original work was in Hebrew,* but modern scholars now regard his Gospel as a composite one, formed partly from a Greek Gospel resembling that of St. Mark, and partly from a collection of our Lord's sayings in Greek, used also by St. Luke; the two documents having been welded together by a third redactor.

St. Luke, as "a physician," had probably belonged at one time to the body of slaves in some wealthy house in Asia Minor.

St. Mark recorded in his Greek Gospel, for Roman readers,† some of the vivid reminiscences of St. Peter, the Galilean fisherman. Not one of the three was in any other respect specially remarkable, and though all three wrote in Greek, their records are tinged with the Aramaic phrases of the earliest oral teaching. It is a gross absurdity to

himself from the Old Testament, not counting those made by our Lord. In St. Mark, who wrote for Roman readers, there is *only one* (or, perhaps, two). In St. Luke, who wrote mainly for Greeks, *three*. In St. John, who wrote for the whole Christian world, there are *nine*. Each synoptist has his own specialties. The subject of Prophecy is prominent in St. Matthew ; of Prayer in St. Luke, who also dwells much on the ministry of angels, and uses the Pauline word εὐαγγελίζεσθαι more than twenty times, and σωτηρία four times. He uses the title ὁ Κύριος for Christ much more frequently than the other Evangelists.

* Euseb. *H. E.* iii. 39 ; Iren. *Haer.* iii. 1 ; Jer. *Pref. in Matt.* St. Matthew alone uses the Hebrew term "the Kingdom of the heavens" thirty-two times ; the other N. T. writers always call it "the Kingdom of God."

† It is no part of my immediate object to enter into the problem of the origin of the Synoptic Gospels—a problem complicated by their close resemblances yet marked divergences. Even the *verbal* differences show that they did not slavishly follow each other. Thus St. Mark expresses "through the eye of a needle" by διὰ τρυμαλιᾶς ῥαφίδος (Mark x. 25) ; St. Matthew by διὰ τρυπήματος ῥαφίδος ; St. Luke, in the best reading, by διὰ τρήματος βελόνης. To my own mind the theory of a common original fund of *oral teaching* best meets the peculiarities of the case. Many special touches in St. Luke seem to come from eye witnesses. The agreements are mostly in the story of the *beginning* and *end* of the life of Jesus. "Of some eighty-three paragraphs which the Synoptists have in common, only about thirty-four come in the same order in all three narratives—that is to say, in some forty-nine instances the Synoptists do not agree in the order of their narratives." (Gilbert, *The Student's Life of Jesus*, p. 36.)

suppose that they, and others like them, could have con-
spired to deceive men by an imaginary character and a
false narrative which, ever since, has altered the destinies
and stimulated the noblest efforts of the world!* "Their
divinity," it has been said, "is in *what* they report, not in
the *way* they report."

There are in the Fourth Gospel more marks of profound
and spiritual genius. It concentrates on the person of the
Saviour all the manifold sources of witness borne to Him
by the Father and the Spirit; and by John the Baptist;
and alike by men who believed and disbelieved in His divine
authority. Far more deeply than the Synoptic Gospels it
reveals the inmost nature of Eternal Life. Its "emphatic
monotony," its mixture of extreme simplicity of language
and grammar with unequalled majesty of thought, exercise
over the mind a mysterious spiritual fascination. After
the brows of the Apostles had been mitred with Pentecostal
flame, when the Fall of Jerusalem came as the consummation of the older æon, and when the progress of years had
shown that the "Dayspring from on high" was destined
to broaden into the boundless noon, the insight of Christians became more intense. The Gospel of St. John is
crowded with internal evidences which prove the external
attestation that it was the work of the Apostle whom Jesus
loved. The "most spiritual Gospel" is also "the most
concrete." In some respects it presents Christ under a
more purely spiritual light than the Synoptic Gospels.
Yet it is in closest agreement with the simpler and earlier
narratives which it was written to supplement—and perhaps, in one or two less important particulars, to correct—
but mainly (in the New Testament sense) to "fulfil," *i. e.*,
to fill with a diviner plenitude of meaning. It dwells
chiefly on the Judæan rather than on the Galilean ministry,

* St. Mark adopted a Latin surname (Marcus), and he has in his Gospel ten
Latin words transliterated into Greek—*centurio, speculator, grabatus, quadrans,
flagellum, sextarius, Prætorium, denarius, legio, census.*

because there is reason to believe that St. John was more familiar with Jerusalem than were the other Evangelists : but in no instance does St. John *contradict* the main particulars recorded by his predecessors. He distinctly recognises the ministry both in Galilee and Peræa, which after the labours of the other Evangelists, it was needless fully to record. In every chapter he confirms the teaching which they preserve, and sets forth in all its majesty, but with more penetrating power, the same character which the Synoptists present. Without the Christ whom they had known, and heard, and loved, the Evangelists in themselves would have been nothing and less than nothing. It is as absurd to say that the Christ of these Gospels is a fiction as it would be to say that one who described the glories of the mountains had evolved out of his own imagination the everlasting hills, or that astronomers have invented the starry heavens.

Fortunately we have direct proof of the incapacity of fiction to touch the life of Jesus without instantly betraying itself to be fiction. The Apocryphal Gospels were works of imagination, written by unwise and ill-instructed Christians who professed to adore Jesus and to believe in His Godhead. They were popularly attributed to great names, such as Nicodemus, St. Joseph, St. Peter, and St. Thomas. Yet in the desire and endeavour to exalt Him they unconsciously drag Him down to the level of those who wrote them. In the attempt to represent Him as sinless and divine, they pervert his ideal by their own marked imperfections. The four Gospels, because they tell the simple facts, do not record one saying or one incident which we should wish to be obliterated, as weakening our faith or diminishing our reverence : the Apocryphal Gospels, because they indulge in fiction, scarcely tell us a single incident which we do not instinctively reject as false. From the first they deceived no one. They were recognised and denounced as apocryphal, and never won a particle of confidence. They depict Christ only to degrade Him, and thereby prove how impossible it was to set Him forth as divine except by the unadorned and simple truth. And we may estimate the force of contemporary evidence from the fact that it revolutionised the whole life and ideal of "a Pharisee of the Pharisees," the pupil of Gamaliel, incomparably the ablest Pharisee of his day—the Apostle St. Paul. Against the struggles of his own will, this great contemporary was driven into irresistible conviction, through doubt and denial. His knowledge of Jesus, which began in the vision on the road to Damascus, was "not the fruit of a blind acceptance of unexamined Christian tradition, but, as the case of his enquiry into the evidences of the Resurrection shows,* was arrived at by means of a lucid, keen, searching, sceptical observation, comparison, collection, and collation of such materials as were accessible to him." †

Surely, then, we may say of the Gospels with the utmost confidence, that " we did not follow on the false track of myths, artificially elaborated," but that we accept the simple truth at the hands of those who neither " trafficked with," nor "adulterated," nor " mutilated," nor " misrepresented " the Word of God. ‡

* 1 Cor. xv. 3–8.   † Keim, i. 521, E. T.
‡ 2 Pet. i. 16 ; 2 Cor. ii. 17, iv. 2.

CHAPTER VI.

THE CLAIMS OF JESUS, AND THE SPELL HE EXERCISED

ἵνα μείνῃ τὰ μὴ σαλευόμενα.—Heb. xii. 27.

"Nemo pen se satis valet ut emergat; oportet manum aliquis porrigat, aliquis educat."—SEN. *Ep.* 52.

WE may, then, be assured of the genuineness of the Gospel narratives, and they prove that Jesus was a Perfect Man. All subsequent experience, and the survey of nineteen centuries of history, suffice (as we have seen) to show that, as a Perfect Man, He stands alone in the annals of the world—unapproachable, unparalleled.

From heathen sources—from Tacitus,* Suetonius,† and Pliny‡—though they all refer to Jesus, nothing is to be learnt. In Jewish sources—Josephus and the Talmudists—we find deliberate silence or frantic calumny. "The True Word" of the Platonist Celsus (A. D. 176) was sufficiently refuted by Origen. Some of these writers merely mention His name as the founder of a religion, and the Talmudists have a few wild and monstrous fictions about Him, but none of them charge Him with sin or crime. The silence of Josephus—for the famous allusion to Jesus in his *Antiquities* (xviii. 3, 3) is either an interpolation, or has been tampered with by Christian writers—was obviously intentional. That it was not the silence of ignorance, but of embarrassment, is certain, for he knew all about John the Baptist,§ and regarded him with high respect; and in speaking of the martyrdom of James, the Lord's brother, if that passage be genuine, he actually attributes

---

* Tac. *Ann.* xv. 44. † Suet. *Nero* 16 ; *Claud.* 16.
‡ Plin. *Ep.* x. 97, 98. §*Antt.* xviii. 5, 2.

the final destruction of Jerusalem to the Nemesis due to that crime. The allusions in the writings of later Judaism —which will not name Jesus, but speak of Him as "the fellow," "the fool," or "he who ought not to be named" —are beneath contempt. The "infamous, multiform, mediæval lampoon" against Jesus, known as the " *Toldoth Jeshu*," gives expression to the screams and curses of a hatred only excusable because it was partly, alas! due to the savage ruthlessness of Christian persecution.

But in what way do the fourfold records of the Evangelists demonstrate this unique sinlessness and perfectness of the Saviour of Mankind? They do so, because in all they narrate they show us One who lived His life amid the ordinary surroundings of men, yet wholly without a trace of evil, or of incompleteness in His moral supremacy.

Jesus lived in the full blaze of publicity. (i.) Many followers had been under His constant teaching. (ii.) Myriads had heard His words and seen His works in Galilee. (iii.) He had thousands of enemies, who hated Him with a singular intensity of that unscrupulous hatred which always exhibits itself in its vilest and most ruthless forms among religious disputants.

His followers, who had seen Him in the most private and confidential intercourse of common life, narrated from intimate knowledge the incidents of His ministry. In all that they narrate we see the glory of Godhead veiled in human form, and we cannot find the least trace of that evil impulse (the *Yetzer ha-rah*) which, the Jewish Rabbis said, divided with the good impulse (the *Yetzer ha-tob*) the whole domain of human existence.*

We see that the sinlessness of Jesus was not a miraculous,

---

* See Hershon, *Rabbinic Commentary on Genesis*, p. 21. *Treasures of the Talmud*, p. 161. In Gen. ii. 7, the word for "He formed" has *two* Iods, which the Rabbis explained of the *two* impulses. On Gen. viii. 21, they remarked that the *Yetzer ha-rah* is implanted in men, whereas the *Yetzer ha-tob* is only a guest. See, too, *Sanhedrin*, f. 64, 1.

but an *achieved* sinlessness. He was perfectly man, as well as truly God. He was tempted in all points like as we are, yet without sin. He was " tempted of the Devil," not only in the wilderness, but to the end; and the temptations would have been no temptations if it had been antecedently *impossible* for Him to have succumbed to them. After the great Temptation in the wilderness the Devil left Him, but it was only " for a season." He had to face those two-fold and opposite influences to swerve from the path of perfectness, which arise on the one hand from the allurements of ease, and on the other from the agonies of suffering. His temptations appealed to His human nature, His human imagination, His human sensitiveness to anguish; they endeavoured to sway at once the desires of the mind and the weakness of the flesh. Jesus was not humanly endowed with an impossibility of sinning—a *non posse peccare ;* but with the power to achieve the complete and final victory over every impulse to sin—a *posse non peccare.* This victory, even more than His miracles, was sufficient to convince His followers of His Divine Nature, so that from the earliest days of Christianity, as we learn from Pliny the younger, they sang hymns to Him as God.*

Be it observed that the superhuman grandeur which seemed to invest Him as with a garment was something wholly apart from all earthly pomp of circumstance, or splendour of endowments. In position He was nothing more than a Galilean peasant, the lowliest of the lowly, "the carpenter" of despised and proverbial Nazareth. The Prophet whom the multitudes saw before them was a nameless youth, seated on a mountain, or speaking to them from a boat. When the world, even the hostile and sceptical world, involuntarily bows before Him, it is not because of any of the gifts or qualities which ordinarily dazzle mankind. Jesus was no Poet, entrancing the souls of men with passionate melodies. He was no mighty Leader like Moses, emancipating nations from servitude,

* Pliny, *Ep.* x. 97.

or, with illuminated countenance, promulgating to them a code of systematic morality. He was no rapt Orator, now stirring them to tumultuous emotion, now holding them hushed as an infant at the mother's breast. He was no Warrior, smiting down his foes in triumphant victory, and breaking from the necks of the oppressed the yoke of foreign bondage. Yet turning away from the choir of immortal Poets; from all "famous men and the fathers who begat us"; from mighty Orators who have played on the emotions of men as on an instrument, and swept them into stormy passion, or moved them to sobs of pity, as the wind sweeps into wild music or into soft murmurings the strings of an Æolian harp; from all magnificent Conquerors; from the Pharaohs in their chariots whirled into battle amid the serried ranks of their archers; from Assyrian monarchs leading their captivity captive, and hunting the lion amid their lords; from Babylonian Emperors with the crumbs gathered beneath their tables by vassal kings; from deified Cæsars in their dizzy exaltation; from Aurungzebe or Haroun, flaming in their jewelled robes and surrounded by kotowing courtiers—the world, abandoning all its own predilections, has felt constrained to drop its weapons, to tear the garlands from its hair, to kneel lowly on its knees before the Son of Man in His meek humiliation—in the faded purple of His mockery, in His crown of torturing thorns!

And His sinlessness is confirmed from every source.

(i.) His own Family witness to it. His mother and His brethren had lived with Him from infancy in the same poor hut at Nazareth; they had eaten and drunk and slept with Him; had been with Him by night, by day, in the most solemn intercourse, at the most unguarded moments, during the bright gaiety of boyhood and the passionate fire of youth, with an intimacy which would have rendered concealment impossible, if, even in His thoughts, He had been unfaithful to God His Father. His ways were not as their ways, nor His thoughts as their thoughts. He set aside their advice; He checked their occasional intrusiveness.[*] He did not adopt their ideals of patriotism; He bitterly disappointed the earthly form of their Messianic hopes— yet they were so convinced of His sinlessness, that, after His resurrection, these *Desposyni* as they were called—these members of our Lord's human family—became, like James the Bishop of Jerusalem and Jude the author of the Epistle, pre-eminent and pronounced believers in His divine supremacy.

(ii.) ST. JOHN THE BAPTIST was united to Him by earthly kinship, and had probably seen something of Him in His earlier years. This prophet of the wilderness was one of the sternest of mankind—an uncompromising foe to all insincerity; a man who did not for a moment hesitate to rebuke cruel autocrats, and, with rude impetuosity, to strip the mask from the hypocritic face of painted Pharisees; a man who, so far from feeling flattered when he won converts among the pompous religionists of his day, bluntly denounced them as "the offsprings of vipers." At the presence of Jesus, though as yet He was but the unknown carpenter of Nazareth, the voice which terrified multitudes and made kings tremble is hushed into accents of humility, and the strong personality which over-awed a proud and passionate nation becomes like that of a timid boy. He who baptised all others, shrank from baptising the Son of Man. Before the ministry of Jesus had begun, or a single miracle had been wrought, John pointed Him out to His disciples as "the Lamb of God which taketh away the sins of the world," and as One whose shoe's latchet he is not worthy to stoop down and unloose.

(iii.) THE APOSTLES lived and moved about with Him under all varieties of outward condition, alike in the sunlight of His early ministry, and amid the deadly hatred and bitter persecution which drove Him forth as a wan-

[*] See Matt. xiii. 46; Mk. iii. 31; Luke viii. 19; John vii. 5, 10.

derer and a fugitive who had not where to lay His head; and though their worldly Messianic hopes were so utterly blighted, though they had to bear for His sake the loss of all which men most desire—yet, with one voice, they speak of Him as the Holy One of God; as One who did no sin, neither was guile found in His mouth; as One who alone had the words of eternal life; as the Christ, the Son of the Living God; as holy, harmless, undefiled, separate from sinners, and made higher than the heavens; as the sinless High Priest, who is faithful and just to forgive us our sins, and to cleanse us from all unrighteousness.*

(iv.) THE PHARISEES, THE SADDUCEES, THE HERODIANS, all hated Christ with that deadliness of malignity which has been invariably exhibited against all the best and holiest men; alike by Priests, Jesuits, and Inquisitors, against all who oppose their own falsities, and by worldings who resent all unswerving sincerity and stainless authority. These enemies laid traps for Jesus; tried to entangle Him in His talk; combined in shameless and clever machinations to entrap and to destroy Him; did their utmost to embroil Him with the rulers, and to disillusion the Galilean multitude of their devotion for Him. They supported their own false judgments by frantic lies. Yet the only charges which they could bring against Him were that He "broke the tradition of the elders"—which He did designedly, because the so-called "tradition" had become a paltry rubbish-heap of quantitative goodness—and that " He had a demon, and cast out demons by Beelzebul, the prince of demons," which was a mere scream of insane hatred, and involved the absurdity of supposing that the prince of the demons was going about as an angel of holiness.

(v.) ONE of His Apostles, Judas Iscariot, giving himself up to the temptation of greed, and probably maddened with sullen wrath at the frustration and disappointment of

---

* Acts iii. 14, viii. 35, xxii. 14; 1 Pet. ii. 21, iii. 18; 1 John ii. 1, 29, iii. 5, 7; 2 Cor. v. 21; 1 Tim. iii. 16.

all his worldly hopes, became a traitor. Perhaps he laid to his soul the flattering unction that there could be no great sin in doing that which High Priests, and Scribes, and Pharisees urged him to do, and paid him for doing. Yet even *after* that humiliating condemnation, which he might have been tempted to regard as the final disproof of His Master's Messianic claims, he was so haunted by the pangs of intolerable remorse that he flung down unspent upon the Temple floor the thirty pieces of silver for which he had sold his soul, and rushed forth to his hideous suicide with the confession that he had been guilty in that he "had betrayed INNOCENT BLOOD."

(vi.) THE SANHEDRISTS, violating the traditional compassionateness of Jewish tribunals, and goaded on by priestly hypocrites, *sought* false witness against Him, and could find none. There was not a single fault or crime which they could establish against Him, and their eager false witnesses utterly broke down. They condemned Him on His true claim—extorted from Him by the illegal adjuration of the High Priest, and proved by the subsequent history of the whole Jewish and Gentile world—His claim to be the Christ.

(vii.) THE ROMAN LADY, Claudia Procula, the wife of Pilate, was so haunted by the thought of Jesus that, terrified by dreams, she bade her husband take no part in condemning "that Just Person."

(viii.) Before PILATE the Jewish priests, with base and shifty malice, brought against Him four charges: (1) that He was a deceiver; (2) that He stirred up the people; (3) that He forbade to pay tribute to Cæsar; (4) that He called Himself a King. All four charges, in the sense in which they were urged, were absolute lies; and Pilate—bad, cruel, blood-stained, wilful as he was—saw them to be lies, born of the deadliest hatred. Awed by the Prisoner's meek grandeur, unoffended even by His majestic silence, trembling before the mysterious spell which He exercised while He

stood before him with the agony of pain and the marks of shame and spitting upon His brow, the haughty Roman Procurator was constrained to utter again and again the emphatic testimony, "I find in him no fault at all."

(ix.) THE CRUCIFIED MALEFACTOR who witnessed the ultimate humiliation of Jesus; who shared in the unspeakable infamy of His last agonies; who had, at first, joined in the taunts of the other malefactor against Him; who had challenged Him—if He were not the *mesîth* whom the priests and religious world of the day declared Him to be —to come down from the cross, and save Himself and His companions in misery;—that crucified robber, who saw Him only in the hour and power of darkness, with the Roman soldiers mocking, and the crowds yelling against Him, and the Hierarchs and Elders passing by and wagging their heads at Him—even that poor robber, overawed to conviction by the triumph of His patient majesty, testified "This man hath done nothing amiss," and called Him " Lord," and prayed that He would admit him into His kingdom.

(x.) THE ROMAN CENTURION, who had seen Him so grievously insulted by the leaders and religious teachers and mobs of His own countrymen; who had watched the whole scene until the tortures ceased in death; who had been in command of the rude quaternions of soldiers—felt the witness wrung from him, " Truly this was a righteous man."

(xi.) The very mobs which had so frantically yelled against Him seem to have been hushed into awe and silence by the sight of a majesty which no ignominy could humiliate, and after His crucifixion returned to Jerusalem smiting their breasts with remorseful misgiving.

Thus, alike the friends and the enemies of Jesus became voluntary or unwilling witnesses to His stainless innocence. His friends not only testified to His perfectness through all the remainder of their days, but demonstrated it by the

simplicity of their truthful records, and the power of their renovated lives. His opponents, with all the will in the world to blacken His name and depr eciate His cha racter, were either constrained to confess is immaculate pu of c or in the charges whi ch they brought against Him were self-convicted of malice, ignorance, and falsehood.

Yet all these testimonies, and even the stupendous results of His life and death, would not necessarily prove His sinless humanity, or His divine prerogatives, had they not been corroborated by His own repeated and unvarying testimony.*

He asked His most raging opponents, " Which of you convinceth Me of sin? And if I say the truth, why do ye not believe Me?" †

The keynote of Christ's inner life was heavenliness.

> " How sour sweet music is
> When time is broke, and no proportion kept ;
> So is it with the music of men's lives."

If the keynote of a man's life be selfishness, earthliness, greed, self-indulgence, his whole life will be full of " harsh chromatic jars." If we imitate Christ, we shall be enabled to join in the perfect diapason, and keep in tune with heaven. For us, as for our Saviour, " the path to heaven will then lie *through* heaven, and all the way to heaven *be* heaven." And this heavenliness of Christ was achieved and exhibited in the common round, the trivial task. He never was what Romanists call " a religious." His life bore no resemblance to those of hermits, monks, or ascetics. His religion was to finish His Father's work amid the common every-day life of men. In that common every-day life, He shifted the centre of gravity of man's existence from earth to heaven. He made it not *geocentric*, but *heleocentric*. For all who walk in His steps, life is not only ennobled ; it

* John iv. 34 ; v. 30 ; viii. 29 ; x. 30 ; xiv. 9, 31 ; xv. 6. 27 ; xvi. 33 ; xvii. 4, 19 ; Matt. xi. 28.

† John viii 46. Stier, *Reden Jesu*, Part IV., p. 428.

is glorified, it is transfigured. " Thou shalt show me the path of life ; in Thy presence is fulness of joy, and at Thy right hand there are pleasures for evermore."

Bearing in mind what He was, only consider the weight of such utterances as these which follow, and consider how —if they had not been so amply justified, both by the short years of His life, and by the nineteen centuries which that life has influenced, and by the ages which it will still influence till Time shall be no more—the fact of uttering them, had they not been the perfect truth, would have lowered Jesus below the level of all other religious teachers ; would have branded Him with the weakness of self-deception and the stain of falsehood.

Consider His seven " I am's."

1. " Jesus said unto them, *I am the Bread of Life.*" *

This He said when the multitude, impressed with His words and works, yet asked of Him a sign to authenticate His claim that the Father had sent Him to bestow eternal life by the food which He could give. They challenged Him to fulfil the tradition that the Messiah should, like Moses, give them manna from Heaven. † They had not realised, as even Philo had done, ‡ that " the heavenly food which feeds the *soul* " is the true bread from heaven. And when they asked for the bread of God which cometh down from heaven, He told them that He Himself was the Bread of Life ; in other words, that they who accepted Him, by faith lived in Him, would never hunger nor thirst, but would have everlasting life. The Apostles showed that they had rightly apprehended His revelation when Simon Peter said, in the name of them all, " Lord, to whom shall we go ? Thou hast words of eternal life ; and we have believed and have come to know that Thou art the Holy One of God."§

---

* John vi. 35. † See Lightfoot, *Hor. Hebr. ad loc.*
‡ Philo, *de Profugis*, § 25, quoted by Bp. Westcott *ad loc.*
§ Christ also spoke of Himself as the source of the Living Water (John iv. 14, vii. 37, 38).

2. *"I am the Light of the World."* *

This utterance was another revelation of His divinity, for God is Light. Christ was "the Sun of Righteousness" of whom Malachi had prophesied that He should rise with healing in His wings. Just as the Pillar of Fire had illuminated the darkness of night in the wilderness, so would Christ illuminate the darkness of the world, and His true disciples should reflect His light.

3. *"I am the Door of the Fold."* †

In Eastern lands separate flocks are often led at night for safety into one large fold. The porter remains to watch over the various flocks, and in the morning the shepherds come and call out their own sheep. The fold is the universal Church—"the blessed company of all faithful people," and none can enter into that safe and holy fold except through Christ.

4. *"I am the Fair Shepherd."* ‡

Christ is the genuine Shepherd of the sheep, and not only the "good," but the "fair" Shepherd—altogether lovely as well as tender—who knows His sheep, defends them from all danger, and lays down His life for them. He has *many* "folds" in His one Flock, but all the sheep shall be gathered at last into the one eternal fold, and become one fold under their one Shepherd. This beautiful image more than any other haunted the minds of the early Christians, as we see from the constant representations of the "Fair Shepherd" on the walls of the Catacombs.

5. *"I am the Resurrection and the Life."* §

Christ is the Eternal Life shared equally by all who live "in Him." Whether they be now living on earth, or living in the new form of life beyond the phase of earthly death, death cannot touch them that have life in Him.

---

* John viii. 12. The words were immediately suggested by the lighting of the great Golden Candelabra in the Court of the Women at the Feast of Tabernacles.

† John x. 7, 9.   ‡ John x. 11, 14.   § John xi. 25.

6. *"I am the true Vine."* *

As all the branches of a vine derive their life from union with the stem and root, so all believers in Christ share His life. As long as they bear the fruit of such union, they need indeed to be pruned—as men are by suffering—but only that they may become more fruitful. It is only the absolutely and hopelessly barren and withered branches that are taken away and burned.

7. *"I am the Way, the Truth, and the Life."* †

Christ is the sole Way whereby we can pass from death to life, and from our evil and perverted self to the Father. He is the Eternal Verity in which all semblances are lost. He is the Life because He is one with the Living Father, apart from whom life is but a living death.

By all these metaphors—of the Manna, and the living Bread, and the Light, and the Door, and the Shepherd, and the Vine, and the Way—did Jesus indicate "the irrevocable saving significance" which He knew that His life and death possessed for mankind.

No human lips have ever uttered claims so immense and fundamental as these. The fact that Jesus made them would brand Him with condemnation had not age after age demonstrated their simple and eternal truth.

Again, consider such invitations as these:

"Come unto Me all ye that labour and are heavy-laden, and I will give you rest. Take My yoke upon you, and learn of Me, for I am meek and lowly of heart, and ye shall find rest unto your souls." ‡

Or sayings so awful as:

"He that hath seen Me hath seen the Father. How sayest thou, Show us the Father?" §

Or,

"All things have been delivered unto Me of My Father; and no one knoweth who the Son is save the Father; and

* John xv. 1.   † John xiv. 6.
‡ Matt. xi. 28, 29.   § John xiv. 9.

who the Father is save the Son, and he to whomsoever the Son willeth to reveal Him." *

These utterances are not *accidental* outcomes of the thought of Jesus. Expressed in every variety of form they are a fundamental part of all His teaching. He accepted worship ; He called Himself the Son of God.† In the lowest abyss of the shame, agony, and failure out-poured upon His short earthly life—and be it ever remem-bered that the man Christ Jesus was a young man even when He died—He could yet tell the maddened, sneering Sanhedrin, with death for blasphemy staring Him in the face as the certain and immediate consequence, that He was the Christ, the Son of the Living God, and that here-after they should see the Son of Man seated at the right hand of God, and coming in the clouds of heaven.

On the cross itself, nailed there in the uttermost humilia-tion of helpless torture and nakedness, with scarcely one friend to care for Him among the millions whom He came to save, He yet, of His own authority, flung wide open the gates of Paradise to the robber who, in punishment for his crimes, was dying by His side.

And all these claims—so vast, of such eternal import— were unhesitatingly repeated and proclaimed, even at the peril of life, by those who had seen and known, and whose hands had handled the Word of Life. ‡

Now, if such claims, promises, and testimonies were the result of monstrous arrogance, or the delusions of pitiful hallucination, they would degrade Jesus into the position of a self-worshipping fanatic, or an insanely arrogant deceiver. Every line which is written of Him, every day of the long centuries which have passed since the day of

* Luke x. 22. Comp. Luke xix. 10 ; John iii. 35, 36, vi. 37, vii. 37, etc.

† John ix. 35-38 ; Matt. viii. 2, ix. 18, xiv. 33, etc.; Mark xv. 19 ; Luke xxiv. 52.

‡ Rom. vi. 23 ; Gal. iii. 13, 22 ; 1 Tim. i. 15 ; Col. i. 14 ; 1 Pet. ii. 24 ; John iii. 35, 36, x. 9, xvii. 3 ; Acts xvi. 31, xiii. 38, 39, etc.

His baptism, stamp either alternative as too outrageous even for blasphemy to utter. As He said to the hostile Jews, His works bore witness for Him. They were the seal of attestation affixed to His utterances by His heavenly Father, whom they knew not. Though He bore witness to Himself, yet was His witness true, for He sought not His own glory.* It was His Father who glorified Him, and consecrated Him, and bore witness to Him, and He did the works of His Father.† The whole ideal and outline of His character, as shewn in all that He said and did, stamps His own witness concerning Himself with an unanswerable force. Liars and deceivers rank among the wickedest of mankind ; self-exalting madmen, who claim to be divine, are among the most abject of human creatures. It might seem as if the earth would yawn beneath the feet of any one who—by rejecting this repeated and most awfully solemn testimony, and in defiance of all truth and reverence —dared to relegate the Son of Man to either class. For has not every claim He uttered been superabundantly justified by the witness of God in the renovation of the world wrought through faith in His name ?

The validity of the words and promises of Christ has been abundantly justified in matters open to the most ordinary tests. He never commissioned His Apostles to write, yet, in the midst of what might have seemed to be utter and shameful defeat, He calmly said to His little ob- scure handful of Galilean disciples that heaven and earth would pass away, but His words would not pass away ; and so it has been.‡ And when He well knew how near was His death of shame, at a feast in the petty Judæan village of Bethany, He promised to Mary's act of fidelity an im- mortal memory over the whole habitable earth ; and to this day, in every region of the habitable earth, that deed is still proclaimed.§

* John viii. 50–54. † John xii. 28, xiv. 13, xvii. 4, etc.
‡ Matt. xxiv. 35. § Matt. xxvi. 13.

There are, as Kant wrote, *two* things which move and uplift and overawe the soul, more than all else of which, by our senses and intellect, we can become cognisant—"the starry heavens above, and the moral law within." But to these two things, it has been rightly said, we must add a third, yet more sublime, namely, the realisation, the fulfilment, the perfect exhibition of that "moral law within" in the life of One who was exalted far above all heavens, yet lived in a tent like ours, and of the same material—the man Christ Jesus. "Sin is a failure, and perversity an apostasy. He alone conquered sin. In Him alone there was no sin."

Yes! God the Father, the Almighty, the Maker of Heaven and Earth, has, in all the consequences achieved by Christ in all the world, stamped His seal of Divine attestation to the mission of His Son Jesus. God has "in manifold figures indicated the unique, irrevocable, saving significance which He knew His preaching to have for men."[*] The comment upon that saving significance is written broad and large over all the subsequent destinies of mankind. Jesus taught but for one or two short years, moving about among the humble peasants of despised Galilee; yet He "became the creator of a new and higher Kosmos, the duration of which is to be reckoned by millenniums and the extent of which is to be conterminous with the whole surface of the earth."[†] "The proof of the grace poured out in His life,"[‡] says Origen, "is this—that, after a brief space of time, the whole world has been filled with His teaching and the faith of His filial love." In vain were Philo and Josephus silent respecting Him; in vain did Tacitus dismiss Christianity as an "*exitiabilis superstitio*," to be classed with all things "*atrocia aut pudenda*";[§] in vain did Pliny characterise it as "*superstitio prava et immodica*;"[‖] in vain

---

[*] Wendt, *The Teaching of Jesus*, ii. 289.   [†] Keim.
[‡] Orig. *De Princ.* iv. 5.   [§] Tac. *Ann.* xv. 14.
[‖] Plin. *Epp.* 10, 97, 98.

did Celsus accumulate his lying slanders;* in vain did Suetonius describe Christians as people of a new and malefic superstition;† in vain did Talmudic and mediæval Judaism heap upon Jesus and those who believed on Him their inextinguishable hatred and monstrous calumnies;‡ in vain did the Middle Ages produce the book *De Tribus Impostoribus;* in vain did Paulus, and Strauss, and Renan, and many more in modern days strive to undermine our faith with their naturalistic explanations, and mythic theories, and historic or philosophic reconstructions—in spite of all these, *Christus vincit, Christus regnat, Christus imperat;* and we still pray with perfect faith, "*Christus ab omni malo plebem suam defendat!*"

---

* See Orig. *c. Cels.* 1, 28, and *passim.* Comp. Justin. *Dial.* 10, 17, 28.

† See Eisemenger Entd. Judenth. Schöttgen. *Hor. Hebr.* ii. 693. Wagenseil, *Tela ignea Satanae.*

‡ Suet. *Nero.* 16.

CHAPTER VII.

THE HUMAN EDUCATION OF JESUS.

" Hearken unto me, ye holy children, and bud forth as a rose growing by the brook of the field ; and give ye a sweet savour as frankincense, and flourish as a lily, and send forth a smell, and sing a song of praise." —Ecclus. xxxix. 13, 14.

τὸ δὲ παιδίον ηὔξανε, " The Little Child grew."—Luke ii. 40.

THERE is in the Evangelists a deep and holy reserve. What they did not know they would not relate. St. Matthew had only become a disciple when Christ called him from the place of toll beside the Lake of Galilee in Capernaum. St. Mark was probably still a youth at the time of the Crucifixion. He had not been a personal witness of the scenes of the ministry, and though he derived his information from St. Peter, yet St. Peter first met Jesus at the Baptism of John. St. Luke may not have been converted till after the death of Christ ; and he frankly tells us that, though he classed himself among those who "from the beginning were the eye-witnesses and ministers of the word," he based his Gospel on what he had ascertained from " having traced the course of all things accurately from the first." St. John did not mean his Gospel for a complete record ; he disavows the intention of recording " many other things which Jesus did." His obvious purpose was to complete the narratives of his predecessors, to supplement what they had left unrecorded of the Judæan ministry, and to present the life and teaching of the Lord Jesus under that more immediately spiritual aspect, which, until years of eventful issue had passed by, could not have been adequately understood.

The only persons who could fully have narrated the early years of Jesus were His mother, Mary, and Joseph, and those who are called " His brethren." But Mary chose to remain silent.* Conscious of overwhelming revelations, she "kept all these things and pondered them in her heart." Joseph, her husband, seems to have died while Jesus was yet a boy. The "brethren"—whatever may have been the exact relation in which they stood to Jesus—were not at first among the number of his avowed disciples, and only became so after His resurrection. Further, we may observe that the importance attached to childhood and youth in many modern records was a thing unknown to antiquity, and that stories of early years are very rarely, or never, mentioned in ancient biographies.

St. Matthew narrates the circumstances of the Virgin-birth of Christ. He tells us of the visit of the Magi; the massacre of the innocents at Bethlehem; the flight into Egypt; and the reason why Joseph—abandoning all thoughts of settling in Judæa under the suspicious and sanguinary rule of Archelaus—retired to Nazareth, in Galilee. Then, passing over some thirty years of the Saviour's life, he proceeds at once to describe the preaching of John the Baptist.

St. Mark, in his brief and vivid Gospel, written for Roman readers,† plunges at once "*in medias res,*" and only professes to give an account of the ministry, which was inaugurated by the vision and descent of the Holy Spirit upon Jesus when John was baptising. All the light which he throws on the childhood, youth, and early manhood of Jesus, is seen (as well as pointed out later) in the flash of a single casual but revealing word.

---

* I have not, in this book, entered into questions of date. Our era *Anno Domini* (A. U. C. 754) was fixed by the Abbot Dionysius Exiguus in A. D. 525. An older tradition fixed the Birth of Christ A. U. C. 750, four years earlier. The question is unsettled, and will probably remain so.

† See such notices as those in Mark x. 12, xii. 42, xv. 1.

St. John, writing at the close of the first century, when the Synoptic Gospels, and others less sacred, were already in the hands of Christians, takes the same starting-point as the three Synoptists. He does not lift the curtain for us, though he probably knew more about the early years of Jesus than the other Evangelists, for he was, by birth, a nephew of the Virgin, and had been as a son to her, and —by the tender care of Jesus for His mother—had taken her in her hour of anguish to his own home.*

In the silence of the New Testament on the earlier years of Jesus, we see the over-ruling restraint of a Divine Providence. It was not intended that the Gospels should gratify a biographical curiosity; they had a far diviner purpose. Had *all* been detailed, St. John says, "I suppose that even the world itself would not contain the books that should be written." As it is, the Gospels have been the parents of a literature ever increasing in extent, and already immeasurably vast. There are cases in which silence becomes the most powerful eloquence, and something of the *significance* of that silence we may see when we come to speak of Christ's unrecorded years.

St. Luke, a Greek-speaking convert of Asiatic origin, was undoubtedly familiar with Ephesus, which he had visited among the companions of St. Paul; and if the tradition be true that the Virgin died at Ephesus, † he may have known

---

* It does not fall within my scope, in this book, to enter for the ten thousandth time into the question of the genuineness and authenticity of the Fourth Gospel. We know at any rate that as early as the day of Tatian (*circ.* A. D. 170) it had taken its place as one of the Four Gospels received by the whole Church; and that (in *Orat. ad Graecos* 13) Tatian (a pupil of Justin Martyr) quotes John i. 5 as sacred Scripture. For the rest I must content myself with referring to the many decisive proofs which have of late years been accumulated by the learned; and especially to the decisive arguments of Bishop Westcott in the Speaker's Commentary.

† Epiph. *Haer*. 78. Her tomb was shown at Ephesus (see *Conc. Eph.* Labbe iii. 574a.) Another tradition is that she died at Jerusalem, and that her latter years were mainly spent in the Cœnaculum, the upper chamber of the Last Supper.

her there, and have learnt from her lips the few details about the infancy of Christ, which, in their ineffable sweetness, seem stamped with the tender grace of a mother's reminiscences.

But among the minor differences between the Gospels, they do not differ in the least in the picture and impression of Jesus which they leave upon our minds. The method of St. John, and the details which he furnishes, diverge in many particulars from the method and details of the Synoptists, but we see on every page alike one and the same Divine Lord.

It is from St. Luke that we learn in a single sentence all that we know of the Divine Infancy. It is that " the Child grew and waxed strong, becoming full of wisdom, and the grace of God was upon Him." *

It is but a single sentence, but it is inestimably precious. It illustrates the truth of the perfect humanity of Jesus. It shows us that Christ was not only " truly God " (as was finally declared by the decision of the Council of Nice), but that also He was (as the Council of Constantinople decided) "*perfectly* ($\tau\epsilon\lambda\epsilon\omega\varsigma$) man." It is a bulwark against the Apollinarianism which denies the full humanity of Christ, a heresy more common in these days, and quite as dangerous as the Arianism which denies His divinity. It shows us the reality of that *kenosis*, that " emptying Himself " of His glory, and of the divine attributes of Omnipotence and Omniscience, of which St. Paul speaks. † It shows us that Jesus grew up simply as a human child, after the common way of all men (as Justin Martyr says), ‡ though the grace of God was upon Him ; and that His *advance* in wisdom was as normal as His growth in strength and stature. It pictures to us a natural but holy childhood, "like the

---

* Luke ii 40. The word $\pi\lambda\eta\rho o\acute{\nu}\mu\epsilon\nu o\nu$ implies, of course, *continuous* advance, like the word $\pi\rho o\acute{\epsilon}\kappa o\pi\tau\epsilon$ in Luke ii. 52.

† Phil. ii. 7. $\acute{\epsilon}\kappa\acute{\epsilon}\nu\omega\sigma\epsilon\nu$ $\acute{\epsilon}\alpha\upsilon\tau\acute{o}\nu$.

‡ Just. Mart. *Dial. c. Tryph.* 88.

flower of roses in the spring of the year, and as lilies by the water courses."

But St. Luke—and there can be little doubt that he heard the story from the lips of the Virgin, whether at Jerusalem or at Ephesus—alone preserves for us a single anecdote of the boyhood of Jesus, which is full of beauty and preciousness.

Twelve silent years glided by—perhaps the twelfth had been completed—and Jesus was considered old enough to accompany His parents to the Paschal Feast.* Of the eight stages into which the Jews divided childhood and boyhood, He had now reached the last. He was a *bachur*, "a full-grown boy." In Rabbinic phraseology, He was no longer animated by the *nephesh*, or "natural life," but by the *ruach* or "spirit"; that is, as we should express it, He had attained to years of discretion—for the boys develop much more rapidly in the East than in our Northern climate. At this age, by the rule of tradition, a boy would begin to learn a trade for his own maintenance, and to wear "phylacteries" (*tephillin*) after presentation by his father in the synagogue on the *Shabbath Tephilin*. It is, however, highly uncertain whether our Lord ever wore, on arm and forehead, these little leather receptacles for texts, or whether they were common among "the men of the people"—the *amharatzim* of Galilee. We have no reference to them in the Gospels, except in Christ's condemnation of the Pharisees for the vain ostentation with which they made them unusually broad.

As Jesus was now, or shortly afterwards became, "a son of the Covenant" (*Bar mitzvah*), or "a son of the Law" (*Benhattorah*), He had already received a considerable part of His early education. What were the most marked features in the training of a Jewish boy of that day?

The Jews were honourably distinguished by the care they took in the education of their children. They re-

* Comp. Jos. *Antt.* ii. 9, § 6.

garded their schools as "vineyards." There is a story in the Talmud how once there had been a long and painful drought, and all the Chief Priests and Rabbis assembled before the people to pray for rain. They prayed, and prayed, but no rain fell. Then rose up one common-looking man, and prayed, and instantly the heavens grew black with clouds, and the rain fell abundantly. " Who art thou," they asked in astonishment, " that thy prayer alone should have prevailed ? " And he answered, " *I am a teacher of little children.*"*

It is probable that our Lord grew up in the habitual use of two languages—Aramaic and Greek. Aramaic, a dialect of Hebrew, was at that time the current language of Galilee. A great part of Palestine was bilingual, so that there can be no doubt that Jesus also learnt to speak Greek, for He could converse with the Centurion, and the Syro-Phœnician woman, and Pilate, and others, without any interpreter. He was of course familiar with the Old Testament in the original Hebrew.† Since our Lord's brethren, James and Jude, show in their Epistles that they were well acquainted with the Apocrypha, we may be sure that our Lord was also. This would be decisively proved by the resemblance of Matt. xxiii. 37 to 2 Esdras i. 30–33, if it were not nearly certain that much of 2 Esdras is interpolated by a Christian writer.

The teaching of children was, however, mainly confined to the Mosaic and Levitic Law. " I lay aside all the trade of the world," said R. Nehorai, " and teach my son only the Law ; for its reward is enjoyed in this world, and its

---

* See the articles on " *Kinder,*" " *Unterricht* " in Winer. Realwörterbuch ; Diestel, *s.v. Unterricht*, in Schenkel's *Bibel-Lexicon ;* Hamburger, *s. vv. Schuler, Lehrer, Schule, Mitzwa.* Kitto, *Cyclopaed., s.v. Education;* Dean Plumptre in Smith's *Dict. of the Bible*, and Schürer, *Div.* ii. 1, 323–326 ; Herzfeld, *Gesch. d. Völkes Israel*, iii. 266–268, etc.

† As seems to be proved by the quotations from the original. Mark xii. 29, 30 ; Luke xxi. 37 ; Matt. xxvii. 46. The knowledge of Hebrew seems to be implied by Matt. v. 22.

capital remains for the world to come." * But the teaching of the Law was mainly an exercise of the memory. The commands of the Law were iterated and reiterated, so that the Rabbinic word for "to teach" (*shanah*) means "to repeat," and the word for "teaching" is *Mishnah* ("repetition"). The highest praise for a pupil was to be "like a well, lined with lime, which loses not one drop." †

The main effort, then, was merely to train the memory. We do full justice to the importance which the Jews attached to education, yet we cannot but admit that their views of education were too narrow. We cannot concede to Josephus that "the Jews by their system of teaching, which combined the teaching of the Law with the practice of morals, surpassed the foremost of the Greeks, since they united the unquestioning obedience of the Spartans with the theoretic instruction of the Athenians." ‡ Jewish boys were taught the Law, as Philo says, by their parents and teachers, from their very swaddling clothes; but, unhappily, the current conception of the Law had been overlaid with deplorable perversions, and was radically erroneous in important particulars.

There can be little doubt that Jesus attended the school which was attached to the synagogue of Nazareth, and that, as He "was continually growing in wisdom," He had from the first been carefully trained by His mother and Joseph. *That* training also was all-but-exclusively Scriptural. The *Kindergarten* of Jewish children—and the Jews sometimes called their schools "gardens"—was the *Beth Hassepher*, or "House of the Book"; and it was only when a child had been well grounded in "the Book" that he passed to the *Beth Hammidrash*, or secondary school. §

* *Peah*, i. 1.
† *Avoth*. ii. 8 ; Gfrörer, *Jahrh. des Heils*, i.; Hamburger, *s.v. Lehrhaus*.
‡ Jos. *c. Ap*. ii. 16, 17. Compare *Antt*. iv. 8, 12 ; Philo, *Leg. ad Caium*. 36.
§ Schools for children are said to have been founded throughout Palestine a century earlier by Simeon ben Shetach (Jer. *Kethouboth*, viii. 14) ; and to have

By that time a boy had been taught to read, and sometimes (though more rarely) to write; to keep the Sabbath; and to fast on the Day of Atonement. A little later he would be taught to repeat the *Shema* and the *Shemoneh Ezreh*. The *Shema*—or "Hear, O Israel!"—consisted of the sections Deut. vi. 4–9, xi. 13–21; Num. xv. 37–41, with various benedictions (*Berachoth*) which were attached to them. The *Shemoneh Ezreh* consisted of "Eighteen Blessings," mostly expressed in the words of Scripture, and beginning with the words "Blessed art Thou, O Lord."*

To this training was added all that a child learnt almost mechanically from his constant Sabbath-attendances at the synagogue, which was meant for instruction as well as for worship. How familiar must Christ have been with that village *Beth Tephilla* (House of Prayer) or *Beth Hakkeneseth* (House of Assembly), as He sat among the other boys of Nazareth in the back seats, behind the chief worshippers! How deeply must He have taken in the divine meaning alike of the *Parashoth*, or 154 sections of the Law, by which the Pentateuch was read through in three years; and also of the *Haphtaroth*, or sections of the Prophets, the reading of which had been introduced in the days of the fierce persecution by Antiochus Epiphanes, when the reading of the Law was punished with death. Not only were the passages read by the appointed person—who might even be a boy—in the original Hebrew, but they were translated, paragraph after paragraph, into the Aramaic by the *Methurgeman*, or interpreter. How deep must have been the expectant interest with which the child Jesus saw the *Rosh Hakkeneseth*, or "Ruler of the Synagogue," receive from the hand of his clerk (*Chazzan*) the roll of the Law, or of the Prophets, and appoint the reader, who took

---

been extended by the order of the High Priest, Jesus Bar Gamala (Bab. *Bavabathra* f. 21, 1).

* For full information, see Hamburger, *Real-Encycl.* II. *s.v. Schemone-Esre.*

his stand behind the elevated *Bema*, and read the lesson, and then sat down to deliver the explanation or sermon (*Derashah*). With what a thrill of heart must He have heard the trumpets (*Shopharoth*) blown at the beginning of the new year and on the solemn feast days.

Thus the human training of the Christ Child involved a thorough acquaintance with the letter of the Holy Scriptures, which rose infinitely above the wooden literalism, the fantastic expansions, the evasive manipulations of the current exegesis. The right apprehension of Holy Writ came to Him from no human teacher, but from His own pure spirit, and His union with that Father of Lights with whom is no variableness nor shadow cast by turning. Yet, early as He may have seen through the hollowness of the interpretations with which Scripture had been overlaid by the current tendencies of His day, we are quite sure that He was utterly unlike the terrible, ungovernable child of the Apocryphal fictions. Towards all His earthly teachers we are sure that He exhibited that sweet lowliness of heart which, as He grew in wisdom and stature, caused Him to advance also in favour with God and man.

The Son of Sirach asks : " How can he get wisdom that holdeth the plough, that driveth oxen—and whose talk is of bullocks . . . so every *carpenter* and workmaster that laboureth night and day? All these trust to their hands ; they shall not be sought for in public counsel. . . They shall not understand the covenant of judgment, and where parables are they shall not be found." * Nevertheless, however simple and elementary may have been the training which Jesus received from the *Mikredardike*, or " teachers of children," in the local synagogue-school, so deep was His insight into the Scriptures—so far deeper than that derived from the traditions of the Scribes—that when Rabbis and Jerusalemite Pharisees encountered Him in lordly opposition, He could at once refute their insolent

* Ecclus. xxxviii. 24–34.

tone of superiority by His searching questions, "*Have ye never read ?*" * We observe, too, that whereas the system of Jewish education was almost exclusively occupied with the study of the Law, our Lord reverts far more frequently to the great Prophets of Israel, and sets mercy far above sac-rifice.

It may be worth while to emphasise in passing the extreme simplicity of the worship in which during all His life the Saviour of mankind, Sabbath after Sabbath, was wont to take His part. The visits to the Temple were few and exceptional, and all His life long He mainly worshipped in the synagogues, which were as bare and as devoid of all ritual, symbolism, or outward gorgeousness as the barest Dissenting chapel. The synagogues were rooms, of which the end usually pointed to Jerusalem (the *Kibleh*, or con-secrated direction of Jewish worship, Dan. vi. 10). On one side sat the men ; on the other the veiled women. Almost the only piece of furniture in them was the Ark (*Tebhah*) of painted wood, which contained the Law (*Thorah*) and the rolls (*Tephilloth*) of the Prophets. On one side was a *Bema* (the Jews borrowed the name from the Greeks) for the reader and preacher, and the "chief seats" of the "Ruler of the Synagogue" and the Elders (*Zekenim*). The only servants of the synagogue, in its severe simplicity, were the clerk (*Chazzan*), the verger (*Sheliach*), and the deacons (*Parnasim*, or shepherds). It is clear therefore that rites and ceremonies—in favour of which neither Christ nor His Apostles uttered a single word—were needless for the most intense and exalted worship which the world has ever seen. The only rubric which the New Testament contains is, "Let all things be done decently and in order."

* Luke iv. 17 ; Matt. v. 18, xii. 3, xiii. 52, xix. 4, xxi. 16, 42, xxii. 31. The Rabbis hardly regarded a country education as worth their notice (Mark vi. 2 ; John vi. 42, vii. 15).

CHAPTER VIII.

THE FIRST ANECDOTE.

Ιησοῦς ὁ παῖς.—Luke ii. 43.

2 Macc. ii. 22. " The Temple, renowned all the world over."

" Take notice that His doing nothing wonderful was itself a kind of wonder. As there was power in His actions, so is there power in His silence, in His inactivity, in His retirement."—ST. BONAVENTURA.

THE other Evangelists give us a passing glimpse of the outer circumstances of the infancy of Jesus, and then pass on to His full manhood.

St. Luke alone, as we have seen, gives us the notice respecting Him—brief, but inestimably precious—when He was " a weaned child." He also furnishes us with " one solitary floweret out of the enclosed garden of the thirty years, plucked precisely there where the swollen bud, at a *distinctive crisis*, bursts into flower." *

Not before the twelfth year, and, as a rule, not till after its completion,† was a boy required to enter into the full obedience of an Israelite, and to attend the Passover. We can imagine how the heart of Jesus must have beat with earnest joy, as, with His parents and the many pilgrims from Nazareth who would attend the Feast, He made His way down the narrow valley from the summit of His native hill. He was doubtless clad in the bright-coloured robes of an Eastern boy—in red caftan, and gay tunic, girded with an embroidered sash, and covered, perhaps, with a loose

* Stier, v. 18.

† *Pirqe Avôth.* v. 21. " At thirteen years of age a boy becomes bound to observe the (613) precepts of the Law."

80

outer jacket of white or blue. What a rush of new associations would sweep through His soul as He traversed those
eighty miles between Nazareth and Jerusalem, and saw the
scenes which were indelibly associated in His mind with
memories of Sisera and Barak, of Elijah and Elisha, of
Joshua and Saul, at Kishon, and Shunem, and Gilboa!
He probably passed between Ebal and Gerizin, and by
Jacob's Well, and so by Shiloh and Bethel to the Holy
City. How often must the thought have been in His
mind, "Our feet shall stand in Thy courts, O Jerusalem!"
And when the city glittered before Him on its rocky water-
shed between the Jordan and the sea, with its three hills of
Zion, Moriah, and Acra, surrounded by walls and stately
towers—when He saw the Temple, with its white marble,
and gilded pinnacles, flaming in the eastern sunlight like a
mountain of snow and gold, and rising before Him, terrace
above terrace—the words of the Psalmist would almost
inevitably be in His mind, " Jerusalem is built as a city which
is at unity with itself. For thither the tribes go up, even
the tribes of the Lord, for a testimony unto Israel, to give
thanks unto the name of the Lord." *

Or, " Walk about Zion, and go round about her, and tell
the towers thereof. Mark well her bulwarks, consider her
palaces, that ye may tell them that come after." † The
Psalms known as the "Songs of Degrees," ‡ were often
sung by the pilgrims as they approached Jerusalem, as they
had been—according to tradition—by the exiles who
returned with Ezra. We can imagine the enthusiasm with
which they would join in such words as :

" Peace be within thy walls, and plenteousness within
thy palaces !

" For my brethren and companions' sakes, I will wish
thee prosperity.

---

* Ps. cxxii. 4. † Ps. xlviii. 13.
‡ Pss. cxx.–cxxxiv. They should properly be called " Songs of Ascents,"
or " of the Goings Up."

" Yea, because of the House of the Lord our God I will seek to do thee good. *

Amid the rose-gardens and pleasances which surrounded Jerusalem,† and under the umbrageous multitudes of palms and olives, and figs and cedars, and chestnut trees, would have been scattered the temporary booths of some of the two million pilgrims who flocked to the city for the great yearly feast from every region of the civilised globe. When the pilgrims from Nazareth had passed along the Valleys of Jehoshaphat and Hinnom, the roads and the streets through which they made their way to the Temple must have been densely thronged with ever-increasing crowds.

Jesus would pass beneath those colossal substructions towering up some 600 feet above His head, and built of vast blocks of stones, still visible, of which some are 20 feet in length and 4 feet in height.‡ Perhaps he crossed the royal bridge over the Valley of the Tyropœon. And at last—at last—He would enter "the Mountain of the House " § by one of the five gates. If He entered by the gate called *Shushan*, or " the Lily Gate," He would see " Solomon's Porch " stretching to right and left, and would stand on the many-coloured pavement of the court of that gorgeous Herodian Temple which was one of the wonders of the world. The scene was doubtless one of extraordinary animation, yet it must have presented many repulsive features which it required an intense enthusiasm to overlook. For the colonnades were thronged with the vendors of sheep and oxen for sacrifice, including thousands of Paschal lambs. Here were seated the sellers of the doves, for the offerings of the poor, with their crowded wicker

---

* Ps. cxxii. 7–9.

† An ancient rose-garden is mentioned (*Baba Kama*, 82, 1), and there were the gardens of Solomon (2 Kings xxv. 4 ; Neh. iii. 15 ; Eccl. ii. 5, etc.).

‡ On the Temple, see Josephus *B. J.* v. 2, and plate in Carr's St. Matthew.

§ הר הבית   Comp. 1 Macc. xiii. 52.

baskets. Here sat and chaffered the two classes of money-changers—those who gave smaller change for gold and silver,* and those who took foreign money, with its heathen emblems and inscriptions, in exchange for the Jewish money, which could alone be used for Temple purposes.† These men drove hard bargains in noisy and often nefarious traffic. At the south end of this huge Court of the Gentiles was the triple royal colonnade—known as "Solomon's Porch"—which was reserved for more quiet gatherings. This Forecourt of the Gentiles was marked off from the more sacred enclosures by the double barriers of the *Soreg* and the *Chel* (חיל). Through one of the openings of the *Soreg* Jesus would climb the fourteen steps to the *Chel*, on which were marble tablets with inscriptions in Greek and Latin forbidding any Gentiles to proceed a step farther on pain of death.‡ Mounting the steps of a terrace which towered sixty feet above the Court of the Gentiles, Jesus would pass, perhaps, through "the Beautiful Gate" and gaze at the Court of the Women, and the Court of the Israelites. In the latter stood the *Lishcath Hag-gazzîth*, or "Hall of Square Stones," to the southeast of the inner forecourt, in which perhaps at that time the Sanhedrin held its meetings. Here, too, was the Treasury, outside of which were the thirteen chests with trumpet-shaped open-

---

* κολλυβισταὶ, John ii. 15. See Matt. xxi. 12; Mark xi. 15; Luke xix. 45.

† κερματισταὶ, John ii. 14; Josephus *B. J.* vi. 2, 4; Philo, *Opp.* ii. 577. Comp. Acts xxi. 28.

‡ One of these marble tablets, which must have been seen by Christ Himself, was discovered by Mons. Clermont Ganneau built into the wall of a Mohammedan house at Jerusalem. It is now in one of the mosques in Constantinople. For the actual inscription see *Rev. Archéologique*, xxiii. pl. x.; Schürer, i. 266. M. Clermont Ganneau gave an account of its discovery in the *Athenæum* of June 10, 1871. The inscription is word for word as given by Josephus, except that he, with his usual complaisance to the Romans, omits the threatened penalty of death to any intruder beyond the δρυφακτὸς which ran round the temple (ἱερον) and enclosure (περιβολή) (Besant, *Twenty-One Years of Work*, p. 167).

ings (*Shopharoth*) * into which alike the rich and the poor cast their Temple-offerings.

Twelve or fifteen steps higher still was the Court of the Priests, on the northwest end of which, on a platform ascended by twelve more steps, rose in white marble " the joy of the whole earth, the Temple of the Great King." † Its doors were open, but the interior was concealed from vulgar gaze by curtains of Babylonian purple. Over its gilded portico was wreathed the huge Vine with its bunches of golden grapes. On its topmost roof were the gilded spikes (" scare-ravens ") to keep birds from settling on it. Within its mysterious recesses was that awful " Holy of Holies " which was trodden by no human foot save that of the High Priest when he sprinkled the blood of the sacrifice, on the great Day of Atonement, towards the place where once had stood the Ark of the Covenant, overshadowed by the outspread wings of the golden Cherubim.‡ And this was the one most hallowed spot of all the world, towards which, for centuries, every Jew had turned his eyes when he knelt down to pray to the God of his Fathers.§

All was as yet entirely new to the Holy Boy, and we can but imagine with what interest He—the unknown heir of David's line—would have listened to the nine trumpet-blasts which announced the morning and evening sacrifice,

---

* *Yoma*, f. 55, 2.

† We cannot always be certain of the exactness of the details.

‡ The Ark had disappeared since the Captivity. Nothing was now to be seen in the Holiest Place but the " Stone of the Foundation " (*Yoma*, f. 53, 2), which was supposed to be the centre of the world (*cf.* Ezek. v. 5, and see Hershon, *Talm. Miscellany*, p. 300). Pompey, when he forced his way into the Holiest, expecting to find some image of an animal which the Gentiles ignorantly fancied that the Jews worshipped, was amazed to find " *vacua omnia.*" According to *Yoma*, f. 21, 2, the five things wanting to the second Temple were : 1. The Ark. 2. The Holy Fire. 3. The Shechinah. 4. The Spirit of Prophecy. 5. The Urim and Thummim. These five missing things were supposed to be indicated by the omission of ה (= 5) in the word ראנבר, " and I will be glorified," in Hag. i. 8.

§ Dan. vi. 10.

and to the sacred songs and solemn litanies of the singers, the sons of Asaph, Heman, and Jeduthun, with their silver trumpets, and harps, and cymbals. He must have watched the army of priests in their turbans and white robes and girdles of purple, and blue, and scarlet, hurrying about the Court of the Priests with their bare feet, and busy from morn till dewy eve in roasting and seething the oxen, and lambs, and kids, and ever washing the gold and silver vessels of the Sanctuary. He would see for the first time the huge altar of burnt-offering standing before the eastern front of the Temple. It was the hugest in the world, forty-eight feet square at the base, and diminishing by stages to its summit. It was built of unhewn stones, untouched by any human tool. It was also approached by an ascent of unhewn stones, and on its broad summit flamed, day and night, the perpetual fire. Beyond it was the great brazen laver in which the priests washed their hands and feet.* In this Court the victims were slaughtered, and there were pillars to which their carcasses were hung, and marble tables on which they were skinned and the entrails washed.

To the ordinary eye this Court must often have looked like one huge slaughter-house, in which amid the wreaths of curling smoke were heard the sound of perpetual prayers and formularies, the bleating of sheep, and the lowing of oxen. But it would seem transfigured to eyes that gazed on it with holy enthusiasm. Jesus could only have seen it from the Court of the Israelites; for, under ordinary circumstances, none but the priestly ministers were allowed to enter into its actual precincts. "Whoever has not seen Herod's Temple," says the Talmud, "has never seen a beautiful structure in his life. How did Herod build it? Ravah replied, 'With white and green marble, so that it appeared in the distance like waves of the sea.'" †

---

* *Baba Bathra*, f. 3, 2. " The Mount of the Temple was 500 yards square." *Middoth*, ch. 2.

† *Baba Bathra*, f. 4, 1. See, for full details, Schürer, i. 280.

But in the Court below, the full stream of the varied life of Judaism must have passed before His eyes. Here He would have seen the High Priest Hanan (or Annas), son of Seth, before whom He was destined to stand as a prisoner. * He would have seen too, the "Captain of the Temple" (the *Ish har hab-Bîth*, or "Man of the Mountain of the House"), with his little army of subordinate Levites, in their peaked caps, and with the pockets which held their Law books. Mingled among the crowd would be solemn white-robed Essenes; Pharisees with their broad phylacteries; Herodian courtiers in their gorgeous clothing; Nazarites with their long hair; beggars—blind and lame—seated before the two great bronze valves of the Gate Beautiful; and here and there, perhaps, in the Court of the Gentiles, some Roman soldier in his armour, looking round him with scornful curiosity, and answering with looks of disdain the scowls of hatred sometimes thrown upon him. At sunset Jesus would perhaps stop to witness the closing of the great bronze gate on the east of the Court of the Gentiles, so heavy that it took twenty men to move it,† though, sixty years later, before the destruction of the Temple, it was said to have opened of its own accord, while Voices, as of departing Deities, where heard to wail in tones of awful warning, "Let us depart hence!" ‡

And then, at evening, in some little wattled booth out-side the city, among the Galilean pilgrims, or in the humble house of some Galilean friends in Jerusalem, the male members of the Holy Family—although not with their loins girded, their staves in their hands, their shoes on their feet, as the ancient custom was—would have eaten the Paschal meal rejoicing, with hymns and benedictions, and would

---

* He was High Priest A. D. 6–15. At later visits Jesus may have seen, in the rapidly changing Hierarchy, Ishmael ben Phabi (A. D. 15, 16); Eleazar, son of Annas (A. D. 16, 17); Simon ben Kamhith (A. D. 17, 18); and Joseph Caiaphas (A. D. 18–36).

† Josephus *B. J.* vi. 5, 3.   ‡ Tac. *Hist.* v. 13.

drink the cups of blessing and thanksgiving which the father of the family passed round.

So the Feast ended, with its tumult of new associations. And then, after this chief event in the whole year, the booths were broken up, the simple belongings of the pilgrims were packed on the backs of asses and camels, and in various groups, the hundreds of thousands of pilgrims, amid psalms and hymns and spiritual songs, began to wend their way back to their own quiet homes.

How easy it would be, in such a scene of bustle, to lose sight of one young boy.* At first, Joseph and Mary did not notice His absence, feeling no doubt assured that, as He must have known the hour at which the caravan would start, He must be safe and happy amid some group of the rejoicing relatives and friends who had accompanied them from Nazareth. The fact that they did not observe His absence illustrates the naturalness and unconstraint of the conditions in which the Boy Jesus had been trained. To this day the incident of separation from friends in these great caravans is a common one, and excites little anxiety.

It was not till the evening of the first day's journey— perhaps when they had arrived at Beeroth, some six miles north of Jerusalem—that they missed Him, and by that time wondered why He had not rejoined them. Then, with intense anxiety, they began to search for Him, and their anxiety deepened to agony when he was nowhere to be found in the little companies of Nazarenes or other Galileans. With hearts full of forebodings, they turned back to Jerusalem, looking for Him all along the route. Still they could hear nothing of Him. He was nowhere to be seen in the entire caravans, nor among the later stragglers. It was not till the third day that they discovered Him in the Temple,† probably in one of the halls or rooms which surrounded the Court of the Israelities, and were used for purposes of teaching. They were amazed to see the gracious

* Luke ii. 43. † Luke ii. 46, " After three days."

Boy " sitting in the midst of the Rabbis, both hearing them and asking them questions." The instruction of the young was a constant function of the leading Scribes, and they always showed ready kindness to any youthful enquirer. It is not impossible that among these Rabbis may have been men so famous as Hillel and Shammai, and Bava ben Butah, in their extreme old age ; and among the younger may have been Rabban Simeon, son of Shammai ; and Gamaliel, son of Hillel ; and Nicodemus, and Jochanan ben Zakkai.

Overawed perhaps at first, Joseph and Mary would hardly venture to thrust themselves into that group of learned officials and Rabbis, surrounded as they were with almost awful reverence ; but they took in enough of the scene to notice that " all that heard Him were astonished at His understanding and answers."

In the Apocryphal Gospels, and in many books, the significance of the scene has been entirely misunderstood. In pictures, also, Jesus has been represented sitting, or standing, in an attitude of authority, as though He were teaching and catechising these Scribes, the most famed for learning in their day. Such a notion is contrary to all that we know of Christ's gracious humility. Anything like forwardness or presumption would have awakened nothing but displeasure in Rabbis accustomed to deferential homage ;* but, on the contrary, the Boy of Nazareth had won their admiration by His modesty and intelligence. He was "sitting" at the feet of the Rabbis, " hearing them," *i. e.*, trying to learn all which they could teach ; and ingenuously, but with consummate insight, "answering" the questions which they addressed to Him. What most astonished

* See *Pirqe Avôth*, v. 12, 15. *Baba Metzia*, f. 84, 2. Similar stories are told of Eliezer ben Azariah, R. Ashi, and Josephus (Vit. 2). Comp. *Baba Metzia*, f. 48, 6, where we are told how Rabbi Elaza, and Rabbi Judah (the Holy) sat on the ground as boys before two great Rabbis, " asking questions and starting objections. The other Rabbis exclaimed, ' We drink of their water ' (*i. e.*, we imbibe their wisdom), ' and they sit upon the ground ! ' Seats were then brought in for the two children."

them was His knowledge of the Scriptures, and the wisdom, beyond His boyish age, which His answers manifested. His parents too—for Mary's awful secret was hidden deep within her heart, and Joseph was regarded as His father— were amazed to see Him so happy, so calmly at ease, in that august assembly. At last His mother ventured to address to Him the agitated question, "Child (τέκνον), why didst thou thus to us? Behold, thy father and I were seeking thee in sorrow?" * To Him—so wrapt up in all that He had seen and heard, and living in inward com- munion with His Father in Heaven—their distress seemed strange. When they first missed Him, where, He asked, would it have been most natural for them at once to seek Him? "Why is it that ye were seeking me? Did ye not know that I must be in my Father's house?" †

The rendering of the A. V., "about my Father's business," may now be regarded as having been finally disproved. It would be, in every way, much more difficult to explain ; for Jesus had been in the Temple, *not* in any fulfilment of His mission, but as a boy, to worship and to learn. His kinsfolk must have observed His rapture as He had spent day after day of the Feast in the Temple Courts. They must have been long familiar with His ardent love for instruction, and with the untroubled simplicity with which He always looked up to God as His Father. "Where then," He seems to ask them, "would it be natural for you at once to seek for me, except *in my Father's House ?*" It was an accident that, when they started homeward, they had not noticed His absence ;—but, having missed Him, surely they might have known the one place where they would be most sure to find Him !

* Luke ii. 48.

† The contrast of the sublime and truthful simplicity of the Evangelists with the unauthorised additions of the Apocryphal Gospels may be seen by reading the very different accounts of this incident in the Gospel of St. Thomas. The attempt to glorify Christ by *inventing* details instantly profanes the Ideal, which nothing but truth could paint.

What could they say? They could not take in the full meaning of His words. The answer came to them like a marvellous gleam of light. They felt that worlds of mystery lay hidden in the depths of the Boy's soul—of mystery which they could not fathom. His mother especially pondered over His words, and kept them in her heart. What would be the end of these things? Whereunto would they ultimately grow?

And yet to His parents the Divine Boy was all tenderness and meek submission. From His earliest years "He was meek and lowly of heart." * He returned with them at once, and without question. They soon found themselves once more in Nazareth, among the poor yet happy surroundings of their Holy Home. There was nothing froward or defiant in the bearing of Mary's Son. His years passed in uneventful calm, as He "kept advancing in wisdom and stature, and in favour with God and man." †

Many of the great Prophets of the Old Testament had lived as He did, through a youth of unknown preparation —as did David among the sheepfolds, and Elijah in the tents of the Bed'awin, and Amos as a gatherer of sycamore leaves at Tekoah, and Jeremiah in quiet Anathoth, and the Baptist in the wilderness. They had waited, as He waited, the call which summoned them to perform in the face of the world the high mission of their lives.

And so, as Irenæus says, " He passed through every age, having been made an infant to sanctify infants ; a little one among the little ones, sanctifying the little ones ; among the youths a youth." ‡ That His childhood and early boyhood were full of happy peace we have every reason to

---

* Matt. xi. 29.

† Comp. Prov. iii. 4. "So shalt thou find favour and good success in the sight of God and man." *Pirqe Avôth* iii. 10. " In whomsoever the mind of man delights, in him also the Spirit of God delights." It is not said that the Baptist grew up in favour *with men*. On the lifelong holy submission of Jesus to the will of His Heavenly Father, see John iv. 34, v. 30, vi. 38, viii. 18, etc.

‡ Iren. *c. Haer*. ii. 22.

infer from the infinite tenderness which He always displayed towards children, and His sympathetic references to their joyous games and trustful gentleness.* His divine nature *deepened*, it did not *quench*, the keenness of His human sympathies for His family, for His nation, for all mankind. His greatness was not the separate greatness of Poet, or Artist, or Orator, or Hero, but the unprecedented greatness of Harmony and Peace, Humility and Majesty. His hatred of sin in its every form, combined with tender compassion for even the worst of sinners, made Him the fairest of the children of men, the most supreme representative of man in that union with God which is the sole greatness that it is open to our nature to achieve by the grace which comes from Him alone.†

* Matt. xi. 16, xix. 13–15.
† On the whole subject, see Ullmann, *The Sinlessness of Jesus*, pp. 50-59.

CHAPTER IX.

LESSONS OF THE UNRECORDED YEARS.

"He shall grow up before Him as a tender plant, and as a root out of the dry ground."—Isaiah liii. 2.

"Having food and raiment, in these we shall have enough."—1 Tim. vi. 8.

"Ecclesia habet quatuor Evangelia, haeresis plurima."—IRENÆUS iii. 11, 9.

" HE went down with them . . . to Nazareth, and was subject unto them." Such is St. Luke's brief epitome. It is the only record left to us of nearly twenty years of the life of Christ, from the time when He had attained the age of twelve till when " He was about thirty years of age."* We are told the one anecdote of boyhood, of which we have been trying to grasp the significance, and, beyond that, only the general facts of His growth in wisdom and stature and favour with God and man, and His sweet filial obedience during His abode in that beautiful Valley of Nazareth. This is literally all that the four Gospels record of all except—at the outside—some three and a half years of the life of the Son of Man and the Son of God.

This is all that they *record;* but in St. Mark, a single casual word—not meant for any part of the biography, but occurring in the most incidental manner in the discontented murmurs of the people of Nazareth—comes like a revealing flash to illuminate the darkness. That word is " *the Carpenter.*"†

* Luke iii. 23, R. V. " Jesus, *when He began to teach*, was about thirty years of age."

† Mark vi. 3. Justin Martyr says, " He used, when among men, to work as a carpenter, making ploughs and yokes." *Dial. c. Tryph.* 88.

Jesus had been teaching in the synagogue so familiar to Him in His early years, and His disciples were with Him. As He taught, the Nazarenes were amazed at His wisdom, and His mighty works, but the humility of His origin was a stumbling-block to them. Was not this man a peasant like themselves? In what respect could He claim any superiority over them? Did they not know Mary His mother, and His four brothers, and His sisters? Had He not laboured among them for His daily bread? Was He not in the eyes of the Scribes a mere ignoramus? How could they accept a teaching so authoritative, claims so lofty? A prophet could expect but little honour in his own country, and among his own kin, and in his own house. "Is not this the Carpenter?" * Christ might have come as a Prince like Buddha, or a Philosopher like Confucius, or a Priest like Zoroaster, or a Warrior like Mohammed; but He chose to come as "the Carpenter of Nazareth." The name of scorn lingered on through the centuries. "What is the *Carpenter* doing now?" sneeringly asked Libanius, the pagan sophist, of a Christian. "*He is making a coffin,*" answered the Christian; and shortly after, Julian, the apostate Emperor, whom Libanius regarded with such proud devotion, was cut short in his brilliant career of statesmanship and victory, and died with the words "*Thou hast conquered, O Galilean!*" upon his lips.†

The innate vulgarity which showed itself in the scoff of

---

* Mark vi. 3. Hence Origen is mistaken when he says (*c. Cels.* vi. 36) that " Jesus has never been described as the carpenter." The Jews, wiser by far in this respect than the Pagans, honoured manual labour, and many of their greatest men—among them Hillel and Akiba—were never ashamed to have once earned their bread by the sweat of their brow. But how deep was the humility of Christ's choice may be estimated if we read Ecclus. xxxviii. 24

† There is a curious passage in *Succah.* " ' And the Lord showed me four *carpenters* ' (Zech. i. 20). Who are these four carpenters? Rav Chana bar Bizna says that they were *Messiah the Son of David;* Messiah the son of Joseph; Elijah, and the Priest of Righteousness." (*Succah,* f. 52, 2 ; Hershon, *Talm. Misc.* p. 77.)

the Nazarenes has been common in all ages, although, again and again, those who have sprung from the humblest ranks among the people—like Mohammed, and St. Francis of Assisi, and Gregory VII., and Luther, and Shakespeare, and Bunyan—have shown themselves to be moving forces in the world. But the low sneer becomes to us an illuminating truth, revealing to us the methods and purposes of God.

The very silence of the Evangelists about those long years is full of eloquence. Contrast it with the profane babblings and old wives' fables of unauthorised invention, and it becomes rich in most blessed significance!

Let us consider what it means.

It shows the *truthfulness* of the Evangelists. It might well have seemed most strange to them, as at first sight it does to us, that He in whom they recognised the Son of God, the Saviour of the world, should have spent in lowly obscurity and unrecorded silence all but so small a fraction of His years on earth. They must have yearned, as we yearn, to lift the curtain of apparent oblivion which had been suffered to rest upon the Life of Lives. But they would not be of the "fools" who

"Rush in where angels fear to tread";

nor would they surround the brow of Christ with a halo of lying miracles. They would record nothing where nothing was given them to record.

Throughout these four narratives they show a great simplicity, which is the most certain stamp of truthfulness. They burst into no raptures, they abandon themselves to no ecstasies, they indulge in no notes of admiration. "*Ils se souviennent, voilà tout !* " *

Yet this reticence is in itself rich in the deepest and most necessary lessons.

"*Fruit is seed.*" What the soil and the grain have been, that will the harvest be. When we see the perfect rose we

* Didon, I, liv.

know at once that there can have been no blight, no imperfection in the bud. So far, then, as the revelation of
Christ's Person is concerned, we recognise, without special
record, that those unrecorded years must have been years
of holy and sinless humility.

But, further, the one word preserved (with such apparent
casualness) by St. Mark, brings clearly home to us that
those long years of Jesus in Nazareth were years of preparation, of poverty, of obscurity, of labor.

(i.) They were years of *preparation :* However deep
must have been the consciousness in the soul of the youthful Christ that He was, in a special sense, the Son of His
Heavenly Father, and that He was born to do His work,
yet, in meekness and lowliness of heart, He would abide
God's good time, He would await the pointing of His finger,
the whisper of His voice. " He shall not strive, nor cry,
neither shall His voice be heard in the streets. A bruised
reed will He not break, and the smoking flax will He not
quench, until He send forth judgment unto victory." * The
life *with* God and *in* God sufficed Him. Men might look
for manifestations of God in the earthquake or the thunder,
or the mighty strong wind which shakes the mountains and
rends their rocks: to Jesus, hidden in the cleft of that
mountain valley, they came, as to Elijah, in the "still,
small voice."

(ii.) And it teaches us a most blessed lesson, that God
Himself, hid in the veil of mortal flesh, should voluntarily
have undergone those long silent years from childhood to
manhood in the lot of poverty, of obscurity, of labour.

Of *poverty*. The Gospel of Christ is a Gospel to the
poor, who are *the many*. Poverty is the normal lot of the
vast majority of mankind. There was nothing squalid,
nothing torturing, nothing degraded in this poverty. It
was the modest competence, earned by manly toil, which
suffices to provide all that men truly need, though not all

* Matt. xii. 19, 20 ; Is. xlii. **2, 3.**

that they passionately desire. It was the poverty which is content with food and raiment. Men, by myraids, strive passionately for wealth. In all ages Mammon has been the god of their commonest worship,—

> " Mammon, the least erected spirit that fell
> From heaven ; for e'en in heaven his looks and thoughts
> Were always downward bent, admiring more
> The riches of heaven's pavement, trodden gold,
> Than aught divine or holy else enjoyed
> In vision beatific."

Men strive and agonise for gold ; they toil and moil, and cheat, and steal, and oppress, and poison, and ruin their brethren to get money ; they sell their souls, they turn their whole lives into a degradation and a lie, because of the false glamour of riches. The old song says rightly :—

> " The gods from above the mad labour behold,
> And pity mankind who would perish for gold."

Yet after all it is but very few who, with all their passionate endeavours, attain to riches. The Dives who is clad in purple and fine linen, and fares sumptuously every day, is but one out of every hundred thousand ; and very often his earthly wealth tends only to ossify and dehumanise his heart. The lesson of Christ's poverty has helped myraids of the humble to say, with brave Martin Luther, " My God, I thank Thee that Thou hast made me poor and a beggar upon earth." And, as the wise king had prayed : "Give me neither poverty nor riches ; feed me with food convenient for me," so Christ, by the example of these long, silent years of poverty, gave deeper emphasis to His own teaching : " Lay not up for yourselves treasures upon earth, where moth and rust doth corrupt, and where thieves dig through and steal ; but lay up for yourselves treasures in heaven, where neither moth nor rust doth corrupt, and where thieves do not dig through nor steal." * In the

* Matt. vi. 19, 20.

workshop at Nazareth, faithful in that which was little, Christ revealed to mankind where to seek, and how to enjoy the true riches. By long example He added force to His own precept: " Be not anxious for the morrow, for the morrow will be anxious for the things of itself." " Be not anxious for your life, what ye shall eat, or what ye shall drink; nor yet for your body what ye shall put on. Is not the life more than food, and the body than raiment." *

(iii.) And it was a life of *obscurity*. Men love fame; they will risk life itself, they will face the cannon which pour forth destruction into the midst of them, to win renown, and " fly victorious in the mouths of men." This passion to win fame is not so grovellingly ignoble as that love of money which is a root of all kinds of evil?†

> Fame is the spur that the clear spirit doth raise
> (That last infirmity of noble minds),
> To scorn delights, and live laborious days ;
> But the fair guerdon when we hope to find,
> And think to burst out into sudden blaze,
> Comes the blind Fury with th' abhorrèd shears
> And slits the thin-spun life."

It is infinitely difficult to disillusion men from this passion, although in age after age the greatest have been among the saddest of mankind. "*Omnia fui, et nihil expedit*," sighed the Roman Emperor, who had risen from lowliness to the topmost summit of earthly grandeur. " All my life long I have been prosperous in peace and victorious in war, feared by my enemies, loved and honoured by my friends," wrote Abdalrahman the Magnificent, in his private diary. " Amid all this wealth and glory I have counted the days of my life which I could call happy. They amount to fourteen ! "‡ Our great dramatist makes his holy king say :—

---

* Matt. vi. 34, 25. † Tim. vi. 10.
‡ Quoted by Gibbon, ch. lii. (ed. Milman, v. 197).

> " My crown is in my heart, not on my head,
> Not set with diamonds, or Indian stones,
> Nor to be seen : my crown is called Content—
> A crown it is which seldom kings enjoy ! "

And again :—

> " I swear 'tis better to be lowly born
> And range with humble dwellers in content,
> Than to be perked up in a glistering grief,
> And wear a golden sorrow."

"I never spent such tedious hours in all my life," exclaimed Napoleon I., as he flung into the corners of the room the superb coronation robes which he had worn when the Pope of Rome, in the Cathedral of Notre Dame, had placed the crown of St. Louis on the brows of him who had, a few years before, been the poor and struggling sub-lieutenant of artillery. "Right well I know"—such are the words which one of the chief poets of our generation puts into the mouth of the mighty Merlin—

> " Right well know I that fame is half dis-fame,
> The cackle of the unborn about the grave.
> Sweet were the days when I was all unknown,
> But when my name was lifted up, the storm
> Brake on the mountain, and I cared not for it."

And so the "Emptiness of emptiness, emptiness of emptiness, all is emptiness!" of the richest, wisest, and most splendid of earthly kings * has been reverberated from century to century; and with that verdict of disillusionment comes the old wise lesson, "Seekest thou great things for thyself? Seek them not, saith the Lord." † Jesus gave to the lesson of this world-wide experience His seal of confirmation by His unknown years at Nazareth; and thus, by example as by His words, He says to us:

---

* Ecc. i. 2.
† Jer. xlv. 5.   Comp. Luke xii. 29 ; John v. 30, 44, viii. 50.

"Come unto Me . . . for I am meek and lowly in heart, and ye shall find rest unto your souls." *

(iv.) And His was a life of *manual toil.* In this respect also how inestimable a boon did He confer upon the toiling millions of mankind:

> "Not to the rich He came, nor to the ruling,
>   Men full of meat, whom most His heart abhors;
> Not to the fools, grown insolent in fooling,
>   Most when the poor are dying out of doors."

There has been a haughty tendency in all ages to despise manual labour, and look down on those who live by it. All trade and mechanic work was to the ancient world despicable (βάναυσον), a thing to be left to slaves, or those but a little above them. So it was in the days of the Roman Empire; so it was even among our Teutonic forefathers. A "base mechanic" was quite an ordinary description, in the days of Queen Elizabeth, for the mass of the people, † and to this day the insolent ineptitude of commonplace vulgarity thinks it an immense disparagement to call a man "a mere tradesman." The Jews alone among the nations rose to a wiser standpoint, though even among them we find such haughty sentence as: "How can he get wisdom that holdeth the plough . . . whose talk is of bullocks?"‡

Even "the sweet and noble Hillel," though he rose from a position of the lowliest poverty, was so tainted by the pride of leisurely sciolism as to say, "No *am-ha-aretz* can be pious." The lot of artisans was, however, indefinitely raised among the Jews by the fact that the greatest Rabbis were taught that it was well to be able to maintain themselves by a trade. What sublimer lesson could Jesus have taught to mankind than by spending thirty unknown years as the humble Carpenter of Nazareth? How fundamentally did He thus rectify the judgments of man's feeble and

* Matt. xi. 29.   † Comp. Shakespeare, *Ant. and Cleop.* v. 2.
‡ Ecclus. xxxviii. 25.

erring day! How did He thus illustrate the truth that
"all honest labour is an honour to the labourer"! How
did He further demonstrate by this example that man has
no essential dignity except that which comes from his
inherent nature as created in the image of God! Shakespeare complains:

> " Not a man for being simply man
> Hath any honour ; but honour for those honours
> Which are without him, as place, riches, favour,
> Prizes of accident as oft as merit."

Buddhism has its Arhats; Brahminism its Yogis;
Mohammedanism its Dervishes; Manichean asceticism has
its monks and hermits. But Christ wished to show that
He who, by His Divine Being, was immeasurably and
inconceivably greater than the greatest in all the world,
lost no particle of His grandeur by living the common
every-day life, and by learning to labour truly, and earning
His bread by the sweat of His brow.

" He who is without friends, without money, without
home, without country, is still at the least a man ; and he
who has all these is no more."* To all alike—to the
poorest, the lowliest, the most oppressed, the most persecuted—God in Christ gives an equal chance of happiness.
Complete earthly insignificance is the lot of the mass of
mankind. Millions might say, " We are the merest
cyphers." All but the very few, when death comes might
murmur:

> " I shall be gone to the crowd untold
> Of men by the cause they served unknown,
> Who lie in the myriad graves of old,
> Never a story, and never a stone."

Some men are inclined to ask why God placed them in
depths where their voices can never be heard. The answer
is that life means something infinitely more precious than

* Sir Walter Scott, *Rob Roy.*

power and fame.   The object of life—as the silent, unrecorded years of Christ's life teach us—is neither to be
known, nor to be praised, but simply to do our duty, and
to the best of our power to serve our brother-men.   The
inch-high dignities of man on the insignificant stage of his
little greatness are annihilated in the infinitude of God, to
whom all human life, apart from Him, is but as "a trouble
of ants 'mid a million million of suns!"   But

> " All service is true service, while it lasts,"

and

> " All service ranks the same with God,
>   Whose puppets are we, one and all ;
>   There is no great and small."

If we realise this truth in the light of Christ's early life, we
add an undreamed-of "grandeur to the beatings of the
heart."   If we live blameless and harmless children of
God without rebuke, we may make our lives as splendid in
the sight of our Heavenly Father as though we stood on
the summits of humanity, clad with angels' wings.   The
Archangel Gabriel thought it as high an honour to help
back to its nest the little struggling ant as to save the great
King from committing a sin.

> " He did God's work, to him all one,
>   If on the earth, or in the sun."

All readers then, will, I trust, agree with me that the
silence of the Evangelists about those thirty years in the
earthly life of the Lord of Glory is the grandest eloquence ;
and that merely by living this unknown life of labour as a
peasant in a Galilean village, Christ set the very example,
and taught the very lesson, which the untold millions of
mankind most deeply need—it was the lesson that life
comes indeed differently to the good and to the bad, to the
wise and to the foolish, but that it has gifts of *equal* blessedness for the low and for the high, for the poor and for the

rich.   To all true men, with no respect of persons, are flung equally wide

> " The Gates of Heaven, on golden hinges moving."

But it is perfectly lawful and reverent for us, though we cannot narrate a single incident of Christ's youth and early manhood, yet to try to realise all that can be ascertained of the outer circumstances in the midst of which that life was spent.

" He went down . . . to Nazareth and was subject unto them."

What was the scenery around the humble home in which Jesus grew up? I need not repeat the description which I have given elsewhere of that little white village on the hill—" *urbs florida et virgultis consita* " *—lying amid its green and umbrageous fields " like a handful of pearls in a goblet of emerald."   Suffice it to say that, while the scenery is by no means grand or overwhelming, it is full of peaceful loveliness.   In this, as in all else, there was nothing *exceptional* in the conditions which surrounded the youth and early manhood of the Saviour.

> " Needs no show of mountain hoary,
>   Winding shore, or deepening glen,
> Where the landscape in its glory
>   Teaches truth to wondering men ;
> Give true hearts but earth and sky,
> And some flowers to bloom and die ;
> Homely scenes and simple views,
> Lowly thoughts may best infuse."

As the boy Jesus stood on the hill-top of His native town, gazing over scenes rich in the historic memories of the Chosen People, and rejoicing as the wind of the mountains and the sea played in His long hair, He would have seen the pelicans, with their great white wings, flying in long lines to the Lake of Galilee ; and the roller-bird, with

* Jerome *in Is.* xi. 1.

its plumage of vivid blue, flash like a living sapphire among
the pale grey olive-trees; and the kingfisher, perched on a
reed beside the waters, fishing eagerly from hour to hour;
and the harmless doves, soiled sometimes as they lighted
on the dustheaps of the streets, but "covered with silver
wings, and their feathers like gold" when they soared once
more into the azure, and reflected the sunlight from every
varying plume. He had watched with loving eye the
eagle soaring with supreme dominion in the cloudless sky;
the vultures which gather round the fallen carcass; the
ravens which lay up no store for food, and yet the Heavenly
Father feedeth them; the innumerable little brown
sparrows which twittered in the over-grown foliage of the
water-courses—so valueless that you could buy two of them
for a farthing, and, if you spent *two* farthings, could get
five, so that one would be thrown in for nothing,* and yet
not one of them falling to the ground without our Father's
love. He had noticed " the hen, with passionate maternal
love, clucking to gather its young beneath the shelter of
its widespread wings; the lambs blithely following their
shepherd, yet going astray, and roaming into the wild";
the sower flinging out the grains of wheat which sometimes
fell on rocky, or trodden, or thorny ground, or sank into
the good soil, to die indeed, but to spring up again in the
hundredfold of golden harvests. He would watch the
green blade passing into the ear, and then into the full corn
in the ear; and the fig-tree in springtide putting forth its
tender leaves; and the vine-branch hung with its rich
purple clusters; and the grain of mustard-seed, smallest of
all seeds, but growing up into the largest and bushiest of
garden herbs, so that the birds of the air took shelter in its
branches; and the rushes whispering and wavering in the
evening wind; and the lilies of the field brightening the
meadows and the mountain sides with blue and purple and
scarlet, like the broidery on the girdle of the High Priest;

* Matt. x. 29 ; Luke xii. 6.

and the many-coloured tulip, the golden armaryllis, the scarlet anemone arrayed more splendidly than Solomon in all his glory. He would notice, too, all the wild creatures with an eager and tender gaze—the sly wisdom of the serpent, the fox creeping to its hole, the wild wolves and prowling jackals, as well as the sheep which hear the voice of their shepherd and follow him when he calls them by their names. He would watch the lightning hurling its flame to earth, or flashing from the East even to the West, and gaze on the sky red with the promise of golden days, or lurid with the menace of the storm. He would listen to the welcome plash of the fertilising rain, and to the rush of the swollen streams, and to the south wind with its burning heat, and to the breeze of which we hear the sound but cannot tell whence it cometh nor whither it goeth. Nature was to Him no blank impervious barrier between the soul and God, but a glorious crystal mirror in which the Creator was reflected; and every one of these sights and sounds of common nature, treasured up in His pure and sinless soul, became parables of spiritual truth and illustrations of eternal wisdom.

> "To Thee all nature's oracles unfold
>   Their wondrous meaning, deep-concealed of old,
> Now by Thy touch of sympathy laid bare :
>   To Thee the richness of their truth they yield,
>   Each sparrow, and each lily of the field,
> Preaching the gospel of a Father's care.
>   The shepherd seeking his lost lambs again,
>   The housewife's bread, the gently falling rain,
> The morning sun that climbs the heavenly height ;
>   The green grass, and the spirits of careless youth,
>   Are all but garments of the living truth
> That through them shines, and fills our lives with light." *

Nor was it otherwise with the commonest sights and sounds and incidents of daily life. To Him all became

* Quoted by Mr. Wicksteed in his translation of H. Van Oort's *Bible for the Young*, v. 198.

fruitful as vehicles of the holiest teaching, which was the more impressive because all alike could understand it, from the highest to the lowest. The form which His teaching took furnishes an indirect proof of His daily familiarity with the common life of the people during the long years which He spent as one of the labouring classes. He had watched the processions of the bridegrooms, and the games of the little ones, and the gay clothing of the courtiers from Tiberias. "He was at home," says Hausrath,* "in those poor, windowless Syrian hovels, in which the housewife must light a candle in the daytime in order to seek for her lost piece of silver.† He is acquainted with the secrets of the bakehouse, ‡ and the gardener, § and the builder, ‖ and with things which the higher classes never see—such as the 'good measure, pressed down, and shaken together, and running over,' of the cornchandler; ¶ the rotten, leaking wine-skin of the wine-dealer; ** the clumsy patchwork of the peasant-woman; †† and the brutal manners of the upper servants towards the lower. ‡‡ A hundred other features of a similar kind are enwoven by Him into His parables. Reminiscences given of His more special handicraft have been found, it is believed, in some of His sayings. The parable of the Splinter and the Beam is said to recall the carpenter's shop; §§ the uneven foundation of the houses, the building-yard; ‖‖ the cubit that is added, His workshop; ¶¶ the distinction in the appearance of the green and dry wood, the drying shed; *** but from the frequency of expressions peculiar to Him, it would be possible to find similar evidence for every other handicraft. Nevertheless the circumstance that His discourses are not

* *New Testament Times* ii. 137.
‡ Matt. xiii. 33 ; Luke xiii. 21.
‖ Luke vi. 48, 49.
** Matt. ix. 17.
‡‡ Luke xii. 45.
‖‖ Matt. vii. 24–27.
*** Luke xxiii. 31.

† Luke xv. 8.
§ Matt. xv. 13.
¶ Luke vi. 38.
†† Matt. ix. 16.
§§ Matt. vii. 3.
¶¶ Matt. vi. 27.

drawn from rare spectacles and unusual processes, but always move in the sphere of the ordinary man's activity, has contributed to establish their special popularity."

We may say then of Jesus, that, for the infinite consolation of the poor, during by far the greater part of His life, He showed by an example more powerful than any teaching, that " Man is as great as he is in God's sight, and no greater."

CHAPTER X

THE HOME AT NAZARETH

"Love had he found in huts where poor men lie ;
His only teachers were the woods and rills,
The silence that is in the starry sky,
The peace that is in the eternal hills."

—WORDSWORTH.

THE hill-town of Nazareth on the southwest of the old tribal district of Zabulon was remote, insignificant, and poor. It was traversed by one of the roads from Ptolemais to Damascus, and was near large and populous townships, like Sepphoris and Tiberias, but it never rose into prominence. It is not once mentioned in the Old Testament, nor in the Talmud, nor in the Midrashim. The recent attempts to make out that it was the centre of a busy commerce are entirely unsuccessful. It is not alluded to by any Gentile writer, nor even by Josephus, though he writes so much about Galilee. The Jews despised it so entirely as to have among them the proverb,* "Can any good thing come out

* The prophecy quoted by Matthew (ii. 23), "He shall be called a Nazarene," is of uncertain explanation. It is probably an allusion to *Netzer* Branch (Is. xi. 1 ; Comp. *T'semach*, Jer. xxiii. 5. ; Zech. iii. 8), or *Notsri*, as Nazareth may perhaps mean " Protectress." The Christians were contemptuously called "Nazarenes." Isaiah (ix. 1, 2) describes the region in which Nazareth stood as inhabited by "those that walk in darkness," and " that dwell in the land of the shadow of death" (John i. 46, vii. 52, xix. 19. Lightfoot, *Hor. Hebr.* 232). Galilee, occupied by so many Phœnicians, Syrians, Arabians, and other Gentiles (Jos. *Antt.* xiii. 15, 4 ; *B. J.* iii. 3, 2 ; Strabo xvi. 2, 34. Comp. Is. ix. 1) was spoken of with great scorn (Acts ii. 7 ; Matt. xxvi. 69, 73), though the inhabitants, in their glad and healthy enthusiasm, were far superior to other Jews. See Tacitus *Hist.* v. 6 ; Josephus *B. J.* 9 ; iii. 3, 2. Barak, Deborah, Elon, Elisha, Hoshea, Jonah, Nahum, Tobit, and many other men of fame sprang from Galilee.

of Nazareth?" And afterwards the brethren of Jesus spoke of work in Galilee as work " in secret." *

The position of an artisan in such a place must have been humble indeed. The picture of a carpenter's shop at Nazareth, drawn by Mr. Holman Hunt, will probably give a very true conception of what such a shop looked like in the days of Christ ; † for in the unchanging East the aspect of things remains the same for century after century. It was probably a house and workshop in one, and lighted mostly from the door, except by night, when the single lamp suspended in the centre was lit, " showing curiously commingled the furniture of the family and the tools of the mechanic." I have noticed in the homes of Nazareth the gay-coloured quilts, neatly rolled up in the daytime, and placed in a corner of the room, which at night are the beds of the family. There is usually no table, but a little circular or octagonal stand, sometimes gaily painted or inlaid, on which is placed the common dish of *libban*, or stewed fruit, and the bread which form the staple meals. The bronze basin and ewer are brought out after the meal by the youngest member of the family, that he may pour water over the hands of all who have been helping themselves out of the common dish.

Such was the home, for thirty years, of the Son of God, the Saviour of the world. He lived amid the most ordinary conditions. He would not seek for Himself an exceptional lot, but one which most closely resembled the common life of men, of whom all but a very few live humble, unknown lives, and earn their bread by the labour of their hands. There was nothing squalid or repellent in such a life, but it served as the most forcible of proofs that the

* John vii. 3–5.

† I saw Mr. Hunt when he was living at Jerusalem, and he drew this interior of a real carpenter's shop at Nazareth to illustrate my *Life of Christ*. Since those days the primitive simplicity of Nazareth is said to have partly disappeared.

true greatness of man consists in the immortal nature which God has bestowed upon him, and not in the adjuncts by which he is surrounded. Christ, by the years of His earthly obscurity, meant to teach us that God judges not as man judges, but that the sole appreciable greatness of any man, be he emperor or peasant, lies in the fact that God breathed into his nostrils the breath of life—that God made him a little lower than the angels, to crown him with glory and honour.

CHAPTER XI.

THE FAMILY AT NAZARETH.

" Home is Heaven for beginners ; the place of peace ; the shelter not only from all injury but from all terror, doubt, and division."

In the humble abode of the carpenter, Jesus learnt the strength and tenderness of human affection which breathes through all His utterances. Joseph and Mary were so poor that the Virgin could only offer at her purification the pair of turtle doves which none but the humblest mothers were permitted by the Law to present in the place of lambs. The fact that she was a descendant of David—which His enemies never denied, and which is even admitted by the Talmud *—made no difference in the lowliness of the position of the Holy Family. The great Hillel is also said to have been of David's race, yet until manhood he was in so humble a lot as barely to be able to earn his daily bread by toiling as an artisan. There is many an obscure working-man in England at this moment who has the blood of the Plantagenets in his veins. A few centuries entirely obliterate any dignity which may be derivable from a royal origin. In Egypt and Arabia we constantly see common beggars who wear the green turban which shows them to be of the family of Mohammed.†

---

* See Derenbourg, *Hist. de la Palestine*, p. 349, who quotes Sanhedrin f. 43, 1 (in editions not expurgated). The late Dr. Schiller Szinessy, however, called Derenbourg an *am-ha-aretz* for understanding the words thus, and said they only meant that Jesus was " influential with the (Roman) Government " !

† St. Peter, very soon after the Crucifixion, and St. Paul—Rabbi and San-hedrist as he had been—speak of Jesus being " of the seed of David according to the flesh," as though it was a fact which could not be challenged (Acts ii. 29-31 ; Rom. i. 3 ; 2 Tim. ii. 8. Comp. Heb. vii. 14 ; Hegesippus *ap.* Euseb. ii. 8, iii. 11, 12, 19, 20).

Joseph, according to tradition, was considerably older than the Virgin Mary, and as he is not once mentioned in the Gospels after the Passover visit to Jerusalem, and as no other trace of him, or allusion to him, has been preserved, except in the Apocryphal Gospel which goes by his name, it is probable that he died soon after Jesus was thirteen years old. The rest of the family consisted of four brothers, and several sisters. They seem to have continued to live together, with Mary and with Jesus. The names of these "brethren" were James, and Joses, and Judas, and Simon.

What was their exact relationship to Jesus? The *Helvidian* theory takes the language of the New Testament in its natural sense, and regards them as full brothers; the *Epiphanian* describes them as elder sons of Joseph by a previous or a Levirate marriage; the *Hieronymian*—which is the weakest and most foundationless—speaks of them as the cousins of Jesus. From the unvarying language of the Gospels about them, we might naturally infer that they were sons of Mary and her husband Joseph, born after the birth of Christ.* The belief in the *Aeiparthenia*, or perpetual virginity of the mother of Jesus, was an afterthought, unknown to the primitive Christians. It does not seem to have been turned into an actual dogma before the third century,† and even then there were some—called the *Antidicomarianitæ*—who followed Helvidius in rejecting this new doctrine. It must be borne in mind that one of

---

* See Luke ii. 7, xxiv. 10; John ii. 12, vii. 2–8, xix. 25; Mark iii. 21, 31, xv. 40; Matt. xxvii. 56, etc.

† Hegesippus (*circ.* A. D. 160) speaks of them as brethren in the natural sense; and Tertullian (A. D. 220) definitely states that they were (*c. Marc.* iv. 19; *De Carn. Christi* 7; *De Virg. Vel.* 61). Origen, indeed, took the view that they were sons of Joseph by a former wife, but could only quote in favour of this view two heretical and apocryphal Gospels. For fuller information, see Bishop Lightfoot's Essay on the Brethren of the Lord in his Commentary on the Galatians; and Dr. J. B. Mayor in his Commentary on St. James; and in Hastings' *Dict. of the Bible*, i. 320. I may also refer to ch. xix. of my *Early Days of Christianity*.

the views most universally current among the Jews was the inherent duty and sanctity of marriage. To the earliest Christians it would have seemed no derogation whatever from the holy dignity of the Virgin, but rather the reverse, if she had added the sacredness of ordinary motherhood to the blessing of one who had been so highly favoured by the Lord.

If, however, these four " brethren of Jesus " were not the sons of His mother, they can only have been (i.) either His cousins, or (ii.) the sons of Joseph by a previous or a Levirate marriage.

The notion that they were the cousins of our Lord—suggested by St. Jerome only as a desperate expedient of argument in which he himself hardly believed *—turns on the supposition that Mary, the wife of Cleopas (Alphæus), was a sister of the Virgin, and that these were her four sons.

That this Mary was a sister of the Virgin is on other grounds probable. The fact that two sisters should have borne the same name is by no means unprecedented, and it could not have been a very uncommon circumstance in days when distinctive names, especially of women, were extremely few in number. But it is fatal to this hypothesis (a) that no one ever seems to have heard of it before Jerome invented it ; and (b) that, if they were Christ's cousins, there is no conceivable reason why the word "cousin" (ἀνέψιος), or " kinsman " (συγγενής), should not have been used of them,† nor why, without a single variation, they should have been called " brethren "; and (c) that two, perhaps four, of the sons of Mary and Alphæus were Apostles of Christ, so that it could not have been said, " neither did

---

* He first made the suggestion, without pretending to quote the least authority for it, about A. D. 383 ; but in later works (*Ep. ad Hedibiam*), and in his Commentary on the Galatians, he holds very loosely to this view, and his *arguments*, such as they are, are beneath notice.

† The word ἀνέψιος occurs in Col. iv. 10 ; and of Symeon, son of Clopas, by Hegesippus, *ap* Euseb. *H. E.* iv. 22. For συγγενής, see Luke i. 36, ii. 44 ; John xviii. 26, etc.

His brethren believe on Him." On the other hand, if they
were sons of Joseph by a Levirate marriage, they would not
have been officially regarded as *his* sons, but rather as sons
of his deceased brother. And if they were sons of Joseph
by a previous marriage,* they, and not Jesus, were the
elder heirs of David's line.

In calling them Christ's "brethren" we adopt the language of the Evangelists, and there is no evidence to justify
us in explaining it away out of deference to later fancies,
which seem to be purely subjective, and derive no support
of any kind from Scripture. If the "Perpetual Virginity"
had been regarded as a doctrine of any importance the
Evangelists would have guarded themselves against language so liable to misinterpretation as Matt. i. 24, Luke
ii. 7.

Of these brethren, the two of most marked individuality—
the only two of whom any record survives—are James "the
Lord's brother," and Jude the "brother of James," to each
of whom we owe one of the Epistles of the New Testament.

St. James was a man of most powerful and independent
personality—pure and holy, yet with a certain natural
sternness of character. If the traditions preserved by
Hegesippus be true, he had been a Nazarite from his birth,
and the long locks of the Nazarite flowed over his shoulders. It is manifest from his Epistle that he was a devoted
Jew. He addresses "the sojourners of the Dispersion"; he
speaks of the Christian assembly as "a synagogue"; his
mind was evidently steeped in Jewish literature, both
Scriptural and Apocryphal. There is a tone of severity in
his moral appeals and objurgations which recalls John the

---

* This was the view of Epiphanius (A. D. 370). Pearson and others have
quoted Ezek. xliv. 2 in this connection, but nothing is more deplorable that
this "ever-widening spiral *ergo* from the narrow aperture of single texts."
If we are to quote the Old Testament in this matter, Ps. lxix. 8 would be much
more apposite. This Psalm, treated as Messianic by St. John (ii. 17), and St.
Luke (ii. 35), and St. Matthew (xxvii. 34). says: "I have become a stranger to
my brethren; and an alien unto my *mother's children.*" See Mayor *l. c.*

Baptist. His Epistle is the least directly Christological in the New Testament, yet Luther made an utter mistake when he ventured to speak of it as a " downright strawy Epistle." One passage in it especially has the profoundest Gospel significance. It is the one in which he says, " Putting away all filthiness and overflowing of wickedness, receive with meekness the Implanted Word which is able to save your souls." *

Still the Epistle shows us one who, while he believed in the Lord Jesus Christ, had not broken loose from the traditions of Judaism. In this respect he carried out the early custom of St. Peter and St. John, who, being Jews, after the Resurrection and after Pentecost still attended the Temple services. Indeed, it is clear, if we accept the story of Hegesippus, that St. James stood very high in the estimation of the Jews, who even called him *Obliam*, or " *The Bulwark of the People* " (*Ophel am*). Yet so absolute was his fidelity to Christ, that, in His name and for His sake, he braved a martyr's death (A. D. 62.) †

Of St. JUDE, who modestly calls himself " the brother of James," we know much less. Tradition has preserved no particulars respecting him, except that he was the grandfather of those descendants of David who were known as " the Desposyni." We have, however, St. Jude's Epistle by which to form some estimate of his character. We find in it the same qualities of moral sternness as in that of his brother; and besides the evident traces of a strict Judaic

* James i. 21.

† See, on the death of St. James, Jos. *Antt.* xx. 9, 1 ; Orig. *c. Cels.* i. 47 ; Euseb. *H. E.* ii. 1, vii. 19. The well-known tradition of his martyrdom is given at length by Hegesippus (A. D. 160), quoted by Euseb. *H. E.* ii. 23. The story may come from an Ebionite book called Ἀναβαθμοὶ Ἰακώβου, of which there are traces in the Clementine Recognitions. The simpler story is given by Josephus (*Antt.* xx. 9). Comp. Orig. *c. Cels.* i. 47; Euseb. *H. E.* vii. 19. There is an interesting allusion to St. James in the spurious letter of Ignatius to St. John. " The venerable James, who is surnamed Just, whom they relate to be very like Christ in appearance, in life, and in method of conduct, as if he were a twin brother of the same womb."

training, it contains uncommon allusions to Levitic institutions,* and the apocryphal legends of the Jewish *Haggadah*.† Some of these are softened down in the *rifacimento* of the Epistle which we find in the second chapter of the Second Epistle of St. Peter.

It is clear, then, that the family of Joseph was trained in the strictest traditions of Mosaism, and it is one of the numberless proofs of the Divine individuality of the Son of Man that He was not swayed by such near and powerful representatives of the Old Dispensation. There is not a whisper or a trace of any disagreement or disunion within the narrow limits of that humble home at Nazareth. But the testimony of the Evangelists shows that when our Lord began His mission, when he claimed the right to speak with authority, and not as the Scribes; when He set aside the Oral Law, which his brethren had been taught to reverence as "the tradition of the Elders"; when He openly broke with the all-venerated religious teachers of His day— His brethren were startled by the immensity of His claims. They even seem to have attributed them to a dangerous enthusiasm, for—dreading, perhaps, lest they should lead to some terrible catastrophe—they induced His mother to join them in the endeavour to put some gentle restraint on what they, with eyes as yet unenlightened, regarded as perilous impulses.‡

And again, on a later occasion, His brethren tried to exercise an unwarrantable influence over His methods and actions, since their eyes were not yet opened to His Divine authority.§ They held to the current conceptions of the coming Messiah, and urged Him to go openly to the Feast of Tabernacles, and show His works, and claim his due posi-

---

* Jude 8–23.   † Jude 6, 9, 14.

‡ Matt. xii. 46 : Mark iii. 31, ἐξέστη; Luke viii. 19. They were no doubt deeply troubled by the fact that the venerated Scribes said that He "had a demon," and cast out demons by Beelzebul. Comp. Mark vi. 4 ; John vii. 20. Beelzebul seems to be the best attested reading.

§ John vii. 3, 5, 10, 14.

tion.   He was compelled, therefore, to set aside their intrusiveness.   He would not go to the Feast with them. He would not follow the wisdom or the ways of this world. He was compelled to repudiate their officiousness, and He did not take them into His confidence.   He went up to Jerusalem, not officially, but privately, after they had departed, and did not appear in the Temple till the midst of the Feast.

We see, however, clearly that if these " brethren of the Lord " were men of somewhat unbending convictions, they were nevertheless men of lofty moral character.   They seem to have been convinced and converted by the Resurrection of Christ; for though, during His ministry, they had not fully or adequately believed on Him, immediately afterwards we find them among his leading disciples.   His brother James, though not one of the Twelve, was elected Bishop of Jerusalem after the martyrdom of James the son of Zebedee.   St. Paul, among six appearances of the Risen Christ, mentions two only which are unrecorded in the Gospels.   One of these is, "after that He appeared to *James.*" *   This has often been supposed to be the appearance, not to the son of Zebedee, but to the eldest brother of Jesus, which is mentioned in the Gospel according to the Hebrews. †   We are told that, after the Crucifixion, ‡ James said that he would neither eat nor drink till he had seen Christ risen from the dead ; and that Christ, appearing to him, said, " Eat and drink, my brother, for the Son of Man is risen from the dead."

The descendants of Jude, known as "members of the Lord's family," are mentioned in the famous story of the

---

* I Cor. xv. 7.   The *separate* appearance to Peter is not described in the Gospels.

†Quoted by Jerome *De Ver. ill.* 2.

‡ Or, i nanother version, " from the hour in which he had drunk the cup of the Lord."   See Mayor, *Ep. of St. James,* xxxvii. n.   See " *Gospel acc. to the Hebrews,*" *ap.* Jer. *De Vir. ill.* 2.

Emperor Domitian, who (A. D. 81), hearing from Josephus and from certain Nazarean heretics that some of the family of Christ in Palestine claimed royal descent, suspected that they might become possible leaders of sedition, and sent for them to come to Rome. But on seeing at a glance that they were only poor peasants whose hands were rough and hard with toil, and hearing from them that they only tilled seven acres of land, he contemptuously dismissed them to their humble Galilean farms.*

In Christian History there is no more mysterious figure than that of THE MOTHER OF OUR LORD. In that carpenter's shop at Nazareth what was her influence over the early years of her Divine Son?

After the events of the Nativity, the Virgin, strange to say, almost disappears, not only from the New Testament, but even from all the records of the Early Church. From the incident in the Temple when Jesus had completed His early boyhood, and from the fact that it was Mary, not Joseph, who addressed Him, we infer that her share in the training of His early years was more marked than was usual in the case of Jewish mothers. We see again in the record of the first miracle at Cana that she occupied a leading position. There is no possible explanation of her remark to Christ, "*They have no wine,*" except that it was an indirect suggestion that by some word or deed of power He should prevent the joy of the wedding-feast from being destroyed by an apparent failure of the sacred duties of hospitality. His answer, "Woman, what have I to do with thee? mine hour is not yet come," sounds to our ears far more harsh than it was. It set aside the right of Mary to direct His actions, yet was an implicit granting of her request. The address, "Woman," † in accordance with

---

* Hegesippus *ap.* Eusebius, *H. E.* iii. 19–21. Julius Africanus (early in the third century) says that he knew some of the Desposyni personally. He was born at Emmaus. Euseb. *H. E.* i. 7.

† John ii. 4, τί ἐμοὶ καί σοι γύναι. In Aramaic this would be the common

ancient idiom, was perfectly tender and respectful, and might be used even to Queens. *   The "what have I to do with thee?" spoken in tones of perfect gentleness, meant merely, "This is a point which *I* must arrange, not thou." The words might have been used by the most gentle and affectionate son of full age, to his mother.   The direction immediately given by Mary to the servants shows that, so far from feeling any sense of a repulse, she anticipated the granting of her petition, which followed, without delay.

The Virgin is prominently mentioned in the Gospels in but one other incident.   It was on the occasion when she came with the Lord's brethren to prevent, if possible, what they regarded as the continuance of a deeply imperilled career. Not only did Jesus decline to see them, but He uttered a remark which seemed most decisively to show that the time had now come when His work as the Son of God tran-scended all the earthly conditions of the Son of Man. Looking round on His assembled hearers at Capernaum, He exclaimed, "Who is My mother, and who are My brethren?"   And stretching forth His hand towards His disciples, He said, "Behold My mother and My brethren! For whosoever shall do the will of My Father who is in heaven, he is My brother, and sister, and mother." †

Another incident tends still more strongly to emphasise our conviction that any form of what has been called "Mariolatry" is entirely alien from the teaching of the pure Gospel of Christ.   Our Lord had been teaching in one of the synagogues, when a woman in the assembly, carried away by the intensity of her feelings, cried out in the hear-ing of all, "Blessed is the womb that bare Thee, and the breasts which Thou hast sucked." ‡   But though that

phrase, *Mah lî velâk*, which is perfectly courteous.   See 2 Sam. xvi. 10, xix. 22 ; 1 Kings xvii. 18 ; 2 Kings iii. 13, etc.

* See John iv. 21, xix. 26, xx. 13, 15.   Thus Augustus addressed Cleopatra in the words θάρσει γύναι (Dio. Cass. ii. p. 305).

† Matt. xii. 46–50 ; Mark iii. 31–35.   ‡ Luke xi. 27.

might have seemed to be the most natural of sentiments, yet our Lord corrects its too material and human point of view. He systematically discouraged the exaltation of mere outward contact with His person, and taught that the presence of His Spirit was something nearer and more to be desired than any relationship with Him after the flesh (John xiv. 16, 2 Cor. v. 16). " How many women have blessed the Holy Virgin," says St. Chrysostom, " and desired to be such a mother as she was! What hinders them? Christ has made for us a wide way to this happiness, and not only women but men may tread it—the way of obedience. This it is which makes such a mother, and not the throes of parturition."

The last time during His life on earth that the Virgin is mentioned is in the intensely pathetic incident when Jesus, as He hung upon His Cross of Shame, saw His mother standing by, and the disciple whom He loved. Thoughtful, even at that supreme moment, for her desolate future, He said, indicating by a movement of His head the Beloved Disciple, " Woman, behold thy son!" and to John, " Behold thy mother!" She had now drunk to the very dregs the cup of anguish. John led her away, and from that hour took her to his own home. In the surmises of which the Lives of Christ are full, this incident has been much discussed. I think the answer to any difficulty lies in some obvious considerations. St. John was " the disciple whom Jesus loved," and was His kinsman. Having been admitted into Christ's closest and most tender friendship, he would be more likely to enter into the unspeakable depth of Mary's feelings than the " brethren " who, up to that time, had never fully accepted His Divine claims. Then again there are indications that St. John was in a somewhat less struggling worldly position than the sons of Joseph the carpenter. Unlike " the brethren of the Lord," he was unmarried. He was familiar with Jerusalem, and probably had a home there, in which, according to one tradition, the Virgin lived from that time until her death.

From this moment the Virgin Mary, though her name is just mentioned among those who formed the assemblies of the early believers, practically disappears from Christian History.* Even apocryphal tradition scarcely so much as mentions her. It is not known how long she lived. It is not certain whether she died at Jerusalem or at Ephesus. She is not referred to as a source of information, still less as a fount of authority, though she could have told more than any living being about the birth of the Saviour, and the thirty long years of His humble obscurity. She "kept all these and pondered them in her heart." But though she must ever be cherished in Christian reverence as the chosen handmaid of the Lord, and " blessed among women," it is impossible not to see in these indisputable facts the strongest possible condemnation of that utterly unauthorised worship of the Virgin, which centuries afterwards, began to corrupt the turbid stream of Christianity. As though by a Divine prevision of the dangerous aberrations which were to come, in which Christians by millions were taught to adore the creature even *more* than the Creator, who is blessed for evermore, the name Mary is scarcely noticed in the whole New Testament after the beginning of Christ's ministry, and indeed after the one incident of His boyhood. In *three* of the instances in which it *is* introduced, our Lord says, " Woman, what have I to do with thee?"; " He that doeth the will of God the same is my mother, and my sister, and my brother "; and, " Yea rather, blessed are they that do the word of God and keep it." It might, therefore, seem as if *special* care had been taken to discourage and obviate the corrupted forms of Christianity

---

* Epiphanius (*Haer*. lxxviii. 11) knew nothing on the subject. Nicephorus (*H. E*. ii. 3) is no authority, for he lived in the middle of the fourteenth century. He says that she died at Jerusalem, aged 59, eleven years after the Crucifixion. There was a tradition, mentioned in a letter of the Council of Ephesus (A. D. 431), that she went with St. John to Ephesus and was buried there. (See Westcott on John xix. 2, 4.) A supposed " Tomb of the Virgin " is shown at Jerusalem, near the traditional Gethsemane.

which have thrust the Virgin Mary into the place of her Eternal Son, and made her more an object of rapturous worship than God, to whom alone all worship is due.

Here we may perhaps revert for a moment to the question on which I have already spoken elsewhere, as to the human aspect of the Lord of Life. The early Christians —looking almost daily for the visible return of Christ in glory, and habitually regarding Him, no longer as "the Man Christ Jesus," who for a few short years moved about upon this earth, but rather as the Divine, the Eternal, the ever-present God—have preserved for us no outline of a picture, not even so much as a passing tradition, of His appearance as a man among men.* The early Christians— feeling that He was with them, and within them, and that He was "God of God, Lord of Lords, very God of very God"—cared nothing for relics, or holy places, or semblances of His mortal face. Hence, as far back as the second century, *nothing whatever was known* which could even decide the question whether He was tall and stately and humanly beautiful, or whether He was the very reverse. Ancient writers could only fall back on the language of Prophecy. Among the Greek Fathers and the earlier Latin writers the tendency was to borrow the conception of His earthly aspect from the prophecies of Isaiah (lii. 14, liii. 23), and to speak of Him as "without form or comeliness," inglorious, nay, even mean in appearance, "short, ignoble, ill-favoured in body." † But later on it began to be felt that such notions were utterly untenable. We may safely infer from the Gospels themselves that there must have been some grandeur about the appearance of Jesus—" *Sidereum*

---

* For full further information on these questions see my *Life of Christ in Art*. See, too, Ullmann, p. 191 ; Schürer, II. ii, 161.

† See the well-known passages : Just. Mart. *Dial.* 14, 36, 85, 88 ; Clem. Alex. *Paed.* iii. 1, 3 ; and others quoted on next page.

quiddam," as St. Jerome says—which on many occasions won His friends and overawed His enemies.* No one who had lived a life of sinless innocence and the supremest moral nobleness could be otherwise than "fairer than the children of men" (Ps. xlv. 3). This was the view of Jerome and Augustine, and it became established in the Church of the West, though Byzantine art continued to depict Him in traditional ugliness.

The two late descriptions of Jesus—that by the pseudo Publius Lentulus, preserved by John of Damascus in the eighth, and that by Nicephorus in the fourteenth century— are very beautiful, but purely ideal. All that we may be sure of is that if "beauty" be "the sacrament of goodness," the Sinless Purity of the Son of Man could not but have created for itself a noble Presence, and a Countenance full of all human sweetness and all Divine dignity. It is certain that pretended likeness of Christ originated among heretics like the Carpocratians (Iren. i. 25), and we must still say generally with St. Augustine, "*Qua fuerit Ille facie, penitus ignoramus.*" † It must be remembered that St. Augustine gave this decisive judgment when hundreds of pretended likenesses were in existence, all of which, he says, differed most widely from each other.

And now the greater part of Christ's human life had passed. The long thirty years were over. As yet He had wrought no miracle, had given no sign, had uttered no revelation of the Divine claims which were part of the teaching destined to revolutionise the world. He had lived

* See, for instances, Matt. vii. 28, xiii. 54, xix. 25 ; Mark ix. 15 ; Luke ii. 47, etc.

† Jer. *Ep.* lxv. *in Matt.* ix. 9 ; Aug. *De Trin.* viii. 4, 5. See Gieseler, i. 66 ; W. H. Lecky, *Hist. of Rationalism*, i. 257 ; Kugler, *Hist. of Art*, i. 15, 16. The chief authorities are Clem. Alex. *Paedag.* iii. 1, *Strom.* ii. p. 308 ; Tert. *De Carne Christi*, 9. *c. Jud.* 14 ; Orig. *c. Cels.* vi. 327 ; Euseb. *H. E.* vii. 15.

unknown and unnoticed, in the small Galilean town, as an ordinary and humble mechanic, not challenging any place among its provincial aristocracy, not interfering even with the extremely modest prerogatives of the officials in its synagogue. He had fulfilled the prophecy of Isaiah :

> " He shall not strive, nor cry aloud;
> Neither shall any one hear His voice in the streets.
> A bruised reed shall He not break,
> And smoking flax shall He not quench,
> Till He send forth judgment unto victory."

We may here sum up the deep lessons involved in these long years of obscure and silent labour. They involve in the most striking of all possible forms a testimony to the value and sacredness of the ordinary life of man. They were destined to furnish the most vivid possible proof that the life is more than the food, and the body than the raiment ; that God created man for incorruption, and made him an image of His own everlastingness ; that to receive Him into the soul is perfect righteousness, and to know His dominion is the root of immortality. The lot of all but the very few in every million of human beings is the lot of struggle and obscurity. The Psalmist sang, ages ago, that

> " As for man, his days are as grass,
> As a flower of the field, so he flourisheth.
> For the wind passeth over it and it is gone,
> And the place thereof shall know it no more."

Christ came to live, in all external respects, the commonest life of man, that the multitude might not regard their lives as mere stubble of the field, and themselves as things of no account with God, because they constitute but

> " Of men, the common rout
> That, wandering loose about,
> Grow up and perish, as the summer fly ;
> Heads without name, no more rememberèd."

For the life which they live, in its namelessness and little apparent value to mankind, was the very life lived by the Son of God Himself, the Lord of Glory, for all but the brief years of His ministry. It sufficed Him, and He thereby taught us how infinite is the inherent preciousness of life itself, apart from those concomitants of pride, success, and riches, which to many men seem alone to make it worth living. Tried by the world's standard, our existence may seem deplorably insignificant ; but what is taught us by the thirty years passed in the shop of the Nazarene carpenter by "the Lord of Time and all the worlds," is that each man has a right to say with humble faith :

> " All I could never be,
> All men ignored in me,
> This was I worth to God, whose wheel the pitcher shaped." *

And in all the early years of His life, with their experiences and meditations, Jesus looked far more on what is good in human nature than on what is evil. He became filled more and more with a boundless compassion for man, springing from absolute love for God. " Here," says Keim, " we are made aware in Him of an ascending effort to get beyond the boundaries of the natural, beyond the limitations of human nature ;—a renunciation of the whole world, a feeling of the nothingness of riches, and of the utter helplessness of all human existence which lives but from the alms, and crumbs, of the Eternal : but yet, instead of the leap of self-annihilation, the plunging of man's nothingness into God's Eternity—a profound repose of the creature in itself; an inward contemplation of inward riches along with outward neediness ; a joyful recognition of the bright light and everlasting worth of a human soul ; a self-confirmation in the right to endless existence ; and belief in the personal elevation and dignity of mankind at large, in such strength of conviction as had never been before, and as

* Browning, *Rabbi Ben Ezra.*

became henceforth the motive-power of all the future life of humanity." * Even the most abject and wretched were, in Christ's apprehension, still sons and daughters of Abraham, still children of the Heavenly Father, of the true and ever-lasting God.

It was Christ's intense realisation of God's infinitude of love which raised Him into the all-embracing love of Man. It was His sense of the infinite grandeur of the Divine Perfection which made Him insist on the nature of true worship as consisting in a communion of the soul with God. The self-deceiving littlenesses of a theatrical externalism hinder rather than promote the depth of that communion of man with God which uplifts our souls at last into that mystery wherein God in man is one with man in God.

* Keim, ii. 170. See Matt. vii. 9–11.

CHAPTER XII.

THE CONDITION OF THE WORLD.

" In whatsoever I may find you, in this will I also judge you."—Unwritten Saying of Christ. CLEM. *Hom*. ii. 5. JUST. MART. *Dial.* 47.

" Divina Providentia agitur mundus et homo."—OROSIUS.

" No incident in the Gospel story, no word in the teaching of Jesus Christ, is intelligible apart from its setting in Jewish History, and without a clear understanding of that world of thought distinctive of the Jewish People."—SCHÜRER, *Hist. of the Jewish People*, Div. 1, Vol. 1, p. 1.

BUT the time had now come, when, in fulfilment of the mission which was to regenerate mankind and to inaugurate the last æon of the Divine Dispensation, Christ had to reveal Himself to the world. Nazareth, secluded as it was, was in a central position for observing the movements and tendencies of the age. The Galileans—an eager and emotional race—were in constant contact with Jerusalem and Samaria, and their hearts thrilled to the religious questions of the day. They were within a short distance from Decapolis, and the heathen or semi-heathen cities of Sepphoris, Hippos, Bethsaida Julias, and Tiberias. Not far from them, in the plain of Esdraelon, was an encampment of Roman soldiers, which still retains the name of " Legion " (Lejjûn). They were under the dominance of the meanest of the Herods, and were well aware that their political existence was ultimately dependent on the will of those whom Herod the Great had called " the almighty Romans " and their deified Emperors. From the hill-top of Nazareth was visible the blue Mediterranean traversed by " the ships of Chittim "—the narrow and open pathway to the Greek and Asiatic world and the Isles of the Gentiles. And though there is no proof that Nazareth itself was in any sense a centre of commercial activity, it was within easy access of the roads from Damascus to the sea, the great Southern road which led ultimately to Egypt, and the Eastern road which led from Acre to Bethlehem.* In the festal visits to Jerusalem Jesus must have mingled among crowds in which there were " Parthians, and Medes, and Elamites, and dwellers in Mesopotamia, in Judæa and Cappadocia, in Pontus and Asia, in Phrygia and Pamphylia, in Egypt and the parts of Libya about Cyrene, Alexandrians and Cilicians, and sojourners from Rome, both Jews and Proselytes, Cretans and Arabians." A Passover crowd in the Temple Courts was an epitome of the civilised world.

Jesus must, therefore, have often meditated on the general conditions of the life of His day, both among the Jews and among the Gentiles. And the epoch was a deplorable one. The darkness was deepest before the approach of dawn.

I. THE GENTILES.

As regards the Gentile world, no epoch could have been worse, no period more deeply plunged into the Dead Sea of corruption, or more despairingly conscious of its own moral degradation. The mimes of Paganism reeked with moral corruption, and the sanguinary amphitheatres were schools of callous cruelty.† Infanticide was so universal that a senator challenged the members of a full Senate to say whether nearly every one of them had not exposed infant children to die. Their very religion was corrupt at the fountain-head. The pictures in the Temples, and the representations of stories of their religious mythology, were potent sources of corruption, such as even light poets

---

* See G. A. Smith, *Hist. Geogr. of the Holy Land*, 413–463.

† Juv. *Sat.* vi. 67 ; Mart. *De Spectac.* 7 ; Sen. *Ep.* 7 ; Tert. *Apol.* 15 ; *ad Nat.* i. 11. See Zosimus, *Hist.* i. 6. Offences against moral purity were regarded even by philosophers as " matters of indifference " (ἀδιάφορα).

observed and bewailed ; * and the dark mysterious recesses of consecrated shrines were scenes of gross demoralisation.† The old Roman virtues had been quenched, partly in consequence of the closer contact of Rome with Greek immorality, partly because the dead weight of military despotism, as represented by the Emperors, had crushed out the old freedom and nobleness. A highborn Roman historian, Cremutius Cordus, was driven to suicide in the days of Tiberius for speaking of Cassius as " *the last of the Romans.*"‡ The age was under no illusion as to its own degeneracy, and it was pervaded by the gloomiest dread. § The lowest of the mob were conscious of the unsurpassable abominations which ran riot in the recesses of the palace, and were envied and reproduced, not only in the houses of the great senators, but even in those of the middle class. How could any nobleness or purity survive the sway of adored and deified monsters such as Tiberius, Caligula, Nero, Vitellius, Otho, and Domitian ? Was ever a more deplorable picture drawn of a state of morals rotten to its inmost depths, than that delineated by such historians as Tacitus and Suetonius ? The picture which our Lord drew in one of His last discourses, of wars and tumults, of nations in perplexity for the roaring of the sea and the billows, and of men fainting for fear and expectation of the things which are coming on the world,‖ is the exact parallel of the description of the same epoch by Tacitus as one "rich in disasters, savage with battles, rent with factions, cruel even in peace ; the swallowing up or overthrow of cities, the pollution of sacred functions, the prevalence of adulteries, the corruption of slaves against their masters, of

---

* Propert. *Eleg.* ii. 5, 19-26.

† Tert. *Apol.* 15 ; Minucius Felix, *Octav.* 25 ; Ovid *Ars. Amat.* i. 77, iii. 393 ; Firmicus *De err. prof. rel.* iv. p. 64 ; Rufinus, *H. E.* xii. 24, cited by Döllinger, *Judenth. u. Heidenth.* p. 644.

‡ Tac. *Ann.* iv. 34.

§ See Tac. *Ann.* vi. 28-51, *H.* i. 3.

‖ Matt. xxiv. 3-14 ; Luke xxi. 10-28.

freedmen against their patrons, and, when there was no open enemy, the ruin of friends by friends." * Could anything be more debased than the tone of vileness unblushingly presented by Juvenal, Martial, and Petronius? Already, in the better days of Augustus, Horace had sung:

> " Damnosa quid non imminuit dies ?
> Aetas parentum pejor avis dabit
> Nos nequiores, mox daturos
> Progeniem vitiosiorem." †

Bad as his age was, the poet thought it might conceivably be worse, and prophesied for future generations a still more irredeemable decadence. But Juvenal, in the days of Nero, with no conscious reference to what Horace had said, wrote that wickedness had now reached its absolute culmination, and that though future generations might be as bad as his was, they could not be more vile.

> " *Nil* erit ulterius quod nostris moribus addat
> Posteritas ; eadem cupient, facientque minores
> Omne in praecipiti vitium stetit." ‡

Their hideous taurobolies and kriobolies—of which the first trace is found on an inscription, A. D. 133—were but vain outward forms of expiation, which neither diminished the violence of their passions, nor cooled the anguish of their accusing consciences. Judaism did not reach them. They fancied that the Jews were descended from lepers who had been driven out of Egypt; that they worshipped, some said an ass, and others the clouds of heaven; that they were a nation of cheats and liars; that they kept Sabbaths on pretence of superstition, but solely as an excuse for idleness;§ and that they hated all men, as all men hated them.

---

* Tac. *Hist.* 1, 2. † Hor. *Od.* iii. vi. 45. ‡ Juv. *Sat.* i. 148.

§ On these ignorant misapprehensions, even of cultivated heathen writers, see Tac. *H.* v. 2, etc.; Juv. *Sat.* xiv. 96 ; Strabo, xvi. p. 670 ; Aug. *Civ. Dei* vi. 1 ; Tert. *Apol.* 23 ; Döllinger, *Judenth. u. Heidenth.* p. 628.

And the anguish of retribution was equal to the wickedness of universal abandonment to vile affections. Insolence, arrogance, greed, and the superabundance of flagitiousness, filled Rome with whisperers, liars, slanderers, professional informers—of whom some, to the common terror, exercised their infernal trade openly, others secretly.* The Emperor Tiberius had sunk to the lowest depths of degradation in his sty at Capreæ, as an "inventor of evil things," so that new words had to be coined to describe his vileness;† and he was, as even Pliny says of him, "notoriously the most wretched of mankind." He himself wrote to his Senate, "What to write, or how to write to you, Conscript Fathers, or what not to write, at the present moment, may all the gods and goddesses destroy me worse than I feel myself to be daily perishing, if I know."‡ The comment of the stern historian on those words is that his crimes and enormities turned to his own punishment; that neither his splendour nor his solitude saved him from suffering the torments and penalties which he confessed; and that he illustrated the wise remark that, if the minds of tyrants could be laid open to view, they would be as visibly lacerated by the scourges of cruelty, lust, and wicked counsels as bodies are by the lash.

This awful condition of things created an unspeakable weariness of life;§ and so deep was the conviction that the life of men is but a matter of indifference, or even a constant comedy in the eyes of the gods,‖ that suicide was no longer regarded as a crime, but had come to be looked upon as a sign of moral nobleness. Nor are these the rhetorical exaggerations of poets, historians, and satirists. Seneca was a grave philosopher, and one who tried to be sincere, and he wrote, "He who denies that we may forcibly end our life, does not see that he is closing the

---

* Tac. *Ann*. vi. 7.
‡ Tac. *Ann*. vi. 6.

† Tac. *Ann*. vi. 1 ; Rom. i. 30.
§ Tac. *Ann*. iv. 1, xvi. 16 ; Cic. *de Off*. i. 4–18.
‖ Tac. *Ann*. iii. 18.

path of liberty. The eternal law hath done nothing better than that it has given us one entrance to life, but many exits."

Self-murder was belauded as an act of real magnanimity by many, both of Greeks and Romans.* Even an Epictetus and a Marcus Aurelius did not rise above this point of view.† Not a few who were counted by the Greeks and Romans among their noblest sons had died by their own hands, and among them such philosophers as Zeno and Kleanthes. "Having gone through every species of wickedness," says Theophylact, "Human Nature needed to be healed."

Thus the Gentiles are convicted out of the mouths of their own writers, and it is proved that when St. Paul, in the first chapter of the Epistle to the Romans, drew, in such deep dark lines, the sketch of Pagan wickedness, and showed how the heathen had "become vain in their reasonings and their senseless heart was darkened," and how they were given up to passions of dishonour and reprobate uncleanness, he was not actuated by feelings of national or religious hatred, but was speaking, with holy dignity, the words of soberness and truth. The worst fact about them was that they were "past feeling"; they had felt once, but now were "hardened in wickedness."‡

II. THE JEWS.

Nor must it be supposed that this leprosy of Pagan wickedness was visible only in great Roman centres and heathen lands. There were many Gentiles, and large contingents of soldiers, in Palestine,§ and the wickedness

---

* See *Ep.* lviii. 34, lxxvii.; Plin. *Epp.* 3, 7.

† Epict. *Diss.* i. 25, ii. 2 ; Marc. Aurel. v. 9, viii. 47, x. 8.

‡ Eph. iv. 19, ἀπηλγηκότες. See, for further proofs, Döllinger, *The Jew and the Gentile ;* Renan, *L'Antéchrist ;* and my *Seekers after God*, pp. 36–53.

§ Since the year A. D. 63, when Pompey had entered Jerusalem with his army, Palestine had been under the dominance of Rome. Even in the days

of "them that knew not God" was not restrained by contact with Judaism. The stories told of things done by Roman soldiers, even in Jerusalem; their close alliance, in the days of Felix, with the murderous Sicarii; the cruel slaughters of the defenceless in which they took a share; the act of gross indecency openly displayed for purposes of insult by a Roman legionary in sight of all the worshippers in the Temple at a great festival; the abominable deeds of brutalism enacted by the soldiers and people after the death of Agrippa, in the cities of Cæsarea and Sebaste*—are incidents which sufficiently prove that the contagion of heathendom was diffused even into the Holy Land.

Herod the Great and his sons were open patrons of idolatry everywhere but in Jerusalem. They were not Jews at all. Herod, who came to the throne in A. D. 39, and held it for thirty-seven years, was the son of an Edomite father and an Arabian mother. He could afford to defy the shuddering hatred of the Jews so long as by flattering subservience and supple complaisance he could retain the favour of his Roman lords. These aliens built temples, in the Holy Land itself, to heathen deities and to deified Emperors. Herod the Great had even introduced into the Holy City the looseness of the theatre and the sanguinary ferocity of the gladiatorial games. Herod Philip, the tetrarch of Ituræa, ruled as a heathen among heathens. He stamped his coinage with the temple of Augustus, and the laureated effigies of Augustus and Tiberius, and he called the town of Bethsaida "Julias" in honour of the infamous daughter of Augustus. Besides this it was universally known, nor was there even a pretence at concealing the fact, that the darkest vices of fallen humanity were practised in the Herodian palaces; and that Herod's sons, while still mere youths, had carried back with them from

of the Maccabees there were πόλεις Ἑλληνίδες in the boundaries of Judæa (2 Macc. vi. 8).

* Jos. *Antt.* xix. 9, I.

Rome, where they were educated, sins which the Mosaic law punished with death. So deeply indeed had this contamination sunk that, for the sake of political dominance, Alexandra, the mother of the beautiful Mariamne and of the young High Priest Aristobulos, had, with the worst purposes, sent the likenesses of her son and daughter to the lewd Mark Antony, in order that she might secure an influence over him by means of his most shameless depravities. And this was the family which, under the protection first of the Triumvirate, and then of Augustus and Tiberius, held in their hands the autocracy of the Land of Israel!

Philip, the tetrarch of Ituræa, was the only one of the Herodian family who was unstained by crimes of lust and bloodshed ; and he, as we have seen, was an open patron of a decadent idolatry. It was in vain for the Rabbis to protest against the *Chokmath Javanith*, or "Greek science," and to say that, since men ought to study the Law day and night, Hellenic books could only be studied at some time which was neither day nor night.* Hellenism, in its literary aspect, deeply affected the views even of Philo; in its practical influences it was felt not only throughout the Dispersion, but in large areas of Palestine itself. In the palace of Herod the Great were to be found cultivated Hellenists like Nicolas of Damascus, a man of most versatile ability, and time-serving fortune hunters of the "*Græculus esuriens*" type, and even a youth like Carus, who represented the lowest decadence of heathen immorality and shame.† There were still righteous and holy men among the Jews; yet very shortly after the days of Christ, St. Paul, a Hebrew of the Hebrews, draws a very dark picture of the moral condition of his countrymen, and accuses them of imposture, impurity, and theft. He says of the Jews: "They please not God, and are contrary to all men "; and adds that though they professed "to dis-

---

* Menachoth, p. 992. Derenbourg, p. 361.
† Jos. *Antt.* xvii. 2, 4.

criminate the transcendent," they caused the Name of God to be blasphemed among the Gentiles.* The Pharisees thought so lightly of the mass of their own people as to call them "accursed."† The Roman writers attach to the name of Jew such epithets as "*gens sceleratissima, teterrima, projectissima ad libidinem.*"‡ Their own historian Josephus declares that the nation had become so wicked and depraved that the Holy City would have been swallowed up by an earthquake, or overthrown by Sodomitic lightning, had not the Romans executed judgment upon it.§ Divorce had become disgracefully common. Adultery was so rife that pretexts had to be devised for getting rid of the fearful ordeal of "the water of jealousy." Judaism had become a "*sentina iniquitatis,*" and Jerusalem was a "*laniena prophetarum.*"

III. THE DISPERSION.

If Heathendom brought its taint into the Promised Land of the People of the Covenant, it might have been hoped that the vast majority of the Jewish nation, now known as the *Galootha*, or Dispersion,‖ which was scattered throughout the civilised world, would have disseminated some higher moral ideals and some knowledge of the true God. It is to be feared that this was not the case. In Rome itself, since Pompey (B. C. 63) had brought back with him his multitude of captives, there had been a large and formidable colony of Jews in the Imperial city, where their ancient burial-places (*columbaria*) may still be seen.¶ They

---

* Rom. ii. 17–29, ix. 3 ; 1 Thess. ii. 21. † John vii. 49.

‡ Seneca. *ap.* Aug. *Civ. Dei* vi. 11 ; Tac. *Hist.* v. 5, 8 ; *Ann.* ii. 85 ; Suet. *Tiber.* 36.

§ Keim i. 314 ; Jos. *B. J.* v. 13, 6, x. 5, vii. 8, 1.

‖ Only a handful of Jews—likened by their own writers to the chaff in comparison with the wheat—returned with Ezra to Palestine, *Kiddushin*, 69, 2. See Hershon, *Genesis acc. to the Talmud*, p. 246.

¶ The Sibylline verses say that "every land and every sea was filled with Jews" (*Orac. Sibyll.* iii. 271), and Strabo, that they had come into every city

were so numerous as at times to create real alarm, and they made themselves specially terrible to returning Provincial Governors who had treated their compatriots with severity. In Cicero's days they assembled in the Forum in such threatening crowds that in B. C. 59 he had to deliver his speech in favour of Flaccus—who was obnoxious to them— in a tone of voice too low for them to hear.* Julius Cæsar had always been their friend, and their mourning ceremonies after his murder were expressive of such unrestrained grief as to amaze the people of the city.† Tiberius had multitudes of them impressed into the army, and sent to the pestilential regions of Sardinia, in accordance with a universal feeling that if they all perished by malaria it would be a very cheap loss. Claudius passed an edict which expelled them all from Rome because they were continually rioting " under the impulse of Christus."‡ They did indeed make some proselytes, but almost exclusively among women. Josephus claims Poppæa, the wife of Nero, as a Jewish proselyte.§ But two circumstances prevented Jews from exercising a beneficent influence over their heathen neighbours. One was the impression they made of being the devotees of a superstition which gave them no moral superiority. Cicero calls their religion " a barbarous superstition," and the elder Pliny brands them as " noted for a contempt of the gods." Coarser stories spoke of them as a nation who worshipped the head of an ass.‖ The vile cheating prac-

---

(*ap*. Jos. *Antt.* xiv. 7, 2 ; Schürer div. ii. vol. ii. p. 321). They were most numerous in Egypt and Cyrene. St. Paul found Jewish synagogues not only throughout Asia Minor, but in Thessalonica, Berœa, Athens, Corinth (Acts xvii. xviii.), Crete, and Rome.

* Cic. *Pro Flacco*, 28.

† Sueton. *Cæs.* 84. In B. C. 4 eight thousand Jews of Rome met the deputation which came from Jerusalem to denounce the Herods.

‡ Suet. *Claud.* 25 ; Acts xviii. 2.

§ Jos. *Antt.* xx. 8; *Vit.* 3. On the whole subject, see Schürer ii. vol. ii. § 31.

‖ Tac. *Hist.* v. 2–4, 13 ; *Ann.* ii. 85 ; Suet. *Tib.* 36 ; Pliny, *H. N.* iii. 4 ; Juv. *Sat.* xiv. 97 ; Pers. v. 184; Plut. *Sympos.* iv. 5, 6 ; Justin xxxvi. 1, 2 ;

tised on a Roman lady in Rome in the reign of Nero greatly deepened the hatred felt for them.* They were regarded as beggars, swindlers, and sacrilegious robbers; and were believed to alienate to their private use the sums of money which were contributed as the " Temple didrachm."

The other impediment to their influence rose from their attitude of habitual disdain and hatred for those around them.† "*Adversus omnes alios,*" says Seneca, "*hostile odium.*" St. Paul, with inspired insight, lays his finger on both sources of failure. " They are contrary to all men," ‡ he says in his letter to the Thessalonians ; and in the Epistle to the Romans he turns on the self-satisfied Jews with a series of crushing questions.§ " Thou therefore that teachest another, teachest thou not thyself ? Thou that teachest that a man should not steal, dost thou steal ? Thou that abhorrest idols, dost thou rob temples ? Thou that makest thy boast in the Law, through breaking the Law dishonourest thou God ? " We see, then, that the Jews as a nation had shown themselves false to the high ideal which had been set before them. Their religion was nothing more than a decrepit survival. They had failed to accomplish the mission which intended them to be the moral and religious teachers of the ancient world. Josephus says (*B. J.* v.-vi. 10) that no age had ever bred a generation more fruitful in wickedness since the beginning of the world.

Philostr. *Apoll. Tycan.* v. 11. Comp. Jos. *Ap.* i. 14, ii. 4–6 ; Rutilianus, i. 887. " Humanis animal dissociale cibis. Reddimus obscenæ convicia debita genti." Tert. *Apol.* 16, etc.

* Suet. *Nero.* 32. Hence St. Paul's questions, " Thou that abhorrest idols, *dost thou rob temples ?* " The notorious case had been that in which some Jews swindled the Roman lady Fulvia (Jos. *Antt.* xviii. 3, 5).

† They applied to the Gentiles, Ezek. xxiii. 20, "whose flesh is as the flesh of asses." Many fierce and contemptuous passages against Gentiles might be quoted from the Talmud. See Rosh Hashanah, f. 17, 1 (Hershon, *Talm. Miscell.* p. 155).

‡ 1 Thess. ii. 15.   § Rom. ii. 17–29.

IV. THE SAMARITANS.

Within the limits of the Holy Land itself there were three closely connected yet often widely antagonistic nationalities—the Jews, the Samaritans, and the Galileans.

The Samaritans were a people of mongrel origin. They had sprung from the mixture of the Israelitish population with immigrants sent into the ancient territory of the kings of Israel by Shalmaneser, king of Assyria, after his capture of Samaria.* At first these immigrants had continued the forms of idolatry to which they had been accustomed ; but on the devastation of the land by lions they asked the king of Assyria to have a priest sent to them who should teach them "the religion of the God of the land." This was done, and they learned to worship Jehovah, though their various communities mingled His worship with that of all sorts of idols,† Nerjal and Ashimah, Nibhaz and Tartuk, Adrammelech and Ananmelech. The Jews looked askance upon them, and called them by the contemptuous name of "lion-proselytes" and "Cuthæans,"‡ and "that foolish people that dwell in Sichem."§ Gradually, however, the descendants of these settlers and the original people of the land shook off the old idolatries, accepted Mosaism, claimed the special heritage of Jacob, and built a Temple on Mount Gerizim, which they (perhaps rightly) regarded as the scene of Abraham's sacrifice of Isaac,‖ and of the meeting of Abra-

---

* 2 Kings xviii. 9, 12–24. The new settlers came from Babylon, Cuthah, Ava, Hamath, Sepharvaim.

† Some most gratuitously see an allusion to this fivefold worship in John iv. 18 : "Thou hast had five husbands."

‡ *Cuthim*—so they are called throughout the Mishna ; and see Jos. *Antt.* ix. 14, 3, xi. 4, etc. Cuth, near Babylon, was one of the cities from which Sargon (B. C. 722) deported the settlers. See Neubauer, *Geogr. du Talm.* 329. They were also accused of worshipping the amulets buried by Jacob under the Enchanted Oak (Gen. xxx. 47). See my *Life of Christ*, p. 149.

§ Ecclus. i, 25, 26.

‖ In Deut. xi. 29, they interpolated the words "*that is, Shechem*" after

ham with Melchisedech,* and as the scene of Jacob's vision. They referred to Deut. xxvii., and to the fact that at Shechem Abrabam had built his first altar to the Lord (Gen. xii. 7). Since Gerizim had been chosen as "the Mount of Blessing," † they regarded it—and not Jerusalem—as being "the place which the Lord thy God shall choose." ‡ Their religion was the earliest form of Judaism, though they accepted only the Pentateuch as their sacred book. They were monotheists; they adopted circumcision; they kept the Sabbath and the chief festivals.

The antagonism between them and the Jews was specially accentuated by the building of their Temple on Gerizim in the days of Alexander the Great.§ It was destroyed by John Hyrcanus in B. C. 110,‖ but the mountain was still their sacred shrine. The breach might have been healed if the Jews in the days Zerubbabel had accepted their offer of co-operation in rebuilding the Temple of Jerusalem.¶ The refusal of this offer led to centuries of embitterment. The Jews did not in general rank them above Edomites and Philistines,** though in a few respects they gave them a grudging recognition. It was not till the days of the Talmud that they were slanderously charged with worshipping a dove.†† The treatment they received at the hands of their

---

"Gerizim," and were accused of tampering with the Books of the Law (*Soteh*, f. 33, 2). In *Chullin*, p. 13 i. we read, "The bread of a *Min* (heretic) is as the bread of a Cuthite; his wine as the wine of idol-worship; his books as the books of wizards." *Sheviith*, ch. 8. "He who eats the bread of a Cuthite, eats as it were the flesh of swine." Many other passages of the Talmud might be quoted.

* Gen. xiv. 17.   † Deut. xi. 29, xxvii. 4, 12.
‡ John iv. 20.
§ It had been originally built by a son-in-law of Sanballat the Heronite. Neh. xiii. 28.
‖ Jos. *Antt*. xii. 9, 1 ; *B. J.* i. 2, 6.   ¶ Ezra iv.
** "The nation that I hate is no nation," Ecclus. l, 25, 26. The Samaritans always showed themselves open to foreign influences, and had become greatly Hellenised.
†† *Demoth Jonah, Chullin*, f. 6, 1. The dove was worshipped at Ascalon,

neighbours caused a bitter hostility, which still raged in our Lord's day. In former times they had purposely caused confusion by kindling fire signals to mislead Jews as to the time of the Easter moon. They frequently annoyed any Jewish Passover pilgrims who ventured to pass through their territory.* The people of En-Gannim (Ginæa),† on the Samaritan frontier, actually refused hospitality to our Lord and the Apostles on their way to His last Passover, "because His face was as though He would go to Jerusalem."‡ Even when Jesus, in His thirst and weariness, asked the Samaritan woman for some water from Jacob's well, she was astonished at so small a request, because "Jews have no dealings with Samaritans."§ It was probably for this reason that, on sending out the Apostles on a mission, Jesus said, "Into any city of the Samaritans enter ye not."

The hatred between the two peoples was raised to white heat, partly by the promise of an impostor (in A. D. 35) to lead the Samaritans to Gerizim, and there reveal to them the buried treasures of the old Temple; ‖ and partly by a detestable act of some Samaritans at the Passover. During the Feast the Temple was kept open at night, and Samaritans had entered the sacred precincts and prevented the possibility of keeping the Passover by scattering dead men's bones about the courts.¶ The Samaritans have now dwindled down to a small community of some sixty souls,

and doves may have been an object of worship among the Assyrians. Most of the relevant passages of the Talmud, some of which breathe an intense hatred, are quoted by Mr. Hershon, *Treasures of the Talmud*, pp. 188 ff. See, too, Schürer, Div. ii., vol. i. pp. 5–8 ; Hamburger, Real Encycl. ii. 1662, etc. Jos. *Antt.* xviii. 2, 2, xx. 6, 1 ; *B. J.* ii. 12, 3.

* Lives were sometimes sacrificed. Jos. *Antt.* xx. 6, 1 ; *B. J.* ii. 12, 13.

† Jos. *B. J.* ii. 12.

‡ Luke ix. 51, 53.

§ John iv. 9. The clause is omitted in some of the best MSS.

‖ Moses was supposed to have buried the old sacred vessels of the Tabernacle in the clefts of Gerizim (Jos. *Antt.* xviii. 4).

¶ Jos. *Antt.* xviii. 2, 2. Coponius, the Procurator, left the crime unpunished.

and it is probable that they may soon disappear altogether. They alone have been able yearly to kill the Paschal lamb, because they regard the summit of Gerizim as the chosen place for that sacrifice, whereas the Jews, since the destruction of Jerusalem, have only been able to observe a " memorial " (μνημονευτικόν) and not a " sacrificial " (θυσιμόν) Passover.

But the same hatred and alienation still exists. A modern traveller relates how he saw a Jew and a Samaritan tugging at each other's beards, and thought that " there were very rough dealings between the Jews and Samaritans." They are still reviled as " worshippers of the pigeon "; and the Jewish traveller, Dr. Frankl, tells us that, on informing a lady in Samaria that he had been spending a morning with the Samaritans, she drew back from him with the exclamation, " *Take a purifying bath !* "

Our Lord utterly discountenanced this spirit of furious bigotry and mutual injuries. Although among the Jews it was the bitterest term of reproach to call a man " a Samaritan "—as when they said to Jesus, " Thou art a Samaritan, and hast a demon " *—He chose the compassion of the hated and heretical Samaritan as an example to Priests and Pharisees, and gladly accepted the hospitality of these detested aliens. This was the more remarkable because the Galileans, no less than the Jews, were on terms of bitterest animosity with them, and Tacitus tells us of " pillaging upon both sides, marauding bands despatched against each other, ambuscades devised, and at times regular engagements." † But Jesus habitually breathed that empyreal air of love towards all men, in which it was impossible that personal or national animosities should continue to exist.

* John viii. 48.
† *Ann.* xii. 54.   See Hausrath, *N. T. Times*, E. T. i. 27.

V. THE GALILEANS.

We must next consider what was the condition of the Galileans among whom our Lord spent the greater part of His life, and to whom the main part of His teaching was addressed.

Galilee (derived from *Galîl*, "circle," or "ring") was a district of some 1600 square miles, measuring about 36 miles from east to west, and about 50 miles from north to south. With its hills and valleys, rivers, lakes and plains, it had every variety of scenery. It was well watered by many streams, which took their origin from the accumulated snows of Lebanon, and even in ancient days it had been famous for its fertility, comprising as it did the tribes of Asher, Zabulon and Naphthali.* It was a densely populated country, which contained, according to Josephus, 204 towns, 15 fortified places, and 3,000,000 inhabitants. It was chiefly remarkable for the mixture of populations which had gained it the name of " Galilee of the Gentiles."

Few Jews had settled in the district after the return from Babylon, and in B. C. 164 Simon the Maccabean had removed them to Judæa.† Many of the population had, however, returned between B. C. 165–135, in the reign of John Hyrcanus. Galilee was crowded with Phœnicians, Syrians, Arabs, and Greeks. Scythopolis, on the road from Jezreel to the Valley of the Jordan, was practically a Gentile city. The great roads which ran through Galilee were constantly traversed by throngs of foreign traders. Sepphoris, so near Nazareth, looked like a Roman city, and at Tiberias Herod Antipas had not scrupled to adorn the frieze of his palace with the figures of animals. The Galileans were much more cosmopolitan in their tolerance, and far less scrupulously bigoted, than the Jews. But the

---

* Deut. xxxiii. 23, 24 ; Gen. xlix. 20 : Hos. xiv. 5 ; Ps. lxxxix. 12.   See G. A. Smith, *Geogr. of the Holy Land*, 413 ff.

† 1 Macc. v. 23 ; 2 Macc. vi. 8 ; Schürer, Div. i. 1, 19.

Syrians had infected them with superstition so that they were specially susceptible to "demoniacal possession." They were gay and quick-witted, and though they did not resist Hellenic and other influences they remained faithful Jews and ardent patriots, whose old traditional bravery and passionate idealism often hurried them into tumults.* Even at Jerusalem their excitability had led to a massacre, in which Pilate had mingled their blood with their sacrifices.

Judas the Galilean, who came from Gamala, had headed the Zealots (A. D. 6), who were the extremest section of the Pharisees. He took for his watchword, "No Lord but Jehovah; no tax but the Temple didrachma; no friend but the Zealot." Judas, indeed, as Gamaliel tells us (Acts v. 37), perished; but not till after a furious struggle, which warned the Romans not to attempt the taxation of the country.

His mantle fell on his sons, James, Simon, Menahem, and Eleazar, who still maintained internecine hostility against Rome. The family of Judas ended with the fearful deed of his grandson Eleazar at Magada, when he and all his garrison died by their own hands, set the fortress in flames, and left nothing for the Roman Conqueror but blackened ruins and half-burnt corpses. Hence, as Josephus says, a Galilean revolt of two months "disturbed Rome for seventy years, turned Palestine into a desert, destoyed the Temple, and scattered Israel over the face of the earth." †

The Jews ridiculed the rough *patois* of the Galileans, ‡ which made them mispronounce the most common letters.§

The Pharisees, with a strange ignorance of history, said

---

* Judg. v. 18.

† Hausrath ii. 81 ; Jos. *B. J.* vii. 8, 1, viii. 6.   For John of Gamala, see Jos *Vit.* and *B. J.* xxi. 1.

‡ Mark xiv. 70 ; Matt. xxvi. 73.

§ Thus they substituted ‏ת‎ for ‏ש‎, and call a man *tth*, not *tsh*.

that "out of Galilee ariseth no prophet." * Even Nathanael had asked Philip, " Can any good thing come out of Nazareth ? " and at Pentecost the amazement of the assembled multitude at the Gift of Tongues was increased by the question, " Behold, are not all these who speak Galileans ? " " Nazarene " was a term of opprobrium even in the first century, and it continues to be the contemptuous designation for Christians in Palestine to this day. † Nevertheless, though they were not without serious faults, and were highly excitable and liable to sudden changes of temperament, and though Josephus describes them as ever fond of innovation, we may say in accordance with both ancient and modern testimony, that " they were still a healthy people whose conscience would not get corrupted by Rabbinical sophistries, and among whom full-grown men were elevated far above their Jewish kinsfolk sickening with fanaticism." ‡ The Talmud itself bears witness that whereas the Jews cared more for money, the Galileans cared more for honour. §

---

* See *ante*, p. 108 (footnote). Not a few prophets like Hoshea, and great leaders like Barak, sprang from tribes included in the district of Galilee, and the glowing poetry of the Song of Songs derives its colouring from the land they occupied. See Hausrath i. 14.

† When I was in Palestine, if ever we came to a village where the inhabitants were specially rude and inhospitable, my dragoman used always to say, " Oh, yes, those people are Nazarenes."

‡ Hausrath quotes Jos. *B. J.* iii. 2, 3 ; Tac. *Hist.* v. 6 ; *Ann.* xii. 5. See too Jos. *Antt.* x. 5, xx. 6, 1 ; *B. J.* xv. 5 ; *Vit.* xvii.

§ See Neubauer, *Geogr. der Talmud*, p. 181.

CHAPTER XIII.

THE STATE OF RELIGION IN PALESTINE.

"Corruptio optimi, pessima."

THE conditions of the world in general woke, then, echoes even in Nazareth, and must have had their influence on the human mind of Jesus during the silent years. Still more would He feel and meditate over the state of things in His own province, and in those which bordered upon it. As regards questions of eternal moment, the thoughts of the people of Palestine, of the countless Jews of the Dispersion, and indirectly of all who were under the sway of Imperial Rome, were affected by the religious views of the Priests and religious teachers in Judæa, and most of all in Jerusalem itself. And there the aspects of religious life and religious opinion, which we must now more closely scrutinise, might well awaken the deepest misgivings.

(i.) Of the ZEALOTS we need say but little further. They represented the extreme wing of Pharisaic fanaticism, and seem first to have acquired their distinctive name in the rising of Judas the Galilean in A. D. 6. In Jerusalem and Judæa the Zealots were rarely able to achieve anything. The destruction of the Golden Eagle which Herod had put over the Temple Gate, by the wild scholars of the Rabbis Judas and Matthias, was punished by wholesale executions. The party became more prominent in later days. Many of them degenerated into mere assassins (*sicarii*) and conspirators, like the forty who bound themselves under a curse (*Cherem*) that they would neither eat nor drink till they had murdered Paul.

(ii.) Nor is it necessary to dwell long on the ESSENES, for the accounts which we have of them vary so much that they must either be inaccurate or refer to different sections of the general body. The very derivation of the name is quite uncertain. Philo seems to connect it with "holy ones." Others derive it from Jesse. Bishop Lightfoot connects it with *chasha*, "to be silent"; Ewald, from *chazan*, "to be strong"; Gfrörer, from *asî*, "healers"; Grätz, from *sacha*, "to bathe." If Philo's account of them in his book, *Quod omnis probus liber*, be correct, they lived mainly in villages, avoided trade, disapproved of war, formed social communities of which all the members ate at a common table, and lived a life of celibacy and labour. * The notion that they worshipped the sun seems to have been a calumny or a blunder. Josephus also speaks of them. He compares them with the Pythagoreans,† and adds such particulars as that they avoided the use of oil, refused to take oaths, and were very scrupulous in all matters of ceremonial cleanness. He mentions Judas the Essene and Menahem as exercising gifts of prophecy, and Simon the Essene as an interpreter of dreams. Pliny the

---

* The fullest information is given by Bishop Lightfoot in his Essay on the Essenes (*Epistle to the Colossians*, pp. 114-179). The original accounts are found in Philo, *Quod omnis probus liber;* and a quotation from Philo in Euseb. *Praep. Evang.;* Pliny, *Hist. Nat.* v. 17; Jos. *Antt.* xiii. 8, 9; ii. 2, xviii. 1. 5, etc.; *B. J.* ii. 8, 2, ff. ; Hippol. *Laer.* ix. 18–28. They were akin in doctrines to the Therapeutæ, of Alexandria, whom Philo describes in his *De Vita Contemplativa.* Some of the statements about them are confused and contradictory.

See, too, the quotation of Eusebius (*Praep. Evan.*) from Philo's *De Nobiltate.* It must be regarded as quite uncertain whether, in his book (if it be his) *De Vita Contemplativa*, he meant to describe the Essenes under the name of *Therapeutæ*.

† Jos. *Antt.* ii. 8, 2, xiii. 5, 9, xv. 10, xviii. 1. Both Philo and Josephus state the numbers of the Essenes at about 4000. Zeller, Keim, and Herzfeld think that they were under Pythagorean influences (as well as Alexandrian) ; but there seems more truth in the view of Frankl, Jost, Grätz, Derenbourg, Ewald, Hausrath, and others, that Essenism is only a peculiar and extreme development of Pharisaism.

Elder describes one of their communities which was settled in the neighbourhood of Engadi and Masada.*

They are not even mentioned in the New Testament, or in the Mishnah, and they do not seem to have exercised any effective influence on the religion of the nation. They were exclusive and self-righteous ascetics, who abandoned the world, which only regarded them with cold and distant curiosity. Their Manichæan tenet that "enjoyment is vile," is utterly unlike the teaching of Christ, who never encouraged self-macerating abstemiousness for its own sake, but "came eating and drinking." "Essenism was in reality only a confession of helplessness against the actual state of things, a renunciation of all attempts to reconstruct a united Israel."

The fancy that John the Baptist was an Essene is sufficiently refuted by the fact that he wore a dress of camel's hair, whereas they dressed in white linen; and that he fed on locusts, whereas they seem to have abjured animal food.† We are not told that our Lord or His Apostles once came into contact with them, and nothing is more absolutely baseless than the notion that He was Himself an Essene. They were Separatists; His life was spent among the multitudes. They were ascetics; He came eating and drinking, and living in outward particulars the common life of men. They were Sabbatarians of the strictest school, whereas He set aside the rules of Pharisaic Sabbatism. They forbade the use and even the manufacture of weapons; He said, "He that hath no sword, let him sell his cloak and buy one."‡ They were vegetarians; He was not.

---

* Plin. *H. N.* v. 17. There are also dubious and unimportant references to them in Epiphanius and in the Talmud. "The Colossian heresy," against which St. Paul wrote, may have been tinged with Essenian as well as Gnostic elements.

† This is denied by Schürer (Div. II. vol. ii. 201), but his arguments do not seem to me entirely conclusive. Perhaps some only of the Essenes were vegetarians.

‡ Luke xxii. 36.

They would never touch food not prepared by the members of their sect; He reclined alike at the banquets of the Publican and of the Pharisee, and swept away hosts of petty *Halachoth* about ceremonial uncleanness. They shunned and despised women; He was followed by a band of ministering women. They washed themselves if a stranger touched them; He suffered the penitent harlot to wet His feet with her tears, and to wipe them with the hairs of her head. So far as they aimed at holiness, and believed in a universal Priesthood, they resembled the Christians, but their religious opinions and practices diverged most widely from the teachings of Christ, and would have been absolutely powerless for the regeneration of the world.*

(iii.) THE SADDUCEES played a far greater part in the politics and destiny of Palestine that the Essenes, and exercised a wider influence over the fortunes of the people. In Jerusalem the Sadducees and Pharisees absorbed or overshadowed all other sects.

The entire religion of Israel underwent a change during the Babylonian Captivity, quite apart from any Persian influences which the Jews imbibed.

Before the Captivity the people had shown an incessant tendency to relapse into idolatry. After the Captivity they abhorred idols with the whole intensity of their convictions.

But the peril of idolatry was replaced by the peril of a dead ritual, and by the ruinous results of substituting an outward and mechanical worship for the service of pure hearts and holy lives.

From the days of Ezra, all the ordinances which may be

---

* See, among other authorities, Gfrörer, *Philo* ii. 299; Uhlhorn, *s.v.* "Essenes" (Herzog's *Real Encyc.*); Hilgenfeld, *Jud. Apocal.* 243–286; Herzfeld, *Gesch. des Volkes Isr.* iii. 368 ff.; Keim, i. 365–393; Ewald, *Gesch. des Volkes Isr.* iv. 453; Wescott, "Essenes" (Smith's *Dict. of the Bible*); Ginsburg, "Essenes" (Kitto's *Cyclop.*); Thomson, *Books which Influenced Our Lord*, 75–123; Lightfoot, *Colossians* (349–419); and the authorities referred to by Hausrath, Schürer, and Hamburger, *s.v.* "Essäer."

summed up under the head of "Levitism"—all the Levitic ordinances of the later Mosaic Law—assumed a new and immense prominence.* During the long centuries from the entrance of Israel into Canaan to the Return from the Exile, there is scarcely the slightest trace that they existed, and certainly they do not attract the least attention. The Day of Atonement, which came to be regarded as the most memorable day of the year, is not mentioned even in narratives where everything would have led us to suppose that it would have occupied a most prominent place. The name of Azazel, the evil spirit to whom the scape-goat was devoted, only occurs in Lev. xvi., and is alluded to nowhere else in the whole Bible. But after the days of Ezra, "ordinances which were not good, and statutes whereby they could not live"†—given to the Jews originally only "because of the hardness of their hearts"; this system of ordinances—against the slavish use of which the great Prophets of Israel had spoken in tones of thunder—became the main religion, and ultimately the almost mechanical fetish of the religionists of the nation. The patriotism, and the fervour for the institutions of Moses, aroused by the cruel persecutions and apostatising Hellenism of some of the Priests, created the party of the Chasidim, or "the Pious." The party which *rejected* legal stringency gradually acquired the name of Sadducees. The origin of the name is uncertain. The Fathers—as Epiphanius and St. Jerome—connected it with *Tsaddîkîm*, "the righteous," but the form of the name perhaps indicates a connection with *Tsadduk*, or *Zadok*.‡ The sons of Zadok formed one of the priestly families, and the name may have been immediately

---

* It is remarkable that the word "Levites" occurs *only twice* in the N. T. : John i. 19 ; Luke x. 32.

† Ezek. xx. 25.

‡ Epiphan. *Panar. H.* 14 ; Jer. *in Matt.* xxii. 23. The double *d* favours this derivation. The word may have been altered from *Tsaddikim* to Tsaddoukim only because of assonance with *Peroushim*, "Pharisees." On the Sadducees, see Taylor, *Pirqe Avôth*, pp. 126, 127.

derived from Zadok, the High Priest in the days of David (Ezek. xl. 46; 1 Chr. xii. 28; Ex. ii. 2); or from Zadok, the pupil of Antigonus of Socho,* and successor of Simeon the Just. Antigonus is said to have left behind him the rule that "we ought not to do righteousness for the sake of reward." As the notion that salvation must be earned by legal scrupulosities was rooted in the system of the Pharisees, the opposition to this view became the mark of Sadducees. The *Chasidim* developed into the *Perushim* (*Separatists*), or Pharisees; and the Sadducees, as representing the Priests, rejected more and more the authority of the Pharisaic Rabbis. They would only accept the Written Law, and ignored "the traditions of the Elders" with which it was overlaid.

But besides the endless disputes which arose between the two parties about the interpretation of Levitic rules, there were other lines of demarcation. The Sadducees were the more aristocratic party, and also the more worldly and cosmopolitan. Almost all the leading Priests were Sadducees,† and this sacerdotal party, contenting itself with sacrificial functions, was always inclined to temporise. Even in the days of Ezra and Nehemiah the Priests had shown a tendency to be at ease amid their privileges and emoluments, to adopt motives of worldly policy, and to relax the most binding ordinances.‡ Thus Eliashib the Priest, in direct defiance of the Mosaic Law (Deut. xxiii. 3, 4), had roused the righteous indignation of Nehemiah by clearing out a chamber in the Temple which had been used for storing tithes and frankincense, and assigning it to the use of Tobiah the Ammonite. In later days the Priests Manasseh and Onias had proved themselves traitors to the nation and its religion in their dealings with the Seleucidæ, and Joshua had openly assumed the heathen name of Jason.

The Asmonæan Priest-Prince Alexander Jannæus, dis-

---

* Abôth de Rabbi Nathan, 5.

† Acts v. 17.   ‡ Neh. xiii. 7.

gusted with the arrogance, insolence, and dishonesty of the Pharisaic leader, Simeon ben Shetach, had joined the Sadducees. He showed his contempt for Pharisaic tradition at the Feast of Tabernacles, by pouring out the libation on the ground, and not on the altar.* The people were always with the Pharisees, and in their fury at this neglect of customary ritual, they pelted Jannæus with the citrons and branches (*lulabim*) which they carried in their hands. This resulted in a tumult and a massacre, but the Priest-Prince became so conscious of the power of the Pharisees that on his deathbed he ordered his widow to reconcile herself with them.†

In the days of Herod the Great, Sudduceeism assumed its fullest dimensions, for then the priests could reckon on the aid of Roman and Idumæan despotism. Herod had summoned to the High Priesthood the obscure Ananeel, of Babylon. After this the High Priesthood, as we shall see hereafter, became the coveted appanage of a few worldly families—the House of Annas, the Boethusim,‡ the Kam. hits, and others. These Priests, while they professed the utmost strictness about sacrificial minutiæ, had the worst reputation among the people for greed, tyranny, and arrogance, and denied such essential elements of religion as the immortality of the soul, the resurrection of the body, the future Messianic kingdom,§ the world of angels and spirits, and even (it is said) the over-ruling Providence of God in the affairs of men.‖ The Sadducees remained to the last the aristocratic and exclusive party, luxurious time-servers, insouciant sceptics, noted at once for cruelty and Epicureanism. Disliked by the nation, and strong

---

* *Succah*, f. 48, 2.

† Jos. *Antt.* xiii. 15, 5 ; *Soteh*, f. 22, 2 ; Derenbourg, *Palestine*, p. 99.

‡ The Boethusim owed their elevation to Herod, who married Mariamne (the Second), a daughter of the Alexandrian Priest Joazar, son of Boethos.

§ Jos. *Antt.* xviii. 1, 4 ; Enoch xcviii. 6, c. 16, civ. 7.

‖ See Jos. *Antt.* x. 11, 7, xviii. 1, 3, xiii. 5, 9 ; *B. J.* ii. 8, 14 ; Acts xxiii. 8 ; Keim, i. 353–365. The Talmud calls them "Epicureans."

only by their alliance with the ruling powers, they had to allow the Pharisees to dominate in the Sanhedrin.* "The eloquence of the Synagogue," says Hausrath, "had won the victory over the splendour of the Temple, but only to dig a pit for the State, in which the Temple and School were together buried." Whatever the Sadducees may have been in their origin, they had, before the days of our Lord, degenerated into "typical opportunists," bent above all things on holding fast their own rights, privileges, and immunities.†

(iv.) THE HERODIANS need not occupy much of our attention. They are only mentioned on two occasions in the Gospels (Mark. iii. 6, xii. 13; Matt. xxii. 16). Josephus defines them generally as "the partisans of Herod" (οἱ τὰ τοῦ Ἡρώδου φρονοῦντες), and it is evident that they were a political rather than a religious party. It is true that Tertullian says that they tried to represent Herod the Great as a sort of *political* Messiah,‡ and they certainly claimed the adherence of so prominent an Essene as Menahem (Manaen), whose son was a foster-brother of Herod.§ But though they recognised in Jesus an enemy to their worldly views, and were ready to plot with Pharisees and Sadducees, and attempted to entangle Him by their insidious questions as to the lawfulness of paying tribute-money to Cæsar, they played no prominent part among the religious sects of Palestine.

(v.) We shall recur to the subject of the distinctive views of the PHARISEES when we have to show our Lord's dealings with them and their system.

The *Perushim* rose into prominence in those times of

---

* 1 Macc. ii. 42, vii. 13, 17; 2 Macc. xiv. 6. See Wellhausen, *Pharisäer und Sadducäer*, 76 ff.

† "Qui Christum Herodem esse dixerunt." Tert. *Adv. Omn. Haer.* I. Jer. *Adv. Lucifer* (opp. Bened. iv. 304), "Herodiani Herodem regem suscepere pro Christo."

‡ See Jos. *Antt.* xv. 10, 5; Lightfoot, *Hor. Hebr.* ii. 726.

§ Acts xiii. i.

priestly Hellenising which were known as the "days of *the mingling*"; and the word *Perishooth*, or "separatism," represents the ἀμιξία of legalised and intentional unsociability (2 Macc. xiv. 3, 38). In the days of Christ they had risen into marked prominence, and are said to have numbered 6000 adherents of their sect.* Their main characteristic was devotion to the Oral Law, with its masses of inferential tradition, and a slavish reverence for the Lawyers, Scribes, and Rabbis, to whose misplaced and microscopic ingenuity the development of this system was due. The Talmud is, of course, a late and most untrustworthy authority. It is utterly unhistoric, and full of confusions, anachronisms, and sheer inventions; yet to a certain extent it represents the continuity of older traditions. The Talmudists leave a false impression when they represent the *Zougoth*, or "Couples"†—that is, the two leading teachers of the Schools in successive generations— as having been the Presidents (the *Nasi* and the *Ab-beth-Din*) of the Sanhedrin—for the *Nasi* was always the High Priest. The leading Rabbis merely held positions in the *non-political* Sanhedrin of the Schools. Those of them who were specially and, so to speak, *professionally*, devoted to the study of the Law, were called "Lawyers," *i. e.,* "Teachers of the Law," or "Scribes,"‡ of whom the Son of Sirach says, "Where subtle parables are, he will be there also. He will seek out the hidden meaning of similitudes, and be conversant in the dark sayings of parables." §

There were many particulars in which Pharisaism was

---

* Jos. *Antt.* xvii. ii. 4.

† The chief "Couples" were: Jose Ben Joezer and Jose Ben Jochanan, Joshua Ben Perachiah and Nitai of Arbela, Jehuda Ben Tabbai and Simeon Ben Shetach, Shemaiah and Abtalion, Hillel and Shammai.

‡ Νομικοί, νομοδιδάσκαλοι, Luke vii. 30, xi. 45, etc. The "Scribes *of the* Pharisees" is the true reading in Mark ii. 16. The *Sopherim* (γραμματεῖς), "Scribes," are hardly distinguishable from "the Lawyers."

§ Ecclus. xxxix. 1-5.

nearer to Christianity than Sadduceeism. The Pharisees believed in the coming of the Messianic Kingdom, though they mistook its nature. They believed in the immortality of the soul, and the overruling Providence of God. But the more they sank into petty ceremonialism—the more extravagantly they valued mere external acts—the more radically did they degrade the conception of the true nature of God. Their religionism led to a hypocrisy all the deeper because it was half unconscious. What shall we think of the Talmudic representation of God, the Lord of Heaven and Earth, as a kind of magnified Rabbi, who repeats the Sh'ma to Himself daily; wears phylacteries on the wrist and forehead; occupies Himself three hours every day in studying His own law; has disputes with the Angels about legal minutiæ; and finally summons a Rabbi to settle the difference? Religion must always suffer in the worst degree when the King of Kings and Lord of Lords, who filleth Infinitude and Eternity, is dwarfed into a small-minded precisionist, to be pleased and pacified by prostrations, genuflexions, ablutions, and infinitestimal minutiæ, as though these paltry externals could be substitutes for that inward holiness which alone He requires.

It is not too much to say that Pharisaism sank more and more into a system which, while it travesticd the burdensome externalities of developed Levitism, ignored all that was noblest and most spiritual in the whole teaching of the Old Testament Scriptures. It nullified and superseded the plainest injunctions of Moses by casuistic *Halachoth* and tricky *Erubhin;* and took into no real account the magnificent and unbroken series of utterances which, in book after book of Scripture, laid it down with unmistakable plainness that such things are to true religion but as the small dust of the balance. With deplorable self-deceit the Pharisees aborbed themselves in numbering the threads of tassels, and tithing the stalks of pot-**herb**s, while for such cheap things they neglected the weightier matters of the Law—Justice, Mercy, and Truth. That was why they drew down upon themselves "the seven-fold flash of Christ's terrible invective." Utterly absorbed in making their "hedge round the Law," they emptied the Law itself—especially its most pure and spiritual elements— of all the deepest significance.* Paralysed by self-induced hypocrisy they showed far less *real* sincerity than the blindest of Pagan devotees, and while they posed as religious teachers, they poisoned religion at its fountain-head, made it petty and unreal, and precipitated the catastrophe which overwhelmed themselves and the nation which they had misled.

The Prophets of the Old Testament furnished a direct antithesis to the current Pharisaism of the Gospel era; their declarations of the inmost will of God are valid for all time, and constitute the final distinctions between conceited will-worship and that religion which is pure and undefiled before God and the Father.

What said the mighty MOSES?

"And now, Israel, what doth the Lord thy God require of thee, but to fear the Lord thy God, to walk in all His ways, and to love Him?"†

What said the holy SAMUEL?

"Hath the Lord as great delight in burnt-offerings and sacrifices as in obeying the voice of the Lord? Behold, to obey is better than sacrifice, and to hearken than the fat of rams."‡

What said KING SOLOMON?

"To do justice and judgment is more acceptable to the Lord than sacrifice."§

What said the inspired gatherer of sycamore leaves—the Prophet AMOS?

"I hate, I despise your feast-days, and I will not dwell in

---

* On the Pharisees, see Jos. *Antt.* xvii. 2, 4 ; *B. J.* ii. 8, 14.
† Deut. x. 12, 13.   ‡ 1 Sam. xv. 22.   § Prov. xxi. 3.

your solemn assemblies. . . . But let judgment run down as waters, and righteousness as a mighty stream." *

What said the sad-hearted HOSHEA, in words which were the favourite quotation of our Lord?

" I desired mercy and not sacrifice ; and the knowledge of God more than burnt-offerings." †

What said the burning ISAIAH, again and again, in words which were like thunder?

" To what purpose is the multitude of your sacrifices unto Me, saith the Lord. . . Bring no more vain oblations ; incense is an abomination unto Me. Wash you, make you clean, put away the evil of your doings from before Mine eyes ; cease to do evil ; learn to do well." ‡

What said the royal DAVID in his broken-hearted penitence?

" Thou desirest not sacrifice, else would I give it ; Thou delightest not in burnt-offerings. The sacrifices of God are a broken spirit ; a broken and a contrite heart, O God, Thou wilt not despise." §

What said the sweet PSALMISTS of Israel?

" Lord, who shall abide in Thy tabernacle? Who shall dwell in Thy holy hill? He that walketh uprightly and worketh righteousness, and speaketh the truth in his heart." ‖

" Who shall ascend unto the hill of the Lord? And who shall stand in His holy place? He that hath clean hands and a pure heart ; who hath not lifted up his soul to vanity nor sworn to deceive his neighbour. He shall receive the blessing from the Lord, and righteousness from the God of his salvation." ¶

What said JEREMIAH, in language startling in its emphasis?

---

* Amos v. 21–24.   † Hos. vi. 6 ; Matt. xii. 7.
‡ Is. i. 11, 16, 17.   Comp. lviii. 6, 7, lxvi. 3, xxix. 13, and *passim*.
§ Ps. li. 16, 17.   Comp. xxxiv. 18.
‖ Ps. xv. 1, 2.   ¶ Ps. xxiv. 3–5.   Comp. Ps. lxxxiv. 11, 12.

" I spake *not* unto your fathers, nor commanded them in the day that I brought them out of the land of Egypt, concerning burnt-offerings or sacrifices ; but this thing commanded I them, saying, Obey My voice, and I will be your God." *

What said EZEKIEL ?

" They sit before thee as My people, and they hear thy words, but they will not do them. For with their mouth they shew much love, but their heart goeth after their covetousness." †

What said the eloquent MICAH ?

" Wherewith shall I come before the Lord and bow myself before the Most High God ? Shall I come before Him with burnt-offerings, with calves of a year old ? Will the Lord be pleased with thousands of rams, or with ten thousands of rivers of oil ? Shall I give my first-born for my transgression, the fruit of my body for the sin of my soul ? He hath showed thee, O man, what is good ; and what doth the Lord require of thee, but to do justly, and to love mercy, and to walk humbly with thy God ? " ‡

What said HABAKKUK ?

" The just shall live by faith," or " in his faithfulness." §

What said ZECHARIAH in answer to inquiries about fasting ?

" Execute true judgment, and show mercy and compassion every man to his brother." " These are the things that ye shall do. Speak ye every man the truth to his neighbour. And let none of you imagine evil in your hearts." ‖

The teaching of the whole New Testament as to the nature of true religion, and as to what God desires, is in closest accordance with these utterances of the Prophets. This must be patent to every one who has not blinded and

---

* Jer. vii. 22, 23.   † Ezek. xxxiii. 31.   ‡ Micah. vi. 6–8.
§ Hab. ii. 4. (John iii. 36 ; Gal. ii. 16, iii. 11 ; Heb. x. 38.)
‖ Zech. vii. 9, viii. 16, 17.

benumbed his own soul by the super-exaltation of traditional nothings. Suffice it to point to the explicit words of
Christ Himself. When the young man asked Him, "What
must I do to be saved?" he received the answer, "If thou
wouldst enter into the kingdom of heaven, keep the commandments." When the Scribe, tempting Him, asked,
"Which is the great commandment of the Law?" He said
that on the two commandments, "Love God with all thy
heart," and "Love thy neighbour as thyself," hang all the
Law, and the Prophets." *

To quote but two of His special utterances, he said :

"Not every one that *saith* unto Me, Lord, Lord, shall
enter into the kingdom of heaven, but he that doeth the
will of My Father which is in heaven." †

And He said :

"Whatsoever ye would that men should do unto you,
even so do unto them: for *this* is the Law and the
Prophets." ‡

Contrast these with some of the Pharisaic utterances in
the Talmud, which constantly confound an easy, useless,
and self-deceiving legalism with the holiness which God
requires.

The Mosaic rule about wearing fringes (Num. xv. 38)
(*Tsitsith*, κράσπεδα, Matt. ix. 20), at the "wings," *i. e.*,
corners of garments, and to put on them a thread § of blue,
is probably of Egyptian origin ; and there was nothing
either burdensome or unreasonable about it, since the white
wool and blue threads might stand as symbols of innocence
and heaven. But to this the Scribes had added a moun-
tainous mass of oral pedantries. The fringe was to be
made of four threads of white wool, of which one was to
be wound round the others first 7 times with a double
knot, then 8 times with a double knot, then 11 times
with a double knot, then 13 times with a double knot;

---

* Matt. xxii. 38 ; Mark xii. 33.   † Matt. vii. 21, xii. 50.
‡ Matt. vii. 12.   § Not as in A. V., "ribands."

because $7 + 8 + 11 = 26$, the numerical value of the letters of Jehovah (יהוה), and 13 is the numerical value of *Achad*, " one," so that the number of windings represents the words " Jehovah is one."

The great Rashi said, " The precept concerning fringes *is as weighty as all the other precepts put together;* for it is written (Num. xv. 39), 'And remember all the commandments of the Lord.'" Now numerically (by what the Rabbis called *Gematria*) the word fringes (*Tsitsith*) = 600; and this with 8 threads and 5 knots makes 613. And Rabbi Samlai had said that Moses gave 613 commandments, namely, 365 *negative* (*Gezaroth*), as many as the days of the year, and 248 *positive* (*Tekanoth*), as many as the members of the human body = 613;* and this he *proved* by saying that Thorah, " Law," by Gematria = 611; which with " I am," and " Thou shalt have no other" = 613.†

Again, Rashi said that " he who observes the precepts about fringes shall have 2800 slaves to wait on him ": for, in Zech. viii. 23, we are told that ten men of all nations shall take hold of the skirt of a Jew, and as there are seventy nations, and four corners of a garment, $70 \times 10 \times 4 = 2800$.‡

In the same Talmudic treatise we are also told that Rabbi Joseph ben Rabba declared that " the law about fringes " was the one which should be most strongly inculcated, and that his father Rabba having once accidentally trodden on his fringe and torn it while he was standing on a ladder, stayed where he was, and would not move till it was mended.§

Our Lord, when He warned the people and His disciples

---

* See the Kabbalistic work *Kitzur Sh'lu*, p. 2, and Hershon, *Talm. Misc.*, pp. 322 ff.

† *Shevuoth*, f. 29, 1 ; *Maccoth*, f. 23, 2. In Deut. xxii. 12 they are called *gedillim*, lxx., στρεπτά, R. V. Marg., " twisted threads." The rule is elaborated in Num. xv. 37, 38.

‡ *Shabbath*, f. 32, 2.

§ *Shabbath*, f. 118, 2. See Rashi on Num. xv. 39.

against the hypocrisy of the Pharisees, said not only that "they enlarge the border of their garments" (which is an allusion to the "fringes"), but also that "they make broad their phylacteries," *Tephillîn.* *

It is at least doubtful whether Moses ever intended these Tephillîn to be worn. He said indeed, "It [the institution of the Passover] shall be for a sign unto thee upon thine hand, and for a memorial between thine eyes"; † and "It shall be for a token upon thine hand, and for frontlets between thine eyes." ‡ There is the strongest probability that the words were only metaphorical, just as in Prov. iii. 3, "Bind them on thy neck; write them on the tablet of thine heart." For there is no trace of any early use of these prayer-boxes, and the passages inscribed on the vellum are by no means the most memorable that might have been selected.§ On these grounds the sensible Karaites rejected the use of them, and St. Jerome rightly explains the passages to mean that the Jews should meditate constantly on these commands. The Scribes and Pharisees, however, attached the most exaggerated importance to the use of them, and made them as showily broad as they could. The arm-phylacteries (*Tephillîn shel yod*) were bound on the left arm, so as to be near the heart; and the head-phylacteries (*Tephillîn shel rosh*) were bound between the eyes. The leather strips by which they were tied were regarded as symbols of "the self-fettering of the Divine commands." On the phylactery of the forehead the four passages were to be written on four strips, and each placed in a separate compartment of the calfskin receptacle, and each was to be tied round with well-washed hair from the

---

* The separate compartments of the *beth* or "house" of the *Tephillîn* were called *Totaphoth.*

† Ex. xiii. 9.

‡ Ex. xiii. 16. Similiarly, the use of Mezuzoth, hollow cylinders with texts in them, was founded on Deut. vi. 8, xi. 18.

§ They were Ex. xiii. 1–16 ; Deut. vi. 4–9, xi. 13–21.

tail of a calf, with the letter Shin, ש, with *three* prongs on the right side (for *Shaddai*, Almighty), and with *four* prongs on the left side. In the "arm-phylactery" the four passages were to be written on a single slip of parchment in four columns of seven lines each, and the thong was to be passed round the arm three times for ש, and then to have seven more twists. Rabbi Simon Hassida deduced from Ex. xxxiii. 23 that God had revealed to Moses the way to make the knot of the phylacteries,* and also that the Eternal Himself wears "phylacteries." So vast was the importance attached to these fetishes that the Rabbis said, "He who has *Tephillin* on his arm, and *Tsitsith* on his garment, and *Mezuzoth* on his door, has every possible guarantee that he will not sin." Yet they said that, since some of the words of *the Law* were "light" and some "heavy," it was venial to deny that phylacteries had ever been enjoined; but since all the words of *the Scribes* were "heavy," *i. e.*, of consummate importance, it was a capital offence to say that the *division* of the prayer-box should have five compartments and not four !† Salvation by works, and by such paltry nothings as these, was the direct contradiction of the righteousness which Jesus taught. Thus we may say of the Pharisees that their fear towards God was taught by the precepts of men.‡

"Mankind," said Bishop Butler, "are for placing the stress of their religion anywhere rather than upon virtue." Nevertheless in virtue—or to use the higher and better words, "in righteousness and true holiness"—all that is essential in true religion is comprised. The vast error both of Sadducees and Pharisees was that they laid more stress on rules which had degenerated into external rites and petty puerilities than on temperance, chastity, and soberness. And

---

* *Beb. Barachoth*, f. 7.

† *Menach.* 33, 6 ; *Jer. Berachoth*, 3, 6.   See Gfrörer, *Jahr. d. Heils* i. 146; Schwab, p. 17 ; Kalisch, *Exodus*, p. 224.

‡ Matt. xv. 9 ; Col. ii. 22.

that was why Christ addressed them as "Ye hypocrites!" and quoted against them the words of the Evangelical Prophet: "This people draweth nigh unto Me with their mouth and honoureth Me with their lips; but their heart is far from Me. But in vain they do worship Me, teaching for doctrines the commandments of men."*

In these pages we have been able to furnish but the slightest glimpse of the religious condition of the Jews in the time of our Lord, as represented by their leading parties. But in the Talmud itself we find the elements of their emphatic condemnation. The people, while they continued to pay conventional honour to the Priests, deeply suspected them of betraying the national interests for their own aggrandisement,† and gave their main confidence to the Pharisees. On the great Day of Atonement, on one occasion, the High Priest left the Temple followed by a crowd of worshippers, just after he had pronounced the promises of God's pardon; but on seeing the Pharisaic "couple" of the day, Shemaiah and Abtalion, the crowd immediately deserted the High Priest to give an escort to the Rabbis. "Greeting to the men of the people!" said the sarcastic and indignant Pontiff. "Greeting," answered the Rabbis, "to the men of the people who do the works of Aaron, not to the sons of Aaron who do not resemble Aaron." ‡

Thus, of the Sadducean families of Priests in the days of the Herods we read:

"Woe to the family of Boethos! woe to their spears!"

"Woe to the family of Hanan (Annas)! woe to their serpent-hissings!"

"Woe to the family of Kanthera! woe to their pens!"

---

* Matt. xv. 8, 9.　　　　　　　　　　　　† Jos. *Antt.* xiv. 3. 2.
‡ *Yoma,* f. 71, 2 ; Grätz, iii. 116 ; Derenbourg, p. 118. See Hamburger, *Real-Encycl.* ii. 1043.

" Woe to the family of Ishmael ben Phabi ! woe to their fists !"

" They themselves are High Priests. Their sons are the treasurers ; their sons-in-law captains of the Temple ; and their servants smite the people with their rods."*

In another passage we read that " the threshold of the Sanctuary uttered four cries, ' Depart hence, ye descendants of Eli ; you defile the Temple of Jehovah !'

" ' Depart hence, Issachar of Kephar Barkai, who only carest for thyself, and profanest the victims consecrated to heaven—[for he wore silk gloves when he sacrificed !]

" ' Open yourselves wide, ye portals ! let Ishmael ben Phabi enter, the disciple of Pinekai.

" ' Open yourselves wide, ye gates ! let Johanan ben Nebedai enter, the disciple of gluttons, that he may gorge himself on the victims ! ' "†

And of the Pharisees, we read :

There are eight sects of Pharisees, viz., these :

1. The *shoulder* Pharisees, *i. e.*, he who, as it were, shoulders his good works, to be seen of men.

2. The *time-gaining* Pharisee, he who says, " Wait a little while ; let me first perform this or that good work."

3. The *compounding* Pharisee, he who says, " May my few sins be deducted from my many virtues, and so atoned for."

4. The *mortar* Pharisee (*medorkia*), who so bends his back with his eyes on the ground, as to look like an inverted mortar.

This seems to be the same as the *tumbling* Pharisee, who is so humble that he will not lift his feet from the ground ;

---

* *Pesachim*, f. 57, 1 ; *Kerithoth*, f. 28. Josephus furnishes a startling comment on the last woe in *Antt.* xx. 8, 9. See also Tosefta, *Menachoth ad fin.;* Geiger, *Urschrift*, p. 118; Derenbourg, *Palestine*, p. 233; Renan, *L'Antéchrist*, p. 51; Raphall, *Hist. of the Jews*, ii. 370.

† Derenbourg, *Palestine*, p. 233. He regards Pinekai as meaning *Self-indulgence*," an ironic variation of Phinehas.

and the *hump-backed* Pharisee who walked as though his shoulders bore the whole weight of the Law.

5. The *tell-me-another-duty-to-do-and-I-will-do-it* Pharisee.

6. The *Shechemite* Pharisee, who is a Pharisee *only for reward.* (Com. Gen. xxxiv. 19.)

7. The *timid* Pharisee, who is a Pharisee *only from dread of Punishment.*

To which Rabbi Nathan adds:

8. The *born* Pharisee.

And some substituted for one of these classes the *bleeding* Pharisee (*kinai*), who shuts his eyes and knocks his face against walls, lest he should happen to see a woman.

In their unbounded self-exaltation, and undisguised contempt for all except their own set, they thrust themselves into the place of God, and identified their small decisions with the very voice of the Almighty. They fostered the "enormous delusion" that sensuous and finical scrupulosities constituted an acceptable service, and could suspend the vengeance of God, which they imagined as ever ready to burst upon those who neglected and despised their "commandments of men." Punctilious trifles were substituted for holy lives, and immorality was concealed under a cloak "doubly-lined with the fox-fur of hypocrisy."

Dr. Emmanuel Deutsch says that the Talmud inveighs even more bitterly and caustically than the New Testament against what it calls "the plague of Pharisaism"— "the dyed ones who do evil deeds and claim godly recompense";* "they who preach beautifully, but do not act beautifully." Parodying their exaggerated logical arrangements, their scrupulous divisions and sub-divisions, the Talmud, among its classes of unworthy pretenders, says that the real and only Pharisee is he who doeth the will of

---

* Jer. *Berachoth,* f. ix. 7, f. 13 ; Bab. *Soteh,* f. 22, 1 ; *Avôth d'Rabbi Nathan,* ch. 37. See Hershon, *Talm. Miscel.* p. 122 ; Derenbourg, *Palestine,* p. 71. In *Soteh,* f. 21, 2, we read : " Foolish saints, crafty villains, sanctimonious women, and *self-afflicting Pharisees* are the destroyers of the world."

his Father in heaven *because he loves Him*. But the charge of hypocrisy against the Pharisees was not new in the days of Christ. Even Alexander Jannæus had warned his wife against " painted Pharisees, who do the deeds of Zimri and look for the reward of Phinehas."

Yet there must be in the human mind an instinctive tendency to substitute outward observance for heart-religion, and to make exaggerated legalism usurp the place of true holiness; for Pharisaism, from its incipient stage in the days of the Scribes of the Great Synagogue till the time when it was codified in the Mishnah, covered a space of six centuries; and, in the grotesque developments of Talmudism, it lasted on, in greater or less degree, down to modern times. The explanation of the tendency is that externalism is easy, and generates a self-satisfaction which enables men to pose as " religious," while they despise others. Nothing is more easy than to live with boundless self-complacency in an elaborate round of functions dictated by some empty *Directorium* of useless and obsolete tradition: but, as even a heathen could say, it is difficult—difficult and not so easy as it seems—to be good and not bad.

CHAPTER XIV.

THE MESSIANIC HOPE.

"Proclaim glad tidings in Jerusalem, for God hath had mercy upon Israel in her visitation. Set thyself, O Jerusalem, upon a high place, and behold thy sons and thy daughters from the morning unto the evening, brought together for ever by the Lord."—Ps. Salom xi.

"All the prophets prophesied of nothing else than of the days of the Messiah."—*Bab. Berachoth*, f. 34, 2.

SUCH was the condition of the world and of religion as Jesus heard of it, and saw it, and meditated upon it, while in holy and obscure poverty He toiled in the shop of the village carpenter. But He was also profoundly conscious of the deep unrest, of the passionate longing for deliverance, which moved the inmost hearts of thousands, and caused so many of the best and holiest to live in constant and yearning hope for "the redemption of Jerusalem" and "the consolation of Israel." *

There are epochs in the world's history when men feel a depressing sense of uncertainty and misery which tends to deepen into despair. At such times they yearn with the whole strength of their being for some fresh communication of the mind and will of God. The lamp of revelation has a tendency to burn dim as the ages advance; not only because it remains untrimmed, but also because the requirements of the ages differ, and that which sufficed the needs of one millennium loses much of its force in another. For this reason God has renewed again and again His communi-

---

* Luke ii. 25, 38, i. 46–55. Comp. Pss. Sol. v. 13 ff.; 2 Esdras xi. 42 ; Orac. Sib. iii. 49, etc. The Book of Baruch and 2 Esdras were probably not written till after the Fall of Jerusalem (A. D. 72), and are doubtless influenced directly and indirectly by Christian hopes.

cations with mankind. From the first dim promise of deliverance to the fallen progenitors of the human race—from the days of Enoch, and Noah, and Abraham, and Jacob, and Moses, again and again has

> " God, stooping, showed sufficient of His light
> For those i' the dark to walk by."

Then came the succession of Prophets, from Samuel to Amos, and Isaiah to Malachi. After five centuries of Scribism, not unenlightened by the appearance of a few noble personalities like Judas the Maccabee and Simon the Just, and by a few great writers like the Son of Sirach, we come down to the Messianic era. The olden prophets had spoken of a coming Deliverer—a Davidic King, who should give victory, peace, and prosperity to His people; or of a Servant of Jehovah, who should bear the sins of many. The Book of Daniel—the favourite book of the days of Christ*—and various Apocryphal books, of more recent date, pointed to the establishment of an everlasting kingdom, and looked for a return of Elijah, or one of the Prophets,† to prepare the way of its Founder. ‡ It was a current belief that Jeremiah might re-appear to restore to the nation the five missing glories of the Temple, some of which he was supposed to have hidden.§ But in parts of the Book of Enoch (B. C. 70), and the Sibylline Prophecies, and in the Psalms of Solomon (B. C. 70–40), the belief in the Advent of a Davidic King had been revived,‖ though

---

* Jos. *Antt.* x. 10, 11, *B. J.* vi. 5, 4. Josephus says that the popularity of the Book rose from the definite calculations which they founded upon it. They saw in the Roman Empire the "fourth Beast" of Daniel, which was to be followed by the Kingdom which should not be destroyed (Dan. vii. 13, 14).

† Mal. iv. 5 ; Ecclus. xxxvi. 15, 16, xlix. 7 ; Mark vi. 15, viii. 28 ; John i. 21, vi. 14, etc.

‡ 1 Macc. iv. 46, xiv. 41. Comp. Deut. xviii. 15 ; Wendt, *Teaching of Jesus*, i. 63.

§ Matt. xvi. 14 ; John i. 21, vi. 14, vii. 40. In 2 Macc. xv. 13 ff. he appears in vision to strengthen his countrymen.

‖ Enoch x. 16–38, xlvi. 1, lv. 4, lxii. 6, etc.; Sibyll. iii. 652–794 ; Pss. Sol.

it is not found in the Assumption of Moses or the Book of Jubilees. The Psalms of Solomon were specially full of a passionate conviction that the day was at hand when the coming Messiah should cleanse Jerusalem with His sanctification, even as it was at the first, so that nations would come from the ends of the earth to behold its glory. *" No evil will prevail among them in those days, for all shall be holy, and their King is Christ the Lord."** The great Alexandrian thinker, Philo, though he moved for the most part in a region of chill philosophical abstractions, yet sometimes dwells on the coming glory of Messianic days. † Josephus, though intensely cautious lest he should offend his Roman patrons, shows that he, too, shared to some extent in the hopes of his people. ‡ Since the days of Queen Alexandra, many like Simeon and Joseph of Arimathæa had been " waiting for the Consolation of Israel " and for the Kingdom of God; so that at the coming of the Baptist§ the people were in expectation, "and many reasoned in their hearts of John whether haply he were the Christ." ‖ The generality of the expectation explains the daring violence of the Pharisaic youths who, at the instigation of Matthias and Judas, destroyed the golden eagle which Herod had placed over the entrance-gate of his new Temple. It also accounts for the multitude of followers who gathered round Simon, Athronges, and Judas of

---

xvii., xviii.; Wendt. *l. c.* It is clear from the Gospels that the conception was prominent in the minds of the people. Mark viii. 29, ix. 13, x. 47, xi. 10, xii. 35, xiv. 61–64; John vi. 69, xii. 34.

*Pss. Sol. xvii. 33, 36. The writer also exclaims : "Behold, O Lord, and raise up for them their King, David's Son, in the time when Thou hast appointed, that he may reign over Israel thy servants." The Psalter of Solomon may be read in Hilgenfeld's *Messias Judæorum.* It refers in many passages to a pure and mighty Messiah, who in Ps. xvii. is described as χριστὸς Κύριος as in Lam. iv. 20 (lxx).

† Philo, in his *De execratione,* and *De præm. et poen.*

‡ *B. J.* v. 1, 3 ; *Antt.* iv. 6, 5, x. 10, 4. See Hausrath i. 199.

§ Luke ii. 25–28 ; Mark xv. 43.

‖ Luke iii. 15.

Galilee, and even such a miserable impostor as Theudas. The multitude clung with convulsive hope or despairing frenzy to almost anyone who seemed to promise any form or possibility of emancipation—to Hyrcanus; to the beautiful young High Priest Aristobulus; to the impostor Alexander; to Agrippa I.;—some Jews even regarded Herod the Great as a Divinely appointed Deliverer;* while Josephus looked, or professed to look, to Vespasian and the power of Rome as a source of hope for the future. It was not until after the final overthrow of Bar Cochba, "the Son of a Star" (A. D. 135), that such movements became impossible for ever. With the enthusiastic Pharisee, Rabbi Akiba, ended the Rabbinic Schools, which expected for Israel a temporal deliverance.

The older Messianic Hope had mainly concerned itself with the future glories of Israel; the later form of Messianic Expectation began to regard the Messiah as the Deliverer of the whole world, and the Comforter of individual miseries. It also enriched and enlarged the horizon of mortal life by the doctrine of a future Resurrection—in which the Pharisees believed, though it was rejected by the Priests and Sadducees. The *Olam Habbah*, or "future æon," was to be in every respect more splendid and happy than the *Olam Hazzeh*, or "present æon." But the happy age was to be preceded by days of immense tribulation, of which the only alleviation lay in the knowledge that they were "the *birth-throes*" (ὠδῖνες: Matt. xxiv. 8; Mark xiii. 8; *B. J.* vi. 5, 4), the *Chebly Hammeshiach*, or travail-pangs of the Messiah (Hos. xiii. 13).

Such expectations had even been disseminated in the heathen world. They have left their traces on the pages of Horace and of Virgil. "In the whole East," says Suetonius, "had prevailed an ancient and fixed opinion, that, at this time, it was a decree of destiny that some who came from Judæa would become masters of the whole world.

* See Keim i. 300 ff. (Tert. *Praescr.* 45).

Events subsequently proved that such a prophecy had some reference to a Roman Emperor ; but the Jews, forcing its interpretation to themselves, rose in rebellion." Josephus was probably the first who gave this interpretation to the prophecy. Tacitus, like Suetonius, attributes the revolt of the Jews to their perverted application to themselves of a prediction which referred to the Roman Conquerors.* The rumoured appearance of the Phœnix in Egypt, after the lapse of many centuries, excited the wildest surmise in an age which felt that the mass of mankind had sunk into a condition too horrible for continuance, and which had been affrighted by endless misfortunes and omens.† Men had also been deeply moved by the story of the cry, "*Great Pan is dead!*"‡ which had been heard by the sailors in the reign of Tiberius, and had evoked a burst of multitudinous wailing. Before things had assumed their worst aspect, Virgil, in his vaticination of the future glories of the son of Asinius Pollio, had sung :§

> " Aspice convexo nutantem pondere mundum
> Terræque tractusque maris, cœlumque profundum,
> Adspice venturo lætantur ut omnia sæclo ! "

The restless belief as to some overwhelmingly important world-crisis, which would have its origin in Eastern lands, affected even the most godless of Roman Emperors. It was the passionate desire of Caius Caligula to set up the gilded colossus of himself in the Temple of Jerusalem. As we have seen, Poppæa, the wife of Nero, was, according to Josephus, a Jewish proselyte ; ‖ and Nero himself had been taught, perhaps by Jews, to look to the East, and even to Jerusalem, as the seat of a future dominion.¶

It was not strange that, amid the deep and ever-deepening darkness, men should be expectant of a coming Dawn.

---

* Tac. *Hist.* v. 13. † Tac. *Ann.* vi. 28–51.
‡ Plut. *De Defect. Orac.* 17. § *Ecl.* iv. Comp. *Orac. Sibyll.* 784 ff.
‖ Jos. *Vit.* 3 ; *Antt.* xx. 8, 11. Comp. Tac. *Ann.* xvi. 6.
¶ Suet. *Nero,* 40. See Keim, i. 326.

It is, however, important to observe that the True Messiah was so little the natural evolution of current Messianic expectations that, coming neither as a King nor as a Victor, nor as a temporal Emancipator of His people, nor as a mere man at all, but as a Divine and crucified Nazarene, He reversed and violated all the most cherished expectations of His land and age. He was not " a more victorious Joshua, a more magnificent Herod, a wider-reaching Cæsar, a wiser Moses, a holier Abraham." He was no burning Isaiah, no vengeful Elijah, no learned Hillel, or passionate Akiba—no ringleader of rising multitudes, like Judas the Gaulonite, or Bar Cochba.

> " He came, but not in regal splendour drest—
> The haughty diadem, the Tyrian vest ;
> Not armed in flame all glorious from afar,
> Of hosts the Captain, and the Lord of war ";

but He came as " the Carpenter," as the meek and lowly, as the wearer of the crown of thorns ; and He established His claim as Universal Victor by means of a few obscure and timid followers, after He had perished amid the banded obloquies of His nation and of His age.

CHAPTER XV.

JOHN THE BAPTIST.

"This is Elijah which was for to come."—MATT. xi. 14.

> "John, than which man a sadder and a greater
> Not till this day had been of woman born;
> John, like some iron peak by the Creator
> Fired with the red glow of the rushing morn."
>
> —F. MYERS.

WHEN the hour has struck—when "the shadow has crept to the appointed line on the dial-plate of destiny"—God calls forth the man.

The chief need of the world is the death-defying courage of true men. The only power which can reclaim the world in ages of sloth, decadence, and self-deceiving religionism is the power of insight and burning sincerity which He inspires into the hearts of saints and Prophets. No prayer is more constantly needed than that God would grant to His Church a succession of *men*,—not of incarnate conventionalities, who think that the truth will perish with *them*, or that it has been frozen for ever in channels of stagnant function. Through such channels the living water flows no longer. The cry which springs spontaneously from our hearts is—

> "God give us men! A time like this demands
> Great hearts, strong minds, true faith, and willing hands;
> Men whom the lust of office does not kill,
> Men whom the spoils of office cannot buy,
> Men who possess convictions and a will,
> Men who have honour, men who dare not lie."

This has been felt even in heathen lands. We know how Diogenes went through the streets of Athens with a lan-

171

tern, seeking for a *man;* and when some of the crowd came
to him he beat them away with the contemptuous exclamation, " I want men; ye are σκύβαλα." Much more has it
been felt in Churches which have stagnated into pretence
and unreality under the ruinous influences of priestly
usurpation. " Run ye to and fro through the streets of
Jerusalem," said Jeremiah, "and see now, and know, and
seek in the broad places thereof, if ye can find a *man*, if
there be any that doeth justly and seeketh faithfulness, and
I will pardon her."* But he could find no such man.
There were many who said, "The Lord liveth," but they
swore falsely, and made their faces harder than a rock even
against chastisement. And if these were mainly the poor
and foolish, the great men and leaders were even worse.
They had altogether broken the yoke and burst the bands.
The nation as a nation continued to trust in dead formulæ
which, so used, had dwindled into lying words. " Ignorant
of God's righteousness and seeking to establish their own,
they did not subject themselves to the righteousness of
God."† Convinced that they were themselves righteous,
and despising others, they had degraded God into the
leader of a sect, and in their opinionated infallibility furi-
ously condemned and did their utmost to suppress, by mean
slanders and by open or subterranean violence, those who
had some glimpses of the true light. Like the snail,
which, as the Hindoo proverb says, " sees nothing but its
own shell, and thinks it the grandest place in the universe,"
so they saw nothing beyond the pettinesses which they
glorified as though they were the essence of holy service.

Out of the heart of this spiritual stagnancy which had
lost sight of righteousness in ritualism, and fancied that a
mass of meaningless minutiæ were essential things; out
of the very heart of this dead and half-putrescent system,
which was abundantly breeding its " offspring of vipers " ‡—

* Jer. v. 1-9.   † Rom. x. 3.

‡ This phrase γεννήματα ἐχιδνῶν (Matt. iii. 7; Luke iii. 7; " serpentes ex

God called a MAN. He was by birth a priest, the son of a priest of the order of Abijah, and was therefore in a position to observe at first hand the moral decay of a sacerdotalism which within was full of extortion and excess. The mission of John expressed a revolt against Levitism, and a republication—as from a new Sinai—of the eternal moral law. It was a declaration that religion means "a good mind and a good life," and that when it ceases to mean this, it means worse than nothing. It was a preaching of the old, simple, obliterated truth that "the righteous Lord loveth *righteousness.*" John came, as our Lord said, "*in the way of righteousness.*"* His mission was a return to the mighty moral teaching of those old prophets who were the glory of Hebraism. John the Baptist did not so much as allude to one of the myriad rules of Pharisaism. Priest and Nazarite though he was, he did not once refer to the ceremonial law to which the current orthodoxy made the Prophets a mere appendage. But he re-echoed, in tones of thunder, the burning messages of the Prophets themselves, and especially of Isaiah. The essence of his teaching was to be found in the messages of "the Evangelical Prophet," of Amos, Micah, Jeremiah, and Hoshea.

His aspect emphasised his message. His preached not in Temple or synagogue, but among the wild rocks of "the appalling desolation" (*Jeshimon*), in the Valley of the Dead Sea, "the haunt of thirst, where the dragons and demons howl." He wore no priestly vestments, but a shaggy skin.† His girdle was a strip of untanned leather—not a girdle of fine linen embroidered with threads of gold and silver, like those worn by such as lived in kings' houses. His food was such as nature supplied. It consisted of the wild honey which exudes from the leaves of tropical plants, or is

serpentibus ") is not found in the Old Testament, but was twice used by our Lord (Matt. xii. 34, xxiii. 33).

* Matt. xxi. 32.

† 2 Kings i. 8; Zech. xiii. 4; Is. iii. 24; Heb. xi. 37.

left by the bees in the clefts of the rocks;* and of the locusts, which the south wind swept from Arabia, and scattered among the valleys of the Dead Sea, but which few could eat without disgust.† John poured open scorn on all luxury. He came like a new Elijah, in all the uncompromising sternness of his prototype.‡ He did not preach smooth things and prophesy deceits, but told of One whose fan was in His hand, who should thoroughly purge His floor, and burn up the chaff with unquenchable fire. This constituted the terribly original feature of his message. "Of all the Messianic passages which we find written in Sibyls, Apocalypses, and Jubilees, not one has struck this tone, which fell like rolling thunder on the ears of the people."

His preaching was avowedly preparative—it was that of a Forerunner. He told the deputation of Priests and Levites which came to him from Jerusalem that he was not the Messiah, nor Elijah, nor the expected Prophet, but that he was "the Voice of one crying in the wilderness, Make straight the way of the Lord, as said the Prophet Isaiah." John baptised with water only, as a preparation for Him who already stood among them, though they knew Him not, who should baptise them with the Holy Ghost and with fire, but who would not be finally manifested except after a time of judgment—"the great and terrible day of the Lord."

John's preaching aimed at religious awakenment. The priests were indolently absorbed in "sacrificing and celebrating," and were sunk in greed, routine, and ambitious worldliness. The masses of the people and of their teachers were trusting in lying words, saying, "We be Abraham's sons"; and in outward privileges—"The

---

* Jos. *B. J.* iv. 8.

† All kinds of locusts are allowed to be eaten in Lev. xi. 22. They were dried and salted. Jer. *in Jovin.* ii. Comp. Plin *H. N.* ii. 29, vi. 30.

‡ Mal. iii. 1–3 ; Ecclus. xlviii. 10, 11 ; Mark ix. 12.

Temple of the Lord, the Temple of the Lord, the Temple of the Lord are these." They were occupied with badges of party, and tithes of mint, anise, and cumin, and with artificial moralities which altogether benumbed the sense of truth and reality. The fogs needed to be scattered by thunder and hurricane. From the sickly and perfumed air of contentment with the infinitesimal, and hypocrisy as to the essential—from the conventional optimism "which sweetened the present, and gilded the future with the lazy fancy of a well-fed piety"—he roused them as with shocks of earthquake. It was not his to say smooth things and prophesy deceits; not his to bow low before the idol of fashionable "views," nor "to glide softly into the hearts of party votaries." His object was to tear off the mask from the pretenders who disguised themselves as angels of light, and to smite them in the face. The preaching of John was "as the sweeping storms of March before the soft rustling of the vernal breezes of the Gospel."

He stood up, an Incarnate Conscience rising in revolt against "the shows and shams of a self-soothing piety." This child—nurtured amid the free winds and lonely grandeur of the wilderness—represented Reality confronting Sham. What he demanded was genuine penitence and amendment of life. He had nothing to say about "bowing the head like a bulrush," offering sacrificial atonements, or being particular about fasts and feasts—but he thundered forth, "Wash you, make you clean, put away the evil of your doings; flee from the wrath to come; bring forth fruits worthy of your repentance." In all this (as we have seen) he was but returning to the central messages of the Old Testament Scriptures before the religion of Israel had been overlaid with the filmy network of Scribism and formality. *

* The inmost essence of the Law is expressed in such passages as Lev. xxvi. 40 ; Deut. iv. 29, xxx. 2 ; Isaiah i. 16, xlii. 24 ; Joel ii. 12 ; and *passim*.

Hence his preaching was necessarily a preaching of repentance in the sternest of tones. Never was there a more fierce denouncer of disguised hypocrisy. "Offspring of vipers," he said to the Pharisees and Sadducees, "who warned *you* to flee from the wrath to come? Bring forth, therefore, fruit worthy of repentance. And think not to say within yourselves, 'We have Abraham to our father,' for I say unto you that God is able of these stones (*Abanim*) to raise up children (*Banim*) to Abraham." He did not speak to Jews as a Jew, but as a man to men, "that *all men* through him might believe." Addressing his hearers quite irrespectively of their nationality or prerogatives, he discouraged the materialised hopes of his people no less than their boasted prerogatives. The things about which they prided themselves, and postured before others, were not of the smallest importance. Their fastings, their casuistical theologies, and multiplied ablutions—their phylacteries, whether broad or narrow—were beneath his notice. Their whole system of religion was but the blighted tree on which the axe, already at its backmost poise, should swoop with a final crash; or as the barren chaff which should soon be burnt with unquenchable fire.

The preaching of John dealt, as all true preaching should, with plain, simple, unconventional holiness. It is not the work of such men to compass heaven and earth to make one proselyte, and then to make him "tenfold more the child of hell than themselves." His work was to preach the "pure, unsophisticated, dephlegmated, defæcated" moral law; to tell the publicans to exact no more than that which was legal; to bid the soldiers be content with their wages, to accuse none falsely, and to do no violence; to convince the people that they must substitute righteousness for idle self-confidence, give alms to their fellow-men with the most ample and generous self-sacrifice, and by love serve one another.*

No wonder that such preaching in the wild desert of

* Matt. v. 40.

Jeshimon—preaching so utterly new, so fearless, so heart-searching—uttered by a man who had broken with the traditional religionism of his day, and desired something deeper and more real than its narcotics, something higher and more heroical than its functions, something more healing and essential than its petty effeminacies—caused multitudes to stream out to "the horror" of the desert, to see this "shocking figure" in camel's skin and leathern girdle, who only cared to sustain life on locusts and wild honey. The religious despots might self-complacently pronounce that "he had a demon," but the multitude heard the message of God in the voice of a true man. Here was a man "whose manifestation was like a burning torch; whose whole life was a very earthquake; whose whole being was a sermon." Here was one who, alone among the teachers of his day, scornfully tore to shreds the rags of hypocrisy, and while he showed men that they were something better than "hungers, thirsts, fevers, and appetites," strove to bring them face to face with the Unseen, and make them realise the grandeur of God, and feel the supremacy of righteousness and true holiness.*

But there was also an element of Hope in his discourses. Sharing in the intense Messianic expectations of the day, he promised the speedy advent of the stern yet righteous Deliverer, who should purify the air infected with heathen influences and Sadducean unbelief,† and pour life into a religion which had become like the thin iridescence over the stagnancy of a putrescent pool.

The career of a Prophet or a true saint—especially if he denounces current unrealities, and shows no respect for dominant religious autocrats—is hardly complete unless it

---

* The simple veracity and authenticity of the Gospels constantly find corroboration from external sources. The account of the Baptist receives an independent support in all essential features from the reticent narrative of Josephus.

† The troubles raised by the Samaritan Messianic impostor (Jos. *Antt.* xviii. 4, 1, 2) may have partly arisen from the tension of mind caused by John's teaching.

be surrounded with the malice, hatred, and all uncharitableness of the world and of the nominal Church. The
normal lot of the loftiest teachers is some form or other of
martyrdom at the hands of all who love falsity. Popularity, and party adulation, and the soft murmur of applause
are not for such, but for those natures who, in self-complac-
ent usurpation of prerogatives which are not theirs, answer
the world according to its idols! The stake, the dungeon,
the torture-chamber, the roar of violent abuse, the viper's
hiss of creeping malice, the subterranean calumnies of religious partisans, the bale-fires of the Inquisitors, have been
the ordinary destiny of the noblest of the sons of God.
Their crown and sceptre have been like those of their
Saviour—a crown of torturing thorns, the sceptre of a
mocking reed. Such is the teaching alike of the Old* and
of the New Testament.† By Priests and Kings, "with
fierce lies maddening the blind multitude," the saints are
stoned, are sawn asunder, are slain with the sword, destitute, afflicted, tormented, because the world is not worthy
of them. And worst of all, much of their work often *seems*
—though only *seems*—to have been in vain.

So it was with St. John the Baptist. First came cold
neglect and indifference, and the sneer of the religious
leaders that he was a demoniac; ‡ then the sword flashed,
and the life of the noblest of the Prophets was shorn away.
The "viper's brood," the Pharisees and the Sadducees, the
adulterous king, the wicked matron, the dancing girl, prevailed; and all that was left of him, than whom no greater
had been born of woman, was a head on a charger in a harlot's hand, and a bleeding trunk in the dungeon of a grim
fortress among the desert hills.

Nevertheless his work lived on. Not only did many,

---

* 1 Kings xix. 10 ; 2 Chr. xvi. 10, xxiv. 21 ; Jer. xxvi. 8, 23.

† See Luke vi. 22, 23, 26 ; Matt. v. 11 : Mk. x. 29, 30 ; John xvii. 14 ;
Acts v. 41, vii. 52 ; Rom. v. 3 ; 1 Thess. ii. 14, 15 ; Heb. xi. 36–38, xiii. 13 ;
1 Pet. iii. 14, iv. 12, 16.

‡ Matt. xiv. 8–12.

even at Ephesus, own his leadership nearly thirty years
later (Acts xviii. 25, xix. 3), but—what was of infinitely
greater importance—he had effectually prepared the way
for Him "whose shoe's latchet he was not worthy to
unloose."

> " The last and greatest herald of heaven's King,
>   Girt with rough skins, hies to the deserts wild :
>   His food was locusts, and what there doth spring,
>   With honey that from virgin-hives distilled ;
>   Then burst he forth, ' All ye whose hopes rely
>   On God, with me among the deserts mourn :
>   Repent ! repent ! and from old errors turn ! '
>   Who listened to his voice, obeyed his cry ?
>   Only the echoes which he made relent
>   Rung from their flinty caves—' Repent ! repent !

CHAPTER XVI.

THE BAPTISM OF JESUS.

οὐχ ὡς ἐνδεᾶ . . . ἀλλ᾿ ὑπὲρ τοῦ γένους
τοῦ τῶν ἀνθρώπων.—JUST. MART. *Dial.* 88.

THE Ministry of St. John the Baptist falls into two well-marked epochs, separated from each other by the Baptism of Christ.*

To Jesus, in His obscure and humble home, the thrill which passed through every section of society at the voice of the Baptist, and the appearance of a true Man among the ignoble shadows and self-satisfied hypocrisies, came as a sign from His Heavenly Father that the time had arrived for His manifestation to the world. For now, by John's work as an avowed Forerunner, the long-slumbering hope was aroused, and, " with mighty billows the Messianic movement surged through the entire people." Was he the promised Forerunner, Elijah, whom in so many respects he resembled? Was he the expected Jeremiah come to restore to them the Ark and the Mercy Seat, and the Urim which he was supposed to have hidden in a cave on Mount Nebo?† Many even wondered whether he might not himself be the promised Messiah. " All men mused in their hearts of John whether he were the Christ or not."‡

In going to listen to the preaching of John, our Lord doubtless followed that inward guidance which was the supreme law of His life. He offered Himself for baptism. The full meaning of this act is beyond our apprehension.

---

* It has not been my object to enter into questions of chronology, endlessly debated, and still undecided. Several modern authorities have concluded that Christ's Baptism took place before the Passover in A. D. 27.

† 2 Macc. ii. 1–7.   ‡ Luke iii. 15.

The baptism of John was no mere Essene or Levitical ablution. It was accompanied by the confession of sins. It was not "a laver of regeneration" (Tit. iii. 5), but "a baptism of repentance." It was a sign that a man desired to cleanse himself from moral defilement, to abandon all righteousness of his own, and "to draw nigh unto God in full assurance of faith, having his heart sprinkled from an evil conscience, and his body washed with pure water." * How, then, could it be accepted by the Divine and sinless Son of Man? To others—but not to Him—could have been applied the words of Ezekiel, "Then will I sprinkle clean water upon you, and ye shall be clean." † All that we know is what the Gospels tell us. We see that the stern Prophet, who was no respecter of persons, but had dared to address Scribes and Pharisees in words of scornful denunciation, was overawed before the innate majesty of the Son of God. This new Elijah, in his shaggy robe of camel's hair with its coarse leathern girdle—this ascetic dweller in the deserts—this herald whose voice rang with sternest rebukes to startle drowsy souls, and stir them to repentance —is at once hushed into timidity at the Presence of the Lord of Love. So far from welcoming the acknowledgment of his ministry by one whom he instinctively recognised as his Lord, he made an earnest and continuous effort to prevent Him from accepting his baptism.‡ He even said, "*I* have need to be baptised of *Thee*, and comest *Thou* to *Me?*" But the only explanation given to us is in the words of our Lord Himself. He overcame John's hesitating scruples by saying, "Suffer it to be so now; for thus it becometh us to fulfil all righteousness." § "He

---

* Heb. x. 22. † Ezek. xxxvi. 25. (Is. i. 16; Zech. xiii. 1.)

‡ Matt. iii. 14, διεκώλυεν. The Baptism of Christ seems to have been a solitary one. It took place apparently "after all the people were baptised" (Luke iii. 21), and may have been in a measure private.

§ This may possibly mean, as Dean Alford says, "to fulfil all the claims or requirements (δικαιώματα) of the Law according to the definition of St. Chrysostom," δικαιοσύνη γάρ ἐστιν ἡ τῶν ἐντολῶν ἐκπλήρωσις.

placed the confirmation of perfect righteousness," says St.
Bernard, "in perfect humility." * Many have supposed
that He only submitted to the baptism as a *corporate* act,
desiring to identify Himself with the nation whose guilt
He came to bear and remove; others that He accepted it
vicariously and solely for the sake of mankind; † others
that He regarded the act for Himself personally as a con-
secration to the Messianic kingdom.‡ Others, again, have
thought that as, to the mass of the people, the immer-
sion in the Jordan and the rising out of the water indicated
a death unto sin and a new life unto righteousness, so to
Christ it marked by way of symbol the close of His former
life of seclusion, and the entrance into that Divine mission
to which he was henceforth dedicated.§ Whatever be the
exact explanation, it was as He went up out of the water,
and stood praying, that both to Him and to the Baptist the
sign was given which had been promised, and which led
John to recognise Jesus as the Messiah, the Son of God.
He beheld the Spirit, probably in some gleam of heavenly
brightness, descending out of the parted heavens as a
dove ‖ with soft and hovering motion, and abiding upon
Him, ¶ while a Voice from Heaven said, "This is my

* St. Bernard, *Serm.* 47 *in Cant.*; St. Bonaventura, *Vit. Christi* xiii.

† This is the oldest explanation, and is found as early as Justin Martyr
Dial c. Tryph. 88. Comp. John i. 29. Our Baptismal office says, " He sanctified water to the mystical washing away of sin " Comp. Ps. Aug. *Serm.*
145, 4 ; Ignat. *ad Eph.* 18 . Maxim *Serm.* 7, *de Epiphan.*

‡ Eph. i. 22. Comp. Ex. xxix. 4 ; Lev. viii. 1–30, xiv. 8.

§ See Is. lii. 15 ; Ezek. xxxvi. 25 ; Zech. xiii. 1.

‖ The text does not say that the Spirit actually took the *form* of a dove.
The σωματικῷ εἴδει. of Luke iii. 22, does not necessarily imply more than a visible appearance. It seems more in accordance with other analogies to suppose
that like the outpouring of the Spirit at Pentecost (Acts ii. 7) the appearance
was "like as of fire" (comp. Matt. iii. 11). The dove was indeed a fitting
emblem of innocence and gentleness; but Irenæus, arguing that the Logos was
united to Jesus at baptism, proves this by Gematria, since περιστερὰ = 801 =
א ת (Rev. i. 8, 11, xxi. 6, xxii. 13 ; Iren. *C. Haer.* i. 14, 6).

¶ ἐρχόμενον ἐπ' αὐτον, Matt. iii. 16 ; Is. xi. 2 ; Luke iii. 22 ; κατάβαινον εἰς
αὐτόν (B. D. etc.), *lit.* " descending into Him," Mark i. 10. " Of all the fowls

beloved Son, in whom I am well pleased." Henceforth Jesus felt Himself finally consecrated by the will of His Father to be the Founder of the kingdom of heaven on earth. As a man He now became fully "conscious of a power of the Spirit within Him corresponding to the new form of His work." *

After this it was destined that Jesus should increase and John decrease. For though John was "the lamp kindled and burning," his work showed the inevitable limitations of all *human* work. He preached the preliminaries necessary for the advent of the Kingdom; it was beyond his power to found the Kingdom itself. Indeed, it is probable that though he differed so widely from the religious teachers of his day in his moral ideals, he may have shared in their special Messianic hopes. He may have looked, not for a suffering, but for a triumphant Christ—for one who should be a magnificent Potentate and Deliverer of His nation—though the establishment of His Kingdom was to be preceded by earthquake and eclipse, such as the Hebrew Prophets had foretold.† Softened in tone as his ministry had evidently been by the appearance of Jesus, it is very likely that he failed to understand a Messiah at whose presence the nations did not tremble, nor the mountains visibly flow down ; who was not outwardly " a consuming fire," and did not do terrible things in His wrath.‡ The humble humanity, and untempestuous quietude of a Deliverer who did not strive nor cry, neither was His voice heard in the streets, became a decided stumbling-block in the path of his Messianic faith.§ Jesus did not attempt to found any such earthly kingdom as John had imagined. The whole ideal of the Saviour's work was different from

---

that are created, Thou hast named thee one Dove," 2 Esdr. v. 26. Ps. lv. 6 ; Is. lix. 11 ; Matt. x. 16. Justin Martyr says (*c. Tryph.* 88) that a fire or light was kindled in the Jordan.

* Bishop Westcott on John i. 34. † Is. xiii. 9 ; Zeph. i. 14.
‡ Is. lxiv. 1–3. § Matt. xi. 6.

that of John. He did not frequent the wilderness, or appear as an ascetic in hairy garb, or hurl thunderbolts. He moved about in lowly simplicity as a man with men— and that among the most stained and despised outcasts, whom Pharisees and Sadducees would not touch with the hem of their garments.

After the Baptist's work had culminated in the pointing out of the Messiah, he seems to have lost much of his power and insight. His disciples, if not he himself, began to mistake means for ends. They did not become direct disciples of Jesus. There austere self-denials did not meet with our Lord's approval. Outward asceticism—like that of the Pharisees—was brought by them into injurious prominence. This was to put a patch of undressed cloth upon an old garment. What was intended to fill up the rent only made it worse. It was to put unfermented wine into old wine-skins. The new wine fermented, in contact with the yeasty particles left adhering to the leather—"the skins burst and the wine was spilled." * There is something infinitely pathetic in the fact that, in the gloomy recesses of his frightful dungeon, haunted by demons and surrounded by inaccessible crags, doubt as to Him whom he had pointed out as the promised Christ seems for a moment to have overshadowed the Baptist's soul. " A reed shaken by the wind " he was not, and could not be ; but he might be compared to " a cedar, half uprooted by the storm." He foretold, he announced, the Kingdom of Christ, but can hardly be said to have entered into it, so that—on the principle *"minimum maximi est majus maximo minimi"*— he who is but little (δ $\mu\iota\kappa\rho\acute{o}\tau\iota\rho o\varsigma$) in the kingdom of heaven was greater than he.† Nevertheless, Jesus pronounced on him the splendid eulogy that " Of them that have been born of women there is none greater than John the Baptist " ; and we may feel sure that any doubt which may have crossed his mind was dispelled by the merciful

* Matt. ix. 14, xi. 14, xxi. 32 ; Luke, v. 33. † Matt. xi. 11.

forbearance of Him whom he had pointed out as the Lamb of God that taketh away the sins of the world. It disappeared for ever in the glorious light of that world where all is judged of truly. There he would learn the meaning of Christ's saying, " The kingdom of God is *within* you," * and that they only can enter it, who enter it in the spirit of little children, with meekness and perfect self-surrender.†

* Ἐντὸς ὑμῶν. Vulg. *intra vos est* (i. e., *in animis vestris*). This meaning seems to be the correct one. Comp. Rom. xiv. 17 ; Deut. xxx. 14. The " Kingdom of God " is not only an external, but an ethical condition.

† Luke xvii. 20, 21 ; Matt. xviii. 3.

CHAPTER XVII.

THE TEMPTATION.

"Thou shalt tread upon the lion and the adder, the young lion and the dragon shalt thou trample under foot."—Ps. xci. 13.

Πέπονθεν αὐτὸς πειρασθείς.—Heb. ii. 18, iv. 15.

Διὰ τοὺς ἀσθενοῦντας ἠσθένουν, καὶ διὰ τους πεινῶντας ἐπείνων, καὶ διὰ τοὺς διψῶντας ἐδίψων —"Unwritten Saying" of Christ.—ORIG. (in Matt. xvii. 21).

"Omnis diabolica illa Tentatio foris non intus fuit."—GREG. M. Hom. i. 16.

> "Thou Spirit that ledd'st this glorious Eremite
> Into the desert, His victorious field
> Against the spiritual foe, and brought'st Him thence
> By proof the undoubted Son of God."
> —MILTON, Par. Reg. i.

LITTLE as we may think it right to enter into the boundless field of speculation, yet the history of the Temptation of our Lord is of such importance to a right understanding of all that is revealed respecting Him in the Gospels as to demand our patient endeavour to understand it aright.

It is narrated most circumstantially in the first and third Gospels. In St. Mark it is compressed into one characteristic but vivid verse, and he alone tells us, both, that " He was with the wild beasts," and that "angels were continuously ministering (διηκόνουν) unto Him." As St. John was not professing to write a complete narrative, but intended only to supplement in certain essential particulars the records of the three Synoptic Gospels, it did not fall within the scope of his work to narrate it once more. Yet, so far was this from being—as it has been falsely represented—a designed suppression intended to exalt the

Divinity of Christ, that St. John, no less than the other Evangelists, shows us that the soul of Jesus could be troubled and perplexed;* and that He regarded His work as a triumph over the Prince of this world,† who, through Him, should be "cast out" when He should draw all men unto Him. St. John also describes temptation as due to the direct influence of Satan;‡ he quotes the words of Jesus—which describe the result of the Temptation—that "the Prince of this world cometh, and hath nothing in Me";§ and says that Christ should "convict the world in respect of judgment, because the Prince of this world hath been judged."

The author of the Epistle to the Hebrews greatly helps us to apprehend the significance of the Temptation when he writes :

"We have not a High Priest who cannot be touched with the feeling of our infirmities, but one that hath been *in all points tempted like as we are,* yet without sin." ‖

And again :

"Wherefore it behoved Him in all things to be made like unto His brethren, that He might be a merciful and faithful High Priest in things pertaining to God, to make propitiation for the sins of the people. For in that He Himself hath suffered being tempted, He is able to succour them that are tempted."¶

"We may represent the truth to ourselves best," says Bishop Westcott, "by saying that Christ assumed humanity under the conditions of life belonging to man fallen, though not with sinful promptings *from within.*"

First then let us consider the occasion, the locality, and the circumstances of the Temptation.

Christ—who "lived in a tent like ours, and of the same material," seeing that, as all the Gospels and Epistles teach us, He was "perfectly man"—must have been swayed in

His human soul no less than in the mortal body by the
conditions which affect humanity. To Him therefore
the Baptism in the waters of Jordan, the opening heavens
which indicated a new relation with God, the Divine Voice
which called Him a Beloved Son, the descent of the Holy
Spirit upon and into Him,* there to abide in plenitude,
were the signs that the hour was at hand to begin His
Messianic work of Redemption. It was, as it were, the
final call to come forth from the Galilean village, and fulfil
His eternal purpose as the Teacher and Deliverer of mankind. In proportion as we realise the stupendous character of the work shall we be able to understand the
profound human emotion with which the Son of Man
contemplated the as yet unknown events and destines of
His earthly mission. In all such high hours of visitation
from the Living God there is, and must be, an intensity of
feeling which pervades the whole being, and creates an im-
perious demand for solitude and meditation. Man must be
alone, and " of the people there must be none with him,"
when he treads the winepress of his decisive hours. We can
therefore understand the expression of St. Matthew and
St. Luke that " then He was led up into the wilderness ";
and that "full of the Holy Spirit, He was led in the Spirit
into the wilderness "; and even the more forcible phrase of
St. Mark : " straightway the Spirit *driveth Him forth* into
the wilderness."†   In the Old Testament, Moses and
Elijah had spent forty days of spiritual crisis in lonely
places, and Paul, after his conversion, retired to Arabia.

"Into the wilderness ":—we cannot say with certainty
what wilderness it was, for the tradition which gives its
name to the desert of the Forty Days (*Quarantania*) is
quite uncertain ; but the awful associations with which
Jewish imagination filled these solitudes would correspond
with the tension of the spirit of Jesus. " He was," says St.

---

* Mark i. 10, εἰς αὐτὸν, *v. l.*   † Comp. Ezek. viii. 3 ; Acts viii. 39.

Mark, " with the wild beasts."* The Prophet Isaiah had
spoken of the *Tsiyyim*, and *Ochim*, and *Iyyim*, " the
droughty ones" and " shaggy monsters and groaners,"
" the daughters of screaming,"† the owls, and the arrow-
snakes, and Lilith, " the night fairy," ‡—half demoniac
creatures which made their homes amid its wild vegetation.
Those rugged and desolate places were also the dwelling
place of Azazel, the demon to whom the scapegoat was dismissed.§ " When the evil spirit is gone out of a man, he
walketh *through dry places*"—through the stony, waterless
deserts—" seeking rest, and he findeth it not."‖ The evil
demon of " the dry places" was associated with the thought
of temptation, and there our Lord was tempted, as in
famine and solitude He wrestled mentally with the vast
problems of His predestined work. He felt an irrepres-
sible impulse to be alone in spirit with His Heavenly
Father, however much He might be surrounded by the
snares of the Evil One. He did not indeed feel the stings
of privation—scant as must have been the nourishment
which the wilderness afforded—till the close of the forty
days ; for it was only at their close—so St. Matthew tells us
—that " afterwards He hungered." But the Temptation,
though it was subsequently concentrated into three mighty
special assaults, was, in its essence, continuous. " He was
in the wilderness forty days, *being tempted by the devil*,"
says St. Mark, and St. Luke uses the same expression. It
was a period of mental strain and moral struggle, and it
involved the decisive victory over the assaults of Satan.
Henceforth it became possible for all to experience the
truth of the promise given by St. James, the Lord's
brother, " Resist the devil, and he will flee from you."

Two truths we must firmly apprehend.

(i.) One is that the Temptation was real, not a mere semblance. Our Lord, under stress of genuine temptation, had

---

* See Job v. 22, 23.   † Is. xiii. 21.
‡ Is. xxxiv. 13–15.   § Lev. xvi. 8, 10, 20.   ‖ Matt. xii. 43.

to win the victory, in man and for man, by evincing self-denial, self-control, disregard for selfish advantage ; absolute renunciation of power, honour, and self-gratification ; and complete self-surrender to His Heavenly Father's will. If the struggle had not been an actual struggle, there would have been no significance in the victory. The Gospels represent Jesus as subject to temptations from without, not only at this crisis, but during all His life. He said to Peter, "Get thee behind Me, Satan : thou art *a stumbling-block* unto Me " ; * and He said to His Apostles, " Ye are they which have continued with Me in my temptations." † The only difference between the temptations of Christ and our own is that His came from without, but ours come also from within. In Him " the tempting opportunity " could not appeal to " the susceptible disposition." With us sin acquires its deadliest force because we have yielded to it. We can only conquer it when, by the triumph of God's grace within us, we are able to say with the dying hero of Azincour, " Get thee hence, Satan ; thou hast no part in me ; my part is in the Lord Jesus Christ."

(ii.) The other truth which must be firmly grasped is that the force and reality of the outward temptation did not impair—nay, it illustrated—Christ's sinlessness. It is, as Luther said, one thing to feel temptation (*sentire tenta-tionem*), and quite another thing to *yield* to it (*assentire tentationi*) ; or, as our own great poet so well expresses it :

> " 'Tis one thing to be tempted, Escalus,
> Another thing to fall."

The temptations came to Christ externally, through the craft and subtlety of the devil, and, in defeating them, He illustrated His own parable about the conquest of the Evil One : " When the strong man, fully armed, guardeth his own court, his goods are in peace ; but when a stronger than he shall come upon him, he taketh from him his whole

* Matt. xvi. 23.   † Luke xxii. 28.

armour wherein he trusted, and divideth the spoil." By His victory He gave power over the demons to all who trust in Him, so that in all the power of the enemy nothing should be able to hurt them. And for this very end has He been manifested, "that He might destroy the works of the devil." * He did not, like the parents of our fallen race, dabble with temptation, or go halfway to meet it, but, by the instant rejection of it with the whole force of His inner nature, He secured His transcendent and perfect victory.

The question how the details of the Temptation became known to the Apostles and Evangelists is not specially important, but the answer to it seems clear. They *could* only have learnt it from the Lord Himself. Nor, again, is it in any way essential for the lessons which the narrative is designed to teach us, whether we suppose that, in reveal-ing it, He clothed the essential facts under the veil of sym-bols or not. If He did so, it was only that we might have a more vivid apprehension of truths which it would have been impossible for us to understand had they been expressed in spiritual or metaphysical terms. Nor need we enter into the discussion as to whether Satan appeared to Christ in a visible shape or not. There is nothing in the form of expression which forces this conclusion upon us, any more than in our Lord's words, " I was gazing on Satan fallen as lightning from heaven." † Even the question as to the personality of the Tempter is one which does not con-cern us here. It is sufficient to say that Satan, the Accuser, the Tempter, the Destroyer, is set before us throughout the New Testament as a really existent and concrete being, and, in any case, there exists for every one of us, as we know by fatal experience, a reality of evil without us, "a force not ourselves" which impels to all sin and unrighteousness, and which it is our perpetual duty, as well as our only safety, to resist to the uttermost.

* 1 John iii. 8. † Luke x. 17, πεσόντα.

It is much more important for us to observe that the three temptations of our Lord fall generally under the comprehensive summary under which St. John sums up all forms of temptation, namely, those that arise from " the lust of the flesh, the lust of the eyes, and the pride of life." * We are perhaps hardly in a position to decide whether the order of the Temptations as given by St. Matthew or that as given by St. Luke is the more exact. In spiritual crises we cannot take note of the ordinary sequences of time; they

> " Crowd eternity into an hour,
> And stretch an hour into eternity."

It is clear from the expressions used by St. Mark and St. Luke† that, though the temptations of Satan came to a head in one great final conflict, they were, in some shape or other, continuous; and our Lord's victory is our example, that we are not to love the world, neither the things that are in the world, for if any man love the world the love of the Father is not in him. "Nothing rises higher than its source. The desire of things earthly, as though they were ends in themselves, comes from the world, and is bounded by the world. It is, therefore, incompatible with the love of the Father."

(i.) The first appeal of Satan was an appeal to the desire of the flesh in its simplest and most innocent form. It was a temptation through suffering. It was not a temptation to φιληδονία, the love of pleasure for its own sake, but rather to the exercise of an inherent power for the extinction of pain. Nothing could seem more plausible than the suggestion that Jesus should appease the pangs of hunger by the exercise of a prerogative which had been conferred on Him. The wilderness abounds in stones, which sometimes look like melons or cucumbers,‡ and sometimes bear the exact

---

* 1 John ii. 16.

† Mark i. 12 ; Luke iv. 2, πειραζόμενος. Comp. xxii. 28, " ye are they who have continued with Me *in my temptations.*" Heb. iv. 15, He " was in all points tempted like as we are, yet without sin."

‡ These stones are known as *septaria.*

appearance of loaves of bread. It would make hunger more keen to see the semblance of food. And had not God fed His whole people with manna in the wilderness in answer to their cry? And had He not sustained Moses during the forty days of awful communion on Sinai? And had not an angel ministered to the needs of the unhappy and fugitive Elijah? And had not a voice from the heavens, which seemed to be bursting open to their depths,* accompanied by the hovering gleam of the descending Spirit, proclaimed Him to be the beloved Son in whom God was well pleased? What could be more natural, what more harmless, than that He should, under these circumstances, work the miracle which was suggested to Him? If He did so would it not be a decisive test whether such a power were absolutely His or not?

He now knew Himself to be called to His work as the promised Messiah. Was it not one popular conception of the Messiah's work that, like Moses, He should again feed His people with bread from heaven?† Was not this a most favourable opportunity to exercise this power for the supply of His own urgent needs, that, having thus tested its reality, He might ever afterwards put it forth for the blessing of the world which He had come to save?

Thus, beyond the mere agony of hunger, there might well be this longing for support, this desire for assurance, this impulse to test what, in the human sphere—though He had laid aside His glory and taken upon Him the form of a servant—might be permitted to Him, in a manner which was in itself perfectly innocent. But whence did the suggestion come? It came from something without Him, appealing to a bodily instinct. Quite clearly it was of the earth, and came from the Prince of the Power of the Air, suggesting to Him an inward doubt, or an open self-assertion. And what was hunger? Could not hunger be borne, if God had sent it? If God desired to satiate

* Mark i. 10. † John vi. 30–35.

hunger by a miracle it was a duty to await His good time, and not to use supernatural gifts for personal alleviation. In any case there is the higher as well as the lower life. The Tempter had indirectly suggested the thought of the manna; but in the wilderness God had suffered His people to hunger, expressly that He might try their faith and constancy before He supplied their needs by the manna which neither they nor their fathers had known.   Jesus, therefore, repelled the temptation by the words which follow in the Book of Deuteronomy—that God had acted thus "that He might make thee know that man doth not live by bread only, but by every thing that proceedeth out of the mouth of the Lord doth man live."* Thus to the Israelites the manna became "spiritual food."† And had not Jeremiah also said, " *Thy words* were found, and I did eat them, and *Thy word* was unto me the joy and rejoicing of mine heart; for I am called by Thy name, O Lord God of Hosts."‡ Our Lord would neither sate His hunger, nor challenge His Almighty Father by putting His own miraculous powers to the test.

Thus, by " the sword of the Spirit, which is the word of God," the first temptation was victoriously encountered, and plainly shown to *be* a temptation through all its subtle speciousness.

(ii.) But the Tempter was not yet foiled. His next temptation should be separate from anything which could seem even remotely to have in it any admixture of selfishness or of personal desires. It should be a purely imaginative temptation, appealing solely to the deep thoughts about His Messianic work, which had been occupying the

---

* Deut. viii. 3.   The idea that the observance of God's commandments tends to life runs through Deuteronomy (iv. 1, 2, 40, v. 29–33, etc.).   See Wright, *Some Problems of the New Testament*, p. 10.   All three of our Lord's answers to Satan were taken from Deut. vi. and viii.   Two of them were texts enclosed in the apertures of the phylacteries (*Tephillîn*).

† 1 Cor. x. 4.

‡ Jer. xv. 16.   Comp. Ps. cxix. 103.

mind of Jesus during His forty days in the wilderness, and
only suggesting that He should put to the test the miraculous endowments which seemed indispensable to the fulfilment of the mighty issues before Him. Appealing this
time to the pride of life, the Tempter suggests, " Thou
hast been proclaimed to be the Son of God, and if Thou
art the Son of God, no harm can happen to Thee. See!
Thou art on the pinnacle of the Temple; * cast Thyself
down. Thy safety will be a glorious, a decisive proof of
Thy Divine origin. Even of God's ordinary human saints
it is written—

> " ' There shall no harm happen unto thee,
> For He shall give His angels charge concerning thee
> To keep thee in all thy ways ;
> And on their hands they shall bear thee up,
> Lest haply thou dash thy foot against a stone.' " †

Thus did the Devil cite Scripture for his purpose, and
clothe his temptation in the most seeming-innocent guise.
But he omitted from his quotations the words " to keep
thee *in all thy ways*," because those words implied that
God's promise did *not* extend to " the precipice in the
Temple, the regions of mid-air, or any devious paths of
mere presumption, but only to the ways of obvious duty."‡

If, as many have supposed—though in the brief narrative
of this spiritual struggle in the two Evangelists no hint of
the kind is distantly suggested—if the temptation was
really one to descend miraculously among the people
assembled in the court below ; to flash upon them as it
were at once in one sudden supernatural Epiphany of
divine power—it might seem to acquire additional force.

* Perhaps on the roof of the *Stoa Basilikè*, or Royal Porch, on the southern
side of the Temple, which looked down 400 cubits into the *wady* of the Kidron
(Jos. *Antt.* xv. 11, 5) ; or the *Stoa Anatolikè* (Solomon's Porch), from which the
Lord's brother, St. James, was afterwards flung. Hegesippus *ap.* Euseb. *H. E.*
ii. 23.

† Ps. xci. 1, 11. ‡ See Mill, *Five Sermons on the Temptation*, p. 116.

What a splendid manifestation would this be? How irresistibly would He thus inaugurate the work which His Father had given Him to do!

But again Jesus saw into the hidden heart of the temptation. It was an allurement to self-will, to self-assertion, to the independent challenge and use of heavenly powers. He repels the allurement by refuting the misapplication of Satan's Scriptural quotation. The promise which the Evil One had quoted was a promise that God would keep His children amid the *inevitable, unsought* dangers of life. Scripture is not to be identified—as it constantly is—with any perversion, to alien ends, of its mere *words :* Scripture *is* solely what Scripture *means.* The Devil can quote Scripture for his purpose, but it is always a *perversion* of Scripture. The Psalmist had never meant to encourage the audacious demand for God's supernatural interferences to enable us to escape from self-created perils. Jesus would not be guilty of *forcing* or of *challenging* God's purposes. His reliance on His Heavenly Father should be one of absolute dependence. He knew that He would never be left alone while He did always the things which were pleasing in God's sight.* So He met Satan's false references to Scripture by another quotation which was of eternal validity. "It stands written again," He said, "Thou shalt not tempt the Lord thy God." † This second answer, like the first, involved the repudiation of all self-will ; the determination to follow only the Divine order, not any promptings, whether subjective or objective, which did not come from the Father of Lights. "Trust in God must be accompanied by humble submission to His will, and is incompatible with the attempt to bring the power of God into the service of one's own caprice." ‡

* John viii. 29.

† Matt. iv. 7 (Deut. vi. 16), γέγραπται, " it hath been written," " it standeth written ; οὐκ ἐκπειράσεις " thou shalt not tempt *to the full* the Lord thy God," *i. e.*, thou shalt not *challenge* the full expression of His power.

‡ Wendt.

(iii.) The form in which the third Temptation is narrated illustrates most decisively that our Lord, in revealing the story of His temptations in the wilderness, threw them into such a form as would bring them most vividly before the minds of His Apostles. The *form* of the story—that Satan set Jesus on an exceeding high mountain, and showed him, in a moment of time, all the kingdoms of the world and the glory of them—is doubtless an anthropomorphic picture which summarises the result of a mental conflict. The offer to give all these to Jesus on the condition "*that He would fall down and do reverence before him,*" is obviously one which, in this form, would have been too coarsely and audaciously crude to have been a possible temptation to the Son of God.* But not so the underlying significance of the picture. Our Lord had been proclaimed to be the Messiah, and He was aware of the nature of the Messianic hopes shared by the whole of His nation. But how could He carry out such hopes? how could He come up to the ideal of One whom John had painted as a Ruler, thoroughly purging His floor with mighty winnowing-fan, and gathering the wheat into His garner, but burning up the chaff with unquenchable fire? Surely the fulfilment of such magnificent anticipations would be impossible so long as He did not rise above the humble worldly position of a peasant and a Nazarene? Conscious of His Divine nature, and His as yet unexercised powers—anxious, as a man among men, to inaugurate the Kingdom—He must have felt how easy it would be to kindle His countrymen into a flame of zeal in comparison with which the enthusiasm aroused by Judas of Galilee would have been as nothing;—into zeal which would have gathered them as one man under one banner, and not only have broken in sunder the galling yoke of Roman dominion, but

---

* The rendering, " fall down and *worship* me," is rather too strong ; it is, rather, " do me *homage* as to a king, the κοσμοκράτωρ." Eph. vi. 12.

have carried Him forward to a world-wide dominion of glory and righteousness.

The "desire of the eyes" could have had no share in this temptation, for to Him the riches of the world and the glory of them must have seemed no better than dross in comparison with the things unseen and eternal. It is only in a secondary and spiritual sense that what St. John calls "the braggart vaunt of life," its vain pomp and splendour, could have had the smallest allurement for One who lived in His Father's presence. But the temptation may have come as a suggestion of the readiest and most triumphant means by which He could subdue the world, and make its kingdoms the kingdoms of God, at no other cost than that of concession to earthly prejudices. The temptation was most ingeniously veiled, as though it involved nothing more than a politic accommodation to outward conditions—the condescension of employing human means for high ends. But this temptation also—this half-hidden offer of the κοσμοκράτορ,* "the ruler of this world"—to promote establishment of a Messianic empire—was decisively rejected. "The god of this world" could not blind the eyes of a Wisdom which came from heaven, nor could his fiery darts remain unquenched on the shield of perfect faith. Decisive and energetic was the rejection of this last assault: "Get thee hence, Satan! for it standeth written, Thou shalt worship the Lord thy God, and Him only shalt thou serve."

After so absolute a defeat, the Devil might well leave Him "until a season," i. e., till he could see some new opportunity for assault ;† and angels came and were ministering unto Him. He left the wilderness with mind determined,

---

* John xiii. 31, xiv. 30, xvi. 11.   The Jews spoke of Satan as *Sar ha-Olam*. But his power was *not*, as he said, "delivered unto him," except by the apostasy of men, for "the earth is *the Lord's*, and the fulness thereof" (Ps. xxiv. 1).

† Luke iv. 13, ἀπέστη ἀπ' αὐτοῦ ἀχρὶ καιροῦ.

with will resolutely fixed, to walk only in God's way—in the path which, step by step, the Heavenly Father should make clear to Him, whithersoever it might lead. The principle which would henceforth sustain His whole life should be to shrink from no self-sacrifice, however awful; to drink the cup, however bitter, which God should send to Him; and to annihilate every prompting which should have its source only in the earthly self.

Finally victorious over all the assaults and blandishments of "the prince of the power of the air," Jesus felt the clear conviction that the path of His Messianic deliverance of Israel and of the world did not lie over the radiant mountain-heights of human glory, but through the deep Valley of Humiliation; and that the one inflexible purpose of every act of His mortal life must be, in absolute self-abnegation, "to do the will of Him that sent Him, and to finish IIis work." The whole narrative of the Temptation is a comment on our Lord's saying, "The prince of this world cometh, and hath *nothing* in me." *

* John xiv. 30.

CHAPTER XVIII.

SCENES OF CHRIST'S MINISTRY.

" In the former time He brought into contempt the land of Zebulun and the land of Naphtali, but in the latter time He hath made it glorious, by the way of the sea. . . Galilee of the nations.—Is. ix. 1.

" Quare Vocatur Gennazar? *ob hortos principum (ganne sarim).*"— LIGHTFOOT, *Cent. Chorogr.* lxxix.

I PASS over the pathetically beautiful events which took place when, on the return of Jesus from the Desert of the Temptation, He once more visited the scenes where John, having left the Wilderness of Judæa, was now baptising. John was at Bethany,* beyond Jordan, near the well-known Peræan ford of Bethabara, within a day's journey of Nazareth. The second stage of His ministry had begun. The Baptist now knew full well that his mission was practically finished, and he was inspired to point out the Lamb of God to some of his own disciples,† openly avowing that *He* must increase, and he himself must decrease. I shall speak farther on of the earliest disciples to obey the call of Christ— Andrew, John, Simon, Philip, and Nathanael. With them He visited Cana and wrought His earliest miracle. At the first Passover of His ministry He cleansed the Temple, and had His nocturnal interview with Nicodemus, the teacher of

---

* " *Bethany,*" the reading of A, B, C, etc., was conjecturally altered by Origen into *Bethabara*, because he only knew of the Bethany on the Mount of Olives. Bethabara means " the House of the Passage," and is within easy reach of Cana. Caspari identifies it with Tiellanije, north of the Sea of Galilee. Condor thinks it may be Makhadet Abarah, northeast of Beisah.

† Is. liii.; Acts viii. 32. There may also be a reference to the Paschal Lamb, as the Passover was near. The thought may have been brought home to him by the sight of the flocks of lambs being driven to Jerusalem as offerings at the coming Feast.

Israel. After this He continued for a time to work in Judæa, and permitted His disciples to baptise, though He himself baptised not. It was at this time that, in answer to the jealous complaints of John's disciples, the great Forerunner bore emphatic witness to Him as to One who cometh from heaven, who spoke the words of God, and to whom the Spirit had been given without measure—nay more, as the Son, into whose hands the Father had given all things.* Soon after this, Herod consummated his crimes by throwing John into the prison at Machærus. Jesus then retired from Judæa into Galilee, and it may have been on this journey— for the exact chronology of events must ever remain uncertain—that He spoke with the Samaritan woman by Jacob's Well. To this first year of His ministry also belonged the healing of the son of the court officer ($\beta\alpha\sigma\iota\lambda\iota\kappa\acute{o}s$) of Capernaum, and His rejection by the Nazarenes when He preached in their synagogue.

That pre-eminently bright and fruitful period of His ministry which has been called "the Galilæan Spring" began with His retirement from Nazareth to Capernaum. No small portion of the Gospels is occupied by the narratives of the work and teaching in the Plain of Gennesareth, beside the Sea of Galilee. Remote and narrow in extent is this corner of Galilee, from which issued forth to all the world the words of eternal life. Yet the scenery eminently suited the Divine teaching, which was addressed to the humble, but was intended to bring new life to all mankind. The words of Jesus had few or none of the thunderous elements which marked the preaching of the Baptist. They were spoken, not in the waste and howling wilderness, nor, like those of Moses, among the more awful aspects of nature, but amid the soft delightful fields which lie on the west of the Lake of Galilee. There is a quiet enchantment about the whole locality. I once rode into the plain from the top of Kur'n Hattîn—the Mount of Beatitudes—down the Wady Hammam, or "Vale of Doves," rich with its Eastern vegetation.

* John iii. 22–36.

The road descends to the lake through the wretched village of El Mejdel (Magdala),* where (a certain sign of squalor) the little children run about naked in the street. So desolate are the shores of the Sea of Galilee in these days, that, as I rode for hours through the tall flowering oleanders, laden with their pink blossoms, there was scarcely a sign of human life. The white-winged pelicans floated on the water, and the kingfishers perched on the reeds beside the lake, and the masses of green entangled foliage along the water-courses were alive with myriads of twittering birds; but, with the exception of a little group of fishermen who were fishing with a drag-net from the shore, and four splendidly mounted Bedouin Arabs, I saw no one during many hours; nor did the whole surface of the lake for thirteen miles from north to south show one single sail of the smallest fishing-boat.

The green plain itself—Gennesareth, "that unparalleled garden of God " †—is but three miles long, and a mile and a half broad. Yet it gave its name to the sea, of which the Talmud has this remarkable eulogy: " Seven seas, spake the Lord God, have I created in the land of Canaan, but only one have I chosen for myself, the Sea of Gennezar." ‡ It was " surrounded by pleasant towns," § and its famous hot springs attracted numerous visitors.

In the days of Jesus Christ the little plain was densely populated, and was far more lovely than now it is in its prolific luxuriance, which perhaps gained it the name of the Garden of Princes. ‖ Then as now the lake abounded in rare and delicious varieties of fish; then as now the grass was enamelled with a profusion of the lilies of the field;

---

* In ancient days indigo grew there, and it was known as " the town of dyers."

† Jos. *B. J.* iii. 3, 2, x. 8.

‡ *Midrash Tillin* iv. 1 (quoted by Sepp. ii. 170).

§ Plin. *H. N.* v. 15.

‖ The derivation of " Gennesareth " is uncertain. Some regard the name as a corruption of the old Hebrew name Chinnereth, " a harp " (Deut. iii. 17; Josh. xi. 2).

then as now the barren basaltic hills of the Eastern shore flung the shadows of their abrupt precipices upon the waters, and the gusts which rushed down their narrow valleys often swept the little inland sea into sudden storm. But the contemporary description given of it by the Jewish historian will show how widely its present desolation differs from the aspect which it presented to the eyes of the Saviour of the World. "The waters," he says,* "are sweet, and very agreeable for drinking; they are finer than the thick waters of other fens. The lake is also pure, and on every side ends directly at the shores and at the sand; it is also of a temperate nature when you draw it up, and of a more gentle nature than river or fountain water, and yet always cooler than one could expect. Now when this water is kept in the open air it is as cold as snow. There are several kinds of fish in it, different both to the taste and the sight from those elsewhere. . . . The country also that lies over against this lake hath the same name of Gennesareth. Its nature is wonderful as well as its beauty; its soil is so fruitful that all sorts of trees can grow upon it . . . for the temper of the air is so well mixed that it agrees very well with the several sorts . . . walnuts in vast plenty . . . palm trees . . . fig-trees . . . olives. One may call this place the ambition of nature, where it forces those plants which are naturally enemies to one another to grow together; it is a happy contention of the Seasons, as if every one of them lay claim to this country." †

"Oh, why," asked a Rabbi, "are the fruits of Jerusalem not so good as those of Galilee?" "Because else," is the answer, "we should live at Jerusalem for the sake of the fruits, and not for Divine service." It was in these regions

---

* Jos. *B. J.* iii. 10, 7, 8. See Stanley, *Sinai and Palestine*, pp. 425-47; Thomson, *The Land and the Book*, p. 402 ; Tristram, *Land of Israel*, p. 431; *Rob Roy on the Jordan* ; Conder, *Tent Work in Palestine*, ch. xix.; Renan, *Vie de Jésus*, 144 ; Neubauer, *Geogr. du Talmud*, p. 48.

† Whiston's transl. (abbreviated).

that the Prophet Hoshea "poured forth his warm and deep-felt words in which the excitable temper of the Galileans especially found expression"; and the Song of Songs had been composed "by a poet, into whose heart the cheerful vicinage had poured its sunniest beams, and whose eyes were open to note how the flowers gleam and the fig-tree puts forth its green figs, and the vine sprouts, and the bloom of the pomegranates unfolds itself." And "amid this luxuri-ance of nature there lived still a healthy people, whose con-science was not yet corrupted by Rabbinical sophistries, and where full-grown men were elevated far above their Jewish kinsfolk, sickening with fanaticism."

The commercial road which ran by the lake to Damascus made Gennesareth familiar to foreign merchants, and vari-ous Gentile elements were to be found among the popula-tion. Tiberias, the new and half-heathen capital of Herod, into which we are not told that our Lord so much as once entered, exhibited to the offended eyes of the Jews its Palace ornamented with Grecian sculptures. Jesus never seems to have visited Sepphoris or Taricheæ or other popu-lous cities; but three village-towns (κωμοπόλεις) of Gen-nesareth were specially familiar with the words and works of the Son of Man—Chorazin, Bethsaida, and Capernaum. These are mentioned by Christ Himself as the main scenes of His ministry in the towns of Galilee.

"Woe unto thee, Chorazin! Woe unto thee, Bethsaida! for if the mighty works had been done in Tyre and Sidon which have been done in you, they would have repented long ago in sackcloth and ashes. . . .

"And thou, Capernaum, shalt thou be exalted into heaven? Thou shalt be brought down unto Hades! for if the mighty works had been done in Sodom which were done in thee, it would have remained unto this day."

So fragmentary is our knowlege of the continuous work of Christ, that, though Chorazin is mentioned first among the towns which Jesus had thus signally endowed with the privilege of witnessing His miracles of mercy,[*] it is not once again alluded to in the Gospels, nor do we know of a single miracle which was wrought in it. Though we learn from the Talmud that it was once famous for the fineness of its wheat,[†] it was deserted even in the fourth century after Christ, and it is only within the last few years that its site has been identified with Kherazeh,[‡] a heap of indistinguishable ruins not quite three miles from Tell Hûm. Its unusually stately synagogue had five aisles, and a quadruple row of columns adorned with Corinthian capitals, and decorative details elaborately carved in hard, black basalt. Over the upheaped and weed-grown *débris* of its forgotten prosperity might well be written the inscription:

" Woe unto thee, Chorazin ! "

The site of Bethsaida is to this day uncertain, though it was the native place of Andrew, Peter, and Philip, and was the frequent scene of the Lord's manifestations. It was near Capernaum and Chorazin, and its name (" House of Fish ") seems to indicate that it was on the shore of the lake. The scanty remains at Ain et Tabijah, " the fountain of the fig-tree," seem to meet the necessary requirements.

The site of Capernaum is also still a matter of dispute, though more than any other town it became Christ's " own city," [§] and was the scene of His constant " signs." It is not mentioned either in the Old Testament or the Apocrypha, but in Christ's day it was " exalted to heaven " by His presence and gracious words. Tell Hûm seems to me to correspond most nearly with the indications of its locality furnished by the Gospels. Capernaum is a corruption of Kaphar Nahûm, " the village of Nahûm," and Tell Hûm

---

[*] Matt. xi. 21 ; Luke x. 13.

[†] *Bab. Menachoth*, f. 85, 1.

[‡] It was discovered in 1842 by the Rev. G. Williams; and by the Rev. W. Thomson, 1857. It was in ruins in the days of Eusebius (A. D. 330). See Neubauer, *Geogr. du Talm.* 220.

[§] Matt. ix. 1 ; Mark ii. 1.

may mean "the ruinous mound of (Na)hûm." It is near Chorazin. Among its ruins still stands the fragment of a synagogue, over the gate of which is carved the pot of manna, which may have turned the thoughts of the people to Moses' gift of "bread from heaven."* This is, perhaps, the very synagogue which the town owed to the munificence of the friendly Roman centurion.† In this city Matthew was called from "the place of toll," and here Jesus had at least a temporary home,‡ perhaps in a house which may have been partly occupied by Simon and Andrew. No town, so far as we are aware, witnessed anything like the same number of miracles. Here great multitudes gathered to Him; here He healed the nobleman's son, and the centurion's servant, and Simon's mother-in-law, and the paralytic, and the unclean demoniac, and the woman with the issue of blood, and raised the daughter of Jairus, and showed many other unrecorded signs.§ Here He taught humility to the disputing disciples by the example of a little child.‖ Here, too, in the synagogue He delivered that memorable discourse about "the Bread of Life," and about "eating His flesh and drinking His blood,"¶ which caused such deep-seated offence, but which He Himself explained to be a metaphor when He said, "*It is* the Spirit that quickeneth; *the flesh profiteth nothing; the words that I have spoken unto you are spirit and are life.*"** If that explanation, given by Christ Himself, had been rightly considered and apprehended, we might have been saved from masses of superstition. "The letter," as St. Paul says, "killeth; it is only the Spirit that giveth life." †† "Nothing can carry us beyond the limits of its own realms. The new life must come from that which belongs properly to the sphere in which it moves." There is no room for a wooden literalism. "*Gratia Dei,*" says St.

---

* John vi. 22–71.   † Luke vii. 1, 8 ; Matt. viii. 8.   ‡ Mark ii. 1.
§ John iv. 46 ; Mark i. 21, 29 ; Matt. viii., ix.; Luke iv. 23, etc.
‖ Matt. xix. 13 ; Mark x. 13, 14 ; Luke xviii. 15–17.
¶ John vi. 22–71.   ** John vi. 63.   †† 2 Cor. iii. 6.

Augustine, "*non consumitur morsibus.*" There is no more excuse for giving a *literal* meaning to "My *flesh* is meat indeed," than for understanding literally the words, "He that believeth on Me, out of his belly shall flow rivers of living water."*

It was first in the synagogues, and then in the market-places † of these cities, and in the highways and the hedges, that the Saviour of the World manifested forth His glory. Here "Oriental misery in its most terrible shape became the dearest object of His care." Here the lepers cried to Him amid the degradation of their hideous deformity, and the helpless crippled beggars—the blind, and the halt, and the maimed. Jesus had nothing but love and healing pity for wretches who lived on the scraps flung out of the rich man's door, and for the wild, naked, howling demoniacs, and the miserable, degraded harlots, and those whom Priests and Pharisees spurned and loathed as the very outcasts of society. Nor did He in the least resemble the self-deceivers who

"Sigh for wretchedness, but shun the wretched,
Nursing in some delicious solitude
Their dainty loves and slothful sympathies."

He never withheld the fulness of His miraculous mercy from the sick and sorrowful, the weary and heavy laden. Yet He came not to these alone, but to all around them; and as He regarded them with His kingly eye of love, He used the simplest incidents of their everyday lives to give point to His parables and vividness to His instruction of the poor. In the common illustrations which He employed, "day labourers are hired in the market, and paid in the evening; with plough reversed the labourer takes his homeward way; even at a distance from the village the singing and dancing

* John vii. 38.

† Not "in the streets," for the narrow, densely-crowded streets of Oriental towns would afford no place for sermons or for acts of healing. Hence the R. V., in Mark vi. 56, rightly corrects the "streets" of the A. V. St. Luke uses "streets" in a *general* sense in xiii. 26.

of the holiday-makers can be heard; in the market-place the children wrangle in their sports; until late at night the noise of revelry and knocking at closed doors continues. The drunken steward storms at, and beats, and otherwise misuses the men-servants and maid-servants. In short, from morning till night life is much occupied, and boisterous and gay, and the busy people find no time for meditating on the kingdom of God. The one has bought a piece of ground and must needs go and see it; the other must prove the oxen that have been knocked down to him; the third has other business—a feast, or a funeral, or a marriage." "They ate, they drank, they bought, they sold, they planted, they builded, they married and were given in marriage." So does Jesus describe the restless, busy life of His native land.

At first Jesus seems largely to have used the synagogues as the scenes of His teaching.* They were, during all His life, the normal resorts of His Sabbath worship, and He required no other adjuncts than the bare simplicity of the desk and platform for preaching, and the cupboard in which the Thorah was kept. But when even in the synagogues He began to be opposed, and worried by the petty legalities of the officials who were instigated to annoy Him by their local Scribes, and by Pharisaic spies sent from Jerusalem to watch and harass His movements, then more and more He deserted the synagogues, and taught under the open air of heaven those outcasts of the world and of nominal Churches from whom He meant to gather the children of the Kingdom.

It is a strange thought that there are but three or four actual spots where we may be certain that the feet of the Saviour of mankind have stood. One is in the rocky road full of sepulchral caves which mounts from the Plain of Esdraelon to Nein (the Nain of the Gospel) up the sides of Little Hermon (Jebel ed-Dûhy), where He raised to life the widow's son. Another is the rocky platform where the

* Matt. iv. 23, ix. 35, x. 17, xii. 9, xiii. 54; Luke iv. 15, 20, 44, etc.; John xviii. 20.

road from Bethany sweeps to the northward round the shoulder of the Mount of Olives, and Jerusalem first bursts on the view. The third is the summit of Kur'n Hattîn, from which Safed, "the city set on a hill," stands full in view, where Jesus uttered "the Sermon on the Mount."

To these we may perhaps add the *Har-ha-Beit*, or "Hill of the House," on the broad platform of which once stood the Temple which was "the joy of the whole earth"; and perhaps Gethsemane, of which the traditional site has much to be said in its favour. But we do not know with distant approach to certainty the sites even of the Crucifixion, or of the Holy Sepulchre. That the sites where events took place which have swayed the whole temporal and eternal destinies of the human race could have been forgotten might well seem passing strange; but the earliest generations of believers, in the days of primitive Christianity, attached no importance to localities or relics. The Lord Christ was to them far less the human Jesus, who, for one brief lifetime had moved among men, than He was the Risen, the Eternal, the Glorified Christ, their Lord and their God. They habitually contemplated Him, not as on the Cross, but as on the Throne; not as the humiliated sufferer, but as the King exalted far above all heavens. They never regarded Him as *taken away* from them, but on the contrary as *nearer to them* than He had been while on earth even to the Disciple whom He loved, and who bowed his head upon His breast. So far from being *absent from them*, He was, as He had expressly taught, ever *with them* and *within them*. To minds pervaded by such thoughts, the scenes of His *earthly* pilgrimage were comparatively as nothing. Their thoughts were with Him in the "far more exceeding and eternal weight of glory" wherein, though He now lived amid "the sevenfold chorus of Hallelujahs and harping symphonies," He was yet no less in the midst of them, wheresoever two or three were gathered together in His name.

CHAPTER XIX.

CHRIST'S METHODS OF EVANGELISATION.

Πτωχοὶ εὐαγγελίζονται.—MATT. xi. 5.

Βραχεῖς δὲ καὶ, σύντομοι παρ' αὐτοῦ λόγοι γεγόνασιν. οὐ γὰρ σοφιστὴς ὑπῆρχεν ἀλλὰ Δύναμις Θεοῦ ὁ λόγος αὐτοῦ ἦν.—JUSTIN MARTYR, *Apol.* i. 14.

THE manner in which the Son of God preached the Gospel of His Kingdom was characterised by the perfect simplicity which marked His whole career. He came to give an example to all mankind of what might be the ordinary state of men, not exalted by any factitious rank, nor glorified by any external magnificence, nor rendered prominent by any adventitious circumstances, but elevated transcendently above the low malarious swamps of common humanity by the sinlessness of that *spiritual* life which He came not only to exemplify but to impart. The High Priest on the Day of Atonement went into the holy place in hierarchic pomp, in his golden garments, encircled with his girdle of blue and purple and scarlet, and the jewelled Urim on his breast ; the Essene affected white robes, and a predetermined look of sanctified asceticism ; the Pharisee, while he was devouring widows' houses, and for a pretence making long prayers, chose the chief seats in feasts and synagogues, loved to walk in long robes, and to pose in saintly attitudes, delighted in ceremonious greetings, sounded a trumpet before him when he did his alms, made broad his phylacteries, enlarged the tassels of his garment, and did all his works to be seen of men. The Lord of Life went about in humble sincerity, wearing neither the mantle of the Prophet, nor the hairy garb and leathern girdle of the eremite, but making His appeal to the hearts of men by the sacred elements of the humanity which was the

common gift of God alike to the rich and to the poor, to
the great and to the lowly.

> "In Himself was all His state,
> More solemn than the tedious pomp that waits
> On princes, when their rich retinue long
> Of horses led, and grooms besmeared with gold,
> Dazzles the crowd, and sets them all agape."

His was that most simple and deep-reaching form of evangelisation which, in the persons of His holiest followers—a
Paul, a Peter, a Francis of Assisi, a Francis Xavier, a Wes-
ley, a Whitefield—has ever been ten-thousandfold more
effective than the most elaborately gorgeous ceremonials
of Popes and Priests. And though He wore the peasant
garb, and associated constantly with the peasant multitude,
and had not about Him a single attribute of earthly state,
there was something so heart-searching in His very look
that it troubled the world-entangled soul of the young
ruler;* and broke the heart of Peter;† and impressed the
arrogant cynicism of the Roman Procurator;‡ and again
and again left an indelible impression on the minds of His
disciples,§ and even of the multitude.

When He was at Jerusalem He taught sometimes in the
Temple—but only in the open courts and porticoes, because
they were the common places of resort where alone in the
Holy City His voice could be heard by the multitudes who
thronged thither to the feasts. But the rites and ceremonies of that desecrated Temple, infinitely elaborated as
they were, received from Him no word of approval. The
wild joy of the ceremony of drawing water in the Feast of
Tabernacles only caused Him to exclaim, "If any man
thirst, let him come unto Me and drink"; ‖ and when the
people were exulting in the glory of the huge golden candelabra and numberless lamps which shed their glow over
the Treasury and the Temple Courts, He said, "I am the

* Mark x. 21, 22.　　　† Luke xxii. 61.　　　‡ John xix. 5.
§ Matt. xix. 26 ; Mark x. 27.　　　‖ John vii. 37.

Light of the world: he that followeth Me shall not walk in the darkness, but shall have the light of life." *

These obvious, but unrecorded, indications that Christ's teaching was suggested by immediate circumstances lead us to suppose that this was constantly the case. The Parable of the Pounds was suggested by the history of King Archelaus, which was brought into our Lord's mind by the sight of the palace which he had built at Jericho. The allusion to the wind which bloweth where it listeth, in the discourse with Nicodemus, would naturally arise from the soughing of the night wind outside the booth. The allegory of the Ideal Vine may have been suggested by the vineyards near the Kidron, or by the Golden Vine over the Temple door.

There are some minds which seem to think that worship must be imperfect if it is not surrounded with splendour and symbolism. Thus a Roman Catholic author wrote: "Oh! then what delight! what joy unspeakable! The stoups are filled to the brim; the lamp of the Sanctuary burns bright, and the albs hang in the oaken ambries, and the cope-chests are filled with osphreyed baudekins, and pyx, and pax, and chrismatory are there, and thurible and cross!"† Strange sources, indeed, to any manly and spiritual mind for such ecstatic rapture! How many millions of true saints have enjoyed the utmost bliss of holy worship without any need of being excited or distracted by " pyx," or " pax," or " chrismatory," or " oaken ambries," or even " osphreyed baudekins!" Such things as the thurible and the crucifix were unknown to, and avoided by, primitive Christians in the centuries when Christianity was most effective and most pure. Artificial religious externalism receives no approval from the lips of Christ. Nothing which remotely resembles it is distantly alluded to, either by Him or His Apostles, as constituting a desirable adjunct of holy worship. Even Levitism, destined to meet the requirements of a people whose hearts were gross,

* John viii. 12.   † *Recollections of A. Welby Pugin*, p. 162.

and their ears dull of hearing, offers no analogy to the spirituality, simplicity, and sincerity of worship which are the sole requirements for our approach to Him who is a Spirit, and who requires them that worship Him to worship Him in spirit and in truth. Alike by His precepts and by His practice, He who came from the bosom of the Father illustrates the truth that sincere devotion can make even the mud floor of the humblest cottage "as sacred as the rocks of Sinai."

Hence Jesus taught sometimes in the house which at Capernaum served Him as a home; * sometimes in Peter's house, or the house of Martha and Mary at Bethany. † Sometimes—as in the house of Simon the Pharisee, and of other Pharisaic rulers—He made an ordinary meal the occasion of some of His deepest lessons, and borrowed His images from bread, and salt, and wine, and the washing of hands. ‡ He taught and healed in the market-places, and at city gates; § and in the broader streets and roads. ‖ Much of His most solemn instruction was given, especially to His Apostles, as He journeyed with them on the frequented highways, ¶ or in lonely places to which He had retired,** or "in the fields as they went from village to to village." †† Some of His richest Parables were addressed to the multitudes who crowded the beach while the little boat, which was always at His disposal, rocked gently on the bright ripples of the lake He loved. ‡‡ Sometimes He spoke to throngs composed of poor pilgrims from every

---

* Mark ii. 1, iii. 20, where εἰς οἶκον (or ἐν οἴκῳ) means that the house was His house.

† Matt. viii. 14 ; Luke x. 38.

‡ John vi.; Matt. v. 13, ix. 17 ; Luke v. 37 ; Matt. xv. 2 ; Mark vii. 2. § Mark vi. 56.

‖ Matt. vi. 2 ; Luke x. 10, xiii. 26.

¶ Matt. xvi. 13.

** Matt. xiv. 13 ; Luke ix. 10, xi. 1 ; Mark vi. 34, 35.

†† Matt. ix. 35, xiv. 15 ; Mark vi. 56 ; Luke xii. 22, etc.

‡‡ Matt. xiii. 1, 2 : Mark ii. 13 ; Luke v. 1–3.

nation, as they sat round Him on the hilltop; and sometimes on the broad and lonely plains whither great multitudes flocked to Him on foot from all the cities.* He loved to speak in the open air under God's blue heaven, and among the lilies of the field. Teaching, with His feet among the mountain flowers, He could point to the golden amaryllis, or the scarlet anemones, or the gorgeous tulips, and tell His hearers to trust in God's free bounty, since not even "Solomon in all his glory" was arrayed like one of these, which were but the perishing "grass of the field." Teaching with the soft wind of heaven upon His brow, He could point the lessons to be learnt from the ravens and the sparrows and the bright or lowering sky. But, for the greater part of His life, the simple worship of the synagogues sufficed Him. "As His custom was He went into the synagogue on the Sabbath day, and stood up for to read"; and "He taught in their synagogues, being glorified of all." †

But it did not seem to make the least difference to the depth and power of His teaching whether He was speaking to the ears of a single auditor, like Nicodemus, the timid *Chakam* who came to Him by night, or the Samaritan woman by the noonday well, or the blind man whom He had healed; or whether He was in the midst of "myriads,"‡ who "pressed, and crushed Him,"§ and "trode on one another" in their eagerness to hear the gracious words which proceeded from His lips.

* Matt. v. 1, xv. 29, xvii. 1. † Luke iv. 15, 16, etc.
‡ Luke xii. - § Luke viii. 45.

CHAPTER XX.

THE FORM OF CHRIST'S TEACHING.

Πολυμερῶς καὶ πολυτρόπως.—HEB. i. 1.

THE form of Christ's teaching was as varied and as simple as were its methods. It was the spontaneous outcome of the requirements of the moment. Whatever was most exactly needed for the defence of a truth, or the blighting of a hypocrisy, or the startling of self-satisfaction into penitence, or the consolation of despondency, was instantaneously clothed in its best form, whether of reproach, or question, or deep irony, or tender apostrophe, or exquisitely poetic image. It was a Πολυπόικιλος σοφία, "a richly variegated wisdom," which, like the King's daughter, was " *circumamicta varietatibus*—clothed in raiment of various colours."* His lessons were not, it would seem, often expressed in long and didactic addresses, to which the Sermon on the Mount offers the nearest approach. There was in them nothing of recondite metaphysics. "What Jesus had to offer," it has been said, "was not a new code with its penal enactments, not a new system of doctrine with its curse upon all who should dare to depart from it, but a sure promise of deliverance from misery, of consolation under all suffering, and perfect satisfaction for all the wants of the soul." And this was set forth, not in gorgeous metaphor, or sonorous rhetoric, but in language of the most perfect simplicity, unencumbered by the pedantry of scholasticism, or the minutiæ of logic. There ran throughout His discourses " the two weighty qualities of impressive pregnancy and popular intelligibility." And to make what He said

* Eph. iii. 10 ; Ps. xlv. 13.

more clear in its brevity, His words were illuminated with constant illustrations, not drawn from remote truths of science, but suggested by the commonest sights, sounds, and scenes of nature, and the most familiar incidents of humble life—the rejoicing shepherd carrying back on his shoulders the recovered lamb; the toiling vine-dressers; the harvesters in the fields of ripe corn; the children busy in gathering the tares for burning; the woman seeking for the lost coin out of her forehead-circlet; the man going to borrow from his neighbour a loaf for his hungry and unexpected guest. He taught by picturesque and concrete examples,* or when He laid down general rules applied them to actual cases. Instead of speaking in the abstract of the beauty of Humility, He took a little child and set him in the midst, and bade the disciples receive the Kingdom of Heaven as that little child.† Instead of warning them that they were liable to constant temptation, He says, " Behold, Satan has desired to have you, that he may sift you as wheat." † Instead of saying, "You must not be content to keep your convictions for your private guidance," He says, " Is the lamp brought to be put under the bushel or under the bed, and not to be put on the stand?" ‡ By multitudes of such pictures He caused a spontaneous recognition of the truth which to every enlightened conscience would itself be as an authoritative command.

" A theoretical philosophy strictly so called," says Schürer, "was a thing entirely foreign to genuine Judaism. Whatever it did happen to produce in the way of philosophy (*Chokmah*, 'wisdom') either had practical religious problems as its theme (as in Job and Ecclesiastes), or was of a directly practical nature—being directions based upon a thoughtful study of human things in order so to regulate our life as to ensure our being truly happy. The form in

---

* Matt. vi. 19, 25, vii. 6, x. 35, xi. 8, xviii. 6, xix. 12 ; Luke vi. 34, and *passim*.

† Luke xxii. 31.   ‡ Matt. v. 15.

which these contemplations and instructions were presented was that of the ' proverb ' or aphorism (*Mashai*), which contained a single thought expressed in concise and comprehensive terms, in a form more or less poetical, and in which there was nothing of the nature of discussion or argument."* Jewish literature possessed a collection of such aphorisms in the Proverbs of Solomon, and the Wisdom of Jesus the Son of Sirach; and later we find them in the Talmudic book, *Pirqe Avôth*, or "Sayings of the Fathers." Our Lord frequently adopted this gnomic mode of instruction in concise sayings, of which these are but a few specimens; although, as a glance suffices to prove, He infuses into them a depth of spiritual meaning which finds no parallel in any other form of proverbial instruction.

" A city set on a hill cannot be hid." †

" Beware of the leaven of the Pharisees." ‡

" God is not the God of the dead, but of the living." §

" Leave the dead to bury their own dead." ‖

" If the light in thee be darkness, how great is that darkness." ¶

" Salt is good ; but if the salt have lost its saltness, wherewith will ye season it ?" **

" Do men gather grapes of thorns, or figs of thistles ?" ††

" If the blind lead the blind, both shall fall into a pit." ‡‡

" It is not meet to take the children's bread, and cast it to the dogs." §§

" He that walketh in darkness knoweth not whither he goeth." ‖‖

" They that are whole have no need of a physician, but they that are sick." ¶¶

" Be ye wise as serpents, but harmless as doves." ***

If these be compared with the sayings of Heraclitus (for instance) among the Greeks, or of Hillel, who furnishes the best specimens which we can find in the Talmud, their immense superiority will at once be recognised. There is

---

* *Hist. of the Jewish People*, div. ii. vol. iii. 24, E. T.

† Matt. v. 14.	‡ Matt. xvi. 6.	§ Matt. xxii. 32.
‖ Luke ix. 60.	¶ Matt. vi. 23.	** Mark ix. 50.
†† Matt. vii. 19.	‡‡ Matt. xv. 14.	§§ Mark vii. 27.
‖‖ John xii. 35.	¶¶ Mark ii. 17.	*** Matt. x. 16.

nothing strained or obscure about them ; they are intensely concrete and picturesque. Their marvellous concentration excludes every superfluous word, yet admits no lurking fallacy. They have the illuminating force of the lightning ; they compress words of wisdom into a single line. A child may understand them, but the wisest philosopher cannot exhaust their infinite significance.

Our Lord taught, it has been truly said, in *ideas*, not in limitations; and the essence of faith is " a permanent confidence in the idea—a confidence never to be broken down by apparent failures, or by examples by which ordinary people prove that qualification is necessary. It was precisely because Jesus taught the idea, and nothing below it, that the effect produced by Him could not have been produced by anybody nearer to ordinary humanity."

Again, in order to arrest the attention and stimulate the jaded and conventional moral sense of His hearers, our Lord often adopted the form of paradox to state " exceptionless *principles*," such as could only be perverted by a stupid literalism. Exceptions which are inevitable, and are a matter of course, may easily be omitted.* In fact, some of Christ's vivid questions and concentrated appeals are thrown into the form which was known to the Greeks as *oxymoron*—which is defined as a saying which is the more forcible from its apparent extravagance. †

Take, for instance, such a rule as :

" When thou makest a dinner or a supper, *call not* thy friends, nor thy brethren, nor thy kinsfolk, nor rich neighbours ; lest haply they also bid thee again, and a recompense be made thee. But when thou makest a feast, bid the poor, the maimed, the lame, the blind. . ."‡

No one of the most ordinary intelligence would fail to see

---

* See Matt. vii. 1, xx. 16, xxv. 29 ; Mark ii. 17 ; John v. 31 (comp. viii. 14), ix. 39, etc.

† See Matt. v. 39, ix. 13 ; Luke xiv. 26 ; John vi. 27, etc.; Glass, *Philology Sacr.* p. 468.

‡ Luke xiv. 12–14.

that the rule is not intended for *literal* application, but that
it was meant to point out that there is no merit in hospitality which is only directed by the "slightly expanded egotism" of family selfishness, or only intended to bring about
a return in kind; but that the highest and most genuine
hospitality is disinterested, loving, and compassionate. It
must also be borne in mind that our Lord naturally spoke
in the idioms of His country, and that in Hebrew "*not*"
often means "*not only*—but also*," or "*not so much*—as." *
In other words, "*not*" is often used to deny, not absolutely, but conditionally and comparatively. †

Again, when He said, "Whosoever smiteth thee on thy
right cheek, turn to him the other also. And if any man
would go to law with thee, and take away thy coat, let him
have thy cloak also," He merely meant to present the essential ideas of forbearance and forgiveness "with the greatest clearness and in the briefest compass." He showed by
His own example—as indeed His hearers would have easily
understood—that He did not mean such paradoxes to be
taken in the letter; for when He was Himself smitten on
the cheek by the servant of the High Priest He did not
turn the other cheek, but addressed to the insolent offender
a dignified rebuke in the words, "If I have spoken evil, bear
witness of the evil; but if well, why smitest thou Me?"

So, too, when He said, "If any man cometh unto Me,
and *hateth* not his own father and mother, and wife, and
children, and brethren and sisters, yea and his own life also,
he cannot be My disciple,"‡ He was speaking to those who
were perfectly familiar with Jewish idioms, which put truth
in its extremest form, and—as a figure of speech—emphasised a precept by the exclusion of all exceptions. §

* See Prov. viii. 10; John vi. 27; 1 Cor. i. 17, xv. 10; 1 Tim. ii. 9, etc.

† See Jer. viii. 22; Joel ii. 13; Matt. ix. 13; Gal. v. 21; Heb. vii. 11.

‡ Wendt (ii. 67) compares the saying of Luther "Nehmen sie den Leib,
Gut, Ehr, Kind, und Weib. Lass fahren dahin!"

§ Luke xiv. 26. We see from Matt. x. 37, that "hate" merely means *in
comparison with* the deeper, diviner love.

This fact is illustrated by the way in which St. Matthew records the saying ;—which is "He that loveth father or mother *more than* Me is not worthy of Me : and he that loveth son or daughter more than Me is not worthy of Me."* Thus, in our Lord's favourite quotation from the Prophet Hoshea, "I desire mercy and *not* sacrifice," neither the ancient Prophet nor our Lord meant to abrogate the whole Levitic law of sacrifice, but only to express the transcendence of the duty of mercy.

In teaching which was pre-eminently intended to arrest the attention and to linger in the memory, the form of expression is of the utmost importance.† Our Lord's discourses were often delivered in the current Aramaic, and if we possessed them in their original form it is more than possible that we should find that they abounded in those assonances and forcible plays on words which often have a hidden power of their own. Thus, the words (Matt. xi. 17),

> "We piped unto you and ye did not dance,
> We wailed, and ye did not beat the breast,"

in addition to their rhythmic and antithetic parallelism would have been still more forcible if the words used for "danced" and "mourned" were *rakedtoon* and *arkedtoon*. The phrase "the gates of Hades" (Matt. xvii. 18) may have acquired impressiveness from the alliteration, *Shaare Sheol.* ‡ Again, what a new light falls on the familiar words, "Come unto Me all ye who are weary and heavy laden, and I will give you rest. For I am meek and lowly in heart, and ye shall find rest unto your souls," when we know the assonances between "I will give you rest" (*anikhkhon*), "meek" (*nikh*) and "rest" (*Nikha*).

* Matt. x. 37.

† Thomas Boys (on 1 Pet. iii.) says : "The intention of these apparent inconsistencies is that we may mark them, dwell upon them, get instruction out of them. Things are put to us in a strange way, because if they were put in a more ordinary way we should not notice them."

‡ On this subject, see Heinsius, *Aristarchus*; and Glass, *Phil. Sacra.* p. 958.

In Matt. iii. 9, St. John the Baptist plays on the assonance between *Abanim* (" stones ") and *Banim* (" sons "). In Matt. x. 30, we read, " The very *hairs* of your head are all *numbered*." This is a paronomasia between *Mene* (" hairs ") and *mamyan* (" numbered"). In Luke vii. 41, 42, the words *chav* (" owe ") and *achab* (" one another") resemble each other. In John i. 5, the Syriac would be, " The light shineth in *darkness* (*Gebal*), and the darkness *comprehended* (*gibbal*) it not."*

It has not perhaps been sufficiently noticed that our Lord sometimes adopted for His teaching the form of spontaneous poetry—engraving the words on the memory of His hearers by adopting the rhythmic parallelism of Hebrew verse, characterised by that climax and *refrain* in which Eastern poetry delights. The parallelism which is the distinctive characteristic of Hebrew poetry falls under three main heads—antithetic, synthetic, and synonymous. We find all three forms utilised in Christ's teaching. We have *antithetic* paralellism in such sayings as

> " Every one that exalteth himself shall be humbled,
> And he that humbleth himself shall be exalted." †

We have *synthetic*, or progressive parallelism in

> " He that receiveth you receiveth Me,
> And he that recevieth Me, receiveth Him that sent Me."‡

Synonymous, or illustrative parallelism is found in such sayings as

> " They that are whole have no need of a physician,
> But they that are sick."
> " I came not to call the righteous, but sinners to repentance." §

The following is a specimen of synthetic parallelism in which the second line not only emphasises but advances

---

* Adduced by Dr. Bullinger, *Figures of Scripture*, p. 322.
† Luke xiv. 11.   ‡ Matt. x. 40.   § Mark ii. 17.

the sense of the first ; and to which in the last two lines is added a specimen of antithetic parallelism :

> " Think not that I came to send peace on earth :
> I came not to send peace, but a sword.
> For I came to set a man at variance against his father,
> And the daughter against her mother,
> And the daughter-in-law against her mother-in-law.
> And a man's foe shall be they of his own household."

. . . .

> " He that findeth his life shall lose it ;
> And he that loseth his life for My sake shall find it."*

Again

> " Every sin and blasphemy shall be forgiven unto men,
> But the blasphemy against the Holy Spirit shall not be forgiven.
> And whosoever shall speak a word against the Son of Man, it shall be forgiven him ;
> But whosoever shall speak against the Holy Spirit, it shall not be forgiven him.
> Neither in this æon, nor in the coming one."

Here two antithetic parallelisms are followed by a strong synthetic conclusion. † Again, in Matt. xxv. 34–46 there is a lovely and powerful rhythmic passage in which " each division consists of a triplet or stanza of three lines, followed by a stanza of six lines, which, in the form of a climax, state the reason of the sentence ; then the response of those that receive the sentence, then the reply of the Judge ; lastly, the concluding couplet describes the passage to their doom of the just and of the unjust." ‡

This poetic structure is often traceable in the Sermon on the Mount, as in the lines of synthetic and introverted parallelism in which the first corresponds to the fourth, and the second to the third.

> " Give not that which is holy unto the dogs,
> Neither cast ye your pearls before swine,

---

* Matt. x. 34–39, xvi. 25 ; Mark viii. 35 ; Luke ix. 24. See, too, Matt. vi. 19, 20.

† Matt. xii. 31, 32. ‡ Carr *St. Matthew*, p. 280.

> Lest haply they trample them under their feet
> And turn again and rend you." *

And in the next two verses there are "triplets with an ascending climax." †

> " Ask, and it shall be given you ;
> Seek, and ye shall find ;
> Knock, and it shall be opened unto you
> For every one that asketh receiveth,
> And he that seeketh findeth,
> And to him that knocketh it shall be opened."

And, not to multiply examples, there is a peculiarly lovely and finished specimen of synthetic and antithetic parallelism in the address of our Lord to Simon the Pharisee. ‡

> " Simon, dost thou mark this woman ?
> I entered into thine house,
> Thou gavest me no water for my feet ;
> But she hath wetted my feet with her tears
> And wiped them with her hair.
> Thou gavest me no kiss ;
> But she, since the time I came in,
> Hath not ceased to kiss my feet.
> My head with oil thou didst not anoint ;
> But she hath anointed my feet with spikenard.
> Her sins, which are many, are forgiven,
> For she loved much ;
> But to whom little is forgiven,
> The same loveth little."

---

* Matt. vii. 6.   For another instance of introverted parallelism see Matt. vi. 24.

† *Id.* 7, 8.   Similiar triplets of synthetic parallelism are found in John x. 27, 28.

‡ Luke vii. 44–47.

CHAPTER XXI.

THE FORM OF CHRIST'S TEACHING (*continued*).

THE PARABLES.

" A parable of knowledge is in the treasures of wisdom."—Ecclus. i. 25.

" Apples of gold in baskets of silver."—Prov. xxv. 11.

" Though truths in manhood darkly join,
  Deep-seated in our mystic frame,
  We yield all blessing to the Name
Of Him who made them current coin."
                                        —TENNYSON.

THE teachings of our Lord, especially after the earliest phase of His Ministry, was more habitually and essentially pictorial and illustrative than that of any other teacher of mankind. The word "parable"—derived from παραβάλλειν, "to place side by side," and so "to compare"—is used in the Gospels with a wider latitude than we ordinarily give to it. The parable differs from (i.) a fable because it only moves within the limits of possibility; from (ii.) an allegory in not being throughout identical with the truth illustrated; from (iii.) a simile, in its more complete and dramatic development. There is no direct parable in the Gospel of St. John, but there are many "symbolic comparisons," of which the majority are drawn from Nature—such as that of the wind blowing where it listeth (iii. 8); the growth of the grain of wheat (xii. 24); sowing and reaping (iv. 35–38); and there are two allegories, those of the Fair Shepherd, and the Vine and its branches. St. John does not use the word παραβολή once, but he uses the word παροιμία (" proverb ") four times (x. 6, xvi. 25, 29). Elsewhere this word only occurs in 2 Peter ii. 22.*

The name, "parable," is given, not only to continuous narratives, but to condensed maxims such as :

"If the blind lead the blind, shall they not both fall into the ditch ?"†
"Physician, heal thyself."‡
"The whole have no need of the physician, but the sick."§
"No man rendeth a piece from a new garment and putteth it on an old garment, or putteth new wine into old wine-skins."‖
"Do men gather grapes of thorns, or figs of thistles ?"¶

In point of fact, the words "parable" and "proverb" are used to some extent interchangeably, and both words are, in the Septuagint, chosen to translate the Hebrew *Mashal.*** In this sense of the word even the Sermon on the Mount abounds in parables, for it contains fully fourteen comparisons, any one of which might have been expanded into a little narrative.

In ordinary English, however, the word "parable" is used to describe the illustrations which, whether derived from nature or from human life, are used as pictorial figures of spiritual and moral truths. These have been divided into *symbolic* (which are the more numerous) and *typical.*†† *Symbolic* parables are those which, like the Parables of the Sower, the Mustard Seed, or the Fisher's Net, are descrip-

---

* The Book of Proverbs is called Παροιμίαι in the LXX., but in 1 Kings iv. 32 we read, ἐλάλησε τρισχιλίας παραβολάς.

† Luke v. 36. Our Lord very rarely used *irony*, as in Mark vii. 9.

‡ Luke vi. 39.

§ Mark ii. 17.

‖ Luke iv. 23. This proverb is found in the Talmud, in *e. g. Tanchuma* f. 4, 2.

¶ Matt. vii. 16, 2–4, xxiii. 24, xxiv. 28. For many others see Mark ii. 21; iii. 27, iv. 21, vii. 27, x. 25 ; Luke xvi. 13, xvii. 31, xxiii. 31 ; Matt. xvii. 25; John iv. 37, etc. Many of these are found in the Talmud ; *Sanhedrin*, f. 100, 1 ; *Baba Bathra*, f. 15, 2, etc.

** Ps. xlix. 4 ; lxxviii. 2 ; 1 Sam. x. 19, xxiv. 14. Comp. Num. xxiii. 7 ; Prov. i. 6 ; Ezek. xii. 22, etc.

†† Goebel, *The Parables of Jesus*, p. 4.

tive pictures set forth in a narrative form ; *typical* parables
are those like the Parables of the Good Samaritan, or Dives
and Lazarus, which convey instruction and warning by the
incidents or histories of human life. The Old Testament
supplies us with one example of each kind.* Nathan's
Parable of the Ewe Lamb is typical;† Isaiah's Parable of
the Vineyard is symbolic.‡ In the Psalms of Solomon, the
Book of Enoch, and in later Rabbinic literature, parables
are found, both symbolic and typical; but whereas not one
of them has seized the imagination of mankind, the parables of Jesus remain to this day a source of delight and of
deepest instruction to all sorts and conditions of men, and
in age after age have exercised over the world a memorable
influence.

It is interesting to observe that our Lord expressly used
parables to instruct the simple and ignorant multitude,
whereas by earlier teachers they had been regarded as the
prerogative of the *Chaberim*, or " pupils of the wise."
Tillers and herdsmen, says the Son of Sirach, are not found
where parables are spoken.§

It is further remarked that, amid all the crude and audacious inventions of the Apocryphal Gospels, they do not
venture to invent a single parable. The Divine Wisdom necessary to offer even a remote parallel to such instruction lay
wholly beyond the sphere of the capacity of crude fabulists.

The parables of Jesus took their tone in a great measure
from the circumstances by which He was surrounded, and
the class of people whom He was addressing.‖ For instance,
the first series, delivered at Capernaum—seven or eight in

---

* The address of Jotham (Judge ix. 7–15) is a fable. The scornful reply of
Jehoash to Amaziah (2 Kings xiv. 9, 10) is a sort of symbolic parable. Comp.
Heb. ix. 9.

† 2 Sam. xii. 1–6.

‡ There are many passages in Ezekiel (xv., xvi., xvii. 1–10, 22–24, xxiii.)
and Isaiah (v. 1–6) which contain parabolic elements.

§ Ecclus. xxxviii. 33.

‖ Goebel, pp. 21–23.

number—deals with *the founding* of God's Kingdom; the second series, mainly given by St. Luke (x.–xix.) describes the progressive development of the Kingdom, and the attitude of its members toward God and toward the world ; the final series, which belong to the last period of Christ's ministry, relates to the future completion of the Kingdom at the end of its temporal development.

One series of these parables was practically consecutive. "The Sower exhibits the rise of the kingdom; the Weeds sown by the devil, its obstacles; the Mustard Seed and the Leaven, its growth ; the Treasure and the Pearl, its appropriation by mankind ; the Net, the separation at the judgment, which closes the history of its development."

There was a reason for the adoption of the parabolic form of teaching, which our Lord explained. His parables resembled the pillar of fire, which to the hostile Egyptians was a pillar of cloud. At first He had spoken to the multitudes in similitudes indeed, but such as explained themselves ; and when He first resorted to parables the disciples were astonished.* In answer to their question He explained the double object of this change of method. It was at once helpful and penal. To the earnest and faithful they gave light ; to the wilful and perverse they were as a veil. To the earnest, the sincere, the humble-minded, in proportion to their faithfulness, the parables were, as Seneca said of fables, "*adminicula imbecillitatis*"; but, to those who cared nothing for the truth, or directly set themselves against it, the indifference which caused them to disdain the truth made of the parables a shroud to hide it from them.† Thus, as Bacon said, "A parable has a double use—it tends to veil, and it tends to illustrate a truth. In the latter case it seems designed to teach ; in the former to conceal."‡

---

* Matt. xiii. 10.

† See the excellent article on Parables by the late Dean Plumptre in Smith's *Dict. of the Bible.*

‡ Bacon, *De Sap. Veterum.* The strong expression of Mark iv. 12, " in

How far any of the typical parables were borrowed from
actual facts which had come under the cognisance of Jesus
we are unable to say, though many of them read like
descriptions of real events.   None of them show any im-
probability ; much less do they even transgress the limits
of the possible.   It is, however, a most interesting fact that
we are able to trace the origin of *one* parable—though of one
only—that of the Pounds.*   It was delivered on the journey from Jericho towards Jerusalem, and unintelligible as
the notion of " a nobleman going into a far country to seek
a kingdom" might seem to *us*, there was not one of our
Lord's hearers who would not at once think of Herod the
Great, and of his son Archelaus, both of whom had done
this very thing.   They could not reign over Judæa without
the permission of the all-powerful Cæsar, and they had to
seek it at Rome.   Jesus had just passed by the splendid
palace reared by Archelaus among the balsam-groves of
Jericho, and the thought of the tyrant would naturally be
brought into His mind.†   The parable recalls some actual
incidents of the Ethnarch's history, and since Christ utilised
these events to convey deep and awful lessons, we are justified in the conjecture that many others of the parables may
have derived fresh force because they were directly borrowed from circumstances which were known to those who
heard them.   This parable also, like those of the Unjust
Judge and the Unjust Steward, proves that the *details* of
parables are not to be extravagantly forced ; for our Lord
here employs the movements and actions of a bad and cruel
prince to shadow forth certain truths in the relations of
God to men.

Absolute simplicity was the characteristic of the preach-

order that seeing they may see, and not perceive," is, in Matt. xiii. 13, " I
speak with them in parables because seeing they see not."   Comp. Hos. xiv.
9 ; Rev. xxii. 11.

   * Luke xix. 11–27.

   † Jos. *Antt.* ii. 4, 5, xvii. 13, 1 ; *B. J.* ii. 6, 3 ; Tac. *Hist.* v. 9.

ing of the Son of God. It is interesting to notice that the first groups of parables are derived from natural facts;* the other three are not narratives, but dwell on single incidents.†

The second group consists of parables mainly drawn from human events, and addressed to the disciples on the way from Galilee to Jerusalem, and before the closing scenes.‡

The last group of parables—which were delivered during the closing days of Christ's earthly life—are all derived from human conduct.§

By far the larger number of parables are recorded by St. Matthew and St. Luke; St. John has no parable, and St. Mark only one which is peculiarly his own—that of the Seed growing secretly (iv. 26). If we compare the parables preserved respectively by St. Matthew and St. Luke, we shall see that (as Archbishop Trench says) "St. Matthew's are more theocratic, St. Luke's more ethical; St. Matthew's are more parables of judgment, St. Luke's of mercy; those are statelier, these tenderer." ‖

In the parables generally we mark "the lessons which we may learn from the natural world on the progress and scope of Revelation, and the testimony which man's own heart renders to the Christian morality."¶ Christ's parables were the exact antithesis to those "subtle" and "riddling" para-

---

* The Sower; the Wheat and Tares; the Mustard Seed; the Seed cast into the Ground; the Leaven. (Matt. xiii.; Mark iv.)

† The Hid Treasure; the Pearl; the Net. (Matt. xiii.)

‡ Such are the Two Debtors; the Merciless Servant; the Good Samaritan; the Friend at Midnight; the Rich Fool; the Wedding Feast; the Great Supper; the Lost Sheep; the Lost Piece of Money; the Prodigal Son; the Unjust Steward; Dives and Lazarus; the Unjust Judge; the Pharisee and the Publican; the Labourer in the Vineyard. (Luke vii., x., xi., xii., xiii., xiv., xv., xvi., xviii.; Matt. xviii., xx.)

§ The Pounds; the Two Sons; the Husbandmen; the Marriage Feast; the Ten Virgins; the Talents; the Sheep and Goats. (Luke xix., xx.; Matt. xxi., xxii., xxv.)

‖ Trench, *On the Parables*, p. 28.

¶ Bishop Westcott, *Introd. to the Gospels*, p. 478.

bles in which the son of Sirach tells us that the Scribes and ideal wise men delighted.* The general teaching of them all is in the direction of that large view of religion which uplifts it entirely above the formulæ and functions with which it has been confused by the majority of mankind. Their one main object is to inculcate holiness, and to show that the only religion for which God cares is the religion of the heart. Again and again they impress on us the great duties of love, watchfulness, humility, and prayer, and show that perfect love toward God is most surely evinced by perfect love towards, and service of, our fellow-men. They set before us the one supreme end of human life, which is to live in the conviction of God's presence, and the knowledge that in His presence is life. And with these eternal lessons are intermingled the awful notes of necessary warning— that man cannot sin with impunity; that our sins will always find us out; that, against all pride, cruelty, hypocrisy, and wickedness, "our God is a consuming fire." These lessons run through the whole of Scripture; but "never man spake like this Man." He taught, says Bishop Jeremy Taylor, "by parables, under which were hid mysterious senses, which shined through the veil, like a bright sun through an eye closed with a thin eyelid." Was it strange that all the people "hanged on Him † as the bee doth on the flower, the babe on the breast, the little bird on the bill of her dam? Christ drew the people after Him by the golden chain of His heavenly eloquence."‡

The parables remain as the most winning, yet at the same time the richest and divinest sources of moral and spiritual guidance. They do not furnish us with scholastic forms of creed, or intricate systems of morality, but they teach throughout one main doctrine—"a consistent view of the right ideal relation between God and men, thoroughly pervaded by the idea of God as the living Father." § Who

---

* Ecclus. xxxix. 1–5.   † Luke xix. 48, ἐξεκρέματο αὐτοῦ.
‡ J. Trapp.   § Wendt ii. 390.

could exhaust the depths of tenderness, and warning, and appeal, and revelation of Him whose mercy endureth for ever, which Jesus compressed into the few thrilling verses that tell the story of the Prodigal Son? Truly, of this parable we may say with special force:

> " For Wisdom dealt with mortal powers,
>   Where truth in closest words shall fail,
>   When truth embodied in a tale
> Shall enter in at lowly doors."

The hard dogmatism and theoretic minutiæ of an arrogant theology vanish like oppressive nightmares before this single parable in which Jesus reveals the heavenly secret of human redemption, not according to any mystical or criminal theory of punishment, but anthropologically, psychologically, theologically, to every pure eye that looks into the perfect laws of Olivet. Were we to be asked to name one page of all the literature of all the world since time began which had caused the deepest blessings, and kindled in the despairing hearts of men the most effectual belief in the possibility and efficacy of repentance, would any one hesitate to name the Parable of the Prodigal Son? It shatters to pieces all the common theological conceptions of God the Father as a wrathful Judge, whose flaming countenance can only be softened by the compassion of God the Son; or who only deals with men in the form of forensic arrangement by means of substitutes, and equivalents, and exact retributive vengeance. It sets Him forth as the All Merciful, whose heart is filled with a Father's love; who is more ready to hear than we to pray; who desireth not the death of a sinner, but rather that he should turn from his sins and be saved. It is the *Evangelium in Evangelio*, and, even after long centuries of Christianity, towers transcendently above the elder-brotherly spirit which so many who " profess and call themselves Christians " display in all their dealings with their fellow-men, and even with their brother-religionists whose belief varies ever so little from their own.

Goebel classifies the parables under the heads of—I. 1. The Founding of the Kingdom, The Sower. 2. The Development of the Kingdom (*a*) in the immediate future; (*b*) in its development to the end. 3. The Consummation of the Kingdom. II. The Right Attitude of the Members of the Kingdom (i.) towards God; (ii.) towards the world; (iii.) to men; (iv.) to worldly goods.

Bishop Westcott has given a classification of the parables in his *Introduction to the Study of the Gospels* (pp. 478–480). In main outline he divides them into—I. Parables drawn FROM THE MATERIAL WORLD—The Sower; The Tares; The Seed growing secretly; The Mustard Seed; The Leaven. [5]

II. Parables drawn from the RELATION OF MAN—(i.) *To the Lower World:* The Draw-net; The Barren Fig-tree; The Lost Sheep; The Lost Drachm. [4] (ii.) *To his Fellow-men*, and in the Family: The Unmerciful Servant; The Two Debtors; The Prodigal Son; The Two Sons. [4] (iii.) *In Social Life:* The Friend at Midnight; The Unjust Judge; The Ten Virgins; The Lower Seats (Luke xiv. 7–11); The Great Supper; The King's Marriage Feast. [6] (iv.) *To God's Service:* The Tower Builders; The King Making War; The Unjust Steward; The Talents; The Pounds; The Wicked Husbandman; The Unprofitable Servants; The Labourers in the Vineyard. [8] (v.) *To Providence:* The Hid Treasure; The Man Seeking Pearls; The Rich Fool. [3]

There are also three symbolic narratives:—The Publican and the Pharisee; The Good Samaritan; and Dives and Lazarus—which illustrate (in opposition to Judaism) the essential spirituality, the universal love, and the outward lowliness of Christianity.

We may further notice that the general characteristics of our Lord's parables were influenced by circumstances. In

the brighter period of His ministry, before the enmity of
the Pharisees had developed into deadly opposition, His
parables mainly dwelt on the growth, holiness, and glory of
the kingdom of heaven (Matt. xiii.). After the Transfiguration, and when He fully foresaw the end which awaited
Him, they have stronger elements of warning mixed with
their exhortations (Luke xi.–xiv.). The third series is
more directly judicial and predictive (Luke xix., and in
Matt. xviii.–xxv.). This is specially true of the Parables of
the Rich Fool, the Barren Fig-tree, and the Great Supper,
which convey the most solemn warnings. On the other
hand, the whole depths of Divine tenderness are unfolded
before us in the three Parables of the Lost Sheep, the Lost
Drachm, and the Prodigal Son.* The duties of righteousness and mercy are enforced in the Parables of the Dishonest Steward, Dives and Lazarus, and the Unmerciful
Servant. The peril of self-righteousness is set forth in a
few powerful touches in the Parable of the Pharisee and
the Publican.

While in every parable there is one main central lesson,
there are many touches and incidental details which are
often rich in instruction. Almost every marked phase in
the history of human life comes within the compass of the
story of the Prodigal Son. Yet we must be carefully on
our guard against pressing every incident into the service
of vast structures of theological dogmatism. It is, for
instance, entirely unwarrantable to force the story of the
Rich Man into the proof of the ghastly dogma of endless
torments in hell fire ; and it is a horrible perversion of the
story of the King's Marriage Feast to distort the incidental
phrase "*constrain* them to come in"—as many Roman
Catholic theologians have done—into a command to

---

* Dr. Edersheim contrasts the teaching of Christ, " There is joy in heaven
over one sinner that repenteth," with that of Pharisaism (*Siphrè*, p. 37, 1),
which said, " There is joy before God when those who provoke Him perish
from the world."

practise the atrocities of the Inquisition, and the hellish crime of burning men alive for their religious opinions.*

* See the wise remarks of Archbishop Trench, *On the Parables*, p. 369. Of course, "*constrain* them to come in" means constrain them by moral suasion (2 Tim. iv. 2 ; Matt. xiv. 22). "*Foris* inveniatur necessitas," says St. Chrysostom, "*intus* nascitur voluntas." Calvin wisely says, "Nihil amplius quærendum est quam quod tradere Christi consilium fuit" (on Matt. xx. 1–16).

CHAPTER XXII.

THE SUBSTANCE OF CHRIST'S TEACHING.

"I am the Way, the Truth, and the Life: no man cometh unto the Father but by Me."—JOHN xiv. 6.

"Regnum cælorum quo emitur? Paupertate, regnum; dolore gaudium; labore, requies; vilitate, gloria; morte, vita."—AUGUSTINE, *De Serm. in Morte.*

THE heart of man—which in its hardness and pride is so naturally prepense to all that is worldly—has shown, everywhere and always, a tendency to corrupt the very elements of spiritual religion. Without incessant watchfulness, and unless God sends to age after age His Prophets and Saints —whose usual reward has been the hate, slander, and persecution of their fellow-men—the tendency of all religions has been to sink into formal religiosity. Men think it sufficient to draw nigh unto God with their mouth, and honour Him with their lips, while their hearts are far from Him; and they worship Him in vain because, with innate hypocrisy, they substitute for His requirements the commandments of men.

The one remedy for erring generations and perverted priesthoods, if they have left in them the faintest elements of sincerity, is to go back from the ever-accumulating masses of false human traditions to the teaching of Him whom they profess to worship as their Lord and their God. Much that to this day is taught and paraded as the doctrine of "the church" is in direct and flagrant antagonism to the teaching and example of the Son of God and of His immediate Apostles.

Now, as far as the outward aspect of Judaism was concerned, there were in Christ's days but two prominent

" schools " of religion, namely, those of the Priests and of the Legalists.

Christ entered into no relations with the Priests. He said nothing in commendation of them, or approval of their ideals, or acceptance of their religious views. They were absorbed in selfish worldliness and a ritualism which their insincerity had emptied of its original subordinate significance. The whole body of Priests were Sadducees who had become unspiritual sceptics and worshippers of Mammon. Jesus thought nothing of their pretensions, or of their system. Apart from an allusion to the High Priest Abiathar, who rightly broke the law by giving the shew-bread to David in his hunger, He scarcely mentions priests at all.* In one parable He described the cold-hearted and supercilious formalist who on the way to perform his functions passed with heartless indifference by the wounded wayfarer;† and He told lepers, whom He had already cleansed by His word, to get from the priests the ordinary legal certificate that their leprosy was healed.‡ Otherwise He has nothing to say either *to* them or *of* them, because they had no connection with the essential truths which He came to reveal. They were not teachers at all; they had sunk into mere functionaries who contributed nothing to spiritual religion, or even to elementary morality.

The more numerous and predominant party was that of the Pharisees. Of them we have already spoken, and shall have to speak again later on. All that need here be said is that Christ rejected Pharisaism so utterly that, whereas to all others His words were full of merciful tenderness, He was compelled again and again to denounce in burning utterances—which have been shown to be necessary in each successive generation—the deep-rooted hypocrisies of these haughty and pretentious formalists.

What Christ with unvarying consistency taught, both by

* Mark ii. 26 ; Luke vi. 4.   † Luke x. 31.
‡ Matt. viii. 4 ; Luke v. 14.

His words and His example, was *inward reality, not outward conformities.* His religious practices were marked by undeviating simplicity. He taught that the kingdom of God is *within* us, and that it consists not in meats and drinks, but in righteousness, peace, and joy in believing. He taught that the kingdom of God is not eating and drinking, but holiness, and love, and joy in the Holy Ghost. He taught that it is not the food which goeth into a man which defiles him, but the evil thoughts which come out of him. Thus, by one word, "He made all meats clean."* He would have said with Jeremiah, "Thus said the Lord of Hosts, Add your burnt offerings unto your sacrifices and eat flesh. For I spake not unto your fathers, nor commanded them in the day when I brought them out of the land of Egypt concerning burnt-offerings or sacrifices: but this thing I commanded them, saying, Obey My Voice."†

Again, the Pharisees delighted in outward ablutions—hand-washings and the washing of cups and platters and brazen vessels and tables. For such practices Christ had no word of recognition, and many words of disparagement. The whole of what He had to reveal bore on the essence of heart-reality and spiritual pureness. We shall see hereafter some of the minute and tortuous regulations on which the Pharisees insisted in the matter of fasts and ablutions. Christ practised no formal fast, and discouraged His disciples from doing so; He despised the hand-washings and ablutions of cups and platters which had nothing to do with cleanliness, but only with religious formalism. For those who desire to learn of Him, religion will be the love of God shown in love to man, and rites and ceremonies will sink into the most infinitesimal proportions. There

---

* Mark vii. 19.

† Jer. vii. 21–23. In other words " though burnt-offerings are usually consumed by fire, as given to Jehovah, yet eat them as though they were mere flesh." They are *nothing* to God without justice and kindness.

is no true piety except such as consists in the bond of union between God and man—that direct and immediate relation of the personal creature to the personal Creator by which all true life can alone be determined.

Without heart-sincerity, and rectitude of life, all forms, however ancient, are worthless. It is dangerous to elaborate and magnify the outward ceremonies of worship when they tend (as they too often do) to breed self-deceit, supercilious arrogance, and opinionated lawlessness. It is of no use to be free from outward crimes if the heart be unclean; it is of no use to abstain from murder if the thoughts be full of hatred, and the words full of rage and slander; it is of no use even to do good works if they are only done to obtain the applause or approval of men. Christ evidently regards the Levitic law, whatever may have been its date and origin, as given to the Israelites because of the hardness of their hearts, and as consisting intrinsically in " weak and beggarly rudiments," fitted only to train the disobedient childhood of the race. He came to abrogate it all. " It hath been said to them of old time—but I say unto you." * The essential conception of holiness from henceforth was to be faith and love towards God and the exhibition of that faith and love in constant service to our brethren who are in the world. And the chief means of attaining to this height was prayer—not formal prayers, verbose, stereotyped, wearisome, and interminable, abounding in vain repetitions and artificial phrases; not prayers accompanied, like those of Dervishes and Stylites, with endless crossings, prostrations, and genuflexions—but brief prayers of humble, simple, and trustful earnestness.

All this teaching had become most necessary. The Jews had abandoned the idolatry of false gods during the seventy years of disastrous exile; but almost from the days of their restoration they began to fall into a new idolatry— the worship of the symbol and the letter. While they

* Matt. v. 21, 23.

professed to deify the Law, they emptied it of all its significance, and with cunning casuistry managed to evade its most searching requirements.* The result was a mixture of arrogant tyranny and spiritual uselessness—it was that common form of religionism which may be defined as "self-complacency flavoured by a comprehensive uncharitableness." Religious attitudinising ended in a hypocritic life; a terrible obliquity of moral precepts and conduct; a deplorable confusion of holiness with Levitic purity, and of sin with ceremonial defilements; a futile attempt to extort Divine favour by a mass of observances while it was disgracefully indifferent to inward holiness.† If any regard this view of Pharisaism as too severe, let me remind them that the Lord of Love characterised its votaries as "fools and blind"; as "the offspring of vipers"; devouring widows' houses, and for a pretence making long prayers; as washing the outside of the cup and of the platter, while within they were full of extortion and uncleanness.

The Sermon on the Mount was the promulgation of the laws of Christ's new kingdom. Conceive what the Sermon on the Mount would have been if it had been delivered by Caiaphas the Priest, or Simon the Pharisee, or any of their modern representatives! Would it not have been full of priestly usurpations, and petty orthodoxies, and the small proprieties of the infinitely little? Would it not have been deplorably empty of moral manliness and spiritual freedom? Christ touched on none of these things. Apart from two sacraments, accompanied by rites of the most elementary simplicity, He did not lay down one liturgical ordinance, or ceremonial injunction, or priestly tradition, or Pharisaic observance. No, but He pronounced beatitudes on the meek and the loving, and precepts of self-denial, and inculcations of tenderness and sympathy. So

---

* See Schürer, i. 313–323, ii. 120–125. *Scribes* (Kitto and Smith).
† See Schürer, ii. 91–106.

broad, so simple, so free, so eternal and natural, are the essentials of real saintliness; so universal are the sole requirements of Him who said, "Learn of Me, for I am meek and lowly of heart, and ye shall find rest unto your souls." To wash the hands in innocency, and so to come to God's altar—that is sainthood. To have the heart sprinkled from an evil conscience, void of offence toward God and toward man—that is sainthood. To behold the face of our brother in love; to be pure, peaceable, gentle; to bring forth the fruits of the Spirit, which are love, joy, peace, long-suffering, gentleness, goodness, faith, meekness, temperance—*that* is the only sainthood of which Christ set the example, which Christ approves, which Christ will reward for ever.

CHAPTER XXIII.

THE UNIQUENESS OF CHRIST'S TEACHING.

τί 'εστί τοῦτο ; Διδαχὴ καινὴ.—MARK i. 27.

" Christianus miser *videri potest, inveniri* non potest."—MINUC.
FEL. *Oct.* 37.

> " What if earth
> Be but the shadow of heaven, and things therein
> Each to the other like more than on earth is thought ? "
> —MILTON.

THE broad eternal characteristic of the teaching of the
Lord of Life was that it ignored all that was not spiritual
and essential. It constantly insisted on two fundamental
truths—the infinite love of God, and the moral duty of man.
We see the depth and uniqueness of Christ's teaching, as
well as the unequalled power of its methods, illustrated
from the first in the eight opening beatitudes with which He
began to train the disciples and the assembled multitudes.
" They may be regarded," says Dr. Plummer, " as an anal-
ysis of perfect spiritual well-being, and nowhere in non-
Christian literature shall we find so sublime a summary of
the felicity attainable by man. They correct all low and
carnal views of human happiness. They do not describe
eight different classes of people, but eight different elements
of excellence, and may all be contained in one and the same
man."

Christ had nothing to say to the wretched questions
which now agitate and distract Church parties. There is
not the slightest allusion to his having ever used a purification for ceremonial uncleanness. His only reference to
Jewish sacrificial worship was **in** His repeated reference to

the Prophet Hoshea, "I will have mercy and not sacrifice."
He swept away with a divine scorn the idolatry of symbols.
He was not in the most distant degree interested in "the
sorts and qualities of sacrificial wood," or "the right burning of the two kidneys and the fat." It is hardly possible
to conceive the immeasurable disdain with which such
questions as crowd the Talmud, and fill whole reams of
religious literature, would have been regarded by the Son
of God. All that He had to say of the formalism which
the ignorant people confounded with saintliness, was that
they who practised it had made the word of God of none
effect by their traditions. His attitude to the ceremonial
Law was that it was obsolete and abrogated. The popular
religion had filled it with falsities and emptied it of meaning. He came to purge it from useless trivialities and to
substitute for it righteousness and true holiness. Nothing
was more abhorrent to Him than the notion that the
Infinite, Eternal, Almighty Father cared for, or was to be
propitiated by external scrupulosities. Of what use, He
asked, was the outward glistering of the whitewashed
grave, which within was full of dead men's bones and all
uncleanness?

We see the essence of His teaching in His first great
discourse. It has been well described as an answer to the
question, "What ought to be a man's daily care upon
earth?" The answer is to be found in the one word,
Whole-heartedness. A double-souled man ($\delta i\psi v\chi o s$) is, as
St. James says, "unstable in all his ways." He falls into
the countless host of trimmers, who are content to be one
hundredth part for God, and ninety-nine parts for themselves and for the world. These are the mammon-wor-
shippers and the self-worshippers, who devote themselves
to greed, envy, self-importance, and the indulgence of their
own guilty passions.

But God will be content with no scant and divided service. Therefore Christ set Himself to teach us, Let your

treasure be with your heart, in heaven. Be in no wise anxious about the things of this world. If you are seeking with all your strength the approval of God, care nothing for the hate or scorn of men. Trust implicitly in God's infinite goodness. For His sake love your brethren who are in the world. Regard *all* men as your brethren, pardoning and loving even the worst, and leaving them to God's merciful judgment, not to that of your own spiritual conceit. Above all, beware of secret hypocrisy. Sanctimonious externalism may deceive men; it cannot deceive God. Religion is not Pharisaism; it is to love God with all your heart and your neighbour as yourself. This is the Law and the Prophets, and he who builds on *this* foundation builds upon a rock, and the house of his life can never be swept away by any earthly storms.

By living up to this teaching we shall find that the Kingdom of Heaven is now established upon earth. It is written, "Seek ye first the Kingdom of God and His righteousness, and all else shall be added unto you." *

And this is illustrated by the attitude of our Lord toward the ancient Scriptures. The people, as they heard Him, might well exclaim, "What is this? A new teaching!" In direct antithesis to the inferences which the tortuous ingenuity of men had forced out of the Law of Moses by putting it on the rack to their own destruction, He taught that all forms of righteousness were worthless, all precepts of righteousness insignificant, unless they rule the conduct, and dominate the heart. So far, indeed, from coming to destroy the Law and the Prophets, His object was to give them their sole valid and permanent significance.

As regards the moral law, which Rabbinism, even in fundamental matters, often contrived to evade, He taught that it could only be fulfilled by fidelity to God in the inmost thoughts. From quantitative extensions of ordi-

* Matt. vi. 33. See Wendt, i. 267.

nance He recalled the thoughts of men to central obligations. Instead of the allegorising casuistry of the Jewish
fourfold exegesis, the Rabbinic PARDES, *i. e.*, the *Peshat* or
explanation, the *Remez* or " hint," the *Darush* or homiletic
inference, the *Sod* or " mystery "—and the fourfold arguments and Seven *Middoth* or " Rules " of Hillel *—He
bade men study the innermost meaning of the word of
God. He appealed most often to the Prophets, and rati-
fied their sweeping depreciation of the whole ceremonial
Law when its requirements are made a substitute for true
religion. Prophecy had long been dead in Israel, as it
always dies when sacerdotalism reigns. " The creative
period had ceased," even "the interpretative period " had
ceased ; what now prevailed was the period of false literalism, mingled with ingenious perversions. The living voice
had long been silent ; it had been replaced by " spent
echoes, broken into confused and inarticulate sound."
The pool of popular religion had become turbid, as it must
do when it is not flushed by the living streams of that
river of inspiration which maketh glad the city of God.
The surface glitter of the Dead Sea shore does but hide
the blight and barrenness beneath. It has been said that
" what Jesus really did was to give utterance to a new
principle, which explains all His teaching and furnishes
the key to the mystery of His own religious genius. This
great principle may be described, according to the side
from which it is approached, as the Worth of Man, or the
Love of God." †

The whole of religion must ultimately and essentially
depend on the ideas which we form of God, and it is in
their mean and narrow conceptions of God that all false
religions, and all perversions and degradations of true
religion, have gone astray.

* Rabbi Ishmael expanded the Rule into thirteen, for which see Hershon,
Talm. Miscell. p. 166.

† Van Oort, v. 221.

If, with the Sadducees, we hold that there is no resurrection, neither angel nor spirit, we shall try to line our pockets well in the world, and with complete insouciance to go through certain functions whether we believe in their efficacy or not ; and with Caiaphas and his brother-priests we shall be ready to commit any crime if we regard it as "expedient" for our interests, or our party, and for the maintenance of the present state of things which we regard as advantageous to ourselves.

If we be cruel and wrathful, we shall conceive of God as the Egyptian conceived of his Typhon, or the Moabite of his Chemosh, and shall suppose that He is a terrific, suprahuman monster, a

> "Moloch, horrid King, besmeared with blood
> Of human sacrifice, and parents' tears ;
> Though, for the noise of drums and timbrels loud,
> Their children's cries unheard who passed thro' fire
> To His grim idol."

If we be jealously wrapped up in the serene infallibility of our own opinionated ignorance, and determined to crush all freedom of thought in order that we may keep our own usurped power over the hearts and consciences of our fellow-men, we shall be ready to rekindle the accursed balefires of Smithfield or of Seville, and to blacken the golden light of heaven with the smoke of hell, to get rid of men who are wiser and holier than ourselves.

If we be dwarfed, and petty, and exacting in our conceptions, we shall multiply fantastic obligations till they become like a mountain suspended by a single hair of false teaching; and we shall slander, and belittle, and persecute all who see deeper into the reality of things than ourselves. We shall look upon our whole relation to God as a sort of small bargaining in which we shall be repaid exact equivalents for all our tithes of mint, and anise, and cumin. What becomes of others who do not pay them we shall not greatly care, but shall say with the Pharisees, "This people that knoweth not the Law is accursed."

If our hearts be full of gloom and self-absorbed individualism—if we never raise our eyes upwards from our own unworthiness, but regard God as a sternly pitiless Avenger, dealing with us after our sins, rewarding us after our iniquities, and never appeased till we have paid the uttermost farthing—then we shall adopt an exaggerated asceticism, and shut ourselves up in a half-dazed seclusion equally injurious to ourselves and useless to the world.

Now He who came from the bosom of the Father to reveal Him repudiated all such corruptions. He taught the Fatherhood of God towards all His creatures. He taught man

> " to turn
> To the deep sky, and from its splendours learn
> By stars, by sunsets, by soft clouds that rove
> Its blue expanse, or sleep in silvery rest,
> That nature's God hath left no place unblest
> With founts of beauty for the eye of love."

This was His essential revelation. He pointed to this as the teaching of Nature. Doth not God cause His sun to shine on the evil and on the good, and send His rain to the just and to the unjust? Doth He not clothe the lilies of the field, though they toil not, neither do they spin, with a glory surpassing the magnificence of Solomon? Doth He not feed the ravens, though they neither sow nor reap, nor gather into barns? Doth He not care even for each one of the millions of feeble sparrows, so that not one of them falleth to the ground without His will?

And if this be the revelation of Nature, how much more is it the revelation of Grace? Hence the Parable of the Prodigal Son represents the essence of Christ's teaching as to the relation of God to men. The wild, dissolute youth had flung away the love and left the holy home of his father; had hastened into the far country; had there lived the life of a riotous, self-indulgent debauchee, disgracing the name he bore, and devouring his living with harlots; and he had sunk by inevitable retribution into contempt and misery.   Deserted by his fair-weather friends the moment when nothing more was to be got out of him, he had passed from extravagant luxury into abject serfdom.   In the lowest abyss of his degradation, he had been sent into the fields to feed swine; and, since it was no longer possible to sate the gnawing of his hunger, he would fain at least have filled his belly with the coarse carob-pods which were the food of swine; yet even of these no man gave unto him.   It was only when he had sounded the uttermost abyss of misery that he thought of his loving father, and of his lost home, and of his willing forfeiture of all that he had received of nobleness and grace, once more took possession of his thoughts.   He " came to himself." He had abandoned, he had done his utmost to destroy and obliterate, his *true* self.   But though the light of grace may dwindle to a spark, and the lamp of the Holy Spirit within us be almost quenched, it cannot be *wholly* lost in this life, or man would sink irredeemably into a beast or a demon.   In this awful catastrophe the poor, lost youth determined to fling himself unreservedly on his father's love, and to plead for readmission into the home of his early innocence—no longer as a son, but as a hired servant.   So he arose and returned; and while he was yet a long way off his father saw him, and ran to meet him with the outstretched arms of infinite compassion, and kissed him tenderly; and when the son had sobbed forth upon his neck the confession of his despairing penitence, the father ordered the best robe to be brought at once to cover his swinish rags, and the fatted calf to be killed for his banquet.

This is the picture of God's full, free, unconditioned forgiveness to all who seek Him, and call upon Him, and repent of their old sins.   There is no question of reparation; no demand for the equivalent payment of a debt; no

claim for the pound of flesh ; no requirement of a "substitute "; no need for the intrusion of intermediaries ; but,
as a father pitieth his own children, even so is the Lord
pitiful to them that fear Him.   The prodigal's anguish of
loving penitence was dearer to the father's heart than the
prim, loveless, quantitative goodness and unlovely spite of
the elder son, who was still far astray and saw no need for
repentance.   And all this, let us observe, was taught with a
simplicity which a child might understand.   It was not expanded into vast folios of a *Summa Theologiæ*.   It was not
thrown into rigid and technical formulæ.   It was set forth
in words exquisitely beautiful as a simple, eternal, transcendent truth, clothed in a form intelligible to the humblest
and least instructed souls, yet full of sublime meanings
inexhaustible by men of the loftiest genius.

Was it wonderful if, after having become familiar with
such teaching, St. Peter should exclaim on behalf of all the
Apostles, "Lord, to whom shall we go? Thou hast the
words of eternal life."

In this relation of *God to man* was implicitly involved the
duty of *man to God*.   The first step towards the Kingdom
of Heaven was to realise the truth that love to God necessitated the feeling of brotherhood to man.   When the can-
did Scribe recognised that the Ten Commandments were
summed up in Two, and said, "Of a truth, Master, Thou
hast well said that there is none other but God ; and to love
Him with all the heart, and to love his neighbour as himself, is much more than all whole burnt-offerings and sacrifices," Jesus said unto him, "Thou art not far from the
kingdom of God."*

This was the practical summary of Christ's earliest teaching.   He pointed out the secret of salvation ; the inmost
essence of love and joy and peace.   This is the Magna
Charta of the Kingdom of Heaven.   The Beatitudes reversed
all the judgments of the world, as well as of the Sadducees
and of the Scribes.   They set forth the four virtues of

* Mark xii. 34.

humility, holy sorrow, meekness, and yearning after righteousness ; and the virtues of mercy, purity, peaceableness,
and the endurance of persecution and reproach.   Thus did
Jesus cancel, revise, or fill with far deeper spiritual reality
the moral teaching of the world.   He showed that what the
world regarded as misery might not only lead to, but actually
be, the present fulness of holy joy.   God's blessing rests not
on the arrogant, and the self-satisfied, but on the seekers
after God, and those who with pure hearts devote their
lives to works of compassion, in saving the world from corruption, and setting a shining example to its slaves and
votaries.   He extended the obligations of the Decalogue to
the thoughts of the heart.   The essence of murder consists
in hatred, in unreasoning anger, and bitter speech ; the true
fulfilment of the sixth commandment lies in peace towards
all men.   The essence of adultery lies in dissolute imagina-
tions, and no sacrifice is too severe which is required for the
attainment of inward purity.   The *lex talionis*—a concession to wild and unprotected times—may be reversed by a
spirit of non-resistance and self-suppression.   Love, which
the Rabbis had confined to love of our neighbours, must be
extended to our enemies.   Ostentation in well-doing, or in
alms-giving, corrupts all its blessedness.   Prayer must be
humble, secret, sincere, free from vain repetitions, the outcome of an intense longing to fulfil God's law.   Desire for
earthly treasure must be superseded by a love for God
which expels minor affections, and a trust in God which
excludes the possibility of earthly anxieties.   For the cen-
soriousness which is ever passing judgment on others, the
children of the kingdom must aim at the sincerity which is
only severe to our own shortcomings.   God's mercy and
lovingkindness are infinite, and as we rely on His bounty
for ourselves, we must show the same to others.   "Narrow
is the gate and straitened the way" which leads to the
attainment of these aims.*   We must never suffer ourselves
to be turned from that narrow gate, or driven out of that

* Matt. vii. 14.

strait path. We must judge of religion not by its demon-
strativeness, but by its fruits. Love, obedience, sincerity,
simplicity—these are the eternal bases of the spiritual life.

The only superstructure of religion which can ever abide
the rush of the whirlwind and the sweeping of the flood is
that which is built on the words and deeds of the Son of
Man. Alike in form and substance His teaching stands
alone. It is at once radiantly simple, and unutterably profound. It is, as St. Augustine said, like a great ocean on
whose surface is the $\dot{\alpha}\nu\eta\rho\iota\vartheta\mu\grave{o}\nu$ $\gamma\acute{e}\lambda\alpha\sigma\mu\alpha$, the " ever-twin-
kling smile " which charms even children, yet whose depths
are unfathomable.* It bears upon it a certain ineffable
stamp of divinity which Priests and Pharisees have often
perverted; but which no human being—no Prophet who
came before Jesus, no Apostle or Evangelist, who followed
Him ; no Gentile philosopher, no Eastern Theosophist, no
self-satisfied Agnostic, no modern enquirer with all the
learning and wisdom of the world to draw from at his will
—has ever been able in the most distant degree to equal,
much less to surpass. Many have uttered wise words, and
written noble books ; but either they have soon been comparatively forgotten, or have only reached the few. The
simplest words of Christ have been as arrows of lightnings
which still quiver in the hearts of millions of every race, as
they have done in every age, and which are blessedly powerful to heal the very wounds which they inflict on the
awakened consciences of men.

* Aug. *Conf.* xii. 14.

CHAPTER XXIV.

THE TITLES OF JESUS AND THE BROTHERHOOD OF MAN.

" The first man, Adam, became a living soul ; the last Adam became a life-giving spirit."—1 Cor. xv. 45.

OUR Lord used various titles to describe Himself.

He called Himself " the Christ," *i. e.*, the Messiah, the Anointed One, anointed by the grace of God to preach the Gospel to the poor.* At an earlier period of the ministry He did not wish His Messiahship to be openly proclaimed (Mark viii. 31), and He separated from the idea of Messiahship the notion of *earthly* kingship.† The Messianic faith was a desire, a hope, a promise, and Jesus fulfilled this idea.‡

He alludes to His Davidic descent, and was often addressed by others as the *Son of David.*§

He sometimes spoke of Himself as the Son of God ; ‖ but this title was generally given Him by others.¶ Once

---

* More distinctly at the close of His ministry (Matt. xxiii. 8, xxiv. 5; Mark ix. 41, xi. 10).

† Mark x. 42; Luke xii. 14.

‡ Hausrath, ii. 223.

§ Matt. ix. 27, xii. 23, xv. 22, xx. 30, xxi. 9, etc.; Mark x. 47, xi. 10; John vii. 42. Com. Rom. i. 3. On this title, see Dalman, *Die Worte Jesu*, pp. 260–266.

‖ Matt. xi. 27, xxvi. 63, 64, xxvii. 43; Mark xiii. 32, xiv. 61; Luke x. 21, 22; John i. 16–18, iii. 35, 36, v. 20–26, vi. 40, viii. 35, 36, ix. 35, x. 36, xiv. 13, xvii. 1. St. Matthew records the prophecy of Isaiah (vii. 14) in which Jesus is called Emmanuel—" God with us "—not merely σύν ἡμῖν (of accompaniment), but μεθ' ἡμῶν (" God *in* the common nature of us all ").

¶ By the Angel Gabriel (Luke i. 35); by John the Baptist (John i. 34): by Nathanael (John i. 50); by St. Peter (John vi. 69; Matt. xvi. 16); by Martha (John xi. 27); by Satan (Matt. iv. 3, 6): by the multitude (Mark xv. 39; by demoniacs (Matt. viii. 29; Mark v. 7); by the centurion (Matt. xxvii. 54); by

only, in St. John, He describes Himself as "the Paraclete," or Divine Advocate.* He does not use of Himself the title of " The Chosen One " (Luke ix. 35, xxiii. 35).†

The remarkable designation of " The Word " is given to Christ by St. John alone (John i. 14). As he opens his Gospel with the phrase, " In the beginning," which is also the first word in the Book of Genesis (*Bereshîth*), the title may be a reference to the truth that "the worlds were made by the Word of God." Christ was the Incarnate Word. Philo had written much of the Logos, but without the most distant approach to any conception that the Word could could ever "be made flesh, and dwell among us." In the Targums—ancient paraphrases of the Hebrew Scriptures—"the action of God is constantly, though not consistently, referred to His Word (*Memra* and *Deburah*)." In the Talmudic writings we find the *Metatron*, a sort of divine intermediary between God and man. In the Apocryphal books of the præ-Christian epoch we find " Wisdom " spoken of repeatedly as a person ; even in the Pentateuch and the Prophets we find mention of " the Angel of the Presence " (Gen. xxxii. 24 ; Ex. xxxiii. 12 ; Hos. xii. 4; Is. lxiii. 9, etc.). St. John was doubtless well aware of these unconscious, or half-conscious, prophecies; but the identification of "the Word" with the Man Christ Jesus transcends all that had previously been thought or written.‡ St. John was inspired to reveal with perfect

the disciples (Matt. xiv. 33; John xx. 31); by the Evangelists (Mark i. 1; John i. 18); by the voice from heaven (Matt. xvii. 5). In the Apocalyptic literature the Messiah is regarded as the Son of God. Enoch cv. 2; 4 Esdras viii. 28, xiii. 32, 37, 52, xiv. 9. See Schürer, ii. 11, 158. Comp. Mark xii. 35–37.

*Comp. Job xiv. 16; Matt. xxviii. 19. The word " Paraclete," or Advocate, is only found in St. John—" Christ as the Advocate pleads the believer's cause with the Father against the Accuser Satan (1 John ii. 1); the Holy Spirit pleads the believer's cause against the world and also its cause with the believer" (John xiv. 26, xv. 26). Westcott.

† Comp. Is. xliii. 10; 1 Peter ii. 4.

‡ On the whole subject, see Bp. Westcott's *Introd. to the Gospel of St. John*, pp. xv. ff.

clearness that "the personal Being of the Word was realised in active intercourse and in perfect communion with God," and at the same time in historic manifestation and nearest spiritual influence upon the hearts of men.

But the designation which Christ ordinarily adopted, and which He chose for Himself, was "the Son of Man."

There may be in this title a dim and indirect allusion to Dan. vii. 13, where the word is *Bar-Enosh*. The phrase is used ninety times of the Prophet Ezekiel, though he never applies it to himself. Christ used it eighty times, and always of Himself. It is only applied to Him by others in passages which, like Acts vii. 56, Rev. i. 13–20, imply His exaltation. But since in Dan. vii. 13 this phrase is explained to be equivalent to "the saints of the Most High," in antithesis to "the beasts" who represent the kingdoms of the world, the allusion to Daniel could only be very indirect. The prophet does not speak of "*the* Son of Man," but of "one *like* a son of man." In the later Jewish Apocalypses—the Psalms of Solomon, the Book of Enoch, and the Apocalypse of Baruch—the Messiah is indeed a Person, a King and Judge; but not in the Book of Daniel. "The Second Man is the Lord from heaven." That the title was not a synonym for "the Messiah" seems to be proved by the question, "Who do men say that I the Son of Man am?"*

Upon the lips of Christ the title had a very deep meaning, which throws light on His entire mission and revelations. He used the phrase "*The* Son of Man" to imply His federal Headship of Humanity, as one whom God had highly exalted because of His self-humiliation in taking our flesh (Phil. ii. 6–11). It called attention to Him as "the Second Adam," who came to restore the Eden lost by the sins of the First Adam. In the Old Testament the phrase "Son of Man" had been constantly used to represent man in his feebleness, man in his nothingness before

* Matt. xvi. 13; Mark viii. 37; Luke ix. 18.

the Majesty of God;* and Jesus adopted it because, in all senses and to the full, He came to bear our griefs and to carry our sorrows, while nevertheless He came as the Ideal, as the Representative, of Humanity in all its possible nobleness, when it has been forgiven, redeemed, and filled with the Holy Spirit of God. "The Son of God," says St. Augustine, "was made the Son of Man, that ye who were sons of men might be made sons of God." He came as the divine yet human Brother of the whole human race; as the Elder Brother in the great family of man. He came to extend to all mankind that infinite tenderness which the particularism of the Jews had supposed to be confined to the sons of their own nation. In the Old Testament God by the voice of His Prophets had addressed words of tender, compassionate affection to the children of Israel. He had said :

> " As an eagle stirreth up her nest,
> Fluttereth over her young,
> Spreadeth abroad her wings,
> Taketh them, beareth them on her wings,
> So the Lord alone did lead him." †

He had said—

" Is Ephraim My dear son ? is he a pleasant child ? for since I spake against him, I do earnestly remember him still. Therefore My heart is troubled for him ; I will surely have mercy upon him, saith the Lord." ‡

---

* Num. xxiii. 19–22; Ps. viii. 4: "What is man that Thou art mindful of him, *and the Son of Man* that Thou so regardest him? Man is like a thing of nought, his time passeth away like a shadow." Job xxv. 6 : "How much less man that is a worm; and *the son of man* that is a worm ? " Is. li. 12: " *The son of man* that shall be made as grass" (comp. Ps. cxlvi. 3) Ezekiel (ii. 1, 3) had, perhaps, chosen this designation to emphasise " the self-reflection as to the distance between God and him." But though the title *Ben-Adam* is applied to him nearly ninety times, he never used it of himself. *Ben-Adam* may apply to any man (Job xxv. 6, etc.). The Chaldee *Bar-Enosh*, " son of man in his frailty," is found in Daniel (vii. 13, etc.). *Beni ish,* " filii viri," is found in Ps. iv. 3, xlix. 2, etc., for highborn or wealthy men.

† Deut. xxxii. 11.   ‡ Jer. xxxi. 20.

He had said—

"They shall be Mine, saith the Lord of Hosts, in that day when I make up My jewels, and I will spare them as a man spareth his own son that serveth him." *

But the Son of Man had come to reveal that God has no favourites ; that He is the merciful and loving Father of *all* the race of man ; that He has not merely flung us into the chaos of a wretched and inexplicable existence by the unimpeded operation of blind laws, "dark as night, inexorable as destiny, merciless as death, which have no ear to hear, no heart to pity, no arm to save" ; but that "His tender mercy is over all His works" ; and that, above all, "the Spirit which He made to dwell in us yearneth over us even to jealous envy," † and "maketh intercession for us with groanings which cannot be uttered." ‡

Nothing could have been more radically subversive of the current Jewish views in their narrow exclusiveness than this teaching of the Son of Man, and the way in which He illustrated it by all the relations of His life. The religion of man is essentially dependent on the ideas which it cherishes of God and of Man. The Pharisees had degraded both conceptions. To them God was a Being who chiefly delighted in nullities ; and on the majority of men they looked down from the inch-high pedestal of their own imaginary superiority.

Alike by all His words and all His deeds the Son of Man came to sweep away this sandhill of pretentious ignorance, and to substitute for it the Eternal Temple of the Living God.§

Hence the unlimited kindness, courtesy, forbearance, respect which He observed always to all sorts and conditions of men, in the world. The poet says that :

---

* Mal. iii. 17.   † James iv. 5.
‡ Rom. viii. 26.   § Hos. vi. 6 ; Matt. v. 17, vii. 18, ix. 13, xii. 7.

> " Not a man for being simply man
>   Hath any honour; but honour for those honours
>   Which are without him, as place, riches, favour—
>   Prizes of accident as oft as merit."

But the bearing of the Son of Man alike to the high and to the low, to the rich and to the poor, to the sick and to the sound, to the gifted and to the ignorant, was always full of that infinite respect for the work of God's hands which founded the brotherhood of men upon the living rock of the fatherhood of God. He called Himself the Son of Man, because, as the representative of all that is beautiful and good in human nature, He came to restore to man that ineffaceable dignity which he had forfeited and lost.*

(i.) Nothing could be more virulent than the hatred of the Jews for the *Samaritans*, which still continues, and which naturally provoked the most violent reprisals. A little tact, a little conciliatoriness on the part of the Jews, even in the days of Ezra and Nehemiah, might have obviated the miseries which arose from this age-long friction. If the Samaritans denied all hospitality to Jewish pilgrims; † if they were ready to refuse even a cup of cold water, which the primary principle of Eastern hospitality required; if they mocked, and attacked, and sometimes slew, those who were on their way to the Jewish feasts; if they caused confusion and irregularity by mock fire-signals at Passovertide; if some of their fanatics had even stolen into the Temple, when the gates were open at midnight during the Feast, to render the Passover impossible by strewing the Temple with dead men's bones,‡—the Jews were in no small measure to blame for this deep-seated animosity. They

---

* Jesus applies to Himself the word ἄνθρωπος (*homo*), a human being (John viii. 40. Comp. 2 Tim. ii. 25). The word ἀνὴρ (*Vir*, a man in his personal dignity) is applied to Him by the Baptist (John i. 30), by Cleopas (Luke xxiv. 19), and by St. Paul (Acts xvii. 31). See Canon Mason, *The Conditions of our Lord's Life on Earth*, pp. 46–48.

† Luke ix. 3.

‡ Jos. *Antt.* xviii. 2, 2. Comp. xx. 6, 1 ; *B. J.* ii. 12, 6. See *ante*, p. 139

had admitted into one of their half-sacred books the passage :

" There be two manner of nations which my heart abhorreth ; and the the third is no nation. They that sit upon the mountain of Samaria, and they that dwell among the Philistines, and that foolish people that dwell in Sichem." *

In our Lord's time, to call a man "a Samaritan" was as bad as to call him a demoniac.† Samaritans were regarded as excommunicate and accursed ; they were denied all share in the Resurrection ; it was doubtful whether it was lawful to partake of any of the produce of their soil ; to eat their bread was like eating the flesh of swine ; and their women were despised as specially abhorrent.‡

Yet the Son of Man, as in the hot noonday He sat "thus" by Jacob's well, did not for a moment hesitate to ask drink of a poor sinful woman of Samaria ; to speak to her with uttermost kindness ; to reveal to her—and to her *first*—His Messiahship ; to preach to, and stay among her hated and heretical countrymen, making no difference between them and the dwellers in Holy Jerusalem. Nay, even when He and His disciples were churlishly rejected, and refused ordinary hospitality at the border village of Engannim, and when "the Sons of Thunder," in their impetuous indignation, wanted Him to call down fire from heaven upon them, even as Elijah did, He at once, without a gleam of resentment against the churlish villagers, turned and rebuked James and John with the words, "Ye know not of what spirit ye are, ye. For the Son of Man came not to destroy men's lives, but to save." § Very shortly after this He pronounced His pathetic eulogy on the only one of the ten cleansed lepers who returned to give Him thanks, and he was a Samaritan.‖ And, more even than

* Ecclus. l. 25, 26.   † John viii. 48.
‡ *Pirqe, R. Eliezer*, 38 ; *Book of Jubilee*, 30, quoted by Hausrath, i. 26. See, too, Schürer, Div. ii. 1, p. 8.
§ Luke ix. 55.   ‖ Luke xvii. 16.

this, He chose the hated and heretical Samaritan as a model of right action to mocking Scribes, cold-hearted Priests, and unmerciful Levites.*

(ii.) For *the Gentiles* also He showed the same large considerateness. He was indeed primarily sent to "the lost sheep of the House of Israel." But when the Gentile centurion of Capernaum came to Him, relying on the mere utterance of His word, and not deeming himself worthy that He should enter under his roof, the Son of Man not only granted his petition, but added, "I have not found so great faith, no, not in Israel." † He seemed, indeed, to chill the urgency of the poor Syro-Phœnician woman, but it was only because He desired to evoke and to crown the indomitable resoluteness of her faith. ‡ He unfavourably contrasted His own generation in their hard unbelief with the people of Nineveh, and the Queen of the South, and the widow of Sarepta, and declared that it should be better for Tyre and Sidon, yea, even for Sodom and Gomorrha, in the Day of Judgment, than for Chorazin and Bethsaida, and His own Capernaum. § And when some Gentiles who had come to His last Passover—"certain Greeks "—came to Philip to find some way of arranging a meeting with Him, so far from coldly and haughtily repudiating their desire, He rejoiced in this sign that the hour was come that the Son of Man should be glorified.‖ He had declared, long before, in language of unprecedented—and to His Jewish hearers, of repellent—strangeness, that "many a Gentile should be admitted into the kingdom of heaven: but the children of the kingdom should be cast out."¶ These were preliminary indications of the vast mission which He left to be carried out after His departure: "Go ye into all the world and preach the Gospel, and make disciples of all the nations." ** The Chosen

* Luke x. 28–37. † Matt. viii. 10. ‡ Matt. xv. 21–28.
§ Matt. xi. 20–24. ‖ John xii. 20–23.
¶ Matt. viii. 12 ; Luke xiii. 28, 29. ** Matt. xxviii. 19.

People had rejected Him, and Crucified Him to their own destruction ; thenceforth His servants were to go forth into the highways and hedges and constrain to come in even the poor, and the maimed, and the blind, and the lame.

In the Eternal Temple of Christ there was no *Chel* or *Soreg*, with inscriptions threatening death to any Gentile who dared to enter, and by entering to pollute, the hallowed enclosure. The middle wall of partition was broken down ; nay, the veil of the Temple was rent in twain from the top to the bottom, and free access was given into its very Holy of Holies to the more genuine priesthood of all who were pure in heart. The Jews regarded all Gentiles as utterly unclean, and all intercourse with them as a source of ceremonial pollution. The Jews, as St. Paul says, were " contrary to all men." * It was unlawful for a Jew to enter the house of a Gentile or to hold any close communion with him.† The Talmudic treatise, *Avoda Zara*,‡ directs that if a Jew brought so much as a stone or a gridiron from a Gentile, it must be made red-hot before it could be accounted clean, and it was illegal even to drink milk if a heathen had milked the cow.§ What a tremendous reversal of such " religious " conceptions was the declaration that Gentiles from the East and the West should be preferred to Jews, and sit down with Abraham, Isaac, and Jacob themselves at the marriage supper of the Lamb !‖

(iii.) No less deep was Christ's tender regard for the poor, the destitute, the ignorant, the physically wretched, those of whom men spoke as " common people," and " the vulgar multitude " :

> " Of men the common rout
> That, wandering loose about,
> Grow up and perish as the summer fly,
> Heads without name, no more rememberèd."

* Thess. ii. 15.　　　　　　　† Acts x. 28 ; John xviii. 28.
‡ Zara v. 12.　　　　　　　　§ *Id*. ii. 6.
‖ Comp. Acts xi. 18. The feeling of the Jews against Gentiles is illustrated in Acts xiii. 45 ; 1 Thess. ii. 14–16.

These were all swept by Pharisaic contempt into one common dust-heap, unworthy of notice—except the drawing back the hem of the garment so as not to touch them. They were disdainfully massed together under the common name of "the people of the land." To these they applied Is. xxvii. 11. "It is a people of no understanding, therefore He that hath made them will not have mercy upon them."* Hence even Rabbi the Holy once exclaimed, "Woe is me! I have given my morsel to an *Am ha-arets!*"—a man who does not recite the *Shema!* a man who wears no *Tsitsith* and no phylacteries, and does not wait on the pupils of the wise!† No parley must be held with such; no *Chaber, i. e.,* no member of the Rabbinic school, must buy fruit from them or sell it to them, or receive one of them as a guest, or travel with them, or regard their wives and daughters as other than an abomination. Nay, they might be "torn open like a fish."‡ Their salutations were only to be noticed by a reluctant nod of the head. No calamity ever befalls the world except through them. If an *am ha-arets* but touched a vine-cluster, the whole wine-press, according to Rabbi Chejah, became unclean; and everything within reach of his hand is defiled.§

It may be imagined, then, how startling was the reversal of current judgments, how absolute the reprobation of Pharisaic prejudices, when the Son of Man came to seek and save those despised and lost ones; mingled with them, ate with them, taught them, healed them, extended His

---

* *Berachoth,* f. 33, 1.   † *Id.* f. 47, 2.

‡ This vulgar piece of Rabbinic bluster occurs (with more to the same effect) in *Pesachim,* f. 49, 1.

§ *Pesachim,* f. 49, 2. *Avôth* ii. 6. Here, even Hillel says, "No boor is a sinbearer; nor is the *am ha-arets* pious." (Comp. John vii. 49, "This multitude that knoweth not the law are accursed.") *Taanith,* f. 14, 2. *Bava Bathra,* f. 8, 1. *Avodah Zara,* f. 75, 2. These passages from the Talmud are collected by Hamburger, *Real. Encycl. für Bibel und Talmud,* ii. *s. v. Am ha-arets;* and Mr. Hershon, in his *Talmudic Miscellany,* pp. 17, 91, 92; *Treasures of the Talmud,* pp. 98, 127; *Tabaroth,* ch. 7; Hershon, *Genesis acc. to the Talmud,* p. 443.

main work of compassion and amelioration to the physically destitute and the utterly ignorant ! The " people
of the land," on whom the religious leaders looked down
with such unutterable contempt, were the normal hearers
whom the Son of Man addressed in Galilee. They might
be chilled and brutalised by contempt, but could only be
uplifted to the true possibilities of human greatness and
goodness by sympathy and tenderness—" by quickening
them to a sense of their own worth, and restoring them to
self-respect." He did not speak to them with lofty condescension, but with brotherly tenderness.

(iv.) If there was one class in Palestine which was more
hated and despised than all others, it was the class of the
Publicans, or tax-collectors.* The strict Jews were sufficiently horrified by the thought that the Holy Land, which
in their view could only be lawfully taxed for *sacred* purposes, should in any way be liable to pay imposts to heathen
conquerors for the use of a heathen state and a heathen
emperor. But the maladministration, cheating, and extor-
tions which prevailed throughout the Roman Empire were
felt in Judæa with peculiar keenness. The tax-farmers—
usually Roman knights, who, singly or in companies, pur-
chased from the government the proceeds of a tax, and then
proceeded to make as much as they could out of it—were
universally regarded even by Pagans with a mixture of dislike and contempt.† Suetonius, in his " Life of Vespasian,"
records that the Emperor's father, whose name was Sabinus,
actually had a statue raised to him by several cities as that
astonishingly exceptional personage, " an excellent publican ";‡ and, in answer to the question, " Which are the

---

* Their name became proverbial (Matt. xviii. 17).

† Cic. *De Off*. i. 42. Lucian (*Menipp*. ii.) classes them among the worst
criminals. See *Ep. Barnab.* 4 ; Celsus *ap. Orig.* ii. 46 ; Keim iii. 267 ; Lightfoot, *Hor. Hebr.* on Matt. xviii. 17 ; Cave, *Lives of the Apostles ;* Hamburger
Realwörterb. ii. 1310.

‡ Suet, *Vesp.* i., καλῶς τελωνήσαντι. Josephus mentions one respectable publican (*B. J.* ii. 14, 4).

worst of wild beasts?" Theocritus answers, " On the mountains, bears and lions : in the cities, publicans and pettifog-
gers." Suidas describes the life of a publican as "Unrestrained plunder, unblushing greed, unreasonable pettifog-
ging, shameless business." Among the Jews, who made it
a question of conscience whether under any circumstances
it was lawful to pay tribute to Cæsar, these feelings were
intensified. In A. D. 17 Roman taxation had caused the
insurrection of Judas the Gaulonite, whose motto was, " No
Lord but Jehovah ; no tax but to the Temple." Judæa
seethed with chronic disaffection. The Jews were con-
fronted on every side with the irritating worry of oppressive demands and illegal extortion. There was the poll-tax,
and the land-tax, which demanded a tenth of the corn and
a fifth of the produce of vineyards and fruit trees ; and there
were endless tolls on the most necessary wares relentlessly
exacted at frontiers, at ferries, at bridges, in markets, and
on roads, of which no small part went, as the cost of adminis-
tration, not to the State at all, but to the wealthy and
greedy publican. The system was radically bad. It put a
premium on dishonesty. The State got the sum it wanted
from the men who farmed the tax, and was selfishly
indifferent to the methods which they and their agents
adopted.

The consequence was, in many provinces, an amount of
misery and bankruptcy analogous to that created by the
same vile methods in the Turkish Empire. The Roman
knights and Company-Directors (*Publicani, Mancipes*) *
necessarily required an army of subordinate agents (*socii*) ;
nd in addition to their own exorbitant demands—for which
they had established a sort of official impunity—the rapacity
of these underlings had to be sated, and was kept in very
inefficient check. If the upper *publicani* were hated, how
much more was this the case with the *portitores* or *exactors*,
to whom fell the daily disagreeable task of enforcing the

* Cic. *Pro Plancio*, ix.

payment which gorged their own avarice as well as that of
their masters! That *a Jew* should accept such a post for
the sake of filthy lucre, or even to get a bare living, placed
him beneath the reach of the utmost capacity for disdain in
the hearts of his stricter countrymen ; and this spirit of detestation for these lower officials was exacerbated by daily
scorn and ingenious annoyances.   They, and all things that
belonged to them, were regarded as hopelessly unclean, and
as a source of pollution which any number of purifications
could hardly clear away.   Now when a class is thus
radically despised it is apt to become despicable, and to
defy contempt by ostentatious vileness.   Hence " publicans "—by which in the Gospel is meant these inferior
portitores—are classed with sinners, harlots, thieves, and
murderers.   They were the worst pariahs of the Holy Land,
whose very existence was regarded as offensive, whose hand
was against every man, and every man's hand against them.
The ordinary tax-collector (*Gabbai*) was hated and scorned,
but the *toll-collector* (*Mokes*) was still more an object of
execration.*

How deeply seated, then, was the amazement at, and
how strong the indignation against, the Son of Man,
when—sent as He was to seek and save those that were
lost—He deliberately chose one of these subordinate tax-
gathers—not even a *Gabbai*, but a *Mokes*—to be one of
His Chosen Twelve Apostles ; took him from "the place of
toll," and sat down at his farewell banquet with other publicans and sinners!   Many loudly murmured at His con-
descending love.†   "With arid heart," says St. Gregory the
Great, "they blamed the very Fount of Mercy."   In all
ages it has been the fault of such religionists that " they
sought not the lost."‡

Yet Christ's action was part of a distinct purpose.   He

---

* See Hamburger, *Realwörterb.* ii. 1–10 ; Buxtorf, *Lex. s. v.*, מכם.
† Luke xv. 2, διεγόγγυζον.
‡ Ezek. xxxiv. 4.

held up the humility of the penitent publican who smote on his breast with the cry of "God be merciful to me the sinner," as an example to the posing Pharisee, who bragged of his immaculate superiority rather than prayed for needed pardon.

(v.) Again, throughout the East generally the position of *woman* is more or less despised and down-trodden, so that in some Eastern countries it was a common prayer, "O God, let not my infant be a girl; for very wretched is the life of women."* Their position in Judæa was not quite so low, yet a Pharisee thought it a disgrace to speak to a woman in public, even if the woman was his own wife.† The Apostles were so much infected with this current spirit of fancied superiority that they were amazed when they saw Jesus talking "with *a woman!*"‡ But He always displayed towards all women the same fine respect and tenderness. Ministering women—Salome, and Mary the wife of Cleopas, and Joanna the wife of Chuzas, Herod's steward, and the Magdalene, out of whom He had cast seven devils—followed His wanderings, and ministered to Him of their substance. When a poor woman stole from Him a work of mercy, by secretly touching the hem of His garment among the throng, and thus communicating to Him her ceremonial uncleanness, so far from sternly rebuking her trembling presumption, He said, "Daughter, be of good cheer, thy faith hath saved thee." §

Nay, more even than this, He did not repulse the

---

* Happy he whose children are boys, and woe unto him whose children are girls," Kiddushin, f. 82, 2. See Hershon, *Gen. acc. to the Talmud,* p. 168.

† Jose ben Jochanan of Jerusalem, "Prolong not converse with woman," *Pirqe Avôth,* 1, 5. There is a better view in *Bereshith Rabbah,* viii. But according to Dr. Frankl, *Jews in the East,* ii. 81, the Pharisaic *Chakams* to this day are specially careful to avoid being touched by any part of a woman's dress.

‡ John iv. 27. To talk with a woman in public was one of the six things which a Rabbi might not do. *Berachoth,* f. 42, 2.

§ Matt. ix. 22.

"woman who was a sinner," whom Simon the Pharisee eyed with such supercilious disgust, regarding it as a proof that Jesus was no Prophet since not repulsing her stained touch, He suffered her to kiss His feet, and wet them with her tears, and wipe them with the hairs of her head. But Jesus calmly rebuked the Pharisee by a parable, and saved the soul of the sinner by compassion.

> "She sat and wept beside His feet ; the weight
> Of sin oppressed her heart ; for all the shame,
> And the poor malice of the worldly blame,
> For her were past, extinct, and out of date.
> She would be melted by the heat of love—
> By fires far fiercer than are blown to prove,
> And purge the silver ore adulterate.
>
> .   .   .   .
>
> She sat and wept, and with her untressed hair
> Still wiped the feet she was so blessed to touch:
> And He wiped off the soiling of despair
> From her sweet soul, because she loved so much."

Nay, even when the Scribes brought to Him a woman taken in adultery, hoping either to get Him into trouble with the Romans by condemning her to death by stoning, or to give them an excuse for accusing Him of violation of the Mosaic Law, He defeated their base plot by sending the arrow of conviction into their own hardened consciences. When, self-convicted, they had stolen away, and He raised His eyes from the ground—to which He had bent them in an intolerable sense of shamed indignation at their coarse cruelty—and found Himself standing there alone, with the guilty woman before Him, He only said to her, "Woman, where are they? Did no man condemn thee? Neither do I condemn thee. Go thy way; from henceforth sin no more." *

(vi.) The Jews did not indeed despise *little children*, but, like all ancient nations, they left them all but exclusively to

---

* John viii. 11. Though this narrative was not in the original Gospel of St. John, the incident is undoubtedly a real one.

the charge of women, repressed them, kept them in the background, did little or nothing to mould their infant years. When the eager, loving mothers brought their children to Christ that He should bless them, the disciples were impatient at what they regarded as feminine intrusiveness, and rebuked those that brought them.* But Jesus was more than usually displeased † at this lack of sympathy. He took the little ones in His arms, laid His hands upon them, and blessed them, and said, "Suffer the little children to come unto Me, and forbid them not, for of such is the Kingdom of Heaven." He held up for an example their gentle innocence and blameless receptivity.‡ He had watched with a loving eye their little games in the market-place, as they amused themselves by playing at marriages or funerals.§ Home, with its commonest incidents, was to Him an infinitely sacred place. When the mothers brought to Him, not only their little children, but "*even their babes,*"|| He did not disdain to take in His arms their helpless infancy, and more than once He rebuked the ambitious selfishness of the disciples in their disputes as to which was the greater of them ¶ by taking a little child, setting him in the midst of them, and bidding them take example from his humble innocence.** As the poet describes it :

> " The twelve disputing who was first and chief,
>   He took a little child, knit holy arms
>   Round the brown, flower-soft boy, and smiled and said,
>   ' Here is the first and chiefest ! If a man

---

* Matt. xviii. 1–6, 10–14, xix. 13–18 ; Mark ix. 36, x. 13–16 ; Luke xviii. 17–18.

† ἠγανάκτησε. The word is only used once of Jesus (Mark x. 14).

‡ Matt. xviii. 2.

§ Matt. xi. 17 ; Luke vii. 32.

|| Luke xviii. 15, τὰ βρέφη.

¶ Not " which should be the greatest," but " which of them is accounted to be greatest," R. V. (Luke xxii. 24), or " who was the greater " (Mark ix. 34).

** Luke xviii. 17 ; Matt. xviii. 1–4.

Will be the greatest, see he make himself
Lowest and least, a servant unto all ;
Meek as my small disciple here, who asks
No place nor praise, but takes unquestioning
Love, as the river-lilies take the sun,
And pays it back with rosy folded palms
Clasped round My neck, and simple head reclined
On his Friend's breast.' "

Thus, by all His words and works did Jesus show that He came to be the representative of Humanity, to save the most fallen, to rescue the most miserable, to inspire the most hopeless, to reverence the very weakest, and as the Son of Man to bring home to every soul the revelation which He came to impart as the Son of God. Nor ought we to ignore, as is almost habitually done, the fact that our Lord's promises are often unlimited in scope. Thus, He said that "God sent not His son into the world to condemn the world, but that *the world* through Him might be saved." And He said, " I, if I be lifted up, will draw *all men* unto Me ; " and He came to be " the Saviour of the world " and " the Lamb of God which taketh away the sins of the world." " The sad realities of present experience," says Bishop Westcott, "cannot change the truth thus made known, however little we may be able to understand the way in which it will be accomplished."

It must not be for a moment supposed that the Divine claims were *veiled* under the title of " The Son of Man " ; for our Lord not unfrequently used, and allowed others to use, the title of " The Son " in a pre-eminent sense, as the Son of the Almighty Father. In St. Mark, indeed, it only occurs in xiii. 32 ; and in the other synoptic Gospels only in Matt. xi. 27, Luke x. 22 ; but it is found twenty-two times, and always in the highest sense and with the most Eternal claims, in the Gospel of St. John. And in the synoptic Gospels, where the title is not directly used, it is constantly referred to and implied. Christ spoke of God

the Father as in a very unique sense *His* Father. Again
and again he speaks of *My* heavenly Father,* in a sense
different from and higher than the phrase *your* Father,
which was also frequently upon His lips.† Stupendous,
indeed, was the revelation that He, the persecuted peasant-
teacher of Nazareth, was not only "*a* Son of God"—as, in
one sense, all men are—but "*the* Son of God." Yet, amid
all His humiliations, at the apparent nadir of His earthly
rejection and defeat, this truth—such was the power of His
daily presence and influence—burnt itself deeply into the
hearts of His poor Apostles. It forced from the lips of
Peter the great confession, "*Thou art the Christ, the Son of
the Living God.*"‡ That acknowledgment was the crowning crisis of Christ's earthly ministry. It proved that His
essential work was now accomplished. And as Keim
strikingly observes, "We do not know which first to
designate great, whether this lofty flight of the disciples
who renounce the Jewish standard, quash the verdict of
the hierarchs, leap over the popular opinion which hung
midway between the two extremes, find loftiness and
Divinity in the downtrodden and insignificant, because,
spiritually to spiritual eyes, it remains something Divine ;
or, that Personality of Jesus which compels such weak
disciples, even under the paralysing influence of all external
facts, distinctly and simply and nobly to mirror back the
total impression of His Ministry." §

* Matt. vii. 21 ; xii. 50 ; xv. 13 ; xvii. 35, xviii. 10, 35, etc.

† Matt. x. 20, xvii. 26, xviii. 14, xxiii. 9, etc. In the sentence, " I ascend
unto my Father and your Father" (John xx. 17), the Greek is πρὸς τὸν πατέρα
μου καὶ πατέρα ὑμῶν, " The Father of me and Father of you." Comp. Heb.
ii 11 ; Rom. iii. 29, xv. 6.

‡ Matt. xvi. 16.

§ Keim, iv. 263.

CHAPTER XXV.

CHRIST'S CONDEMNATION OF PHARISAIC RELIGIONISM.

"There is a generation that are pure in their own eyes, and yet are not washed from their filthiness."—Prov. xxx. 12.

"Which say, '*Stand by thyself; come not near to me, for I am holier than thou!*' These are a smoke in my nose, a fire that burneth all the day."—Is. lxv. 5.

"Beggarly elements."—Gal. iv. 9.

'Απεραντολογία.—ORIGEN, *Opp.* i. 119.

"Stupenda inanitas et vafrities."—LIGHTFOOT, *Ded. in Hor. Hebr.*

ALREADY in a previous chapter we have seen something of the wretched series of minutiæ into which the Pharisees had degraded the Levitic System, though that system consisted, as St. Paul says, of " weak and beggarly rudiments," and was nothing more than " a yoke of bondage," necessitated by ignorance and hardness of heart.[*] The fundamental differences between the religion of the letter and of the spirit, between the righteousness of the law and " the righteousness which is through faith in Christ," [†] will be found summarily described in the answer of Christ to the Scribes and Pharisees from Jerusalem, who came to act as spies upon His ministry. [‡]

The Pharisees were the only body of the Jewish people with whom Christ entered into a position of direct antagonism, forced upon Him by their subterranean baseness, as well as by the paltriness of their conceptions and the arrogance which resulted from their fundamental misapprehension of what is and is not truly sacred in the eyes of God.

[*] Gal. iv. 9, v. 1. [†] See Phil. iii. 9.
[‡] Matt. xv. 1-20 ; Mark vii. 1-23.

Their system was an elaborate "externalization of holiness"; _His_ teaching was that "God is a Spirit, and they that worship Him must worship Him in spirit and in truth." It was the main object of the Lord of Life to bring to erring men that true life which they can only acquire by union with God.   Formalities of every kind, will-worship, even severities of the body, are easy; but, as St. Paul so emphatically says, they are of no value against the indulgence of the flesh.*   It is easy to bow the head like a bulrush, but _not_ easy to offer from the depths of a penitent heart the prayer of the Publican, "God be merciful to me, the sinner."   The Pharisees called their Rabbis "Uprooters of Mountains," "Lights of Israel," "Glories of the Law," "The Great," "The Holy," but the mass of the people were in their eyes mere boors, "empty wells," "people of the earth," "who knew not the Law and were accursed." †   Yet "the boldest religionists and mock-prophets," says Henry More,‡ "are very full of heat and spirits; and have their imagination too often infected with the fumes of those lower parts, the full sense and pleasure whereof they prefer before all the subtle delights of reason and generous contemplation."

Always kind, always courteous, always forbearing even towards meddling spies—ready to meet their quibbles, ready to answer their questions, ready to accept their supercilious hospitality, ready with the most gracious courtesy to meet their hard and calumnious criticisms—Jesus was compelled at last "to break into plain thunderings and lightnings" against them, in order to strip bare their hypocrisies, and to blight the influence they exerted over hosts of

---

* Col. ii. 23.

† In Luke xviii. 10-12, we read the brag of the posing Pharisee, and it is exactly analogous to a prayer of R. Nechounia ben Hakana in _Berachoth_ (see Schwab, p. 336).   But

> "Humble we must be if to heaven we go;
> High is the roof there, but the gate is low."

‡ _Conject. Cabbalist._, p. 231.

deluded followers and proselytes, whom, to use His own terrible expression, they "made tenfold more the children of Gehenna than themselves."* He could not reveal to the world the unchangeable truths which constitute the Alpha and Omega of genuine holiness, without showing how mean a parody was substituted for it by these "shallow and selfish men, bigots in creed and in conduct, capable of no sin disapproved by tradition, incapable of any virtue unenjoined by it; too respectable to be publicans and sinners, but at once too ungenerous to forgive any sin against their own order, and too blind to see the sins within it; who remain for all time our most perfect types of fierce and inflexible devotion to a worship instituted and administered by man, but of relentless and unbending antagonism to religion, as the service of God in spirit and in truth." †

The Pharisees were the Tartuffes of ancient days. The Gospel system could not be established without the overthrow of that which had become the corporate expression o' the cardinal sin of Judaism, the corruption of man's worship of God to a mere outward service by acts formal and artificial, through instruments and articles sensuous, external, purchasable. ‡ Shammai, the rival of Hillel, was a luxurious and selfish man; yet so particular was he about senseless scrupulosities that he almost starved his little son on the Day of Atonement, and made a booth over the childbed of his daughter-in-law that his first-born grandson might keep the Feast of Tabernacles! § If they had understood the most elementary teaching of the Psalms, ‖ the Prophets, ¶ and even of their own Law,** they would not have

---

* Matt. xxiii. 15.   † Fairbairn.

‡ Jost., *Gesch. d. Juden.* iv. 76 ; Gfrörer, *Jahrh. d. Heils*, i. 140 ; Lightfoot, *Hor. Hebr.* on Matt. iii. 17.

§ *Succah.* ii. 9.

‖ Ps. vii. 10, xxiv. 4, l. 8, li. 12, 18, cxxxix. 23.

¶ Is. i. 10, lviii. 1, lxvi. 1; Jer. vi. 20, vii. 21, xvii. 10, xxxi. 32 ; Mic. vi. 6; Amos v. 21 ; I Sam. xvi. 7.

** Deut. vi. 5.

elaborated their eye-service of men-pleasers which usurped the place of that singleness of heart without which forms and ceremonies are but as a booming gong or a clanging cymbal. They ordained rites which corresponded to nothing, and made their scrupulosities a cloak of maliciousness. Christ extended the Decalogue itself to the thoughts of the heart, and summed up all the Commandments in the Law of Love. And in point of fact this was not in disaccord with their own best teaching in their saner moments, for we read in *Soteh* (p. 14, 1), "The beginning of the Law is benevolence, and in benevolence it ends. At the beginning God clothed the naked (Gen. iii. 21), at the end He buried the dead (Deut. xxxiv. 5, 6)."

What was the so-called Oral Law which the Pharisees so extravagantly valued? The first sentence of the *Pirqe Avôth* tells us how Moses received the Thorah from God on Mount Sinai, and that through Joshua, the Elders, and the Prophets it was transmitted to the men of the Great Synagogue, who, in accordance with the literal translation of Lev. xviii. 30 ("make a *Mishmereth* to my *Mishmereth*") handed it down as a duty to "make a fence to the Thorah" (*seyyag la-Thorah*). The Rabbis held that Moses received two Laws on Sinai, both the Written (*Thorah Shebektab*) and the Oral Law (*Thorah shebeal Peh*)—"the law on the lip." * Hence they described the Mishnah as "the Halachah" (or "Rule") given to Moses on Sinai; and Rabbi Simon Ben Lakdeh assigned a Mosaic origin even to the Gemara,† including Halachoth, Haggadoth, and Midrashim.‡ Nay, they exalted their tradition *above* the writ-

* The phrase is borrowed from Ex. xxxiv. 27, where *al Peh* is rendered "*after the tenor.*"

† *Gittin*, f. 6, 2 ; Hershon, *Talm. Miscell.*, p. xv. On the great synagogue, see Taylor's *Pirqe Avôth*, pp. 125, 126.

‡ This they deduced in their own way from Mich. ii. 6, 7. In *Baba Metzia* (86a) God summons Rabbi Bar-Nachman to settle a controversy which has arisen between Him and the angels. Comp. f. 59, 6 ; *Shemoth Rabbah*, ch. clvii.; *Berachoth*, i. 7.

ten Law, and said, " The words of the Scribes are more
noble than the words of the Law."   In the *Baba Metzia*
we are told that to read the Mishnah and Gemara is far
more meritorious than to read the words of Scripture.
" The sayings of the elders," they said, " are weightier than
those of the Prophets." *   Not to read the Shema, according to Rabbi Abba Bar-Eshera, in the name of Rabbi
Judah Bar-Pari, deserves but a slight punishment, for it
only breaks an affirmative precept ; but not to read it
according to the rule of Hillel deserves capital punishment, for " whoso breaketh a hedge (the *Seyyag la-Thorah*)
a serpent shall bite him " ! (Eccl. x. 8).   If a man's father
and his Rabbi are carrying burdens, he is to lighten the
Rabbi first.   If both are in captivity he must first ransom
his Rabbi.†   Pride went hand in hand with littleness.
They loved the chief seats in synagogues and the upper-
most place at feasts, and greetings in the market places,
and to be called of men, Rabbi, Rabbi.   Modern criticism
has proved it to be at least possible that much of the
Levitic system did not assume its present form until after
the Exile.   The futile elaborations of this Levitism—
imperfect and secondary as it was—had their origin in the
endeavour to separate Israel from all contact with the
nations by a network of traditions.   The Scribes had
developed it into a sort of *abracadabra* without limit and
without end.   " The whole history of religion proves that
a ceremony- and tradition-ridden time is infallibly a
morally corrupt time—artificial ceremonies, whether origin-
ating with Jewish Rabbis or Christian ' priests,' are of no
spiritual value.   Recommended by their zealous advocates,
often sincerely, as tending to promote the culture of
morality and piety, they often prove fatal to both.   Well
are they called in the Epistle to the Hebrews ' dead works.'
If they have any life at all, it is life feeding upon death, the

* See Schürer II. i. 3.
† *Avôth* iv. 12 ; *Kerithoth*, vi. 9.   See Schürer II. i. 3.

life of fungi growing on dead trees; if they have any beauty, it is the beauty of decay, of autumnal leaves, sere and yellow . . . when the woods are about to pass into their winter state of nakedness." *

Let us see how Jesus dealt with this state of things in separate instances.

(i.) The Oral Law attached immense importance to the *ceremonial purifications*, which occupy no less than twelve treatises of the sixth Seder of the Mishnah, including *Yada'im* or "Handwashings," and *Migvaoth*, "the water used for baths and ablutions, and for the stalks of fruit which convey uncleanness." †

Our Lord said to the Pharisees, " Now do ye Pharisees cleanse the outside of the cup and of the platter, but your inward part is full of extortion and wickedness." ;‡ or, as it is in St. Matthew, " but within they are full from extortion and excess." § The Pharisaic rules about the washing of " cups and platters" were ludicrously minute. In the treatise *Kelim* we read that the air in hollow earthen vessels, like the hollow of the foot, contracts and propagates uncleanness, so that they must be broken, and if a piece be left large enough to anoint the little toe with, it is still " a vessel," and therefore capable of defilement. They are to be accounted as " broken " if there be a hole in them as large as a medium-sized pomegranate! Hillel caused endless trouble throughout the Dispersion by deciding, in accordance with the rule of Joseph Ben Jezzer and Joseph Ben Johanan, that even glass vessels were capable of conveying defilement. This legalised and intentional unsoci-

---

* See Bruce, *Training of the Twelve*, p. 82.

† See Winer, *s. v. Reinigkeit;* Herzog, *s. v. Reinigungen ;* Schürer II. ii. § 28.

‡ Luke xi. 39.

§ Matt. xxiii. 25. St. Mark (vii. 4) speaks also of the washing of pots, and brazen vessels, and tables, or couches. As to the latter we read in *Kelim* that if one or two of the legs of a three-legged table are broken it is clean, but if the third foot is gone, it becomes a board, and is susceptible of defilement.

ability (Perishooth, *αμιξία*) did infinite harm to the Jews and prevented them from fulfilling the Divine mission which they might otherwise have accomplished for the ennoblement of the world.* Such puerilities could only excite contempt in any healthy mind.

Again, as we know, the Jerusalemite spies, Scribes and Pharisees, had seen some of the disciples "eat bread with *defiled* (*lit.* common), *that is, unwashen hands*," whereas they themselves, following the tradition of the Elders, washed their hands *πυγμῇ* (diligently ?), which is by some interpreted to mean "up to the elbow," or "with the fist," and by others "up to the wrist." † The rule given in the Talmudic book *Soteh* (f. 4, 6) is that "He who eats bread without having first washed his hands, commits as it were fornication." According to *Shabbath* (f. 14, 2) a Bath Kol, or voice from heaven, had pronounced Solomon blessed when he instituted the laws respecting hand-washings; and when a man washes his hands he is to first wash the right hand, then the left, whereas in *anointing* the hands he is first to anoint the left hand, then the right.‡ " If a man poured on one hand one gush his hand is clean ; but if one gush on both hands R. Meir pronounces them unclean, until one poured out a quarter log of water upon them." § Moreover the scribes said it were better to cut off the hands than to touch the nose, mouth, and ears with them without having first washed them, as this causes blindness, deafness, foul breath, and polypus. According to R.

---

* See many more of these paltry minutiæ in Schürer, *l. c.*

† Heb. לִבְרָךְ ; Mark vii. 3. See Lightfoot on Matt. xvi. 2 ; Hamburger, *Real. Ency. Handewaschen.* The word *πυγμῇ* probably refers to the rule that the hand was to be held up, with closed fist, so that the water poured on it streamed down to the elbow. There were additional rules as to the sort of water to be used, from what vessel it was to be poured, who was to pour it, etc. Vulg., *crebro.* Epiphanius (*Hær.* 15) *ἐπιμελῶς*, " carefully." Erasmus suggested a reading *πυκνῇ*. The reading of א is *πυκνά*. The word occurs in the LXX.; Ex. xxi. 18 ; Is. lviii. 4.

‡ *Shabbath*, f. 61, 1.   § *Yadayim*, ch. 2, 1.

Nathan an evil spirit named *Bath Chorin* haunts the hands at night, and only departs if they are washed three times!* Akiba preferred to die of thirst rather than not wash his hands. The treatise *Yadayim*, in four chapters, is mainly devoted to this subject. According to another treatise—the *Kitzur Sh'lah*—a man who does not wash his hands before eating will have as little rest as a murderer, and will be transmigrated into a cataract; and in this treatise we are taught that the proper way to wash the hands is to stretch out the fingers, turning the palms upwards, and say "Lift ye up your holy hands."† Further, every one should have a vessel of water by his bed, and if he walks four ells without washing his hands after getting up "he has forfeited his life as a Divine punishment."‡ Most truly may it be said of the Rabbinic writings, as Lightfoot says of them, "*Nugis ubique scatent.*"

It should be observed that the question was not in the least a question of health or cleanliness, but only of imaginary and incidental defilements; and our Lord swept aside this whole mass of contemptible traditions in the one sentence, "to eat with unwashen hands defileth not a man." Between Christ's teaching of spiritual simplicity and the boundless ἐθελοπερισσοθρησκεία (as Epiphanius admirably calls it) of the Pharisees, there could be no middle term.§

(ii.) Again, the Scribes and Pharisees had developed from the Levitic law reams of inferential littlenesses about the distinction between clean and unclean meats. According to the Mishnah, God, in giving the law to Moses, had assigned forty-nine reasons in every case for pronouncing one thing unclean and another clean.‖ Seven hundred kinds of fish and twenty-four kinds of birds were pronounced unclean. Our Lord made very short work of all

---

* *Yadayim*, p. 109, 1.   † Ps. cxxxiv. 2.

‡ *Kitzur Sh'lah*, f. 43, 2.   See Hershon, *Talmudic Miscellany*, p. 333.

§ *Hær.* xvi. 34

‖ *Sopherim*, xvi. 6.

these laws of *Kashar* and *Tame* (which still prevail in Jewish
communities) * when he said, "That which proceedeth out
of the man—out of the heart of men—that defileth the
man . . . whatsoever from without goeth into the man
cannot defile him." † This he said, making all meats clean.
He bade the disciples simply to eat such things as were set
before them, ‡ just as St. Paul told his Gentile converts
to eat whatsoever was sold in the shambles, "asking no
questions." §

(iii.) To *fasting* the Pharisees ascribed an exaggerated
and most mistaken importance. The ninth treatise of
the second Seder of the Mishnah is devoted to fasts. In
the Levitic Law only one fast day was appointed in the
whole year (Lev. xvi. 29)—the *Kippur*, or Day of Atonement.‖ By the time of Zechariah four yearly fasts had
come into vogue (Zech. viii. 19), but the Prophet declared
that they "should be to the House of Judah joy, and gladness, and cheerful feasts," and when he was consulted
about them he in no way encouraged their observance
(vii. 1–14), but, in their place, enforced the duties of mercy
and compassion. Over and over again the great Prophets
of Israel had taught the uselessness of a fasting which had
not the least connection with goodness and charity.¶ In

---

* Jos. c. *Ap.* ii. 17 ; *Chullin*, f. 63, 2. One specimen of the littleness of
their exegesis is shown in the prohibition to eat flesh and milk together because
of the law, " Thou shalt not seethe a kid in its mother's milk ! "

† Mark vii. 18–23.

‡ Luke x. 8.

§ 1 Cor. x. 25.

‖ See, too, Numb. xxix. 7. The fact that this single fast and its ceremonies
is never referred to elsewhere in the Old Testament—not even in such passages
as Ezek. xl.–xlviii. and Neh. viii.–x., taken in connection with critical arguments, constituted a decisive proof that the Day of Atonement was a Post-
exilic ordinance. See Dr. Driver, *s. v. Day of Atonement* (Dr. Hastings'
Dict. of the Bible).

¶ Is. lviii. 3–6; Mic. vi. 6–8; Amos v. 21–24, etc. Even in the *Megillath
Taanith*, which emanated from the *early* Rabbinic School, there is only a list
of days on which fasting is *forbidden*. Fasting was chiefly developed in the

the age of Christ the Pharisees had established two weekly
fasts, one on Thursday, when Moses was supposed to have
ascended Sinai, and one on Monday, when he descended,*
and they plumed themselves in a manner which the Lord
heartily disapproved upon these empty observances.
They probably became mere sham functions, fasting of
the effeminate amateur kind, in which case they were
beneath contempt; or if they were real fasts, they were
a needless and injurious burden. The Scribes made them
still more injurious by parading their sanctimoniousness
and regarding it as a means for extorting Divine favours.
But when, on one of these fast-days, they, with the disciples of the Baptist, who in the imperfection of his views
had adopted the practice, came to complain, in all the carp-
ing fretfulness which fasting produces,† that neither our
Lord nor His Apostles took the least notice of this "tradition of the Elders," our Lord pointed out to them the only
conditions under which fasting becomes natural—the conditions of overwhelming sorrow. He Himself "came eating and drinking"—that is, not depriving our human life
of the necessary support and innocent enjoyments which
God supplies and permits. This He did so openly as to
give to those who thought it right "to lie for God," the
excuse for the abhorrent calumny, "Behold a gluttonous
man and a wine-bibber." His disciples, "sons of the Bride-
chamber,"‡ could not fast while the Bridegroom was with

Post-exilic age. It is absurdly magnified in the Book of Judith iv. 13, viii. 6,
17-20. Comp. Tobit i. 10 ff. xii. 8.

* *Baba Kama*, f. 82, 1.

† Mark ii. 18, ἦσαν νηστεύοντες. " The principle underlying this graphic representation is that fasting should *not* be a matter of fixed mechanical rule, but
should have reference to the state of mind. . . Fasting under any other circumstances is forced, unnatural, unreal. Bruce's *Training of the Twelve*, 72.
In the New Testament the words " and fasting " are an ascetic and Manichean
interpolation of Scribes in Matt. xvii. 21; Mark ix. 29; Acts x. 30; 1 Cor.
vii. 5.

‡ *Beni habachunnah*, the nearest friends of the wedded pair.

them, but should fast, not of necessity, but in heaviness of heart, when they had seen Him die on the Cross, and in the coming days of overwhelming persecution. To interpret "the days when the Bridegroom shall be taken away from them," of the whole Christian Dispensation, and on that misinterpretation to found the false inference that Christians ought continually to fast, is one of the most egregious of the many egregious blunders of ignorant will-worship. It ignores the innermost revelation of the Saviour that His physical absence was actually "expedient" for His disciples, involving, as it did, the richer blessing of a closer spiritual nearness. Hence the characteristics of the early Christians were *not* gloomy anguish and morose asceticism, but, on the contrary, exultation and simplicity of heart.*

(iv.) Again our Lord entirely discountenanced the whole method of Rabbinic exegesis with its "ever-widening spiral *ergo*," drawn from the aperture of single texts. He never referred except with disdain to Halachoth, which were but masses of cobwebs spun out of their own fancy. He ignored the *Midrash*, which was far less an explanation of the Law and the Prophets than an inverted pyramid of distortions built on its isolated phrases. In Ps. lxii. 11 we read

"God hath spoken once ;
Twice have I heard this ; "

and this was interpreted by Rabbi Akiba to mean "God spake one thing ; what I heard is twofold," which wrests the whole passage from its true meaning. This is in accordance with the common Rabbinic comment, "Read not thus, but thus." But our Lord's comments are always on what the Bible *means*, not on those ingenious perversions of it for party purposes which constituted no small

* Acts ii. 46, "Breaking bread at home, they did take their food ἐν ἀγαλλιάσει, "in exultation" (the strongest of all words for abounding joy) "and simplicity of heart."

part of current exegesis. He held with the saner Rabbis that "Scripture speaks in the tongue of the sons of men."[*] Jesus charged the Scribes with deliberately setting at nought by their traditions the very Law round which, as the most sacred object of their lives, they professed it to be their duty to "make a hedge." They explained it "in as many ways as a hammer dashes a rock into fragments."[†] He never referred to the "decision of the Scribes,"[‡] nor to the Kabbalistic mode of interpretation known as *Geneth*,[§] nor to one of their unprofitably minute precepts. But He did upbraid them with their hypocrisy.[||] Thus by means of their *Erubhin* (or "mixtures")[¶] they nullified some of the Mosaic laws which they professed most profoundly to respect,[**] so much so that in *Menachoth* Moses himself is represented as standing amazed at the fatuous inferences established by R. Akiba from the horns and tips of letters.[††] Well might Christ say to them, "Ye search the Scriptures, because ye think that in them ye have eternal life, and those very Scriptures testify of Me; yet ye will not come to Me that ye may have life."[‡‡]

For instance, the law of the Sabbatic year was regarded as fundamental. But as time went on, it was found to be very inconvenient for commerce, so Hillel got rid of it by a subterfuge called *Prosbol*, a preconcerted farce for the

---

[*] *Berach.* 31, 2.　　　　　　　　　　　[†] *Sanhedrin*, 34.

[‡] דִּנְרֵי סוֹפְרִים.

[§] Namely (1), Gematria (Geometria), inferences from the numerical value of the letters of words. (2) *Notarikon*, the deducing of sentences from the letters of words. (3) *Themourah*, the interchange of letters by Athbash, Albam, etc. Those who wish for further explanations may find them fully furnished in my papers on Rabbinic exegesis in *The Expositor*, vols. v., vi. (First Series).

[||] Mark vii. 5-13.

[¶] In the first instance the word seems to be used for "the binding together of several localities," in order to get rid of the supposed law that they might not walk more than 2000 ells on the Sabbath.

[**] Weil, *Le Judaisme*, iii. 268.

[††] *Vajikra Rabba*, f. 162, 1. Quoted by Schöttgen on Matt. xv. 18.

[‡‡] John v. 39, 40.

evasion of the law, by which the creditor *said* to the debtor, " *This being the Sabbatic year I release you from your debt*," and the debtor replied (as had been pre-arranged), " *Many thanks, but I prefer to pay it !* " Thus did they honour God with their lips, but denied Him in their double heart. Long prayers, and devouring of widows' houses; flaming proselytism and subsequent moral neglect; rigorous stickling for the letter, bound-less levity as to the spirit ; high-sounding words as to the sanctity of oaths, and cunning reservations of casuistry ; fidelity in trifles, gross neglect of essential principles; the mask of godliness without the reality ; petty orthodoxy and artificial morals—such was Pharisaism. It was a false system, based on egotism and self-seeking ; a semblable goodness swayed by " a tame conscience," which had no power over the heart.* And that was why the Pharisees were " the only class which Jesus cared publicly to expose."

* See Canon Mozley, *Univ. Sermons*, pp. 28–51.

CHAPTER XXVI.

CHRIST AND THE SABBATH.

IT was as regards the non-observance of the traditions of the Elders about *the Sabbath* that the Pharisees raised the fiercest clamour against Christ. They had established a number of arbitrary rules, whereas the principle and the practice of Christ was that of the olden Law, that "the Sabbath was made for man, and not man for the Sabbath." The Sabbath of the "Book of the Covenant" had been greatly altered in the later priestly laws.* No one on that day was to walk more than 2000 yards, because, in Ex. xvi. 29, a Jew is forbidden "to go out of his place" (*Makom*), but, in Ex. xxi. 13, the homicide may fly to the Levitic suburb, which was 2000 yards from the camp; hence, by one of Hillel's *Middoth* (known as "analogy"), every one might walk 2000 yards on the Sabbath.† But supposing a Pharisee wanted to dine with another on the Sabbath, was he to forego his pleasure on this account? Oh, no! By putting up sham lintels and doorposts, the whole street, even if it were miles long, becomes a part of their own house!‡ And no man might carry anything more than four ells on a Sabbath; but at the end of the four ells he might hand it to another and he to another, and so get it conveyed a hundred miles if necessary.

Again, no man might buy anything on the Sabbath, but he might go to a shopkeeper and say, "*Give me this or that*," and call and pay for it next day. No Jew might

* See Montefiore, *Hibbert Lectures*, p. 338.

† *Rosh Hashanah*, f. 21 ; 2 *Erubhin*, f. 42, 1.

‡ This particular evasion was called the *Erubh. Techumîm.* See Maimonides, *Hilchoth Erubhin*, vi. 6 ; Montefiore, *Hibbert Lectures*, p. 562.

carry any burden on the Sabbath, however small, not even a pocket-handkerchief; but he might tie a pocket-handkerchief round his knee, and *regard* it as a garter! This ἀπεραντολογία, as Origen calls it, has lasted for ages, for even in the third century the Jews had decided that on the Sabbath a man might wear one kind of shoe, but not another.*   Our Lord denounces such mean modes of trying to deceive God, in the matter of the Corban, in the rule about hating enemies, and on the subject of divorce. He taught on the principle that Scripture does *not* cover any number of inferences which can be extorted out of isolated expressions, but that we are to abide by all that is permanent in the plain meaning of Holy Writ.   Scripture *is* what Scripture *means*. To quote a phrase, and attribute to its *literal* significance a meaning which it never had, and never *could* have had, is a mere trick of ignorant hypocrisy.

We read in the Book of Jubilees (50), "Every one who desecrates the Sabbath, or declares that he intends to make a journey on it, or speaks either of buying or selling, or he who draws water and has not provided it upon the sixth day, and he who lifts a burden in order to take it out of his dwelling-place, or out of his house, shall die. And every man who makes a journey, or *attends to his cattle*,† and he who kindles a fire, or rides upon any beast, or sails *upon a ship* on the sea upon the Sabbath day, shall die." The rules about the Sabbath were divided into *Avôth*, "fathers," ‡ and *Toldôth*, "generations"—*i. e.*, primary and derivative rules.

The *Avôth* were thirty-nine in number,§ and they forbade all such works as sowing, ploughing, reaping, binding

---

* Orig. *Opp.* i. 179.   The Sabbatic fanaticism of the Jews attracted the notice of Pagans.   Ovid, *Ars Amat.* i. 415 ; Juv. *Sat.* xiv. 98–100.

† Some Rabbis who "bound" with Shammai, rather than "loosed" with Hillel, had decided that if a sheep fell into a water-tank on the Sabbath it was *not* to be drawn out.   See Hausrath i. 95.

‡ ἀρχηγικώτατα αἴτια.   Philo, *De Vit.* 686.

§ *Shabbath*, f. 78, 1.

sheaves, threshing, etc. To these rules the Pharisees of
Christ's day seem to have *added* another, that no one was
to be healed on a Sabbath day, so little did they recognise
in their blindness that charity is above rubrics, and mercy
better than sacrifice. Now, our Lord, in order to combat
this folly, performed no less than seven miraculous healings
on the Sabbath Day. To refute their fanatical formalism
He appealed not only to His inherent authority as " Lord
of the Sabbath" (Mark ii. 28; John v. 17–47), but also to
Scripture precedents (Luke vi. 3–5), as well as to common
sense and to eternal principles (vi. 9). Sometimes, too, He
used, with crushing force, the *argumentum ad hominem*,
showing the selfish insincerity with which they applied and
modified their own regulations.

The rules of the Rabbis were so minute in what Origen
calls their "frigid traditions" that you might put wine *on
the eyelid* on the "Sabbath," but not into the eye, because
that is healing;* and you might put vinegar into your
mouth for a toothache, but might not rinse the mouth with
it! Yet our Lord never violated even *their* best *principles :*—for they said, " The Sabbath may be broken when
life is in danger—a child, for instance, may be saved from
drowning."† They distinguished, however, between saving
life and doing any other work of mercy; for instance, if a
woman has a toothache she may keep a piece of salt in her
mouth, but only on condition that she has put it in the day
before !‡ " In no case was *this miserable micrology* carried
to greater lengths."

Our Lord wished to restore the two divine principles that
God loves mercy rather than sacrifice; and that God desires our service solely because He desires that we should
be happy. He desired for the sake of Mankind to redeem
the Sabbath from a miserable fetish into the blessed boon
for which God had intended it. Therefore, on the Sabbath

---

* *Shabbath*, f. 108, 2.

† *Yoma*, f. 84, 2.   ‡ *Shabbath*, f. 64, 2.

days He healed the Demoniac;* and Simon's wife's mother;† and the man with the withered hand;‡ and the woman bound by a spirit of infirmity; § and the man with the dropsy;‖ and the paralytic at Bethesda;¶ and the man born blind.** The Jews vehemently denounced Him for these deeds of compassion, even though they involved no labour. Our Lord showed the inherent hypocrisy of their denunciations by pointing out that, in far smaller matters *they* violated their own professions, since none of them hesitated to loose his ox or ass from the manger and lead him away to watering; or to draw out on the Sabbath an animal that had fallen into a pit. When Shemaiah and Abtalion had found Hillel almost frozen on the outer window-sill of their lecture-room on a Sabbath, they had not hesitated to spend a considerable amount of labour to rub, and warm, and rouse him; †† and so far from being blamed for this, their remark that "he was worthy that the Sabbath should be profaned on his behalf" had met with universal approval. So too, when their opponents were not concerned in the matter, the Talmudic writings can praise Rabbis for even bearing burdens on the Sabbath! In the *Midrash Koheleth*,‡‡ Abba Techama is praised for carrying a sick man into a town, and going back—though it was the Sabbath—to fetch his bundle.

The rule laid down by our Lord with perfect distinctness was, "It is lawful to do good on the Sabbath."§§ Could there be a stronger contrast to the Rabbinic inanity, which *allowed bathing* on the Sabbath, but *not* in the Dead Sea or the Mediterranean, because the waters of those seas were supposed to be medicinal, and healing is unlawful on the Sabbath Day!‖‖

The objection to the Sabbath healings was sometimes

---

* Mark i. 23–26. † Mark i. 30, 31. ‡ Matt. xii. 10.
§ Luke xiii. 11. ‖ Luke xiv. 2. ¶ John v. 8, 9.
** John ix. †† *Yoma*, f. 35, 6. ‡‡ *Yoma*, f. 91, 2.
§§ Matt. xii. 12. ‖‖ *Shabbath*, f. 109, 1.

complicated by the fact that Jesus had broken one of the trivial Pharisaic *Toldôth* or *derivative* rules. Thus He had bidden the healed man to take up his bed and walk,* and the Jews "sought to *slay* Him because He had done these things on the Sabbath day." But the so-called "bed" was a mere mat or pallet, the carrying of which was necessary for the man, and involved no labour. The act bore no relation to the real meaning of Jer. xvii. 21, 22, "Take heed to yourselves, and bear no burden on the Sabbath day, neither carry forth a burden out of your houses," which was spoken to prevent the profanation of the Sabbath by daily toil and commerce. Although, therefore, the Rabbis had decided that "to carry anything from a public place to a private house on the Sabbath" rendered a man liable to death by stoning,† our Lord intentionally ignored the literalism which strained out a gnat yet swallowed a camel.

Again, when Jesus healed the man born blind, the *miracle* went for nothing in the obstinate perversion of the Pharisees; but, because He had effected the miracle by anointing the man's eyes with clay moistened with saliva, they declared that "He was not of God, because He keepeth not the Sabbath;"‡ and said, "We know that this man is a sinner."§ Clay and saliva ‖ were both regarded as therapeutic agents, and our Lord had used both as helps to the faith of those whom He cured.¶ The Jews themselves

---

* John v. 10, 16 ; Mark ii. 11, vi. 55, κράββατος, *grabatus;* Heb., *mittah;* Luke v. 24, κλινίδιον ; Attic, σκίμπους ; Fr. *grabat.* It was a mere *palliasse,* or even sometimes an *abeijah* (outer robe) folded up, as we see from Ex. xxii. 27, where it is forbidden to take a man's upper robe in payment for a debt because it is "that whereon he sleepeth" and "his only covering." Comp. Virg. *Mor.* 5. " Membra levat sensim *vili* demissa *grabato.*"

† *Shabbath,* vi.1.

‡ John ix. 16.   § John ix. 24.

‖ Tac. *Hist.* iv. 81 ; Suet. *Vesp.* 7 ; Plin. *H. N.* xxviii. 7. Comp. Mark viii. 23, vii. 33 ; *Shabbath* xiv. 4 (where the healing application of saliva to the eyes on the Sabbath is distinctly forbidden).

¶ Matt. xii. 5.

held that there was "no Sabbatism in the Temple," and
therefore that the Priests "profaned the Sabbath in the
Temple and were blameless."* To Christ the Temple of
God was the Temple of infinite, all-embracing compassion.

Again, on a certain Sabbath the disciples, in their
poverty and hunger, as they were making their way
through the cornfields, began to pluck the ears of corn, and
to rub them in the palms of their hands. Now, by two of
the thirty-nine *Avôth* or primary rules, all reaping and
threshing on the Sabbath were forbidden ; and one of the
numberless *Toldôth* or "derivative rules" regarded plucking the ears of corn (even to satisfy hunger!) as a *kind*
of reaping, and rubbing them as a *kind* of threshing. Immediately, therefore, the Phariasic spies came down on
them with their contemptuous censure, "Why do ye do
that which is not lawful on the Sabbath Day?" and going
at once to Jesus, who seems to have been walking apart
from the Apostles, they said, "See" (pointing to the
Apostles,) "why do *they* do on the Sabbath Day what is
not lawful?" The vitality of these artificial trivialities
among the Jews is remarkable. Abarbanel relates that
when in 1492 the Jews were driven from Spain, and not
allowed to enter the city of Fez, lest they should cause
a famine, "they had to live on grass, but 'religiously'
avoided the violation of their Sabbath by plucking the
grass with their hands!" Yet in order to keep the small
regulation, they gave themselves the infinitely greater
Sabbath-labour of *grovelling on their knees, and cropping the
grass with their teeth!* But our Lord at once defended
His poor Apostles from censure by reminding these literal-
ists how on the Sabbath no less a saint than their own
David had illustrated the principle that physical necessities
abrogated ceremonial obligations, and had fearlessly violated the letter of the law by eating the sacred shew-bread
with his companions, though it was "most holy," and was

* See Matt. xii. 5 ; Numb. xxviii. 9.

expressly reserved for the Priests alone.* Mercy is always a thing infinitely more sacred than "miserable micrology."

After the narration of this incident in Luke vi. 1–7, we find in the Cambridge Uncial Manuscript D. the famous *Codex Bezæ*, the passage: "On the same day, observing one working on the Sabbath, He said, 'O man, if indeed thou knowest what thou art doing, thou art blessed, but if thou knowest not, thou art accursed, and a transgressor of the Law.'"†

The authority of a single manuscript is, of course, insufficient to establish the genuineness of this passage as a part of St. Luke's Gospel; but there is much to be said for the authenticity of the fact recorded. A man would not indeed have dared to work *openly* on the Sabbath, for then he would have incurred the certainty of being stoned; but if he had been compelled in some way—say in his own house—to toil for some purpose of necessity, piety, or charity, then his toil was perfectly justified by our Lord's own teaching. Even the wiser Rabbis agreed that it was better to work *seven* days in the week than to beg one's bread. No less a personage than Rabbi Jochanan said—"in the name of the people of Jerusalem"—"*Make thy Sabbath as a week-day rather than depend upon other people.*" ‡ In any case, if there be any basis for the story, in some *agraphon dogma* of Christ current in early Christian days, His meaning could only have been, "If thy work is *of faith*—if thou art thoroughly persuaded in thine inmost heart and conscience that thy Sabbath work is justifiable—then thou art acting with true insight; but if thy work is *not* of faith, it is sin."§

---

* Lev. xxiv. 9, xxii. 10. See 1 Sam. xxi. 6. The scene took place in the Tabernacle at Nob, and Abiathar may have been assisting his father Ahimelech. Mark ii. 26. The words "in the High priesthood of Abiathar" are omitted in D, and some old Latin MSS.; and if the reading τοῦ ἀρχιερέως in A. C., etc., be right, the words might mean "in the times of *Abiathar*."

† On this reading, see Westcott, *Introd. to the Gospels, Appendix C.*

‡ *Pesachim*, f. 113, 1 ; Hershon, *Treasurer of the Talmud*, f. 194.

§ See Rom. xiv. 22, 23 ; 1 Cor. viii. 1.

Not all the Pharisees were scribes or lawyers.*   In Mark ii. 16 we read of " The Scribes of the Pharisees." They were the " doctors " or " theologians " of the Pharisaic party, and were held in the highest honour. When one of them complained that, in His strong denunciations of the Pharisees, Jesus insulted *them* also,† He emphasised His disapproval by pointing out their supercilious tyranny (Luke xi. 46), their insincerity and persecuting rancour (47–51), and their arrogant exclusiveness (52).‡ But His eight-fold " woe " on the Pharisees was even more severe. He upbraided them for their frivolous scrupulosity (Luke xi. 39, 40), mingled with hypocrisy (41); for their gross lack of *reality* in religion (42); for their pride, ambition, and self-seeking (43); and for their hidden depths of corruption, which made them like tombs glistering with whitewash, or graves over which men walked without being aware of the putrescence underneath (44). In the seven great " woes " pronounced in the Temple on the last day of His public ministry, He spoke yet more fully of their blind folly, which carefully strained out the gnat, yet swallowed the camel; which tithed the stalks of pot-herds, yet neglected justice, mercy, and faith; which professed external scrupulosity, while within they were full from extortion and excess; which bound heavy burdens on men's shoulders, and would not move them with one of their fingers; which shut the gate of the kingdom of heaven against men, and neither entered nor suffered them to enter; which compassed sea and land to make one proselyte, and then made him tenfold more a son of Gehenna than themselves; which devoured widows' houses, while for a pretence they

---

* There does not seem to be much distinction between " Scribes " and " Lawyers " or " Teachers of the Law." See Luke xi. 52, 53 ; Matt. xxiii. 13. The name " Scribes " for those who wrote out and studied the Books of the Law begins with Ezra.

† Luke xi. 45.

‡ " Ye have caused many to stumble at the Law."   Mal. ii. 8.

made long prayers. * Severe as are these denunciations, they are amply supported by many scathing passages in the Talmud. To this day in Jerusalem, "You are a *Porish*" (*i. e.*, a Pharisee) is, says Dr. Frankl, a Jewish writer, "the bitterest term of reproach." "They proudly separate themselves," he says, "from the rest of their co-religionists. *Fanatical, bigoted, intolerant, quarrelsome, and in truth irreligious*, with them the outward observance of the ceremonial law is everything; the moral law little binding, morality itself of no importance." † And the results of Pharisaism were wholly bad. Formalism killed religion, as the strangling ivy kills the oak round which it twines. "At last over the whole inert stagnation of the soul there grew a scurf of feeble corruption. Petty vices, meannesses, littlenesses were rife, and there appeared at last nothing to mark the religious man except a little ill-temper, a faint spite against those who held different opinions, and a feeble, self-important pleasure in detecting heresy."

If the Pharisees had only listened to the words of Eternal Wisdom, how different might have been the course of history! But, although Jesus had at first tried to win them by gentle courtesy, they set their faces as a flint against Him, and tried in every way to thwart His efforts and stir up the multitudes to kill Him. They displayed the deadliest insolence—treating with continuous and scornful jeers even His warnings against their besetting avarice.‡ The words of most just judgment which had at last to be uttered by the lips of love, involved the final breach between Him and the self-constituted religious teachers of His day. At the close of one of these utterances, the Pharisees, in a scene of violence almost unique in His ministry, began to press vehemently upon Him, and

---

* Matt. vi. 7, xxiii. 1–36 ; Mark xii. 40 ; Luke xx. 47.

† Frankl, *The Jews in the East*, ii. 27.

‡ ἐξεμυκτήριζον, Luke xvi. 14, xxiii. 35. Comp. 2 Sam. xix. 21 ; Psalm ii. 3–4.

tried to catch grounds of accusation against Him about very many things by treacherous questions, lying in wait for Him to hunt something out of His mouth,* until the very multitude, in alarm and excitement, gathered for His personal protection round the door of the house in which the scene had taken place.

But He came "to cast fire upon the earth"—the fire which is salutary as well as retributive; which warms and purifies as well as consumes. One of the most remarkable of the "unwritten sayings" is "He who is near Me, is near the fire." †

Can there be the least doubt, we ask, after this survey of the invariable teaching of Christ, wherein pure religion does, and wherein it does not, consist? May it not be summed up even in the words of the Old Testament—"He hath shown thee, O man, what is good; and what doth the Lord require of thee, but to do justly, and to love mercy, and to walk humbly with thy God?" St. Paul is emphatic in teaching that in Christ Jesus neither circumcision availeth anything nor uncircumcision, but faith working by love. The revelation of Christ's will is unmistakably plain, His commandments are summed up in the one word "love." He said that to do unto others as we would they should do unto us *is* the Law and the Prophets; that to say, "Lord, Lord," is nothing, but to do the will of His Father in heaven; that if we would enter into life we must keep His commandments; that he who heareth the Word of God and keepeth it, the same is His brother and His sister and His mother. If we care at all for what Christ taught we shall think less than nothing of the devotee's will-worship, or the ascetic's self-torture, or artificial absolutions, or vestments, or shibboleths, or Church exclusiveness, or hierarchic usurpations. What we shall desire will be simple faithfulness in "the daily round, the common task," the humble prayer

---

* Luke xi. 53, 54, ἀποστοματίζειν. . . θηρεῦσαί . . . δεινῶς ἐνέχειν.
† Preserved in Ignatius, Origen, and Didymus.

offered in secret, the sweet silent charities of common life—the imitation of Christ, learnt, not from corrupt manuals, or ecclesiastical traditions, but from His own lips, and His own life, and His own Spirit shed abroad in the hearts of all of every communion who humbly desire to be His true servants, and who prefer His teaching and His example to the intrusive inventions and tyrannies of men deceiving and self-deceived.

CHAPTER XXVII.

THE MIRACLES OF CHRIST.

"Miraculum voco quicquid arduum aut insolitum supra spem vel facultatem mirantis apparet."—AUGUSTINE, *De Util. Cred.* 16.

" Quisquis prodigia ut credat requirit, magnum est ipse prodigium, qui, mundo credente, non credit."—AUG. *De Civ. Dei*, c. 22.

"Prima miracula *confestim* fecit, ne videretur cum labore facere ; postea quum auctoritatem satis constituerat, moram interum adhibuit salutarem."—BENGEL.

I SHALL not here pause to enter once more into the question of the credibility of the Gospel miracles. Enough for us to say that the attempt to account for all Christ's miracles by hallucination or exaggeration breaks down in every direction before the utter simplicity of the Gospel narratives, which differ *toto cœlo* from the portents of the Apocryphal Gospels, and from those invented to glorify mediæval saints. Had the Apostles been capable of deceitful intentions, their narratives would not have been marked by such extreme sobriety and moderation. The miracles which Christ wrought were not denied by the Pharisees, and are admitted even in the Talmud. The Evangelists regarded John the Baptist as the great Forerunner, as the promised Elijah. Yet they acknowledge with the frankest truthfulness that " John did no miracle," and they represent the Son of Man as habitually repressing and restraining His miraculous gifts (Matt. xxvi. 53) ; as only exercising them for definite ends ; and as forbidding many of those who received them to blazon them abroad. He only appealed to His works as giving further emphasis to the grandeur of His words. To all believing Christians the one surpassing, overwhelming miracle is that of the Incarnation.

Christ being what He was, miracles wrought out of com-passion would radiate from Him as naturally as sunbeams from the sun.

In the endeavour to grasp the essential characteristics of our Lord's miracles, and the relation in which they stand to His whole work, we may learn important lessons from the names by which they are ordinarily described. It will be seen at once that they all involved deeds of mercy, or con-veyed lessons of truth, and do not bear the slightest rela-tion to the senseless prodigies of Eastern invention, or Apocryphal romance.

1. In the Synoptic Gospels they are often called "*Powers*" ($\delta\upsilon\nu\acute{a}\mu\varepsilon\iota\varsigma$);* seven times in St. Matthew, and twice in St. Mark and St. Luke; and the word "Power" (A. V. "Virtue"†) is applied to the source from which they emanated. By this designation they are represented as the outcome of a divine gift.

2. The word "*wonders*," or "*portents*" ($\tau\acute{\varepsilon}\rho\alpha\tau\alpha$), is only used of them three times, and always in connection with "signs."‡ This word describes them by the effect of amazement which they produced upon the minds of those who witnessed them. The rousing of astonishment was the lowest and poorest result of our Lord's exercise of His divine gifts, and one which He always discouraged. His object was to lead men beyond the miracle to the facts it was designed to prove.§

3. The word "*Sign*" and "*Signs*" ($\sigma\eta\mu\varepsilon\tilde{\iota}\alpha$) is used fre-quently in the Gospels, and is the designation ordinarily employed by St. John. This word indicates the main pur-

---

*Sometimes rendered in the A. V. "mighty works," "wonderful works," or "miracles." It is not used by St. John.

† 2 Mark v. 30 ; Luke vi. 19.

‡ Matt. xxiv. 24 ; Mark xiii. 22 ; John iv. 48.

§ Matt. viii. 27, ix. 8, 33, xv. 31, etc.; John vi. 26. The name $\theta\alpha\upsilon\mu\acute{a}\sigma\iota\upsilon\nu$ only occurs in Matt. xxi. 15, and $\pi\alpha\rho\acute{a}\delta\upsilon\xi\upsilon\nu$ (something abnormal) only in Luke v. 26 (comp. Mark. ii. 12). Christ recognised this element of the value of miracles. John v. 36, xi. 15, xx. 31 ; Mark ii. 10, 11 ; Matt. xi. 20, 21.

pose for which they were wrought. They were the *credentials* of Christ's divine power, and of His unity with the Father.

4. The fourth name, " *Works*," is almost peculiar to St. John, where it occurs many times.* It is the deepest and most characteristic of the four terms. It represents the miracles as the natural outcome of Christ's relation to the Father, who was the real doer of the works. " They are the periphery of the circle of which He is the centre. The great miracle is the Incarnation ; all else, so to speak, follows naturally and of course. It is no wonder that He whose name is 'Wonderful' (Is. ix. 6) does works of wonder; the only wonder would be if He did them not." † They were the normal fruit of the heavenly tree; the effluence spontaneously irradiated from the Sun of Righteousness. In the miracle of His personality all that might otherwise startle us in the story of His miracles is completely absorbed. The influence of a higher nature finds expression in " works " which are not contrary to, but are beyond, and above, the ordinary working of earth's natural laws.

It is important to observe that miracles do not seem to have been primarily intended as evidences of Christ's divinity, but rather as adding emphasis to His teaching, and calling attention to His unity with the Father. Our

---

* John vi. 28, vii. 21, x. 25, 32, 38, xiv. 11, etc.   But it also occurs in Matt. xi. 2.

† Trench, *On Miracles*, p. 8.   Ullmann, *Sinlessness of Jesus*, p. 193. Ammonius, quoted by Theophylact, misses the force of the word σημεῖον entirely in the definition τέρας παρὰ φύσιν, σημεῖα παρὰ συνήθειαν γίνεται. Schleiermacher (*Leben Jesu*, p. 206) rightly says, " In σημεῖον the most prominent thing is the significance of what we should deduce from the result ; in δύναμις, ' power,' the chief thing is the nature of the actor—that he has in himself such a power ; and in τέρας, ' wonder,' the comparison of this result with other results."   In Acts ii. 22, St. Peter, using the three words, says that " Jesus of Nazareth was approved of God unto you by powers, and wonders, and signs, which God did by Him in the midst of you, even as ye yourselves know."   See Steinmeyer. *On Miracles*, p. 42 ; Col. i. 19.

Lord was well aware that miracles will not convince the obstinate and the hardened.* His miracles were forms of Revelation.† Had they been meant to prostrate opposition, or to *enforce* belief, their characteristics would have been different; nor, in that case, would our Lord have persistently refused to exhibit the startling and overwhelming "sign from heaven"—the miracle of constantly-descending manna to supply bodily needs, or the portent in the sun or moon or stars—which the Pharisees and the multitude demanded. In all true and transforming faith there is a moral and spiritual element, and Jesus taught that it was a higher thing to believe in His words, and to recognise that the words which He spake were Spirit and were Life, than to believe for the works' sake.‡ The miracles were not acts of His divinity working apart from His humanity. He was truly God, perfectly man, indivisibly God-Man, distinctly God and Man; and He appeals to His works only to prove that the Father dwelt in Him, with whom He was indissolubly united.§ He was co-ordinately the Doer of the works.‖ Hence the miracles "belong properly to the believer and not to the doubter. They are a treasure rather than a bulwark. They are in their inmost sense instruction and not evidence." ¶

All of our Lord's miracles fall under the three heads of miracles on Nature, on man, and on the spirit-world.

1. The miracles exercised in the world of Nature are, for reasons already indicated, the rarest. With the exception

* Luke xvi. 31. Comp. John. xii. 37, xi. 45, 46.

† St. Thomas Aquinas distinguishes between *miracula quæ sunt ad fidei confirmationem*, and *miracula de quibus ipsa est fides*. See Steinmeyer, *On the Miracles*, p. 7; Wendt ii. 192–197.

‡ Theophylact wisely wrote, " Preaching is confirmed by miracles, and miracles by preaching."

§ John xiv. 10.

‖ John v. 17, 19.

¶ Westcott, *The Gospel Miracles*, p. 7. Gerhard says, " Miracula sunt doctrinæ tesseræ et sigilla; quemadmodum igitur sigillum literis avulsum nihil probat, ita quoque miracula sine doctrina nihil valent."

of the two miracles of the multiplication of the loaves and fishes—of which, perhaps, the real character was scarcely understood by most of the 5000 and of the 4000 for whose benefit they were wrought—the Nature-miracles were only directly witnessed by Christ's nearest disciples. These were the changing of water into wine, the stilling of the storm, the walking on the sea, and the withering of the barren fig-tree. The miracles of the two draughts of fishes are probably to be regarded rather as instances of supernatural knowledge than as supersessions of the normal course of natural laws.*

2. The miracles on man were, without exception, works of mercy to relieve the sick and the suffering. They are healings of the blind ; † of the deaf and dumb ; of the impotent ; of the sick ; of lepers ; of the palsied ; of the dropsical ; of the fever-stricken ; of the man with the withered hand ; of the woman with the issue. They were granted either to the faith of personal suppliants, or to the intercession of their parents or friends.

3. The miracles on the spirit-world are chiefly those extended to men or women possessed of the demons,‡ who

---

* Luke v. 1–11 ; John xxi. 1–23. The story of the *stater* in the fish's mouth stands in all respects alone. It is not said that any miracle was wrought. It taught no spiritual truth, and did not arise from pity, nor depend on faith. The meaning of the words has probably been misunderstood. On this subject I must refer to what I have said in *The Life of Christ*.

† Found in the Gospels only in Mark viii. 23 ; Matt. ix. 29, xi. 4, 5, xv. 30, xx. 34, xxi. 14 ; Luke vii. 22 ; John ix. 6.

‡ Δαιμόνια, always "demons" (Heb. *Shedîm*). It is a pity that even the Revised Version preserved the erroneous version "devils." Josephus, in accordance with the general view of that day, defines "demons" as "*the spirits of wicked men, entering into, and slaying, the living.*" See *Antt.* vi. 8, 2, ii. 3 ; *B. J.* viii. 6, 3. For a full discussion of the nature of demoniac possession, see Jahn, *Archæologia Biblica*, E. T., pp. 200–216. Weber, *Syst. d. altsynag. Paläst. Theol.* The Talmud describes "demons" as resembling men. *Pesikta*, i. 504. In the Book of Enoch (xv.) they are regarded as fallen angels (comp. 1 Cor. x. 20). If the account of an exorciser in Josephus (*Antt.* viii. 2, 5) be compared with the Gospel narratives it will be seen at once how free from superstition, and stamped with the mark of truth, are the latter.

afflicted them either with wild and convulsive madness, or with grievous physical calamities. There were also three instances in which Jesus raised the dead—the daughter of Jairus; the young son of the widow of Nain; and Lazarus whom he loved. The whole series of miracles, of which thirty-three are recorded by the Evangelists,* was crowned by our Lord's own Resurrection and Ascension, when by death He had conquered him that hath the power of death—that is the Devil.

It is not unnatural to ask how it came about that such miracles of power and mercy, and many which were wrought collectively, and on a large scale, did not—even apart from our Lord's teaching—exercise a more decisive effect in hushing all criticism, and overcoming all opposition. The answer seems to be twofold. On the one hand, miracles, or what passed as such, were not unknown in the Eastern world.† Various Rabbis are said to have wrought miracles, and our Lord Himself tells us that exorcism was commonly practised among the Jews themselves. " If I by Beelzebul cast out demons, by whom do your sons cast them out? Therefore shall they be your judges." ‡ Indeed, according to Josephus, the power to eject demons has been specially bestowed upon his people, and he tells one remarkable story respecting it. What was known as demoniacal possession often showed itself in forms of violent nervous excitement, by which the sin-polluted mind swayed the functions and temperaments of the degraded and weakened body. Such emotional conditions are capable of being affected by the influence of stronger wills and

---

* St. Matthew narrates twenty miracles; St. Mark, eighteen; St. Luke, nineteen; St. John, seven.

† Jos. *B. J.* vii. 6, 3; *Antt.* viii. 2, 5; *Dial. c. Tryph.* i.

‡ Matt. xii. 27; Mark iii. 22, etc. The true reading seems to be Beelzebul. Beelzebub was the name of the god of Ekron, like Zeus *Apomuios*, " the averter of flies," 2 Kings i. 2. Beelzebul may mean " the lord of the (celestial) habitation," or, as a Jewish name of scorn, " lord of dung."—See Jahn, *Archæologia Biblica.*

holier personalities.* It was easy, within certain limits, even for an impostor to excite a belief in his possession of supernatural powers, as was the case with Theudas, who led hundreds of deluded followers to feel confident that he could divide the Jordan before them, and lead them over dryshod; † and during the procuratorship of Felix no less than 30,000 had assembled on the Mount of Olives in the belief that another impostor would throw down the walls of Jerusalem before their advancing footsteps. The Pharisees, without the smallest tendency to believe in Christ, yet admitted, and were forced to admit, that He *did* work miracles, and that His miracles were works of love and mercy.‡

But, secondly, the Pharisees nullified the effect of them on the minds of the multitude by attributing them to the co-operation of evil spirits. They constantly averred that Christ " had a demon," who conferred on Him the power of doing wonders. They challenged Him to perform some " sign *from heaven*," such as no demon could perform ; but He refused to meet a challenge which would not, even if it had been performed, have really swept away their doubts ; and He pointed them to His teaching, and the sign of the Prophet Jonah. The preaching of Jonah had converted the Ninevites ; the Queen of the South had come all the way to Jerusalem to hear the wisdom of Solomon ; if they refused to listen to one greater than Jonah or Solomon they would harden their hearts even to the end.

His Miracles of Mercy, the course of which seems to have begun with the healing of the demoniac at Caper-

---

* " Demons" were supposed to be the spirits of the wicked dead. Jos. *B. J.* vii. 6, 3. The Jews attributed all sorts of moral failures and physical calamities to demons (as is still the case in the East, where they are called *devs*). See Ps. xci. 6, lxx.; Targ. Cant. iv. 6.

† Jos. *Antt*. xix. 5, 1. Comp. *B. J.* c 13, 4.

‡ John xi. 47, xii. 19. Miracles which could not be denied were attributed to *kîshoof*, " magic." *Sanhedrin*, vii. 13, 19. See Derenbourg, pp. 106, 361.

naum,* were in the great majority of instances miracles of simple compassion.   Jesus suffered with those whom He saw suffer, and St. Mark records how, at the sight of human infirmity, a sigh was wrung from His inmost heart.†
"*I have compassion on the multitude,*" was a feeling which always filled the Saviour's soul. ‡   His miracles all look back to the Incarnation, and forward to the Ascension, now bringing God to man, and now raising man to God, as signs of the full accomplishment of his earthly work. §   They differ fundamentally from the legends and miracles of other religions.   Each miracle was also the revelation of a mystery, and all tend to raise us from a blind idolatry of physical laws to the consciousness of a nobler presence, and of a higher power.   Thus they are a prophecy of a more glorious world, and a revelation of a near God unseen—an Epiphany of sovereignty and of mercy.   They involve a revelation of hope, of restoration, of forgiveness.   The same powers which conquered sickness and death are not less mighty to overcome their spiritual antitypes, "the blindness of sensuality and the leprosy of caste, the fever of restlessness, the palsy of indolence, the death of sin."

I have already pointed out that it is no small indication of the simple truthfulness of the Gospels that although John stood among the greatest of the Prophets they do not attribute to him a single miracle.   "John did no miracle," yet he exercised over the people a stupendous influence. The Evangelists only attribute to Christ these works, and signs, and powers, because they narrated things as they were, with no desire to suppress any more than to invent.

* Mark i. 21–34.   † Mark vii. 34.
‡ Mark i. 41, viii. 2.   Comp. Matt. ix. 36, xiv. 14, xx. 34 ; Luke vii. 13.
§ I here refer to the wise teaching on this subject in Bp. Westcott's *Characteristics of the Gospel Miracles.*

CHAPTER XXVIII.

THE GLADNESS AND SORROW OF THE CHRIST.

τὸ δάκρυον αὐτοῦ χαρὰ ἡμετρά.—ATHANASIUS, *De Incarn.*

" Crede mihi, res severa est verum gaudium."—AUGUSTINE.

IT has been an error, and one not wholly devoid of disastrous consequences, to regard the life of our Lord on earth
as a life of continuous and almost overwhelming sorrow.
This has arisen from too exclusive a contemplation of His
last year of flight and rejection, and of the anguish of His
death and passion ; and it has led to the overlooking of the
indications which point to the many gladder hours of the
Son of Man. He did, indeed, "bear our griefs and carry
our sorrows"; * but man's life is not an unbroken misery,
and Jesus had the deepest sympathy with all natural and
innocent sources of gladness. Nay more, He often called
attention to the truth that, in despite of earthly trials and
persecution, the Christian's joy shines on like a lamp,
unquenched by the darkness of the tomb. In the midst of
the worst misfortunes which the devil or the world could
inflict, He bade His followers to be not only patient in
tribulation, but also to rejoice in hope ; †—to "rejoice and
be exceeding glad," for great was their reward in heaven ;
nay, even to recognise their deep blessedness and " to leap
for joy." ‡ He never intended to reduce the natural
blessedness of life to an artificial monotony of woe-begone
abjectness. It was one of the objects of His life to give to
men " the oil of exultation for mourning, the spirit of joy

* Is. liii. 4 : Heb. ix. 28 ; Matt. viii. 17. " Himself took our infirmities
and bare our diseases."

† Matt. v. 12.   ‡ Luke vi. 23.

for the spirit of heaviness"; * by His gift they should exult " with joy unspeakable and full of glory." †

When the seventy returned with joy at the proof that even demons were subject unto them in Christ's name, He bade them to rejoice still more that their names were written in heaven. ‡ The word ἀγαλλίασις, " exultation," means " abounding and overflowing joy," and not only did Jesus bid His disciples "to exult," but in witnessing the success of their simple-hearted ministrations He Himself " exulted in spirit." §

Must we not feel confident that, during the thirty almost unrecorded years of life, in the lovely country, in the pure and happy home, in the humble and honourable toil, Jesus must have tasted of the most limpid well-springs of human happiness? This happiness must have been immeasurably increased because His heart, unstained by any shadow of guilt, reflected the very blue of heaven. Let any one consider how much our human life is darkened by the deceitfulness of sin; by the stings of shame; by the voice of a self-reproach which cannot be silenced; by the memory of wasted hours and desecrated gifts; by erring jndgments; by the constant sense of moral failure and unworthiness— and he will then be able to estimate what must have been the boyish and youthful happiness of one whose thoughts were ever—

> " Pleasant as roses in the thickets blown,
> And pure as dew bathing their crimson leaves."

But do not we further see the constant elements of simple gladness throughout our Lord's ministry? He discounte-

* Heb. i. 9, ἔλαιον ἀγαλλίασεως. Comp. LXX.; Ps. xlv. 7, 8.

† John xvi. 22 ; 1 Peter i. 6, 8, iv. 13 ; Rev. xix. 7 ; Acts ii. 26 ; Jude 24.

‡ Luke x. 20.

§ Luke x. 21, ἠγαλλίασατο τῷ πνεύματι (the opposite extreme of emotion to ἐνεβριμήσατο τῷ πνεύματι in John xi. 33). In the spurious letter of P. Lentulus to the Senate, it is said that " He wept oft, but no one had ever seen Him smile." This is an instance of the erroneous conception and groundless tradi- tion which I have pointed out.

nanced the showy abstinences of the Pharisees; He practised no form of Essene rigorism; He had nothing of the
habitual fulmination and stern asperities of the Baptist:
He neither practised fasting Himself, nor encouraged His
disciples to do so. His whole attitude towards life show
us that "self-chosen, self-inflicted suffering, where it is not
a wise discipline, is ingratitude to God, or rather it is
partial suicide. The suffering in itself is nothing worth,
the moral end for which it is the means gives it its
value." *

He only recognised fasting as the natural expression of
natural grief. He was radically opposed to the conception
which looked upon self-inflicted burdens as a method for
extorting God's approval. He compared the ministry of
John to children playing at funerals in the market-places,
among companions who would not mourn; and His own
ministry to the games of merry children, playing at wed-
dings, and piping for sullen comrades who would not dance.
Throughout His life Jesus must have had in His heart pure
fountains of perennial joy. He never knew, He could not
know—except by keen sympathy with the lost—the accumulated miseries of selfishness, and its inevitable disappoint-
ments. He never knew, He could not know, those terrors
of a fearful expectation of most just judgment when
" Iniquity hath played her part, and Vengeance leaps upon
the stage "—when " man's gifts begin to fade as though a
worm were gnawing at them "—when " the gnawing conscience reawakens the warning conscience "—when " Fear
and Anguish divide the man's soul between them, and the
Furies of Hell leap upon his heart like a stage "—when
" Thought calleth to Fear, Fear whistleth to Horror; Hatred
beckoneth to Despair, and saith, ' Come and help me to
torment this sinner.' One saith that she cometh from this
sin, and another saith that she cometh from that sin—so the
man goes through a thousand deaths and cannot die. Irons

* Westcott, *The Victory of the Cross*, p. 82.

are laid upon his body like a prisoner. All his lights are put out at once." *

These worst tragedies of human existence could never be personally experienced by Him who was " holy, harmless, undefiled, separate from sinners, and made higher than the heavens."

All that we read of His ministry illustrates the noble words of the poet :

> " Gladness be with Thee, Saviour of the world !
> I think this is the essential sign and seal
> Of goodness, that it ever waxes glad,
> And more glad, till the gladness blossoms forth
> Into a rage to suffer for mankind
> And recommence at sorrow."

It was almost exclusively after the culmination of His ministry that sorrows burst like a hurricane upon the life of the Saviour of the world. His afflictions came from the wickedness of men, and always, in our human career,

> " Man is to man the sorest, surest ill."

Yet we have learnt from Him that "*our* light affliction, which is but for a moment, worketh for us, more and more exceedingly, an eternal weight of glory, while we look not at the things which are seen, but at the things which are not seen." † We must remember that, far more than is the case with us, Christ, in the midst of things temporal, and the worst trials which they could bring, was living in the constant realisation of the things unseen and eternal. The human privations—the homeliness of Him who had not where to lay His Head, the poverty, the wanderings, the intense, bitter, unscrupulous hatred and opposition of the religious leaders of His day, the calumnious meanness of those who called Him " a gluttonous man and a wine-bibber," " a Samaritan," " a blasphemer," " a Sabbath-breaker," and said that He had a demon, and was the agent

* Henry More, *The Betraying of Christ*. † 2 Cor. iv. 17.

of Beelzebul—these He could lightly disregard.   They
simply arose from the fact that—

> " The base man, judging of the good,
>   Puts his own baseness to him, by default
>   Of will and nature."

It has never been otherwise in any age or nation.

> " It is the penalty of being great
>   Still to be aimed at " ;

and even Plato wrote, " The just man will be scourged,
racked, bound, blinded and after suffering many ills, will
be crucified " ($\grave{\alpha}\nu\alpha\sigma\chi\iota\nu\delta\upsilon\lambda\epsilon\upsilon\vartheta\acute{\eta}\sigma\epsilon\tau\alpha\iota$).*

Calumny and misrepresentation pained Him, not at all
on His own account, but out of pity for the wretches who,
under pretence of religion, could be so grossly guilty of
such slanderous lies.   That men who proposed to teach
truth should revel in falsehood ; that men who claimed to
be sources of light should live in a self-chosen darkness ;
that men who ought to have set the example of love and
humility should use every power they possessed to dis-
seminate an arrogant hatred—these were thorns in His
crown of sorrow ; and

> " Face loved of little children long ago,
>   Head hated of the Priests and Elders then,
>   Say was not this Thy sorrow—to foreknow
>   In Thy last hour the deeds of Christian men ? "

Christ bore the worst which a bad world and a corrupted
Church could inflict upon Him ; yet, through His invisible
aid and presence, His followers in all ages have learnt how
to be in need as well as how to abound.   Amid the utmost
evils with which men could torture them, they have known
how to be " pressed on every side, yet not straitened ;
perplexed, yet not unto despair ; pursued, yet not forsaken ; smitten down, yet not destroyed ; always bearing

* Plato, *De Rep.* ii. 362.

about in the body the dying of the Lord Jesus, that the
life also of Jesus may be manifested in their body." *

There was one trial which, most of all, made the iron
enter into Christ's soul. When the gleam of enthusiasm
which welcomed His early preaching had died out ; when
the people took wilful offence at the words which they
would not understand ; when he began to doubt whether
even His beloved disciples might not fall away from Him ;
when He could hardly speak in any Synagogue without
seeing the Scribes and Pharisees, who came to spy upon
Him from Jerusalem, scowling at Him in bitter envy, or
regarding Him with supercilious smiles of fancied superiority ; when He heard their

> " Blind and naked Ignorance
> Delivering brawling judgments all day long
> On all things unashamed " ;

when He, in His Divine, ethereal loftiness of soul, was
thrust into daily contact with every form of meanness and
misery, in the vulgarities, the garrulities, the disgraces,
the insinuated slanders, the infinitesimal littleness of fallen
human souls, which boasted of their immaculate upright-
ness ; when He was hardly safe from personal molestation
even in the towns and villages of Galilee ; when He heard
that " the fox " Herod Antipas † had designs to seize Him ;
when He learnt that not only *the disciples* of John, but
even the Baptist himself, in his rocky dungeon, were beginning to yield to doubts respecting Him ; when flight
into heathen lands and concealment in distant cities
became a necessity ; when on every side He encountered
opposition and unbelief ; when He witnessed around Him
the ravages of disease and the triumphs of the Evil One,

---

* 2 Cor. iv. 8, 9, 10.

† Literally, " Go ye and tell *this she-fox* " (τῇ ἀλώπεκι τάντῃ) 'Αλωπεκίζω in
Aristophanes (*Vesp.* i. 241) means " to make *covert-attacks*." It is remarkable as being the only recorded word of unmitigated *contempt* which our Lord
ever used.

and looked out over a Dead Sea of human debasement, whose raging and swelling waters cast up mire and dirt; when He saw "faces with the terrible stamp of various degradation, and features scarred by sickness, dimmed by sensuality, convulsed by passion, pinched by poverty, shadowed by sorrow, branded with remorse, broken down by labour, tortured by disease, dishonoured with foul uses;" when He saw religion itself degraded into petty feebleness and rotted with conceit and posturing hypocrisy; when He saw "intellects without power, hearts without life, men with their bones full of the sin of their youth;" when instead of what should be the true nobleness of Humanity, with

> "Its godlike head crowned with spiritual stars
> And touching other worlds,"

He saw the pretence of religion conjoined with the depths of wickedness:—then, that which was far more full of anguish to the perfect holiness of Jesus than the sting of death itself, was trembling pity for the victims of the world, the flesh, and the devil, in their apparently hopeless overthrow; in their awful, and, to all love short of the Divine, their apparently *irremediable* degradation.

It is interesting and deeply instructive to consider the words used by the Evangelists to indicate the emotions of Jesus as He was brought face to face with these all but universal indications of human weakness, misery, and sin— of false religion and of hopes vain or vile.

1. One of the commonest feelings attributed to Him is *Pity.** St. Paul tells his beloved Phillippians how he longed after them all "in the tender mercies of Jesus Christ"; and we are told again and again in the Gospels of the yearning compassion of Jesus over human beings in

* Σπλαγχνίζομαι. The word σπλάγχνα, "tender compassion," in several passages of the Authorised Version, is with disastrous literalness rendered "bowels," 2 Cor. vi. 12, vii. 15; Phil. i. 8; Col. iii. 12; Philem. 7. 12, 20 1 John iii. 17.

their afflictions.   Thus, when He saw the multitudes in the cities and villages, "He was moved with compassion for them because they were harassed * and scattered,† as sheep when they have no shepherd."   And when the great multitudes had followed Him on foot out of their cities into a desert place, He had compassion on them, and healed their sick, and would not let them depart in hunger, but

> " He fed their souls with bread from Heaven
> Then stayed their sinking frame." ‡

Again, on the eastern side of the lake, after healing the lame, blind, dumb, maimed, and many whom they cast down at His feet, He said, "I have compassion on the multitude," and, once more, miraculously provided for their needs.§   He had compassion on Bartimæus and his blind companion at Jericho ; ‖ and on the leper who came beseeching Him as He descended from the Mount of Beatitudes,¶ and on the Demoniac Boy,** and on the widow of Nain.†† We cannot doubt that His heart was thrilled by incessant pity. We cannot fathom the depths of His sympathy. But *this* sorrow had its own alleviation, for it was the intensest joy to Him to relieve the sufferings of men.

2. We are also told of the "*wonder*" or "*surprise*" of Jesus. This was sometimes awakened by the happy discovery of faith in unexpected quarters, as, for instance, in the Gentile Centurion at Capernaum.‡‡ More often His wonder was mingled with deepening regret at the unbelief

* ἐσκυλμένοι.   The original meaning of the verb is " to flay," and then " to worry."

† ἐρριμένοι, " outcast," utterly neglected (by their proper teachers).

‡ Matt. xiv. 14, 15 ; Mark vi. 34.

§ Matt. xv. 32 ; Mark viii. 2.

‖ Matt. xx. 34.   ¶ Mark i. 41.

** Mark ix. 22.

†† Luke vii. 13.   The word is not found in St. John's Gospel.

‡‡ Matt. viii. 10; Luke vii. 9.

of those who should have known Him, and who prevented
all possibility of His doing many good works among them
by their lack of faith. This was the case at His own city,
Nazareth, and here it must have grieved him most.*

3. Sometimes this surprise deepened into *grief* and
anger. In the synagogue, when He was about to heal the
man with the withered hand, and came into collision with
the obstinate, conceited, sham-infallibility of the small-
minded sticklers for religious convention, " He looked
round about on them with anger, being at the same time
grieved at the callosity of their heart." † Jesus also felt
most deeply the sting of thanklessness in those who had
been the recipients of inestimable gifts. He sometimes
felt as if all His mercies were " falling into a deep, silent
grave," and He might have said :

> " Blow, blow, thou winter wind,
> Thou art not so unkind
> As man's ingratitude." ‡

This the only passage in which " *anger* " (ὀργή) is directly
attributed to Jesus ; and the only other scene in which His
"*grief*" is spoken of is when in the Garden of Gethsemane
His soul was " exceeding sorrowful even unto death." §

4. It is interesting to observe that the verb " He *was
much displeased*," or, more accurately, " *was indignant* "
(ἠγανάκτησε), is used of our Lord but once (Mark x. 14).
It is used of the Apostles,‖ and of the Chief Priests, ¶ and
of the foolish ruler of the synagogue ;** but only once of
Christ. And what was it that thus kindled the indignation
of the " Blessed One " ? Simply the fact that the Apostles
in their lack of sympathy had gone so far as to " rebuke "

---

* Mark vi. 6. † Mark iii., 5, συλλυπούμενος ἐπὶ τῇ πωρώσει.
‡ See Luke xvii. 18.
§ περίλυπός. Matt. xxvi. 38 ; Mark xiv. 34. Comp. ἐκθαμβεῖσθαι, Mark
xiv. 33.
‖ Matt. xx. 24, xxvi. 8 ; Mark xiv. 4. ¶ Matt. xxi. 15.
** Luke xiii. 14.

the mothers who brought to Jesus the little children whom He so tenderly loved. Nothing so deeply stirs the heart of the Lord of love as the lack of love in those whom He loves.

5. We find, however, a strong and expressive verb (ἐμβριμάομαι) used to indicate His self-restraint amid the impulses of holy indignation.* In the Authorised and Revised Versions it is rendered "*He groaned in the spirit*" (Vulg. *infremuit spiritu*), and in the margin, "He was moved with indignation in the spirit." † This feeling was caused by the heart-rending spectacle of the wailing of the Jews, and of Martha and Mary, for the dead Lazarus. It perhaps implies emotion "at the sight of the momentary triumph of evil, as *death*, or the devil, who had brought sin into the world, and death through sin, which was here shown under circumstances of the deepest pathos."

6. It is followed by the word, "*He was troubled*," or (more literally) "*He troubled Himself.*" This is a peculiar and striking expression. It is true that in other passages St. John merely says that our Lord "was troubled in Spirit;" ‡ but still the phrase "He troubled Himself" seems to imply His entire control over all the impulses of His own heart. His emotions never swept Him away, as ours do, with a resistless force, but were firmly under His

---

* On this word, see Matt. ix. 30; Mark i. 43, xiv. 4, and comp. Lam. ii. 6 (LXX.). It perhaps means that He put constraint on His Spirit in John xi. 33.

† John xi. 33. In Matt. ix. 31, it is rendered "He strictly" (or "sternly") "charged them," where it is used of the injunction to the blind men not to spread abroad the news of their healing. So in Mark i. 43 of the leper. In Mark xiv. 4 it is used of the "indignation" of Judas and others against Mary of Bethany. In Classical Greek it is used of the roaring of a lion, or the snorting of a steed (Æsch. *Theb.* 461); and then of vehement threats (Ar. *Eq.* 855). *Brime* or *Brimo* was a name for Persephone, "the Angered." See Trench, *On the Miracles*, p. 432. Euthymius explains the verb ἐμβριμάοαι, by "a stern look, accompanied by a shake of the head." It is used by Aquila and Symmachus to render Ps. vii. 11; Is. xvii. 13.

‡ John xiii. 21 (comp. xii. 27.)

own power. The emotion of Jesus shows that though He did not approve of the Stoic *apathy*, His feelings were always kept under the holy bonds of self-restraint.* " *Turbatus est*," says St. Augustine, " *quia voluit*."

As regards the outward expressions of emotion, we are told once, and once only, that Jesus " *sighed deeply*," once only that He " *wept*," once only that He was well-nigh " *stupefied with grief*," once only that He " *wailed aloud*."

7. He sighed, or perhaps "*groaned*," † at the sight of the helplessness of the blind man whom He healed, for He never looked with indifference on the spectacle of human infirmity.

8. He shed " *silent tears* " at the grave of Lazarus, ‡ not only " because He loved him "—as the Jews surmised, for He knew that He was about immediately to recall him from the grave—but because He then saw, on every side of Him in the wailing Jews and the wailing family, the proofs of ruined earth and sinful man—the outcome of that first transgression which lost for man his primæval Paradise, and " brought sin into the world and all our woe."

9. The word ἀδημονεῖν, a word which expresses the crushing and stunning weight of *overwhelming sorrow*, is only used of the Agony in the Garden. It swayed His human spirit with awful power. §

10. He " *wailed aloud*" (ἔκλαυσεν) but once, and again it was from the sense of profoundest pity. It was when, from the rocky plateau at the turn of the road from Bethany to Jerusalem, the glorious guilty city burst suddenly upon His view, rising out of the deep umbrageous valley with its "imperial mantle of proud towers." There

---

* The μετριοπάθεια of the Peripatetic philosophers.

† ἐστέναξεν, Mark vii. 34. Here only in the Gospels (but see Rom. viii. 23 ; 2 Cor. v. 2, 4,), and ἀναστενάξας τῷ πνεύματι, Mark viii. 12.

‡ ἐδάκρυσεν, John xi. 35.

§ In Aquila this verb is used in Job xviii. 20 ; Ps. cxvi. 11. Jesus is only recorded to have used the word "soul" of Himself in Matt. xxvi. 38 ; John xii. 27.

stood the Temple with its pinnacles and gilded roofs, re-
flecting the morning light with such fiery splendour as to
force the spectator to avert his gaze. And well might He
wail aloud! Was not the city of Jerusalem the most
" religious " city in the the world? Was it not wholly
devoted to religion, or, at any rate, to religionism? Could
not its Temple Service number its white-robed array of
40,000 priests, and its endless army of attendant Levites?
Did not the blast of silver trumpets announce daily its
morning and evening sacrifices? Did not the High Priest
enter its Holy of Holies every year with the golden censer
and the blood of Atonement in his hands? Were not some
2,000,000 pilgrims, from every region of the world, with
Gentile proselytes among them, streaming on that very day
to its Paschal Feast? Ah, yes! there was sumptuous ritual
enough, and more than enough, but no righteousness;
abundant externalism, but no religion pure and undefiled;
and to His eyes the city was but as a glistering sepulchre,
a hollow sham. He knew that the Priests and Levites, and
Scribes and Pharisees, were, at that very moment, on the
verge of the deadliest sin in all the world, and that that sin
would involve the ultimate doom of them and of their
whole nation, amid the death-throes of an agony more
everwhelming than any which History has ever known.
All this He knew—and for the only time in all His life
He wailed aloud. For:

> " There is an hour, and Justice marks the date
> For long-enduring Clemency to wait :
> That hour elapsed, the incurable revolt
> Is punished—and down comes the thunder-bolt ! "

The scene which burst upon His view, and caused Him to
stop the progress of the humble, joyful procession of those
who loved Him, and believed in Him, and were so full of
hope, was the most visible proof that He had " come unto
His own possessions, and His own people received Him

not." * In the concentrated agony and bitterness of that conviction—the conviction that, in spite of His unbounded tenderness and infinite self-sacrifice, their House would so soon be left unto them desolate—He wailed aloud.† He would fain have gathered their children together as a hen gathereth her chickens under her wings; but now they should be covered indeed, but by "the desolating wing of abomination."‡

He "wailed aloud" out of deep pity; but, afterwards, all the unspeakable agonies of His coming doom, and all the forms of exquisite torture and brutal insult, could not wring from Him one single groan. Personal anguish and affliction could not affect even His humanity half so deeply as the sight of human degradation and the fore-knowledge of all the miseries which sin involves, and of all the deadly catastrophes which it precipitates so unceasingly on the heads of its miserable and deluded votaries.

Forty years afterwards Jerusalem perished amid unspeakable horrors of slaughter and conflagration; and Josephus says that so awful were the calamities that fell on the guilty nation that "their misery was an object of commiseration not to Jews only, but even to those that hated them, and had been the authors of that misery." §

---

* John i. 11, τὰ ἴδια . . . οἱ ἴδιοι.

† There is a remarkable parallel to our Lord's description of His tender yearning for Jerusalem in 2 Esdras i. 30–33.

‡ 1 Dan. ix. 27.

§ 2 Jos. *B. J.* iii. 10, 8.

CHAPTER XXIX.

THE APOSTLES.

" I know Mine own, and Mine own know Me."—John x. 14.

AMONG the many decisive proofs of the Divine Supremacy and Eternal Mission of our Lord, one is the colossal
work effected in the world by the twelve humble Galilean
peasants who were the chosen few. In themselves they
were nothing, and less than nothing. The lordly Priests
and supercilious Pharisees of the Sanhedrin contemptuously
set aside their greatest leaders—Peter and John—as ignorant nobodies and common peasants,* only fit to be thrust
into ward, and threatened, and on due opportunity got rid
of. They were wholly outside the sphere of Roman notice.
Over and over again their lack of apprehension, their un-
imaginative literalism,† their slowness of heart to believe,
their struggles for precedence, their disputes as to which
was the greatest,‡ together with the dulness of their understanding and the selfishness of their individual claims,
wrung from the very depths of His heart—wrung from
Him, in spite of His compassion and love for them, such
sad complaints as, " Why reason ye because ye have no
bread ? Perceive ye not yet, neither understand ? Have ye
your hearts yet hardened ? Having eyes see ye not, and
having ears hear ye not ? Do ye not remember ? How is
it that ye do not understand ? "

* Acts iv. 13. The first five Apostles were of Bethsaida.

† Our Lord's remarks, "I have food to eat that ye know not of," "Our
friend Lazarus sleepeth," "Beware of the leaven of the Pharisees," only called
forth such wooden rejoinders as " Hath any man brought Him aught to eat ? "
" Lord, if he sleep he shall do well " ; " It is because we have no bread."

‡ Matt. xviii. 1–35 ; Mark ix. 33–50 ; Luke ix. 46–50.

On one occasion He exclaimed to them, "O faithless generation, how long shall I be with you? how long shall I suffer you?"* He addressed them as "O ye of little faith." He had to shame their worldly-mindedness by the rebuke, "Verily, I say unto you, except ye become as the little children, ye shall not enter into the Kingdom of Heaven." † They did not grasp His abolition of the distinction between clean and unclean meats. They could not comprehend His teaching about His death and earthly humiliation, and were too much awestruck to ask Him.‡ To their leader He had to say, " Get thee behind me, Satan ; thou art a stumbling-block unto me, for thou mindest not the things of God, but the things of men ; " § and again, "Simon, Simon, Satan obtained you by asking, that he may sift you as wheat." ‖ James and John pained Him by their request for pre-eminent thrones,¶ and by the vindictive fierceness of their Elijah-spirit in desiring to call down fire on the the offending Samaritan village.** Even "the disciple whom He loved " incurred rebuke by forbidding the exorciser who used His name, but "followed not them," to cast out demons. There was something full of charm about the characters of Philip and Thomas, yet to one he had to say, " Have I been so long time with you, and dost thou not know me, Philip?" †† and to Thomas, " Be not faithless, but believing." ‡‡ At the very last, in the hour of His overwhelming peril, His nearest and dearest could not even watch with Him for one hour, and at the terrible moment of His arrest "all the disciples forsook Him and fled." And though He had so often indicated to them His Resurrection from the dead, they treated the earliest reports of those who had seen Him as mere λῆρος—mere idle talk.

* Mark ix. 19. On these rebukes to the Apostles, see Mark iv. 13, 40, vi. 52, viii. 17, 18, 26, 33, ix. 6-19, 32, 34, x. 24, 32, 35, xiv. 40.

† Matt. xviii. 2.

‡ Mark ix. 32. § Matt. xvi. 23. ‖ Luke xxii. 31.

¶ Matt. xx. 22. ** Luke ix. 55, 56.

†† John xiv. 9. ‡‡ John xx. 27.

It is no small testimony to the simple truthfulness of the Gospels that the Apostles and Evangelists thus humbly recorded their own low rank, imperfect education, and utter inadequacy, and handed down the memory of the rebukes which they drew upon themselves by their blank dulness, petty quarrels, and unworthy self-seeking.* Yet because they loved Him, and believed in Him, and had remained with Him in His trials, and wandered with Him over the fields of Galilee, and in His flight to heathen lands, in poverty and hunger, and amid the manifold taunts, brutalities, and scorn of men; because they did not leave Him when men took up stones to stone Him in the Temple courts; because they shared with Him the burning noontides and the homeless nights, He made them blessed above kings and wise men, and sent them forth to ennoble and regenerate the whole wide world. He spent much of the time of His ministry in training them for their high task. He made them His Apostles—*Sheloochim.*† He " sent them forth " to be His authorised delegates among mankind, His fishers of men. He called them His " children,"‡ " His " little flock," His " friends " and " chosen companions," " the salt of the earth," " sons of light," " a city set upon a hill." § Men might despise them and call

---

* Matt. iv. 18, viii. 14, 26, xiii. 52, xiv. 27, 31, xv. 16, xvi. 9, xviii. 1, xx. 20, 26, xxvi. 40 ; Mark xiv. 51.

† The word " Apostle " is used thirty-six times by St. Luke, twenty-one times by St. Paul. Elsewhere only in Mark vi. 30 ; Matt. x. 2. In the LXX. the word only occurs in 1 Kings xiv. 6, where Abijah speaks of himself as commissioned to deliver a stern message to the wife of Jeroboam. The Jews gave the name to the collectors of the Temple tribute. Christ Himself is called " the Apostle and High Priest of our confession " (Heb. iii. 1), as having been commissioned and sent forth by the Father. But the name is not confined to the Twelve. It is given to James, the Lord's brother, and Matthias, and Paul, and Barnabas ; and in Rom. xvi. 7, Andronicus and Junia are said to be " of note among the Apostles." It also means " Messenger " in Phil. ii. 25.

‡ John xiii. 33.

§ Luke xii. 4, 32 ; John xv. 14, 15 ; Matt. v. 13, 14 ; John xii. 36.

them " Beelzebul,"* " as they had called their Master, but
their infinite reward was that they became the soldiers, the
servants, the beloved emissaries of the Lord of Glory. At
His touch, like the gems on the oracular Urim, the character
of each of them gleamed into the most heavenly lustre, and
in a reality more lofty than the metaphor they sat on thrones,
judging the tribes of Israel.† He gave them the fullest
instruction on their commission, their trials, their consolation and their reward, and they were privileged more than
any men to enter into the inmost heart and mind of the
Son of Man.

The lists of the Apostles, as given by the Evangelists, fall
into three well-marked tetrads, ranged in the order of their
nearness to Christ, and the special closeness of intimacy
into which He admitted them.‡

1. The first tetrad consisted of the two pairs of brothers
—Simon and Andrew, James and John. They were the
θεολογικώτατοι, the ἐκλεκτῶν ἐκλεκτότεροι, the *ecclesiola
in ecclesia*, the inmost circle of Christ's friends. Andrew
seems to have been the link of communication between Him
and the others.§ As the first of all the disciples to accept
Jesus,‖ he deserved the high honour of being among the
most chosen, a position for which this fisherman of Bethsaida was well fitted by his humble, blameless, contemplative character. The other three of the first tetrad—Peter,
James, and John, are sometimes called "the Pillar Apos-

---

* The name " Beelzebul" (which is a better attested reading than " Beelzebub ") is possibly a *nickname* of the demon-god of Ekron by the alteration of a
letter. But some of the theories about it seem to be dubious. See Dr.
Cheyne, in *Encycl. Bib. s. v.* " Baalzebub " (2 Kings i. 2) means " Lord of
flies." See p. 298.

† Matt. xix. 28 ; Luke xxii. 30.

‡ Matt. x. 2–4 ; Luke vi. 14–16 ; Mark iii. 16–19, vi. 7 ; Acts i. 13. The
number Twelve is symbolical of completion. It is the number of the Tribes of
Israel. Ex. xxviii. 2 ; Rev. xxi. 14.

§ On two occasions Philip and Andrew are brought together. John i. 44,
vi. 8, xii. 22.

‖ John i. 40.

tles."* They were the only ones admitted to be with Christ at the raising of Jairus' daughter, at the Transfiguration, and at Gethsemane.† James and John were the sons of Zebedee, and of Salome, who, it is nearly certain, was a sister of the Virgin Mary.

2. The second tetrad consisted of Philip, Bartholomew, Thomas, and Matthew. Philip may have been closely connected with Bartholomew; and Thomas, whose surname was "Didymus," or "the Twin," may possibly have been a brother of Matthew.‡

3. The third tetrad consisted of two fathers and two sons—James, the son of Alphæus, and his son Jude (also called Thaddæus and Lebbæus); § Simon the Zealot, and his son Judas Iscariot. If Alphæus, or Clopas ‖ (Chalpai), was, as tradition says, a brother of Joseph, the carpenter of Nazareth, then James was our Lord's first cousin, and Jude His first cousin once removed. It is therefore possible, and not improbable, that in this band of twelve there were four sets of brothers—Simon and Andrew; James and John; Philip and Bartholomew; Matthew, Thomas, and James, sons of Alphæus; and that there were two sets of Apostles who stood to each other in the relation of father and son— namely, James, son of Alphæus, and Jude; Simon the Zealot and Judas Iscariot. It is also a deeply interesting and far from improbable view, that no less than six of the Apostles—James, John, Thomas, Matthew, James the Less, and Jude Thaddæus—were cousins of our Lord.¶

---

* From St. Paul's expression in Gal. ii. 9.

† Mark v. 37 ; Luke viii. 51 ; Matt. xvii. 1, xxvi. 37.

‡ John xi. 16 ; xxi. 2.

§ Jude " of James " is sometimes called " the brother of James," but though the ellipse of the word " brother " is not unprecedented, it is much more probable that " the *son* of James " is intended.

‖ John xix. 25.

¶ Some have supposed that Simon Iscariot was also a son of Clopas. If so *eight* of the Apostles were cousins of Christ. These conclusions are, however, very uncertain.

They were all Galileans with the possible exceptions of Simon the Zealot and Judas Iscariot, who were, perhaps, Jews from the little town of Kerioth *—Kuryetein—ten miles south of Hebron. †

Of some of these Apostles we know next to nothing individually. No incident is recorded of Simon the Zealot,‡ or of James the son of Alphæus, called by St. Mark (xv. 40) "the Little," or "Short of Stature." Nothing is told us about Jude the son of James, except his one perplexed question at the Last Supper. § In spite of the nearness of Andrew to Jesus, little that is distinctive is told us about him, though he was the earliest disciple,‖ and one of the four who specially spoke to Jesus on Mount Olivet.¶ Philip became one of the earliest disciples by the special call of Jesus, ** but after his call (John i. 44) he is only mentioned by St. John in two little incidents—one being the interesting occasion when the Greeks came to him desiring to see Jesus ; †† and another, the remark, "Lord show us the Father, and it sufficeth us." ‡‡ Matthew, or Levi, is only spoken of in connection with his office and his call, §§ but

---

* Josh. xv. 25.

† Simon is called " Iscariot," by the MSS. ℵ B, C, G, L, in John vi. 71, xiii. 26. The MS. *D* often reads, for " Iscariot," ἀπὸ καριῴτου. It is not impossible that Simon *may* have been a Galilean, who, for political reasons, fled southwards to the remote and obscure Kerioth.

‡ ὁ Κανavαῖος does not mean " the Canaanite," or " the man of Cana," but "the Zealot," from " *Kaenna*," " to be hot," *Kineatic* zeal (Ex. xx. 5). The name was taken from the dying words of Matthias, father of Judas Maccabæus, " Be ye zealous for the Law " (1 Macc. ii. 27, 2 iv. 2).

§ John xiv. 22. He is " the three-named disciple." The name Lebbæus is derived from *leb*, " heart "; and the name Thaddæus from *thad*, " bosom." It is another form of Theudas. James and Jude were among the commonest Jewish names.

‖ John i. 40.   ¶ Mark xiii. 3.

** John i. 43. There does not seem to be any traceable significance in the fact that Andrew and Philip have Greek names ; the Jews not unfrequently adopted Hellenistic names.

†† John xii. 20–22.

‡‡ John xiv. 8.   §§ Mark ii. 14.

it is an intensely significant fact that Christ should have chosen for His immediate follower on the one hand a man who had belonged to the fierce uncompromising national party of the Zealots, and on the other a man who had not only accepted the Roman domination, but held the despised and detested office of a *Mokes*, or toll-gatherer.   The character of Thomas, at once faithful and despondent, is depicted for us in a few delicate touches by St. John,* but we see that even when he took the darkest view of the future he was still ready to die with Christ.

In the case of Bartholomew, who was undoubtedly the same as Nathanael, we are only told that he was of Cana in Galilee;† and that our Lord, when He gained him as a disciple by reading the inmost thoughts of his heart, described him as " an Israelite indeed, in whom is no guile." He was one of the happy band of seven to whom the Risen Lord appeared on the shores of the Sea of Galilee,‡ " when the morning was come."

Thus little do we know of the great majority of those whom Christ bade to " be wise as serpents yet simple as doves "; to whom He promised the Spirit of His Father ; and whom He bade to go forth and face the very worst that the world could do to them, certain that through Him they could do all things, and should receive at last their unimaginable reward.§

But is it not an immensely powerful ratification of all that we believe of Jesus as the Son of God, that, with instruments so feeble—by the agency of men humble, poor, unknown, insignificant in the judgment of the world—He should have subdued kingdoms, wrought righteousness, and altered the entire conditions and destinies of the race of

---

* John xi. 16, xiv. 5, xx. 24–29, xxi. 2.

† John xxi. 2.   Nathaniel, like " Theodore " and "Adeodatus," means " the gift of God."   Bartholomew means " son of Tolmai."

‡ John xxi. 2.

§ Matt. v. 12, x. 16, 22, 42.

man? Truly "God chose the foolish things of the world that He might put to shame the wise ; and God chose the weak things of the world to confound the strong ; and the base and despised things of the world, and the things that are not, to bring to naught the things that are." *

The poet makes Cassius say of the great Cæsar:

> "Ye gods! it doth amaze me
> That man of such a feeble temper should
> So get the start of the majestic world,
> And bear the palm alone."

But what works did the mighty Cæsar accomplish which are distantly comparable in eternal significance to the renovation of mankind, the overthrow of the entire conditions of the ancient world, and of the ancient religions, by the agency of this handful of Galilean peasants? Is there any thing parallel to this in the entire history of the world?

> "Such is His will—He takes and He refuses,
> Chooseth Him ministers whom men deny ;
> Great ones nor mighty for His work He chooses—
> No! Such as Paul, or Gideon, or I."

Whence did they derive this unequalled force, this amazing influence? Not from themselves, but solely from the training of their Lord ; from the enthusiasm and the conviction which He had inspired ; from the memory of His sinlessness ; from His words of eternal life ; above all, from the outpouring of His Spirit upon them at Pentecost. After that day, indeed, we lose sight of most of them, and the stories of their travels and their martyrdoms are only recorded by unauthenticated legend. Nevertheless, they sowed the little seed which sprang into the living and mighty tree of Christianity ; and :

* 1 Cor. i. 27. 28.

" The seed,
The tiny seed men laughed at in the dark,
Has risen, and cleft the soil, and grown a bulk
Of spanless girth, that lays on every side
A thousand arms, and rushes to the sun.
There dwelt an iron nature in the grain;
The glittering axe was broken in men's arms,
Their arms were shattered to the shoulder-blade.
Its enemies have fall'n, but this shall grow,
A Night of Summer from the heat, a breath
Of Autumn, dropping fruits of power—and rolled
With Music on the growing breeze of Time
The tops shall strike from star to star, the fangs
Shall move the stony bases of the world."

Apart from Christ they were feeble and insignificant. All their strength, all their wisdom, all their influence came from Him, and Him alone.

CHAPTER XXX.

ST. PETER, ST. JOHN, AND JUDAS.

"Let both grow together until the harvest."—Matt. xiii. 30.

PERHAPS it may be said that though the rest of the Apostles remain but little known, two of them at least were men of unique endowments—Peter and John. I do not add the name of James, because this other "Son of Thunder," though he shared the early fiery impetuosity of his brother, is never mentioned in any incident apart from him. He was indeed the first Apostolic Martyr, as John was the last survivor of the band,[*] and the fact that he was chosen to be the head of the Infant Church in Jerusalem is one illustration of his "light and leading," just as the traditions of his martyrdom illustrate the sweet and tender elements in his character.[†] Yet we cannot trace any results of the influence which he exercised which are at all comparable to those achieved by St. Peter and St. John.

The character of PETER—Symeon, or Simon, the son of John or Jonas [‡]—stands out before us with strange distinctness alike in its strength and in its weakness, in its elements of heroic fidelity and of deplorable fear, of entire self-sacrifice and of self-seeking vulgarism. The quick susceptibility and impetuous eagerness of this warm Galilean heart are again and again illustrated. The Fathers spoke of him

---

[*] Acts xii. 2 ; John xxi. 22.

[†] He was martyred A. D. 44 by Herod Agrippa I. The legends about his conversion of his accuser are found in Euseb. *H. E.* ii. 9 (quoted from the *Hypotyposes* of Clem. Alex. Bk. vii.).

[‡] Symeon (Acts xv. 14), or "Simon," means "hearer." John is a shortened form of Johanan, "the mercy of God" (John i. 42, xxi. 16), and is another form of Jona.

as "the symbol of practical life," whereas St. John was
"the symbol of *theoria*," the contemplative life. St.
Chrysostom calls him "the ever-impassioned, the coryphæus
of the choir of the Apostles." *   He it was who, when so
many were deserting Christ, said, "Lord, to whom shall we
go? Thou hast the words of eternal life." He it was who
justified the name of Kepha which Christ gave him, by
earning chief prominence among the Apostles, often speaking in their name, answering when all were addressed,† and
taking a marked lead among them after the Ascension.‡
He it was who formulated the great confession, "Thou art
the Christ, the Son of the Living God." §   Yet immediately
afterwards he incurred sternest rebuke as "a Satan," and a
stumbling-block. He accepts the early call of Christ, but
at the second call cries, "Depart from me, for I am a sinful
man, O Lord." He wishes to walk to meet his Master over
the stormy waters, yet immediately he began to do so his
faith fails, and he cries out, "Lord, save me: I perish!"
He refuses Christ's act of infinite tenderness in kneeling to
wash his feet, yet immediately afterwards cries, "Lord, not
my feet only, but also my hands and my head." He strikes
the first and only blow for his Master at Gethsemane, yet
the very same night, at the questioning of a servant-maid,
denies Him with oaths and curses. He does not recognise
Christ on the shore after the Resurrection so soon as John,
but the moment he does so he girds his fisher's coat about
him, and plunges into the sea to swim to Him. He is the
first, with consummate boldness, to baptise, and eat and
drink with, a Gentile convert, yet long afterwards, at
Antioch, afraid of "certain who came from James," with
timid lack of candour, he belies his former courage in

* Chrys. *Hom.* liv.

† Matt. xvi. 16, xix. 27 ; Mark viii. 29 ; Luke xii. 41, xxii. 31. Comp.
Matt. xvii. 24, 25, xxvi. 35, 37.

‡ Acts i. 15, ii. 14, iv. 8, v. 29.

§ His brother Andrew had from the first spoken to him of Jesus as the
Messiah, or Anointed of God (John i. 41, 49, vi. 69).

mixing freely with the Gentiles, and carries Barnabas away
with him in his dissimulation. This surely is sufficient to
show that if *he, individually*, was "the Rock" on which
Christ built His Church, the rock was one which was often
as shifting sand ; and that the expression on which so huge
a superstructure of fraud, tyranny, and superstition has
been built, referred only to the fact that, in reward for his
quick insight and bold confession, he was regarded as being
in some ways a leader—though by no means an exclusive
or finally authoritative leader—among the Apostles,* and
that to him was granted the glorious prerogative of prepar-
ing for the evangelisation of the whole world by being the
first to admit the Gentiles into the fold of Christ's Church.
But it was only in this secondary and metaphorical sense
that Christ built His Church on Peter as a rock ; † for elsewhere we are told that the Church is built on the foundation, not of one erring man, but of all the Apostles and
Prophets, and still more on Christ Himself, who is at once
the Foundation and the Chief Corner-stone.‡ We may well
ask with David, and with Isaiah, "Who is a rock, save our
God?" and say with St. Paul, "Other foundation can no
man lay than that which is laid, which is Christ Jesus." §

---

* As is clear from John xxi. 19–23 ; Luke xxii. 24–26 ; Gal. ii. 9, etc. The
building of the claims of the Church of Rome on this phrase is, says Dean
Plumptre, "but the idlest of fantastic dreams, fit only to find its place in that
Limbo of Vanities which contains, among other abortive or morbid growths,
the monstrosities of interpretation."

† This passage is the only one in the Gospels in which Christ uses the word
"Church" (Heb. *Kahal*), for in Matt. xviii. 17, the word only means the local
congregation. (Comp. Acts xix. 32, 41.) Everywhere else He speaks not of
His "Church" but of His "Kingdom."

‡ 1 Cor. iii. 11.

§ 2 Sam. xxii. 32 ; Is. xxviii. 16, xliv. 8 ; 1 Cor. iii. 11, x. 4. In the Old
Testament the metaphor of a Rock is applied always to God, not to a man
(Deut. xxxii. 4, 18 ; Ps. xviii. 2, 31, 46 ; Is. xvii. 10 ; etc.). In Is. li. 1
Abraham is called "the rock" (*Tsur*) whence Israel was hewn. St. Paul certainly recognised no supremacy of Peter, for he calls himself "not a whit
behind the very chiefest Apostles" (2 Cor. xi. 5, xii. 11), and he openly
rebuked Peter for timid unfaithfulness (Gal. ii. 11).

Nor, in any case, has the privilege granted to St. Peter the most distantly remote bearing on the colossal usurpations of the Church of Rome.

ST. JOHN'S faults—his jealousy of "outsiders,"[*] his vindictiveness,[†] his passion to have the pre-eminence [‡]— are set forth with the same unvarnished faithfulness as those of St. Peter; yet it will be his glory to all time to have been "the disciple whom Jesus loved," the disciple who, at the Last Supper, leaned his young head upon His breast. To the last, as is proved by the rich traditions respecting his later years, he retained his burning energy, his impetuous horror against wickedness and apostasy which gained from Christ the name of "Sons of Thunder" (*Benî Regesh?*) for the brothers whose life was often as lightning and their words as thunder.[§] It is in the Apocalypse, in his Gospel, and in his Epistles that we learn to understand the depth, force, and loveliness of this disciple's character; his rare combination of meditativeness and passion, of strength and sweetness, of imperious force and most tender affection. We lose sight of him for many years, which he doubtless spent in preparation for the work which he would have to do when the call came, and in devoted care of the Virgin Mother, whom Christ had so specially entrusted to his charge.[||] Who can measure the

---

[*] Mark ix. 38.   [†] Luke ix. 54.   [‡] Mark x. 35-45.

[§] The Greek Church calls John βροντόφωνος, "the Thunder-voiced." The form of the word *Boanerges* is perplexing and difficult of explanation, as it can hardly be a phonetic corruption of *Benî Regesh*. It never came into common use. See Dalman, *Die Worte Jesu*, 39.

[||] In his own Gospel he generally alludes to himself as "the other disciple" (xviii. 15, xx. 2, 3), or "the disciple whom Jesus loved" (xiii. 23, xix. 26). The account of the origin of the Gospel, quoted by Eusebius (*H. E.* vi. 15), is very interesting. I have not thought it necessary to enter once more into the genuineness of St. John's Gospel. It may be regarded as finally established by modern criticism. The *internal* evidence in its favour is overwhelming; and as for *external* evidence, we know that, in the second century, it is attested by Irenæus (a disciple of Polycarp) at Lyons; by Tertullian at Carthage; by Clement at Alexandria; by the Muratorian fragment at Rome; by the Peshito

value of the elements which he contributed to the age-long dominance of Christianity by the burning Apocalypse, and the spiritual Gospel and Epistles, in which he seems to be soaring heavenwards on the wings, now of the eagle which has been chosen for his appropriate symbol, and now of the dove which is covered with silver wings and her feathers like gold?

In the Apocalypse we still trace the passionate energy of his convictions; in the Gospel they have become as the lightning which slumbers in the dewdrop. "The Son of Thunder," says Weiss, " became, through the training of the Spirit, refined and matured into a mystic, in whom the flames of youth had died down into the glow of a holy love." *

It is strange—amid this little band of men who, in spite of their original weaknesses, were noble and pure-hearted enthusiasts,—to find the dreadful, sullen, saturnine figure of JUDAS, "who became a traitor" †—

> " That furtive mien, that scowling eye ;
> Of hair that red and tufted fell."

We shudder at the depth of wickedness involved in such a crime; at the desperate blindness and callosity of heart, mingled with almost demoniac madness, which, after belonging to that holy fellowship, after spending those years with the sinless Son of Man, after hearing His words of eternal wisdom, after such close familiarity with the

Version in Syria ; by the old Latin in Africa ; by Tatian in his *Diatessaron*, etc. See Lightfoot, *Contemp. Rev.*, Feb., 1876 ; Westcott, *Introd. to St. John's Gospel;* Sanday, *The Fourth Gospel;* Watkins (Ellicott's *New Testament Commentary*, i. 377).

* Nothing can be made of the legend that James and John were of High Priestly descent, or that they wore the πέταλον (Ex. xxviii. 34 ; Euseb. *H. E.* iii. 31 ; Epiphan. *Hær.* xxix. 4). For the later legends of St. John, see Tert. *De Praescr. Hær.* 36 ; Iren. *c. Hær.* v. 30.

† Luke vi. 16, ὃς ἐγένετο προδότης. In the Apocryphal Gospel of the Infancy, Judas, as a boy, was a demoniac who was healed by the presence of the Boy Jesus.

divine beauty of His daily life—could for "thirty pence" betray Him into the scheming, tyrannous, greedy hands of Priests and Pharisees! All that we can suppose was that Judas was not *always* "the traitor." Could not Christ read the hearts of men? Undoubtedly He could.* He could see—

> "In the green the mouldered tree,
> And ruined towers as soon as built."

The depraved, hardened sinner is a very different being from the youth who has not yet been stereotyped in wickedness, and who still has within him the boundless possibilities of good. We might well exclaim, " *O quam dissimiles hic vir, et ille puer !* " The Judas whom Christ chose among His twelve was not *yet* the same man as he "who also *became* a betrayer." We only see him in the poisonous crimson flower and deadly fruitage of his wickedness, in the concentrated degradation of slavery to a mean temptation. But he was once an innocent child ; he was once, perhaps, a bright-hearted boy,† an ardent youth, capable of noble aspirations, not yet possessed by the seven devils of a brooding sullenness and an unresisted temptation.

> "We are not worst at once. The course of evil
> Begins so slowly, and from such slight source,
> An infant's hand might stem the breach with clay.
> But let the stream grow wider, and Philosophy,
> Aye, and Religion too, may strive in vain
> To stem the headlong current."

Judas remains to all time an awful incarnate warning against the peril of yielding to a besetting sin. We are left to surmise the incidents of his career. If he was the son of Simon the Zealot, he may have shared as a

* See Matt. xii. 25 ; Mark ii. 8, xii. 15 ; John i. 43, 48, ii. 25, vi. 64, 70.
† No weight whatever can be attached to the fictions in the Arabic Gospel of the Infancy (xxxv.).

youth the wild impulses of patriotism, and the glowing anticipations of a temporal Messiah—who should shatter the yoke of Rome, and restore the kingdom to Israel— which fired the untamed hearts of Judas of Gamala, and of his sons and followers. If so, we can imagine how the gradual chilling and final quenching of such Messianic hopes had worked in his heart side by side with the growth of a petty, dishonest greed, fostered by the fact that he carried the bag* which contained the little common store of Jesus and His poor Apostles. The heart of Judas was one

> " Which fancies, like to vermin in the nut,
> Have fretted all to dust and bitterness."

To this was added the fact that he could not be unaware that Christ saw through him, penetrated the guilty secrets of his heart long before his fellow-disciples had learnt to do so. He could not miss the significance of some of the allusions by which Christ strove to check him in his awful career.† The climax came when he was robbed of the chance of getting, and partly appropriating, " the three hundred denarii " for which the precious pistic spikenard might have been sold, with which Mary of Bethany with glorious wastefulness anointed the head and feet of the Lord whom she loved. It was the spasm of dreadful disappointment thus caused to his avarice which drove him to the consummation of his crime. He felt that, at all costs, he must indemnify himself—were it only by thirty

---

* John xii. 6, γλωσσόκομον (in Luke, βαλλάντιον.) A *glossokomon*, according to Hesychius, is a box in which flute-players kept the tongue (or reed) of their flutes. It is used by the LXX. in 2 Chron. xxiv. 8 ; by Aquila in Ex. xxxvii. 11.

† " Did not I choose you the twelve, and one of you is a devil ? " (διάβολος) John vi. 70. Probably the expression in the Aramaic (סַטְנָא) was less fearful, but Judas must have felt that Christ's warnings against avarice (Matt. vi. 19–21, xiii. 22, 23 ; Mark x. 25 ; Luke xii. 15, xvi. 11) had a special meaning for him.

shekels—for the loss of a larger chance of gain.* The
Priests weighed out to him the thirty pieces of silver, and
we know all that followed. We know how Christ washed
the traitor's feet; how, in answer to the cold, formal question, "Rabbi, is it I?" He whispered to him the discovery of his guilt;† how He privately indicated to John
and Peter that He was conscious of the man's nefarious
plot; how the traitor led the Roman soldiers, and Temple-
guard, and High Priest's servants to Gethsemane and
said, "Rabbi, Rabbi, hail!" and covered Him with kisses;‡
we know, lastly, of the awful overwhelming revulsion of
feeling, the sickening horror with which he became aware
of the transcendent deadliness of the crime into which he
had fallen; the frantic passion of remorse with which,
when he realised the anguish to which his foul deed had
doomed his Lord, he flung the hated silver—which now
seemed to burn his hands—upon the Temple floor, and
rushed away to hideous suicide. His crime kindled in his
heart a lurid glare by which he first realised its awful
enormity. "*Perfecto demum scelere, magnitudo ejus intel-
lecta est,*" as the Roman historian so strikingly observes.§
The very horror, intensity, and hopelessness of his remorse
may perhaps help us to gauge what his better feelings
must once have been. Who can say whether after he had
gone to "his own place," he may not, even in that abyss,
have been reached by the Divine tenderness and pardoning
compassion of his Lord, and, like the healed demoniac,
have sat at His feet at last, clothed and in his right mind?
A son of perdition ‖ indeed he was; in the most terrible of
earthly senses "he perished" because he was "a son of

---

* Thirty shekels only amounts to £3 13s., and was the lowest price of a
slave (Ex. xxi. 32).   But vast crimes have been committed for far smaller sums.
† Matt. xxvi. 25.
‡ Matt. xxvi. 49.
§ Tac. *Ann.* xiv. 15.   Comp. Juv. *Sat.* xiii. 238.
‖ John xvii. 12.

perishing ": but it is doubtful whether our Lord meant to pronounce over him the terrible sentence that "it would have been better for him never to have been born "; for the curious order of the words, and the context, make it at least possible that what our Lord meant was, "Good were it for Him (the Son of Man) if that man had not been born." *

* This more merciful view of the ultimate destiny of Judas was taken long ago by Origen (*Tract. in Matt.* 35) and Theophanes (Suicer, *s. v.* 'Ιούδας).

CHAPTER XXXI.

"We are ambassadors, therefore, on behalf of Christ . . . we beseech you on behalf of Christ, be ye reconciled to God."—2 Cor. v. 20.

IT was to His little band of Apostles that Jesus gave His great Commission, and on them He conferred the rich spiritual prerogatives metaphorically expressed in the words, "The Keys of the Kingdom of Heaven," and the powers to "loose" and "bind," to "remit" and "retain" sins. It was not till after His death—it was not till their hearts had been filled with the Spirit and their brows encircled with hovering flame that they sprang to their full spiritual stature, and began first to understand the words of Christ and their full significance.* Nor must we forget that from two—it may practically be said, from three of them—emanated the Four Gospels which contain the richest treasures of our knowledge of Christ. The Gospel of St. Matthew, of which the nucleus seems to have been (as Papias tells us) a collection of the Sayings (*Logia*) of Christ, was perhaps the earliest which became current, and may have assumed its present form some thirty-seven years after the Crucifixion.† It is the Gospel for the Jew, the Gospel of the Messiah, the Gospel of the Past, the Gospel of Prophecy fulfilled. The Gospel of St. Mark, as we know alike from internal evidence and ancient tradition, in its brief, vivid, practical delineation, reflects the memories of St. Peter, and is the Gospel for the Roman, the Gospel of the Present. The Gospel of St. Luke reflects the mind of St. Paul, and is the Gospel for the Greeks. The Gospel of St. John is "the Spiritual Gospel," the last utterance of the last survivor, and of "the best beloved,"

---

* John ii. 22, xii. 16, xiii. 7, xiv. 7, xx. 9.

† See Weiss, *Life of Christ*, p. 39.

of the Apostolic band, who could look back over nearly a century, and could interpret the Gospel of Eternity in its final meaning. It is the Gospel of the Church of all time.

I have already mentioned that Christ only once used the word " Church." The exclusiveness which is too often connected with the boast of " *Churchmanship* "—the contemptuous tone towards others so frequently adopted by those who delight to call themselves " Good Churchmen "—is entirely alien from the teaching of Christ. He described Himself as coming to establish *a Kingdom* in which all are alike the subjects of the one King. And by His Church He did not mean this or that body of exclusive claimants, but all the many folds in the one true flock; in the language of our Prayer Book, " the blessed company of all faithful people; " " all true Christians dispersed throughout the world; " *all* who love our Lord Jesus Christ in sincerity and truth; " all who in every place call on the Name of our Lord Jesus Christ, both theirs and ours."

1. What is called " the power of the keys " is a symbol only explicable by its current meaning among the Jews. The key was not a sacerdotal emblem. It was a sign of authority,* and in the highest sense that Key was retained by Christ Himself.† But it was granted to Peter—as one of the Apostles‡—because, just as the Jewish Scribes were supposed to have the key of the treasuries of wisdom and knowledge stored up in Scripture and in tradition, so the Apostles were authorised to admit men into the kingdom of Christ, and to lay open before them its eternal riches. But the keys were not entrusted to Peter individually. " *Claves datæ sunt,*" says St. Augustine, " *non uni sed unitati.*" The keys, the powers to loose and bind, the power to remit and retain sin, refer neither to individual priests nor to sacerdotal caste, but to the didactic, the legislative, and the prophetic powers of *the whole Church of God.*§

2. The power " to loose " and " bind " was also a familiar Jewish metaphor of the day, which was not applied to Priests, but only to Rabbis. " To loose " was to remove the yoke of

---

* Is. xxii. 22. Comp. Luke xii. 41, 42. † Rev. iii. 7.
‡ Matt. xiii. 52, xvi. 19, xviii. 18. § See Hooker, *Eccl. Pol.* iv. 4, 1, 2.

some legal or traditional precept: " to bind " was to enforce its obligatoriness. It was a Jewish saying that " Hillel loosed " and " Shammai bound," because in some respects Hillel and his school were inclined to take a lenient view of traditional obligations, whereas Shammai insisted on their most punctilious observance. In the days of the Primitive Church the Apostles were naturally appealed to, in all uncertain questions, to decide what rules of Judaism were still incumbent on Christians, and what rules were now abrogated. St. James and the Council of Jerusalem exercised the powers both of " loosing " and of " binding " in their decisions about what was necessary for the Gentile Churches ;* and while Paul frequently " bound," he exercised the prerogative of " loosing " on a stupendous scale when he pronounced the Gentile Church to be free from the yoke of the Levitic law, and—taking the ordinance to which the Jews attached the most immense importance—declared thrice over that " circumcision is *nothing,* and uncircumcision is *nothing,*" but " a new creature ; " but " keeping the commandments of God ; " but " faith energising by love."

3. A still loftier prerogative was conferred by the *words spoken, not to the Apostles only*—this is a point of consummate importance, which is habitually ignored—but *to the disciples generally,* as we are expressly told by St. Luke—" to the eleven, and those that were with them." As my Father hath sent Me (ἀπέσταλκε), Christ said, " even so am I sending (πέμπω) you ; " and then, after breathing on them, He added, " Take ye the Holy Spirit ; whosesoever sins ye forgive they are forgiven unto them ; whosesoever sins ye retain they are retained.†

Dangerous errors have risen in the Church from the failure to observe that the commission was given, not to Apostles only, not to ordained ministers only, but *to the whole Christian community;*—to the Church *as* a Church, not to any class or caste within it. It is only by the gift of the Spirit, only by the prophetic insight which the Spirit can alone bestow, that the Church can " remit " or " retain " sins *by declaring the conditions on which God remits or retains them,* and deciding whether those

* Acts xv. 19.   † John xx. 23 ; Luke xxiv. 47.

conditions do or do not exist. It is " Ye "—the Christian Community—who alone possess this power, and it is exercised on men collectively rather than on individual sinners. Christ conferred upon the Church the right, not indeed of deciding whether this or that man shall be saved or lost, but of declaring what men she can admit into, or reject from, her community. The claim of " priests " that *they* can *absolve from sin* entirely perverts the true meaning of Christ's words. All that priests can do is to state—not by their individual authority, but solely in agreement with the mind of the whole Church—the *conditions* on which sin can alone be forgiven. Those conditions the Church may set forth. They are the conditions of sincere repentance and genuine amendment. If any one fulfil these conditions, he not only *will* be, but *is* forgiven, and *has* everlasting life. If a man *have not* fulfilled those conditions he is *not* forgiven, though all Popes and priests should pronounce their absolutions over him, and call him " Saint." Apart from a miraculous power of reading the heart, any " absolution " which is not *simply declaratory and hypothetic* is a false pretence, founded on the perversion of a phrase which has no such meaning—a pretence more meaningless than the idle wind. Who can forgive sins but God only?

The following remarks of Bishop Westcott should be carefully considered by those who, on this subject, have been misled into false conclusions by relying on an isolated and misinterpreted phrase, and who pay no attention to certain truths. " The main thought is that of the reality of the power of absolution from sin granted *to the Church, and not of the particular organisation* through which the power is administered. *There is nothing in the context to show that this gift was confined to any particular group* (as the Apostles) among the whole company present. The commission, therefore, must be regarded properly as *the commission of the Christian Society, and not as that of the Christian Ministry.* As the promise formerly given to the Society (Matt. xviii. 18) gave the power of laying down the terms of fellowship, so this gives a living and abiding power to declare the fact and conditions of forgiveness. The *con-*

ditions refer to character (Luke xxiv. 47). The gift and the refusal of the gift are regarded *in relation to classes and not in relation to individuals. It is impossible to contemplate an absolute individual exercise of the power of 'retaining'; so far it is contrary to the scope of the passage to seek in it a direct authority for the absolute individual exercise of the 'remitting.'* At the same time the exercise of the power must be placed in the closest connection with the faculty of *Spiritual discernment* consequent upon the gift of the Holy Spirit." * It does not need much observation to see that priests, in all ages, have been in no respect more richly endowed with anything which can be called "spiritual discernment" than whole classes of men whom they despise.

* Bishop Westcott on John xx. 23.

CHAPTER XXXII.

ORDER OF EVENTS IN OUR LORD'S LIFE.

And so the Word had breath, and wrought
With human hands the creed of creeds,
In loveliness of perfect deeds
More strong than all poetic thought.
—TENNYSON.

I SHALL not here enter into the difficult details of chronology on which I have already spoken in my " Life of Christ," and in the notes on St. Luke's Gospel.* After the mass of close investigation which has been devoted to this question, it may be regarded as *probable*, even if it cannot be established as certain, that our Lord was born in the winter of B. C. 4. Our present mode of calculation, which fixes the birth four years later, was only introduced by the Abbot Dionysius Exiguus, in the sixth century (A. D. 525), and was founded on the necessarily imperfect knowledge of his day.† The question is an open one, for there is no agreement in the traditions of the Church as to either the year, the day, or the month of our Lord's Advent.‡

It is still a stranger fact, and one even more to be regretted, that there is no agreement among Christian scholars as to the

* On Luke iii. 1, p. 125 (Greek edition).

† The Biblical data on which the date of the Nativity depends are found in Luke iii. 1, 2 (where a sixfold date is given), 23 ; John ii. 13, 20. Owing, however, to the difficulty of obtaining absolutely certain information, various dates have been fixed upon. There have been wide differences of opinion. Thus Pearson and Hug fix the Nativity in B. C. 1 ; Scaliger in B. C. 2 ; Baronius, etc., B. C. 8 ; Ussher and Petavius in B. C. 5 ; Adeler and Sanclemente in B. C. 7. (See Archbishop Thomson in Smith's *Dict. of the Bible*, ii., p. 1701.) But the opinions of most authorities now agree in the date B. C. 4 (Lamy, Bengel, Auger, Wieseler, Cresswell, etc.). The main element in the decision is the death of Herod in the early part of A. U. C. 750, in March or April, B. C. 4.

‡ Lichtenstein in Herzog, *Real. Encycl. s. v.* " Jesus Christ."

length of our Lord's ministry.   Many of the Fathers,* building
their conclusion wholly without reason on the phrase of Isaiah,
" the acceptable year of the Lord," † confine the period of His
active work to a single year.   Others consider that the ministry lasted one and a half years, or two years and one or two
months.   But most inquirers are now agreed that our Lord's
public work extended over about three and a half years, or, at
any rate, three years and some weeks or months.‡   The question is further complicated by the opinion of some of the
Fathers that our Lord, at His death, was between forty and
fifty years old.   This is a mere mistake of tradition, based on
the surprised question of the Jews (in John viii. 57), " Thou
art not yet fifty years old, and hast thou seen Abraham? "   On
this verse, Chrysostom, Eythymius, and others adopt the reading " forty," which, again, in all probability is a mere conjec-
tural correction of the text.   It is a curious fact that Irenæus§
—the scholar of Polycarp, who is said to have received the tradition directly from St. John—says that our Lord was about
fifty at the time of His passion.   Such an error is, however,
easily accounted for by mistaken inferences from this text.
The view that our Lord lived fifty years would be subversive
to all our records.‖   The Jews only mentioned fifty years as a

* Eusebius (*H. E.* iii. 24) Clemens of Alexandria (*Strom.* I, xxi.).   Origen
(*Princip.* iv. 5) says, ἐνιαυτὸν καί που καὶ ὀλίγους μῆνας ἐδίδαξεν, but does not
seem to be quite consistent with himself (*c. Cels.* ii., p. 29) in Matt. xxiv. 15.
So, too, Tert. *c. Jud.* 8 ; Lactant. iv. 10 ; Aug. *De Civ. Dei*, xxviii. 54 ;
Gieseler, *Ch. Hist.* E. T. I, 55 ; Hase, *Leben Jesu*, p. 21. But Melito,
Irenæus, and others take a different view. This opinion has, however, been
strongly, if unsuccessfully, supported by Mr. Browne in his *Ordo Sæclorum* (pp.
342–391).

† Is. lxi. 2.

‡ Some have seen a reference to this in Luke xiii. 7, 8.   " *Tres.*   Numerus
quodammodo decretorius.   *Tertium docendi annum* incipiebat Dominus, ut
vera docet Harmonia Evangelistarum.—Bengel.

§ c. *Hær.* ii. 22, 5.

‖ I am bound, however, to note, though with surprise, that Bishop Westcott
seems to consider such an opinion possible.   He says (*ad loc.*), " However
strange it may appear, some such a view is not inconsistent with the only fixed
historic dates which we have with regard to the Lord's life, the date of the
birth, His baptism, and the banishment of Pilate."

round number for complete manhood.* Hippolytus was a pupil of Iranæus, yet even he mentions thirty-three as the age at
which our Lord died; and Eusebius, Theodoret, Jerome, and
other Fathers agree with him.†

The main elements on which we must decide what was the
length of our Lord's ministry are derived from St. John, who
groups his entire narrative round the Jewish festivals, to which
he makes six allusions.

1. " The Passover of the Jews " (xi. 13).
2. " A [or the] Feast of the Jews " (v. 1).
3. " The Passover, the Feast of the Jews " (vi. 4).‡
4. " The Feast of the Jews, the Tabernacles " (vii. 2).
5. " The Feast of the Dedication " (The *Encænia*) (x. 22).
6. " The Passover of the Jews " (xi. 55).

It may, then, be regarded as certain that St. John mentions
three Passovers. This necessarily implies a ministry of two
years; and if (as seems probable) there was one Passover during the ministry which our Lord did not attend, or if the unnamed feast of John v. 1 was this Passover, we should have
clear *proof* that the ministry lasted three years at least.§ But
as St. John distinctly mentions the Great Feasts by name, it is
unlikely that he should not have called this Feast by its name if
it was either the Passover or the Feast of Tabernacles. It was
possibly the Feast of the Purim, which he would not be likely
to mention by name, as it was (unlike the *Encænia*) unfamiliar

* The Levites were to serve in the Temple " from thirty years old and
upwards, even until fifty years old " (Num. iv. 3).

† Euseb. *H. E.* i. 10. See Wordsworth *ad loc.*

‡ Although τὸ πάσχα is *conjecturally* doubted by some, and even by Westcott
and Hort (*Greek Testament*, pp. 77–81) it is unquestionably genuine, for it is
found " in every known MS., whether of the original Greek or of the versions."
I have not dwelt on the arguments drawn from incidental notices like John iv.
35, vi. 10 ; Mark vi. 39, etc. As to the *years* A. D. no conclusion can as yet be
regarded as at all proven.

§ In John v. 1 there is another reading, " *the* Feast " (which would mean the
Passover or the Tabernacles), which was found in MSS. as early as the second
century, and is the reading of ℵ C, L, but as it is not found in A, B, D, in
Origen, and in many later copies, it is probably spurious.

to the Greeks.   This is inferred by many commentators from a comparison of John iv. 35: " Say ye not, There are yet *four months,* and then cometh harvest? " with vi. 4: " Now the Passover, a feast of the Jews, was nigh." Bishop Westcott, however, thinks that St. John meant the Feast of Trumpets, which was held on the new moon of September, the beginning of the Jewish civil year.   It was suggestive of thoughts which might seem to be reflected in the subsequent discourses, and we know from the incidents at the Feast of Tabernacles—when the discourse on the Living Water was suggested by the Feast of Drawing Water from Siloam, and that on the Light of the World by the illumination of the Temple with great candelabra—that Christ often drew the colouring of His addresses from the sourrounding circumstances.

These details do not, perhaps, admit of a *certain* interpretation; nevertheless the Gospels do give us a clear picture of the main outlines and divisions of Christ's public ministry.

We know the events of His infancy.   The birth in the manger was followed by the circumcision on the eighth day after the birth; by the purification and presentation in the Temple; by the visit of the Magi; the massacre of the Innocents; the flight into Egypt; the return; and the settlement of the Holy Family in Nazareth of Galilee.

Of His childhood we have no record beyond the statement that " He grew, and was waxing strong, becoming full of wisdom, and the grace of God was upon Him."   Of His boyhood nothing is recorded but the visit to the Temple at the first Passover, and the fact that on His return to Nazareth He lived in humble submissiveness to His parents, and advanced in wisdom, and age, and in favour with God and man.

Of His youth and early manhood, as has been shown, we know nothing except that He worked in Nazareth as a village carpenter, living in the humble abode with His mother, and with those who were always regarded as his brethren and sisters.

Then, when He was about thirty years old, He began his public life by going to the Jordan, and accepting the Baptism of John, and receiving the Heavenly Sign that his time was come. Immediately afterwards He went, under the influence of the Spirit, into the wilderness, to be tempted of the Devil for forty days.

From this point begins His active ministry; and, amid all difficulties of detail, we see that it falls into four periods. The first was that of initial work; the second was the period of successful preaching, which has been called "the happy blossoming-time in Galilee"; the third was the period of struggle and opposition, culminating in flight into heathen regions, and including a slow progress to Jerusalem, followed by a time of deep retirement; the fourth includes the journey to the last Passover, the final discourses in the Temple, the Last Supper, betrayal, trial, and Crucifixion. The precise arrangement of all details in the varying order adopted by the Evangelist is impossible, but the broad outlines of the ministry as thus arranged are now generally accepted.

FIRST PERIOD.

On His return from His victorious resistance to temptation, Jesus stayed for a short time in the district about the trans-Jordanic Bethany, where John was baptising. He there attracted round Him the first little group of five disciples—Andrew, John, Simon, Philip, and Nathanael. With them He took his departure to the marriage festival at Cana of Galilee, where He wrought His first sign—the turning of the water into wine—which was not only a work of gracious kindness, but also a symbol and a prophecy of the New Dispensation which was now dawning on the world.

From Cana, accompanied by His mother, His brethren, and His disciples, Jesus went down to Capernaum, on the shores of the Lake of Gennesareth, where He stayed not many days. From thence He went to the Passover at Jerusalem. It was on this occasion that He cleansed the Temple of the crowd of huckstering profaners of its sanctity,* and startled the Jewish

---

* On the *kermatistai* who gave small change, and the *kollubistai* who gave the Temple shekel for heathen money, charging five per cent. (and as much

authorities by His enigmatic words, " Destroy this Temple, and in three days I will raise it up." The saying was treasured up against Him, but even the disciples did not understand that " He spake of the sanctuary of His body " until after He had risen from the dead. The only other event recorded of this visit is the night interview with the eminent Sanhedrist, Nicodemus.

But though there is no other account of what occurred during this part of His ministry, there are indications that Jesus had been met by a stolid and watchful hostility.* He therefore retired into Judæa, and there permitted His disciples to baptise, though He Himself never performed the rite. John the Baptist was at Ænon,† on the borders of Galilee and Samaria. The baptism by the disciples of Jesus was carried on at some part of the Jordan valley which belonged to Judæa. Some unknown Jew seems to have gone from this scene to Ænon, and there to have raised a question with John's disciples " about purifying "—perhaps about the relative significance of the baptisms of John and of Jesus. The Baptist's disciples, with something of bitterness and jealousy for their Master, came to John and said, " Rabbi, He that was with thee beyond Jordan, to whom thou hast borne witness, behold the same *baptiseth, and all men come to Him.*" They only elicited from the Baptist the noble answer that he was *not* the Bridegroom, but only the friend of the Bridegroom; that " He must increase, but I must decrease."

But this successful inauguration of His ministry on the banks of the Jordan had other effects. It kindled still more the animosity of the Pharisees, to which sect " the Jew " who had disputed with John's disciples may have belonged. Further than this, the news reached Jesus that Herod Antipas had now

---

more as they could get) by way of *kolbon* or *agio*, see Lightfoot, *Hor. Hebr.* in Matt. xxi. 12. These noisy traders were truly as " the Canaanite (*Targ-Jon*, ' *trader* '), in the House of the Lord," who, as Zechariah said (xiv. 21), should be there no more.

* John iv. 1.

† John iii. 23. Now *Aynum*, not far from Nablous.

seized John, and cast him into his dungeon at Machærus.* It was, therefore, obviously wise to avoid unnecessary peril, and He left Judæa, and departed through Samaria into Galilee. It was during this journey that He had the memorable conversation with the Samaritan woman by Jacob's well, in which He first clearly announced His own Messiahship. At the earnest request of the Samaritans of Shechem He stayed with them two days, and won many disciples. He then made His way to Galilee, and first visited Cana, where His healing of the courtier's son by a word filled the mouths of all men with his fame.†

The Galileans had seen what He had done at Jerusalem, and received Him with enthusiasm as He taught in their synagogues, journeying towards His native town of Nazareth. But "He Himself testified that a Prophet hath no honour in his own country," and at Nazareth He was not only received with jealousy and hatred, but the inhabitants, stung by his reproach, tried to hurl Him over the brow of the hill on which their city was built. They were, however, overawed by the calm majesty of His bearing, and he left them, perhaps never to return. Henceforth Capernaum by the silver waves of Galilee became His home, so far as we can speak of the home of One who often had not where to lay his head.‡

SECOND PERIOD.

His main work in Galilee now began. It was by far the brightest and most triumphant part of His ministry, and in its radiant hopefulness and beneficence has been called "the Galilean Spring." He called Peter and Andrew, James and John, to a closer relation to Himself, and a more continuous ministry of self-sacrifice, astonishing their minds by the miraculous draught of fishes, and promising to make them fishers of men.

---

* Matt. iv. 12 ; Mark i. 14, vi. 17.

† John iv. 46. The βασιλικὸς, or "courtier," was perhaps Chuzas, the steward of Herod Antipas (Luke viii. 3). This is probably not the same event as the healing of the *centurion's servant* (Matt. viii. 5), which seems to have taken place later.

‡ " His own city " (Matt. ix. 1. Comp. iv. 13, 16, xi. 23, xvii. 24).

His first Sabbath at Capernaum was a memorable day. He preached in the synagogue, amazed the listeners by His wisdom and authority, and healed the demoniac. He went thence to the house of Peter, and healed his mother, who was lying ill of a fever. In the evening the people of the city thronged densely round Peter's house, bringing their demoniacs and their diseased. He " who bore our griefs and carried our sorrows " moved among them, pitied them, and healed them. After this He went away to a secluded place to spend the night in quiet prayer; but the multitudes searched for Him, and Simon with his friends almost " hunted " for Him,* and sought with gentle force to detain Him in their midst. He may have spent one more day with them, preaching perhaps from the little boat upon the shore; after which He went around the villages of Galilee in circle. It was soon after this that He selected His Twelve Apostles for their great work, and promulgated the laws of his new kingdom in the Sermon on the Mount. As He descended from the Mount of Beatitudes He healed the leper. His fame had now grown so great, and He appeared to be immersed in a life of such incessant work and excitement, that even his kinsmen, influenced probably by the instigations of Priests and Pharisees, made a too bold and irreverent attempt to interfere with and restrain His movements.

It was this year of His Galilean ministry which was mainly marked by a succession of miracles: such were the healing of the centurion's servant; the opening of the lips of the dumb, and the ears of the deaf; the raising of the widow's son at Nain; and the miracles performed on those whom He cured in order to strengthen the overclouded faith of the imprisoned Baptist. One great section of this part of his life circles round the feast given to Him by Matthew, one of the hated toll-collectors whom He summoned to be His apostle.† He healed the paralytic let down to Him from the roof, raised the daughter of Jairus, and healed the blind men and the woman with the issue of blood. Another great phase of work commences with the sermon in the boat to the multitude on the shore, when He

* Luke iv. 42, ἐπεζήτουν.   Mark i. 36, κατεδίωξαν αὐτόν.   † Matt. ix. 1-34

delivered the Parable of the Sower, and began His parabolic teaching. After this, in the urgent desire for rest, He set sail for the more lonely Eastern shore, and on the way had brief interviews with the three imperfect aspirants for discipleship.* Then followed the stilling of the storm on the lake, which had risen while He lay sleeping the sleep of deep weariness on the steersman's cushion.† After He had landed He healed the wild naked demoniac of Gergesa, and at the request of the Gergesenes, who were terrified by the loss of their swine, He returned to Capernaum.

But the burning enthusiasm of the Galilean multitudes was gradually cooled by the open opposition and secret machinations of the Pharisees, and was beginning to be replaced in the hearts of many by suspicion, dislike, and even hostility. It was perhaps towards the close of His first year of ministry that Jesus heard the terrible news that John had been beheaded in prison. A deputation of religious spies from Jerusalem began to watch his conduct and dog His footsteps. Nevertheless His work had produced deep results, and about this time He personally traversed the cities and villages in Galilee, in deep pity for the multitude, whom He regarded as sheep harassed by wolves, and lying in the fields thirsty and neglected because they had no shepherd. At the close of these journeys He despatched the Twelve Apostles, two and two, with a special commission to heal and teach. During their absence He seems to have continued His work nearly alone, perhaps as He slowly made His way to the unnamed Feast at Jerusalem which is mentioned in John v. 1. This, as we have seen, was probably the Feast of Purim, and it is quite possible that our Lord's visit to the Holy City was mainly with reference to the Passover which occurred a month later.

But that Passover He never attended. For at the pool of Bethesda,† by the sheep gate, He performed the miracle of the

---

* See Luke ix. 57–62.   † Mark iv. 38, ἐπὶ τὸ προσκεφάλαιον.

‡ Possibly the Fountain of the Virgin in the Wady Kidron Bethesda may mean "House of Mercy" or "House of the Portico," or, if it be a corruption of Bethzatha, "House of the Olive." See Dalman, *Die Worte Jesu*, p. 6.

healing of the impotent man, which, having been done on the Sabbath, roused the still more furious hostility of the Pharisees. Their rage was goaded to fury by the lofty rebukes which He addressed to their materialism and ignorance. His discourse created such bitter exasperation that they began a systematic persecution, and persistently sought an opportunity to kill Him,* on the double charge that He was a breaker of the Sabbath and a blasphemer against God, whom " He had called His Father, making Himself equal with God."

So dangerous a plot compelled Him to return to Galilee without waiting for the celebration of the Passover. In Galilee He seems to have ministered again to eager multitudes,† until He retired once more in order to secure rest for Himself and His Apostles in "a desert place" near Bethsaida Julias, at the northeastern corner of the lake. But His departure had been observed, and thousands of Galileans, and others who were on their way to the Passover at Jerusalem, went round the end of the lake on foot and awaited the arrival of His little vessel. He taught them all day long, and, in the evening, compassionating their hunger, He fed the five thousand with the five barley loaves and two small fishes. Then He dismissed them and His disciples, and went up alone to the mountain to pray. A great storm followed, and He came to them walking on the sea, and arrived with them at Capernaum once more.

The next day He delivered the great discourse on the Bread of Life, in the synagogue at Capernaum.‡ This led to a decisive crisis in His career. It caused many who had hitherto been His disciples to abandon Him, and it alienated the multitude by His refusal to grant them the sign which they had been instigated to demand. Had they been in the least degree sincere, it would have been easy for them to understand that the

---

* John v. 16, 18.

† St. John says that " a great multitude was following Him " (vi. 2).

‡ Perhaps the pot of manna carved on the tympanum of the entrance door may have suggested to some of those present the remark (John vi. 31), " *Our fathers ate the manna in the wilderness*, as it is written, He gave them bread out of heaven to eat."

words of Christ were merely descriptive of the full spiritual
appropriation of His life and of His death. The offence they
chose to take was wilful. The metaphor, " Except ye eat the
flesh of the Son of Man, and drink His blood, ye have not life
in yourselves," had been used centuries before in their own sacred writings to imply the fulness of acceptance, and incorpora-
tion.* " *Crede et manducasti,*" said St. Augustine. Truly
and wisely to believe, *is* to eat. Christ removed all excuse for
coarse materialism when He uttered the words, " *The flesh
profith nothing;* the words which I have spoken unto you are
spirit and are life."

From this time the clouds gathered more and more densely
around Him. Many of His disciples, St. John tells us, walked
no more with Him. In spite of His works of miraculous healing, He was more and more pressed with criticism and calumnies. He had given deep offence by saying to the paralytic and
others, " Thy sins be forgiven thee," and was charged with
arrogating to Himself the attributes of God. Because He and
His disciples fasted not, they called Him " a gluttonous man
and a wine-bibber," as well as " a friend of publicans and sinners." His Sabbath healings, His defence of His hungry

---

* John iv. 32, 34. Compare Ps. xix. 10, cxix. 3 ; Is. iii. 1 ; Prov. ix. 5 ;
Ezek. ii. 8, 9, etc. In the *Midrath Koheleth* (188, 4) we read, " *Every eating
and drinking in the Book of Ecclesiastes is to be understood of good works.*" " I
have *food to eat* that ye know not of." " Thy words were found, and I did *eat*
them " (Jer. xv. 16 ; comp. Ezek. ii. 8, iii. 1–3). " He that *eateth* me (Wisdom) shall even live by me " (Wisd.). " The just *eat* of the glory of the
Shechinah " (a Rabbinic saying). Moses on Sinai was *fed* by the music of the
spheres (Philo, *de Somn.* 1, 6). " Prayer shall be *my meat and drink* " (Gospel of St. James). There is not the least excuse for the coarse and fetish-wor-
shipping materialism which has corrupted the pure spiritual sacrament of the
Lord's Supper. " The Law," said the Rabbis, " speaks to us with the tongue
of the sons of men " ; and so does the Gospel. This is no more excuse for
taking literally the words, " *This is my body,*" than for taking literally, " I am
the *water* of life," or " I am the Door." The notion of drinking the blood of
Christ (in *any* material sense whatever) would have been naturally abhorrent to
them, and the drinking of blood had been imperatively denounced again and
again in the Old Testament (Gen. ix. 4 ; Lev. iii. 17, vii. 26, 27, xvii. 10–14,
xix. 26 ; Deut. xii. 16, 23, 24, xv. 23 ; 1 Sam. xiv. 32, 33 ; Ezek. xxxiii. 25.
Comp. Acts xv. 29).

Apostles for plucking the ears of the corn on the Sabbath and rubbing them in their hands, made the Judæan spies denounce Him as an open violator of the Law. His neglect of ceremonial ablutions led them to brand Him as one who openly ignored " the traditions of the Elders." His persistent enemies explained His casting out of demons by calling Him an ally of Beelzebul, prince of the demons. He continued His discourses and His parables, but the Pharisaic spies were always able to interrupt Him with their " Master, we would see a *sign* from Thee." At last, on one great day of incessant conflict, when the Scribes and Pharisees openly threw off the mask and began shamefully " to press on, and worry him," * He was troubled in spirit, and when the myriads gathered suddenly about the door for His protection, He went out to them and strongly denounced the hypocrisy of the Pharisees before the agitated multitude.†

THIRD PERIOD.

Thus did the Galilean ministry, which had begun so brightly, end in clouds and darkness, and Jesus went forth with His Apostles to wander for months of flight in heathen and semi-heathen lands as far as the coasts of Tyre and Sidon. Of His works and teaching during this period we are told but little. His main miracle was performed to reward the heroic faith of the poor Syro-Phœnician woman.‡ It is probable that He was occupied almost wholly in the training of His Apostles for their mighty mission in the world.

On his return to Decapolis He healed the deaf and dumb man, and being once more received by multitudes, Jews and Greeks, who had flocked and stayed to hear His words, He

---

* Luke xi. 53.   † Luke xii. 1.

‡ We may note that the rebuff, " It is not meet to take the children's bread and cast it to the dogs," does not sound harsh (1) if used to call out a victorious faith ; or (2) if regarded merely as a current proverb, like " Charity begins at home." Further (3), κυνάρια, " little household dogs," is a much less severe term than κυνές. See Dean Plumtre on Matt. xv. 26 in Ellicott's *New Testament Commentary*.

performed His second miracle of feeding a multitude by dis-
tributing the seven loaves and a few fishes among the four
thousand.

He then returned to Galilee, but being once more met by the
hostile emissaries from Jerusalem, with their demand for " a
sign *from heaven,*" He sailed away. After healing a blind
man at Bethsaida Julias, He went towards Cæsarea Philippi.
It was during this journey that He put to His Apostles the mo-
mentous question, " Who say ye that I am? " and heard from
Peter the answer which showed that now His main work was
accomplished, " Thou art the Christ, the Holy One of God." *
Then first He began plainly to tell them of His coming death,
and uttered His terrible rebuke to Peter for trying to put a
stumbling-block on the destined path of His humiliation. This
was one of the most decisive events in the whole ministry. It
was the full relisation and acceptance of the fact that the path
of His glorification and the redemption of men led through the
awful valley of the shadow, and that by the endurance of shame
and death He must overcome the powers of death. He had
prepared His disciples for some great manifestation by telling
them that " some of them should not taste of death till they had
seen the Son of Man coming in His kingdom." Ascending
Mount Hermon with Peter, James, and John, He was transfigured before them. On their descent from the scene of this
vision of glory, He healed the demoniac boy. Perhaps the
sense that something great had happened † kindled the selfish
ambition of the disciples, and caused that unseemly dispute as
to " which was the greatest " ‡ which He reproved by setting
the little child in the midst of them, and telling them that the
highest place in the kingdom should be the reward, not of soaring ambition, but of humility, love, and unselfish service. It

---

* This is the reading of ℵ, B, C, D, L, in John vi. 69.

† His appearance—perhaps some lingering traces (as Theophylact thought)
of the Transfiguration glory—amazed the multitudes.

‡ Mark ix. 3 ; Luke ix. 46, xxii. 24. The dispute was not " which of them
should be," but " which of them is accounted to be greater," or, " who *was* the
greater."

may have been during a brief rest at Capernaum that the incident occurred of His payment of the Temple tribute.

After this—setting aside the intrusive advice of His too presumptuous brethren—He went privately to Jerusalem to the Feast of Tabernacles. Here again He encountered a most deadly opposition. The Pharisees scornfully represented Him as an ignoramus—not a *Chaber*, who had attended the schools of the Rabbis, but an *Am ha-arets*, who had never learnt " letters " in their sense;—a " mesith " who was leading the multitude astray.* To His mention of the fact that some of them were going about to kill Him, they answered that " He had a demon." They again engaged Him in acrimonious Sabbath disputes, and it was constantly on their lips that He was " a Samaritan " and a demoniac. Yet He went on teaching as He sat in the Treasury, the most frequented part of the Temple. With reference to two great events in the Feast, the joy of the Festival of Drawing Water, and the illumination of the Temple with great golden candelabra—which originally commemorated the smitten rock and the pillar of fire—He uttered His memorable discourses on the Living Water and the Light of the World.† It was at this feast that the incident occurred of the dragging into His presence of the woman taken in adultery,‡ after which His enemies were so roused to fury by His reproaches, and revelations of His Eternal Being, that they took up stones to stone Him. Shortly after this He opened the eyes of the man born blind, who, as a result of his faith in, and gratitude to, One whom they denounced as a sinner, incurred the ban of their excommunication.

From Jerusalem He returned to Galilee. Before He bade His last sad farewell to the cities and country which had heard His sermons and parables and witnessed most of His wonder-

---

* John vii. 12, πλανᾷ, 49.

† See Ex. xvii. 6 ; Num. xx. 11 ; Is. lviii. 11 ; Zech. xiv. 8 ; and, for the metaphor of Light, Is. xlii. 6, xlix. 6 ; Mal. iv. 2 ; Luke ii. 32.

‡ An undoubtedly authentic incident, though, perhaps, taken from Papias, and not a part of the original Gospel. It was in the Gospel acc. to the Hebrews (Euseb. *H. E.* iii. 40). It differs in many particulars from the style of St. John, and is absent from the oldest MSS., and obelised in others.

ful works, He uttered the " woe " on Chorazin, Bethsaida, and Capernaum, which was afterwards so terribly fulfilled.* It seems to have been at this time that He sent the Seventy on their mission.

The Pharisees warned Him of a pretended design of Herod Antipas to seize Him, but He saw through their machinations. He then set out on His journey to Jerusalem, and the greater part of the two months between the Feast of Tabernacles and that of Dedication seems to have been occupied with that slow journey of which the details are furnished to us only by St. Luke. He had meant to go through Samaria, but was churlishly refused hospitality by the Samaritans of En Gannim, where He rebuked the vengeful wrath of the Sons of Thunder. Turning to the road which led by the other route to Jerusalem, through Peræa, He cleansed the ten lepers, of whom one only—and he a Samaritan—returned to express his gratitude. During this journey He preached in various synagogues, healed the bowed woman, and the man with the dropsy, and once again refuted the ignorant and self-satisfied Sabbatarianism of small-minded local officials. It was perhaps during this journey that He " exulted in spirit," cheered by the return of the Seventy from their mission; and amid deep discourses and solemn warnings He enshrined some of His most solemn parables—such as the Parables of the Good Samaritan, Dives and Lazarus, and the Prodigal Son.

At the close of His progress through Peræa, we find Jesus domiciled at Bethany, in the quiet home which was very dear to Him, the house of Martha and Mary, and Lazarus whom he loved. It was here that He taught to the eager, busy Martha that " one thing is needful "; and it was from this house that He walked over the Mount of Olives to the Temple, to be present at the Feast of the Dedication, which was kept about December 20. It was during this visit that He spoke the alle-

---

* See the terrible description of the state of stench, pestilence, shipwreck, and desolation to which Galilee was reduced—a state so awful as even to stir the commiseration of those who had caused it. In Jos., *B. J.*, iii. 10, 8. See, too, Renan, *L'Antéchrist*, p. 277.

gory of the Fair Shepherd, who would protect not only His own sheep, but also those other sheep which were not " of His fold," (αὐλή), but which should nevertheless be united hereafter into " one flock " (ποίμνη). Here, as He paced up and down the splendid eastern porch of the Temple, the Pharisaic party and their leaders suddenly surrounded Him, and imperiously demanded of Him whether He was the Messiah or not. In reply He referred them to His teaching and His works; and in the course of his address used the words, " I and My Father are one." * The result was a burst of fury, and they took up some of the heavy stones which were scattered about for the yet unfinished restoration of the Temple, that they might stone Him to death. But they were overawed by the calm majesty with which He continued His appeals and arguments; and, alone and defenceless though He was, they did not even dare to seize Him. He now felt that it was useless to continue His words to men who only glared upon him with fierce hatred on their scowling faces. He retired therefore into comparative seclusion, to the Bethany beyond Jordan, where John once baptised, and where many accepted His teaching.†

It was perhaps during, or just before, this last stay in Peræa that the touching incident took place of " the great refusal " made by the eager young ruler who had sought for something higher and more heroical in religion than the current religionism offered, but who failed to meet the test which he had sought. In the deep discourses which followed this scene, and in answer to the question of Peter, " Lo, we have forsaken all and followed Thee; what shall we have, therefore? " He told the Parable of the Labourers in the Vineyard.

While he was still living in semi-retirement at the Peræan Bethany, He received from the sisters at the other Bethany the urgent message, " Lord, he whom Thou lovest is sick." Then followed the memorable scenes and revelations in connection with the raising of Lazarus from the dead, described by St. John

---

* Lit. " one *thing* " (ἓν), *i. e.*, of one substance.

† John x. 41, 42. " So the narrative of the Lord's ministry closes on the spot where it began."—WESTCOTT.

with such characteristic vividness. The rumours of so stupendous a miracle fanned into white heat the jealous rage of the Sadducees, and at a private meeting of Sanhedrists, the High Priest, Joseph Caiaphas, son-in-law of Annas—a thorough Sadducee, who had gained his High-Priesthood by bribery—propounded the hideous suggestion of political expediency that Jesus must at all hazards be seized and slain. This secret fiat became known, and thenceforth He was living with a price upon His head. He again retired into the still deeper secrecy of a little obscure town called Ephraim, on the edge of the wilderness, and there He stayed till His last Passover.*

FOURTH PERIOD.

Jesus knew that His only chance of even temporary protection from the hierarchs at Jerusalem lay in the presence of the numerous Galilean pilgrims, of whom so many loved and believed on Him. When, therefore, from the hill of Ephraim He saw them streaming down the Jordan valley on their way to the Holy City, He set forth to join them, walking before His disciples in such a Transfiguration of self-sacrifice as to fill them with terror and amazement, especially when, for the first time, He revealed to them the crowning horror that He was not only to be rejected and put to death, but that He was to be *crucified*. This they could not or would not understand; but—perhaps led into earthly hopes of a speedily coming Messianic splendour —James and John, with their mother Salome, chose this most inopportune moment to ask for thrones on His right hand and His left hand in His kingdom. This gave Him the opportunity to impress yet more deeply on the minds of the throne-seekers, and of the Apostles who were indignant with them for their forwardness, the eternal rewards of humility and love.

So they advanced to the environs of Jericho, the city of roses and palms and balsam gardens. Here Jesus healed blind Bar-

---

* Ephraim is, *perhaps, Et Taiyibeh*, twenty miles from Jerusalem, not far from Bethel, called Ophrah in Josh. xviii. 23 ; 2 Chron. xiii. 19 ; 1 Sam. xiii. 17, iv. 9 (Robinson, *Bibl. Researches*, i. 444).

timæus, and with a few words of mercy transformed Zacchæus from a greedy publican into a true and generous son of Abraham. During the progress towards Bethany the sight of the splendid Herodian palace built by Archelaus led Him, as we have seen, to weave some incidents in the history of that worthless tyrant into the Parable of the Pounds.

CHAPTER XXXIII.

THE CLOSING DAYS.

" Greater love hath no man than this, that a man lay down his life for
his friends."—JOHN xv. 13.

THE records which follow the arrival of Christ at Bethany
are devoted to the history of the closing scenes in the life of
Christ, which occupy so large a space in the collective records of
the Gospels.

Jesus and His Apostles, escorted by large numbers of Galilean pilgrims, reached Bethany probably on the evening of
Thursday, Nisan 7, or Friday, Nisan 8 (March 31, A. D. 30),
six days before the beginning of the Passover.* He spent the
Sabbath in quiet, and in the evening they made Him a supper,
at which Mary anointed His head and feet with the precious
spikenard, which she had perhaps reserved from her brother's
funeral. Jesus protected her from the murmurs of the disciples
who, instigated by Judas, denounced this act of loving gener-
osity as a meaningless waste.

How marvellously has His promise been fulfilled, that the
act of love performed at a humble feast in an obscure Judæan
village should be commemorated ever afterwards through all
the world! We may say of Mary of Bethany, " Because of the
perfume of thy sweet ointments thy name is as ointment poured
forth."

This, as I have said, was the turning-point in the career of
Judas, because it goaded into terrible force his besetting sin.
Obviously his chances of gain were over, for Jesus spoke of

* Nothing *certain* can be affirmed as to the exact date. It has already been
shown that those who have examined the chronology with the minutest care
have arrived at widely different conclusions. It forms no part of my object in
this book to enter into minute discussions of uncertainties.

His approaching burial, and this was the death-blow to all possibility of earthly Messianic hopes. Thus did " the tempting opportunity " meet " the susceptible disposition."

It was on the next day—Palm Sunday—that Jesus, mounted on the ass's colt, rode in the humble procession of which the exultant joy was over-shadowed when He paused at the turning of the road to wail aloud over Jerusalem and its coming doom. Once more He cleansed the Temple courts of the noisy traffickers; * defended the Levitic choir boys, with whose Hosannas the Pharisees were displeased; and probably admitted to an interview the Greeks who had gone to Philip desiring to see Him. Then He heard, for the third time, the Voice from Heaven, which uplifted and cheered His soul.† He explained its significance to the people who did not dare to confess Him, because to do so was to face the ban of the Sanhedrin. In the evening He left the Holy City, and went to bivouac with His disciples somewhere under the shadows of the Mount of Olives.

The Monday of Passion week was a day of parables. In the morning took place the *acted* parable of the barren fig-tree. He met the challenge of the Priests as to His authority by His counter-question as to the mission of John, and during the course of the day addressed to the listening multitudes the Parables of the Two Sons; of the Rebellious Husbandmen; of the Rejected Corner-stone; and of the Marriage of the King's Son. The obvious import of these parables filled His enemies with madness, and they would gladly have seized Him then and there; but they were still afraid of the multitude, and Jesus once more retired unmolested to the Mount of Olives.

The next day (Tuesday in Passion week) was the day of temptations—the last, and in some respects the most memorable, day in the earthly ministry of Christ. On the previous evening various machinations, in the form of dangerous and entangling questions, had been secretly contrived against Him

---

* See Zech. xiv. 21, where the Targum of Jonathan reads, "There shall be no more the *trader* in the House of the Lord."

† At His Baptism, Matt. iii. 17; at the Transfiguration, Matt. xvii. 5; and now, John xii. 28.

by each main class of His enemies. First came the plot of the Herodians to entrap Him by the question about the lawfulness of paying tribute money to Cæsar.* Then followed the poor, casuistical question of the Sadducees about the seven-fold widow. The sovereign wisdom with which He defeated these subtle conspiracies, and the divine lessons which He appended to His demonstration of the errors of His enemies, won the admiration even of some of the Scribes. One of them, however, wishing to test Him further, asked Him the common Rabbinic question: "Master, which is the great commandment of the Law?" Our Lord needed only to remind the questioner of the passages transcribed in his own phylacteries, which summed up the whole essence of the Law in love to God and love to our neighbour. The Scribe so fully acknowledged the justice and wisdom of the answer that Jesus said to him: "Thou are not far from the Kingdom of Heaven."

But now, to show the Pharisees how little they were endowed with wisdom, He convicted them of being "blind leaders of the blind," by exposing their inability to answer the question, "How He whom David called his *Lord* could be his *Son?*" And then, "since Love had played her part in vain, Vengeance leaped upon the stage," and He uttered against the Scribes and Pharisees, hypocrites, His eight-fold "woe." His spirit must have been terribly agitated by hours of such manifold excitement, but the last incident and the last words in the Temple were peaceful. He saw the rich ostentatiously casting their offerings into the *Shopharoth*, or trumpet-shaped alms-boxes,† and among them came one poor widow who had nothing to give but two mites, which make one farthing. This, He said, was the true charity, for out of her penury she "had cast in all that she had."

After this He left the Temple; and when the disciples called His attention to its stateliness and splendour, He prophesied

---

* It is probable that the Roman poll-tax could only be paid in *denarii*, which were current in Palestine (Matt. xx. 2), and this was a decisive proof that the land acknowledged Cæsar as its ruler.

† *Yoma*, f. 55, 2.

that not one stone of it should be left upon another. As they sat on the Mount of Olives they asked Him, " When shall these things be, and what shall be the sign of Thy coming, and of the end of the world? " In answer to this question He delivered His great eschatological discourse, dealing first with the destruction of Jerusalem, and the awful catastrophes with which the Old Dispensation should come to an end, and glancing beyond it to the close of " the coming age," and the final end of the world. To deepen their sense of the need of watchfulness, He told them the exquisite Parables of the Ten Virgins and of the Talents, and ended by warning them that " after two days was the Passover, and the Son of Man is betrayed to be crucified." Such were the thoughts which occupied our Lord and His disciples on that last sad walk towards Bethany.

The Wednesday in Passion week was evidently spent by our Lord in seclusion from the world, in company with His chosen Apostles. Alike His friends and His enemies may have expected to see Him as usual teaching in the Temple courts, and doubtless the Priests and Sadducees had hatched fresh plots of their own, in conjunction with Judas. But Jesus came not. It was necessary for Him to prepare His soul for the awful baptism of blood; and doubtless He rejoiced to be for one day at peace, unassailed by the tempting questions and subtly dangerous malignities of priestly hypocrites. Who can say what infinite peace and refreshment He gained from that day of holy intercourse with His Father in Heaven, and in the society of those whom He could trust and love?

On the morning of Thursday—" Green Thursday," as it used to be called—His disciples asked Him where they should prepare for Him the Paschal Feast, and He gave them a secret and mysterious sign which would lead them to the house (as has been conjectured) of the father of St. Mark, who was probably a secret disciple. Thither they would go after sunset, when the shadows of the evening began to fall; and there (so far as they knew and expected) after the evening meal of that day—known as the *Chagigah,* or " Thanksgiving," to which a quasi-Paschal character was given—they could the next day

eat of the real Passover, and sacrifice the Paschal Lamb.* But
it was not so to be. It was written in the decrees of Eternal
Providence that our Lord was *not* to eat the Paschal Lamb,
but Himself to be sacrificed, " that the reality might correspond
to the figure, and the true Lamb might be slain on the same
day as the lamb which was His antitype." †

* " May we not then suppose that the preparation, which the disciples may
have destined for the next day, *was made the preparation for an immediate
meal, which became the Paschal meal of that year when the events of the
following morning rendered the regular Passover impossible.*"—WESTCOTT,
Introd., p. 344.

† Maldonatus. Comp. 1 Cor. v. 7, xi. 23. I have entered fully elsewhere
(see Exc. X. in my *Life of Christ*) into the question whether the Last Supper
was the real Paschal meal or only an *anticipated* Passover to which our Lord
knowing the doom which immediately hung over Him, gave a quasi-Paschal
character. The *Chronicon Paschale* says distinctly, " *He did not eat the
Paschal Lamb*, but was Himself the Genuine Lamb." Additional and
repeated study convinces me that—as seems to be so indubitably indicated by
St. John (xviii. 28, xix. 14, 31, 42)—it was *not* the Passover that was eaten on
the night previous to that feast ; and that the allusions of the Synoptists, which
seem to indicate that it *was* the Passover, are partly due to certain Jewish cus-
toms and expressions and partly counterbalanced by other indications (Mark
xv., 21, 46 ; Luke xxii. 52, 55, xxiii. 26, 56). Each of the Evangelists says
that our Lord suffered on the day which they call " a " or " the Preparation "
(παρασκευή, Matt. xxvii. 62 ; Mark xv. 42 ; Luke xxiii. 54 ; John xix. 31), and
the word *Paraskeue* undoubtedly means " Friday," which in that year was the
day on the evening of which the actual Passover was observed, as St. John
expressly says (xix. 14 : comp. xix. 38, 42) ; and with this, Jewish tradition
agrees. Moreover, " early Christian tradition is almost unanimous in fixing
the Crucifixion on Nisan 14, and in distinguishing the Last Supper from the
Legal Passover " (Routh, *Rell. Sacr.* i. 168 ; Westcott, *Introd. to the Gospels*,
p. 343). For many more proofs of the position I have taken I may refer to
my *Life of Christ*.

CHAPTER XXXIV.

THE LAST SUPPER.

"No longer do I call you servants . . . but I have called you friends."—JOHN xv. 15.

ON that Thursday evening they met in the upper room—probably the same which was afterwards the scene of Pentecost. To us it might seem almost incredible that, when they began to recline for the feast, a dispute should arise among the Apostles about precedence. We can only account for it by the fact that, though a deep gloom seemed to overshadow them, because they were all conscious that some awful crisis was at hand, they yet cherished the conviction that, however that crisis might end for the moment, it could not but finally issue in that promised glory when, in figurative language, they should sit on twelve thrones judging the Twelve Tribes of Israel. Perhaps with the more reprehensible self-seeking was mingled a longing, in the heart of each of them, to be as near as possible to his Lord. But Jesus rebuked their murmured jealousies by the loveliest of acted parables. "Though He knew that the Father had given all things into His hands, and that He came from God, and was going to God," He arose from supper, and, "taking upon Him the form of a slave," laid aside His upper garments, the *simchah* and *cetoneth,* girt Himself round the waist with a slave's apron, and kneeling down began without a word to wash His disciples' feet, and wipe them with the towel wherewith He was girded. He washed—oh, unfathomable love and compassion!—even the traitor's feet; and explained to the impetuous Peter that if He washed not his feet, he had

no share in Him,* but that " he that hath been bathed needeth
not save to wash *his feet.*" †

The story of that Last Supper is one of the divinest and most
tender of all human records. Pages of more moving and exquisite instructiveness were never written than St. John's narrative of its incidents, and of those discourses " so rarely mixed
of sorrows and joys, and studded with mysteries as with
emeralds." The declaration that one of them should betray
Him; the eager, passionate questions, " Lord, is it I?" followed by the cold, formal " Is it I, Rabbi?" of the betrayer;
the whispered questions of Peter to John; the quick change
of attitude of the young disciple whom Jesus loved, and who
was at the right of Jesus, reclining with his head upon His
breast; ‡ the giving of the sop to Judas, and his stepping forth
into the night—were incidents which occurred in quick succession. No sooner was Judas gone than the spirits of all the
little band seemed to be freed from a terrible incubus. Calling
them His " little children," § Jesus founded the Lord's Supper
as a continual memorial of His death and passion by a par-
ticipation in what St. Paul calls " spiritual food " and " spiritual
drink." Then He began to give them His last revelations. He
bade them love one another; and trust in his and His Father's
ever-present love.‖ He assured them that by His Holy Spirit
He would be with them always, " even to the end of the world."
The golden stream of His utterance was broken by an occasional question from one or other of the disciples. " Lord,

---

* How powerfully this act of lowliness affected the mind of St. Peter we see
from his indirect reference to it many years later, in the words, ἐγκομβώσασθε
τὴν ταπεινοφροσύνην, *Tie* humility of mind round you *like a slave's apron* fastened
with knots (*Komboma*), 1 Pet. v. 5. Κόμβος means " a band," or " girth."

† John xiii. 10.

‡ John xiii. 22, 25. As the guests rested at table on the left arm, John's
head would rest on Christ's robe; and when he suddenly moved to speak to
Jesus, his head was touching Christ's breast.

§ Τεκνία. Only in John xiii. 33. In xxi. 5 it is παιδία.

‖ John xiii. 34, xiv. 21. Judas seems to have been present at the distribu-
tion of the bread (Luke xxii. 19), but not (perhaps) at the blessing of the
sacramental cup.

whither goest thou?" asked St. Peter, and "Why cannot I follow Thee now?"* and in answer he received a warning of the deepest solemnity, yet also of the most loving tenderness. To the last the Apostles often mistook the real force of His words, as they showed by the ignorant literalism of their remark, "Lord, here are two swords." "Lord, we know not whither Thou goest, and how can we know the way?" asked the perplexed and despondent Thomas.† "Lord, show us the Father, and it sufficeth us," said Philip.‡ Judas Lebbæus evinced his perplexity by the question, "Lord, how it is that Thou wilt manifest Thyself unto us, and not unto the world?"§

When the Lord had answered these questions, and dwelt on the further thoughts which they suggested, He said, "Arise, let us go hence." Before starting they joined in singing a hymn, probably a part of the Great Hallel (Ps. 136). Perhaps the allegory of the True Vine was spoken on the way to the Kidron, and suggested by the vineyards through which they were passing; or, as some conjecture, the little band went to the Temple, which at the Passover was opened at midnight, and the allegory may have been pointed by the sight of the Golden Vine over the Temple door. After speaking to them of union with Him, and of the Promised Comforter, and of the issue of sorrow in joy and of defeat in victory, He received the expression of their earnest thankfulness. At first they could not understand all He said, and were afraid to ask Him; but as He clothed His revelations in clearer and clearer form, He called forth their gratitude in the words, "Lord, now speakest Thou plainly, and speakest no proverb. Now know we that Thou knowest all things, and needest not that any man should ask Thee; by this we believe that Thou camest forth from God." Alas! did they indeed now believe? He asked. The hour was close at hand when they should all abandon Him. Yet He had spoken to them that in Him they might have peace, and though in the world they should have tribulations, let them be of good cheer, for He had overcome the world.

---

* John xiii. 36–38.   † John xiv. 5–7.
‡ John xiv. 8–14.   § John xiv. 22–24.

Then Jesus lifted up His eyes to heaven, and uttered the great High-Priestly prayer for Himself, and His loved ones, and for all who should believe through their word. After that they walked on under the moonlight, and followed Him under the moonlit-silvered leaves of the olives with an awful dread brooding over their spirits, as He walked before them with bowed head on the way to the Garden of Gethsemane.*

* Luke xxii. 39, 40, τόπος; John xviii. 1, κῆπος; Matt. xxvi. 36, χωρίον. Gethsemane means " oil-press."

CHAPTER XXXV.

GETHSEMANE.

"Is it nothing to you, all ye that pass by? Behold and see if there be any sorrow like unto my sorrow."—Lam. i. 12.

AND now the night deepened, and Jesus knew that the awful hour was close at hand. He told the majority of the Apostles to sit down in the garden while He Himself withdrew for prayer. They sank into sleep, weary with the burdens and trials of the day; but He had slept His last sleep on earth. He took with Him the three nearest and dearest of His chosen followers —Peter and James and John—because His awfully agitated human spirit felt in that supreme hour the need for human sympathy. He bade them to watch and pray for Him. But now the flood-tide of unspeakable anguish began to roll its waves over His soul. Even the presence of the three was more than He could bear, and, telling them that His soul was very heavy, even unto death, He tore Himself away from them, and again urging them to watch and pray, went about a stone's throw from them, and falling upon His knees, and then upon His face, prayed in an awful intensity of suffering that, if it were His Father's will, the cup might pass from Him. And in the passion of His emotion the sweat poured down from His uplifted countenance as in great gouts of blood.* Thrice He prayed thus, and thrice going back to the most chosen of His chosen, He found them sleeping from grief and utter weariness. He might have cried in the words of the Psalmist: " Thy rebuke hath broken My heart, I am full of heaviness; I looked

---

* It should, however, be noticed that the verse about the "bloodlike sweat " and the angel (Luke xxii. 43, 44) are not *certainly* genuine, since they are not found in MSS. ℵ A, B, etc. They are doubly bracketed in Westcott and Hort's New Testament.

for some to have pity upon Me, but there was no man; neither found I any to comfort Me." An angel from heaven strengthened Him. Ere long the power of His willing self-sacrifice, of His absolute acquiescence in His Heavenly Father's will, won the complete and final victory over the tornadoes of His agony, and when He returned to His disciples it was to tell them, with a perfect and untroubled calm, which remained undisturbed until the end, that now His hour had come, and the betrayer was at hand.

The light of many torches and lanterns began to twinkle through the olive grove; the tramp of soldiers echoed along the rocky paths; there was a clank of swords and of armour, and the hoarse murmur of an advancing crowd. Judas had discovered where He was; the High Priest had ordered the attendance of the Captain of the Temple * and his myrmidons; Pilate—warned that there might be a tumult—had lent some of his soldiers from Fort Antonia, under their *Chiliarch* or Tribune.† They were now near at hand—both Jews and Gentiles. Judas hurried forward with the words, "Rabbi, Rabbi!"‡ and saluted Jesus with fervent and over-acted kisses. "Comrade!" said Jesus sternly; "that for which thou art come . . ." § Then followed the rash blow of Peter; the supernatural terror of the crowd; the seizing, the binding, and leading away of Jesus;.‖ the flight of all His disciples, and of the young man—probably St. Mark—who fled away naked when the captors took hold of the *sindôn* which he had thrown loosely over his shoulders.

But Jesus had won His final triumph over the hour and power of darkness. He had only a few more hours to live, but

---

* Known as the *Ish har ha-Beit*, " the man of the mount of the house," or *Sar ha-birah* (2 Macc. iii. 4).

† If σπεῖρα means "a maniple," that was 200 men, the third part of a cohort. But probably the word is used quite generally.

‡ Mark xiv. 45.

§ Matt. xxvi. 50, ἑταῖρε, "companion"; *not* φίλε, "friend." The sentence, ἐφ' ὃ πάρει . . . seems to be left unfinished. It does not seem to be a question.

‖ John alone mentions the binding (John xviii. 12).

from this moment no brutalism of insult, no refinement of mockery, no outburst of rage and scorn, no complication of torture and agony, ruffled for one instant the divine serenity of that majesty which, in spite of themselves, sensibly overawed and impressed even the most recklessly unscrupulous of His enemies. The complicated intensities of His sufferings only served to bring into more supernatural lustre the unapproachable brightness of His glory.

CHAPTER XXXVI.

THE TRIALS BEFORE THE JEWS.

" I gave My back to the smiters, and My cheeks to them that plucked off the hair; I hid not My face from shame and spitting."—Is. l. 16.

" It cannot be that a Prophet perish out of Jerusalem."—LUKE xiii. 33.

I HAVE, elsewhere, minutely followed and endeavoured to illustrate, from history and from other sources, the full and fourfold narratives of the Gospels respecting the various phases of the trials of Christ before the High Priests and Sanhedrin, and before the Roman Procurator. I shall here only endeavour to summarise and to point the significance of the events recorded.

We are struck first with the monstrous illegality of the mock trials as they were carried out by Annas and Caiaphas and the chief Priests, by the Sudducean priestly party in general, and by the Pharisees, who, though they no longer took a prominent part in the proceedings, yet must have consented to them, since they, at this time, constituted the majority of the Sanhedrin.* We know of two only—Nicodemus and Joseph of Arimathæa —" who had not consented to the will and deed of them." Even Rabban Gamaliel, the famous grandson of the great Hillel, must have been among those who allowed complicated irregularities to proceed without any public protest against them.

One of the awful warnings to be derived from this most terrible event in the history of mankind is the blindness, the vanity, the capability of unutterable wickedness which may co-exist with the pretentious scrupulosities of an external religionism. The Priests and Pharisees had sunk into hypocrisy so deep and habitual that it had become half-unconscious, because it had

* Hence we read in John xi. 47 that " the chief Priests *and the Pharisees* " gathered the Council at which it was decided to put Him to death.

narcotised and all but paralysed the moral sense. They were infinitely particular about peddling littlenesses, but, with a hideous cruelty and a hateful indifference to all their highest duties to God and man, they murdered on false charges the Lord of Glory. A vile self-interest—the determination at all costs to maintain their own prerogatives, and to prevent all questioning of their own traditional system—had swallowed up every other consideration in the minds of men whose very religion had become a thing of rites and ceremonies, and had lost all power to touch the heart, or to inspire the moral sense. " The religion of Israel," it has been said, " falsified by priests, perverted from the service of the Living God into a sensuous worship—where the symbol superseded the reality, the Temple over-shadowed the God, and the hierarchy supplanted His law—could find no love in its heart, no reverence in its will, for the holiest Person of its race; met Him not as the fruition of its hopes, and the end of its being, but as the last calamity of its life, a Being who must perish that it might live." *

How many of the nominal Pontiffs who, at the will of the Romans and the Herods, had " passed the chair " of the High Priesthood, and may have taken part in the trial of Jesus, we do not know.† Besides Annas and Caiaphas, there may have been present Ishmael ben Phabi; Eleazar (a son of Annas); Simon ben Kamhith; and of those who subsequently became High Priests, Jonathan, Theophilus, and Matthias (sons of Annas), Simon Kantheras, Joseph ben Kamhith, and others. Even among the Jews, as we have already seen from the Talmud, the names of these worldly and avaricious Pontiffs were held in detestation.

Annas and his son-in-law, Caiaphas, were the leading spirits in this evil conclave. Josephus, in one passage, calls Annas the most fortunate of men because " he had five sons who had

---

* Fairbairn, *Studies*, p. 307.

† Josephus tells us (*Antt.* xx. 10, 1) that there had been twenty-eight of these avaricious, simoniacal, and unworthy desecrators of the priesthood in 100 years.

all held the office of High Priest,* as well as Caiaphas, his son-in-law." †

He had been appointed High Priest A. D. 6 by Quirinius, and deposed in A. D. 15 by Valerius Gratus. His youngest son, Annas the second, was the murderer of James, the Lord's brother. For this crime—impudently committed during the interregnum between two procuratorships—Albinius deposed him. Later on, the long-delayed vengeance fell on him. During the Jewish war the house of Annas was destroyed by a furious mob, this last son of the house was scourged and beaten to his place of murder, and his dead body flung out naked to be the food of dogs and wild beasts.‡

The name of Hanan (Annas) means " merciful "—the exact opposite of the man's real nature. The High Priest who bore it has left a disastrous record of himself and his family. The Sadducees as a body were notorious for their cruel severity, and this family was among the worst.§ Though now an old man, Annas was an astute, avaricious worldling.‖ Josephus tells us that there was, in this age, a sedition between the High Priests and the chief leaders of the people. Each party had violent adherents who often interchanged not only reproachful words, but showers of stones, and produced an epoch of misrule in Jerusalem. " And such," he says, " was the impudence and boldness that had seized on the High Priests, that they had the hardness to send their servants to the threshing floors to seize tithes due to priests, so that the poorer sort of priests died for want." If the priests resisted, they beat them.¶ Besides these acts of au-

---

*On Annas see Jos., *Antt.* xx. 9, 1. His sons were ; Eleazar A. D. 16 ; Jonathan A. D. 36 ; Theophilus A. D. 37 ; Matthias A. D. 42–43 ; Annas the younger A. D 62.

† Joseph Caiaphas (another form of Cephas) A. D. 18–36. He was deposed by Vitellius A. D. 37. He continued to persecute Christians (Acts iv. 6).

‡ Jos. *B. J.* iv. 5, 2.

§ Jos. *Antt.* xx. 9, 1. περὶ τὰς κρίσεις ὡμοὶ παρὰ πάντας τοὺς Ἰουδαίους (speaking of the trial of James). Josephus also calls them ἀπηνεῖς καὶ οὐκ ἀνεκτοὶ πλήθεσιν (*Antt.* xviii. 1, 4). He speaks of the son of Annas, who executed James, as unusually audacious and turbulent (*Antt.* xx. 9, 1).

‖ *Antt.* xx. viii. 8. Josephus calls him Ananus.   ¶ *Antt.* xx. 9, 2.

dacious tyranny, the members of the house of Annas were universally condemned for greed.* Wealthy as they were, they
had set up four booths (*Chanuyôth*) on the Mount of Olives
for the sale of materials for sacrifice, and especially for the sale
of doves—the offerings of the poor—from which they extracted
great gain. It is said that the Sanhedrin, after ceasing to meet
in the *Lishcath Haggazith*, or " Hall of Square-stones," † used
to hold their assemblies in these *Chanuyôth*, whence—after the
" booths " had been destroyed at the time of the murder of the
younger Annas—they returned to Jerusalem.‡ The house of
Annas as the most influential Sadducean and High-Priestly
family was mainly responsible for the invasion of the Temple
courts by the greedy traffickers whom Christ drove forth both
at the beginning and at the end of His ministry.

I.—THE TRIAL BEFORE ANNAS.

It was into the presence of this cunning and powerful hier-
arch that our Lord was first taken after the night arrest. Although Annas had ceased to be High Priest *de facto*, he was
still regarded by strict Jews as High Priest *de jure*, as it was
only by the Roman Governor that he had been deprived of his
office. Whether he still held any official position in the Sanhedrin—such as *Nasi* (in the High Priest's absence), or *Chakam*,
or *Ab-beth Din*—is uncertain, but in any case his influence was
predominant, since all the highest functions were still carried on
by his nearest relatives. Everything, therefore, depended on
the view which Annas would take, and the course which he
would approve, after his preliminary investigation of the charge
against Jesus.

The minor details are not narrated by the four Evangelists
with sufficient precision to enable us to arrive at certainty; but

---

* *Id*. vii. 8. † *Sanhedrin*, f. 88, 2.

‡ *Rosh Hashanah*, 3, 1, 6 ; *Taanith*, iv. 8. There is, however, much uncertainty about these *Chanuyôth*. Derenbourg (*Palestine*, p. 465) accepts the
view that they were (at any rate *originally*) on the Mount of Olives. They are
said to have been destroyed three years before the Fall of Jerusalem, *id*. p,
468.

the majority of those who have written since the publication of my *Life of Christ* have come in the main to the same view as is there presented. Annas, who seems to be alluded to as "the High Priest" in St. John xviii. 19,* asked Jesus about His disciples and His doctrine. In thus acting he was adopting a course which was flagrantly illegal. He was acting as a sole Judge, though the Jewish rule was, "*Be not a sole judge, for there is no sole judge but One*"; † he was conducting a private investigation, whereas Hebrew justice demanded the utmost publicity; he was trying to entrap the Accused by his own admissions, in spite of the distinct requirement that "*one man shall not rise up against a man for any iniquity.*" ‡ It was against these gross violations of the law that our Lord made His calm and majestic protest, in return for which an insolent menial, unreproved by his vile superiors, first profaned with a blow of his brutal hand the face on which angels desire to look.§ From this circumstance Jesus saw that the whole proceeding was to be one glaring travesty of justice, and to these Jewish Priests and Sanhedrists, until adjured by the name of God, He uttered no further word. This preliminary examination was probably held between two and three o'clock at night.

II.—THE TRIAL BEFORE CAIAPHAS.

No law was more stringent than the Jewish as to the necessity of assuming innocence until guilt was proved; yet, as though Jesus had been a legally convicted criminal, Annas sent Him *bound* to Caiaphas. Another night examination, in defiance of Hebrew law, ensued; and it is probable that Caiaphas was supported by at least a committee of Sanhedrists.|| These unjust judges, instead of waiting till witnesses spontaneously came forward, deliberately *sought* for witness, and even for

---

* Comp. John xviii. 23, 24.   † *Pirqe Avôth*, iv. 8.

‡ Deut. xvii. 6, xix. 15 ; Num. xxxv. 30.

§ The Talmud complains of these Priests that "their servants *strike* the people with their rods" (*Pesachim*, 57).

|| Not the "Sanhedrin *gedolah*," or "great Sanhedrin" of 70, but the "Sanhedrin *kethannah*," or "smaller Sanhedrin" of 23.

false witness, against their victim. Yet, eager as they were to fix on Him some charge of blasphemy, the witnesses broke down. Their testimony did not agree. It was too flagrantly loose, discordant, and invalid to be used even by men bent on injustice and murder. At last false witnesses came whose testimony might seem to be more available. But the only definite charge which they could bring against Him was the " sign " which He had offered to His questioners in the first year of His ministry about rebuilding the Temple in three days. Some witnesses declared that He had said, " *I will destroy this Temple.*" Others, that He had said, " *I am able to destroy* this Temple." In point of fact, He had used neither of these incriminated phrases, but had said, " *Destroy ye* this Temple, and I will raise it up in three days" ; in other words, Consummate *your* work, and I will accomplish Mine.* No other charge was brought against Him, and justice was again defied, since they called no witnesses in His favour. Still the accusation, indirect as it was, had broken down. Nor could they in any way establish the charge that Jesus was a *Mesith*—a " seducer " or " misleader " of the people. Caiaphas and his party began to feel that, after all, their enemy might escape from their clutches, in spite of their determination—in the cause, not of right, but of that " expediency " which they interpreted to be the maintenance of their own unhallowed predominance and vile gains —to put Him to death. Moreover, they were perplexed and overawed by the majestic silence which Jesus maintained. They felt that His silence was their condemnation ; that the Accused was justly sitting in judgment on His own unjust judges. Yet they knew that His teaching, even if they could not bring it under the charge of constructive blasphemy, had involved claims of supernatural, though of purely spiritual, pre-eminence. What was to be done? How was the awful silence of the Accused, which shamed and overawed their souls, to be goaded into speech? There was but one way. It was disgracefully unfair, disgracefully illegal. But did that matter, when

---

* Λύσατε τὸν ναὸν τοῦτον (John ii. 19). Ye have begun to desecrate and undermine the Temple by your greed and profanity. Complete your work !

the night trial, and the private examination before Annas, and the seeking for false witnesses, and the suppression of any one to support the cause of the Accused, and every other feature in the entire proceeding, were equally unjust? The hard, worldly, unscrupulous High Priest came to their rescue. Defying the most initial principle of Hebrew Law—which was that no one was to be condemnèd to death on his own confession *—he made to Jesus a tremendous appeal. " I adjure Thee by the Living God," he cried, " that Thou tell us whether Thou be the Christ, the Son of God." So adjured, our Lord could not refuse to answer. He replied: " Thou hast said: and hereafter ye shall see the Son of Man sitting at the right hand of Power and coming in the clouds of heaven." Then the High Priest, in well-acted mock agitation, cried, " Blasphemy ! " and rent his priestly *Ketoneth* of fine linen, and the assembly shouted, " He is *Ish Maveth!* " (a man of death). Then followed the derision by the menials of the Sanhedrin, during the time that elapsed before the morning of Friday when the full Sanhedrin could legally meet. But even this meeting was again illegal, for, after a preliminary condemnation, the Law required that a whole day should intervene before the final judgment.

III.—THE TRIAL BEFORE THE SANHEDRIN.

At earliest dawn Christ was led before this full assembly of seventy members, assembled in the *Beth Din,* or House of Judgment.† He was set before them as a condemned criminal. There a similar scene occurred. The Sanhedrin desired to condemn Him out of His own mouth; and His most determined and unscrupulous enemies kept urging Him with the furious question, " *Art Thou the Christ? tell us.*" He answered not. But at last, to end the unholy farce, He said, " If I tell you ye will not believe. And if I also ask you "—if I question you as

---

* Mishna *Sanhedr.* vi. 2. The Jewish historian Jost admits that all the legal forms were disgracefully violated by these priests (*Gesch. Judenth.* i. 283, 403).

† The *Lishcath Haggazith*, or Hall of Squares, seems to have been abandoned. They *may* have met in the Beth Midrash on the *Chel* or partition wall ; or in the Booths (See *ante*, p. 370). The details must remain uncertain.

to your authority for these proceedings—if I press *you* also with questions—" ye will not answer Me." And they all said: *" Art Thou then the Son of God?"* And He said unto them, " Ye say that I am." After that, He was once more formally condemned to death; and as He had been derided and misused by knaves and menials, so now—which was harder to bear— He was coarsely insulted by Priests and Pharisees.* Although the merciful custom was to regard a condemnation to death by the Sanhedrin as a deplorable event, even when justice required it—and so deplorable that after such a verdict the day should be spent in fasting †—they could not repress their savage delight at having at last got into their power the Prophet whom, again and again, they had vainly endeavoured to seize and slay. " How is the faithful city become an harlot! She that was full of justice! Righteousness lodged in her: but now murderers." ‡

So ended this shameful mockery of justice, illegal at almost every stage and in almost every particular. It was illegal (1) because it was conducted by night; (2) because the Hebrew Law required that every effort should be used to secure the acquittal of a prisoner, whereas every effort had here been used to secure his condemnation; (3) because witnesses had been sought for the accusation, and none called for the defence; (4) because after the witnesses had broken down—which ought to have been followed by the immediate acquittal of the Accused —Jesus had been adjured, by the name of God, to answer a question which might give the false judges an opportunity to condemn Him out of His own mouth; (5) because a claim which—setting aside its truth—was *not* blasphemy, or only *constructive* blasphemy—was treated as a capital offence; (6) because no proper interval of a full day was allowed to intervene between the hasty, illegal, night-condemnation before the Committee of Sanhedrists and the formal condemnation before

---

* Matt. xxvi. 67. The word ἐκμυκτηρίζω, *subsannare, naso suspendere,* is expressive of the extremest scorn.

† *Bab Sanhedr.*, f. 63, 1.

‡ Is. i. 21 ; 1 Thess. ii. 15.

the Sanhedrin as a body; * (7) because the Victim had been misused, smitten, insulted, without any interference, by the lacqueys of the Priests and by the Priests and Sanhedrists themselves; (8) because Jesus was tried on a capital charge on a Friday, not only on the day before the Sabbath (which was unlawful), but before a Sabbath which, as being at the beginning of the Passover, was in an unusually sacred sense a High Day.†

* *Sanhedrin*, iv. 1, v. 5; Schürer, ii. 1, p. 194.   † John xix. 31.

CHAPTER XXXVII.

THE TRIAL BEFORE PILATE.

"Auctor nominis ejus, Christus, Tiberio imperitante, per Procuratorem Pontium Pilatum supplicio affectus erat."—Tac. *Ann.* xv. 44.

THE account of the trial of Christ before Pilate, especially as given by St. John—brief though it is—is unparalleled in the whole world's literature for its vividness and verisimilitude. I shall not relate it at length, but only indicate its varying phases. How varied and agitating those phases were, and how powerfully the presence of Jesus, in His sleeplessness and misery, affected even so hard a heart as that of Pilate, may be seen from the fact that the Procurator, no less than three times, entered into the Prætorium to question Jesus apart from His enemies (xviii. 33-37, xix. 1-3, 8-11), and made four or five strong and separate attempts to rescue One whom he recognised to be incomparably truer, nobler, and more innocent than the crowd of lying Priests, and the multitude whom they hounded to His destruction.

The Jews had condemned our Lord to death, but, according to the best historic authorities, had no power to carry into execution their own decree. A tumultuary murder, like that of St. Stephen, might, indeed, have been overlooked by the contempt of Roman insouciance, especially in a matter which the haughty Gentile rulers might despise as one of words, and names, and of Jewish law.* But the Priestly party could not have stoned Christ without many difficulties and dangers; and, further, they desired to inflict on Him the most abject and awful form of death, which could only be sanctioned by the Romans. They wished also to overawe those whom they regarded as His violent but deluded Galilean followers, by show-

* Acts xviii. 15.

376

ing that He was condemned by their Roman governors as well as by their religious authorities. Their object was to inflict upon Him an accumulation of shame and horrible agony which should be witnessed by the whole multitude assembled to keep the Passover. They thought that such a fate would finally extinguish every attempt to represent Him as a Divine Teacher. And, as is always the case, they most effectually carried out the purposes of God by the human wickedness with which they strove to render them impossible.

Besides all this, the matter was not one which could be hastily hushed up. It is evident that it had already come under the cognisance of Pilate, since otherwise they could not have used the Roman tribune and part of his cohort as agents in the arrest.

1. While it was still early morning, therefore, the imposing body of High Priests, Priests, and Sanhedrists, headed doubtless by Annas and Caiaphas, accompanied Jesus to the tribunal of the Procurator. He was led—a bound and weary prisoner, after so many hours of sleepless anguish and excitement— across the bridge which spanned the Valley of the Tyropœon, to the splendid Herodian palace now occupied by the Procurator.* Greatly as they feared and detested the Roman knight who had thrice been involved in deadly conflict with them and their nation,† they assumed that they would easily overawe him by the pomp of their sacred authority. They thought nothing of the guilt of shedding innocent blood; but since they meant that evening to keep the Passover, their religious scruples prevented them from facing the ceremonial uncleanness involved in entering a house from which leaven had not been removed. In scornful condescension Pilate came out to them from the Prætorium. But he was clad in all the stupendous

---

* It is, however, *possible* that Pilate may have been residing in Fort Antonia.

† At an earlier time the Procurators only ruled for a year or two. Tiberius thought it safer, and kinder to the subject races, to employ them for a longer period (Tac. *Ann.* i. 80; Suet. *Tiber.* 32; Jos. *Antt.* xviii. 6, 5). Valerius Gratus had held office for eleven years (A. D. 14–25); Pontius Pilate ruled for ten years (A. D. 26–36).

power of the Roman Empire, being a direct representative of
Tiberius Cæsar, and he had, amid all his crimes, the stern
sense of Roman justice which made him disdain to condemn to
death a man in whose trial he had had no share. He knew what
sort of men the Priests were, and had not the smallest respect
for their profession of integrity. He asked them, " What accusation bring ye against this man?" This took them by surprise. They did not want a fresh trial; they only wanted Pilate
to crucify One whom they had brought to him as "a malefactor." When they sullenly told him that they had a law, and
by their law He ought to die, Pilate's contemptuous reply was,
" Then deal with Him yourselves." They reminded him that
they had no power to put a man to death, and since the charge
of " blasphemy," on which they had condemned Him, was one
which Pilate would have disdainfully refused to examine, they
heaped up a mass of false accusations, in which three are spe-
cifically discernible, namely, that—

(i.) He was a ringleader of sedition—a *Mesith,* or " deceiver," who was seducing and perverting the nation.

That charge broke down totally and *ipso facto,* for Pilate
was perfectly well aware that there had been no tumults or
signs of insurrection connected with the name of Jesus. He
also knew well that none of the political rulers—not even the
suspicious Antipas, who lived close beside the central scene of
the ministry of Jesus—had ever made the slightest complaint
against Him.

(ii.) He had (they said) forbidden the people to give tribute
to Cæsar.

This charge was a most flagrant falsehood, and was in fact
the very reverse of the truth, since Jesus only two days before,
when an attempt was made to entrap Him in the Temple, had
openly said, " Render unto Cæsar the things that are Cæsar's."
It was also grossly hypocritical; for they themselves abhorred
the indignity of paying tribute to Cæsar, and would have hailed
any chance of throwing off the Imperial yoke. Pilate saw
through their falsity, and it deepened his utter contempt for
them.

(iii.) He had said that " He Himself is Christ, a King."
This charge might be regarded as true *in a sense*, although, as they were well aware, it was *not* true in the sense in which they wished it to be understood; and

> " A lie that is half a truth is ever the greatest of lies."

They intended Pilate to understand the charge in a seditious and temporal sense, though they knew that Christ's Kingdom was "not of this world," and had no bearing on Roman dominion. If, however, they could get Pilate to accept unexamined this accusation of *læsa majestas*, they felt that it was the most deadly which they could possibly bring.

But Pilate was a Roman, and the Romans knew what justice meant. He would not hand Jesus over to death untried and uncondemned, and ordered Him to be led into the palace to be questioned, for he was amazed that He should have stood in calm silence amid these storms of furious false witness. He therefore put to Him the question, "Art *Thou* the King of the Jews?" He received an answer such as confirmed the feeling, which became deeper in his mind every moment, that this was no ordinary prisoner, but a man of transcendent innocence, about whom some awful shadow of the Unknown seemed to hang. He heard from the lips of Jesus a gentle and courteous explanation as to the true nature of the Kingdom which He claimed. Pilate did, indeed, brush aside, with the hard, practical shrewdness of a commonplace intellect, the allusion which Christ had made to " the Truth." This he probably regarded as a piece of harmless transcendentalism, with which he, a Roman Governor, had nothing to do; but, filled with the conviction that the detested Jews were hounding to death One who was infinitely nobler than themselves, he strode out of the palace again, and emphatically pronounced to the raging hierarchs his conviction that the Victim for whose blood they thirsted was absolutely innocent.

2. Amid the roar of denunciations which this acquittal provoked, he heard the name " Galilee," and, catching at any straw to get rid of this bad business, inquired " if the man were a

Galilean?" Being informed that He was, he sent Jesus to Herod. The Sanhedrists accompanied Him to the old As-monæan Palace in which Herod Antipas was living, and re-newed their vehement denunciations:—but there also Jesus maintained His unbroken silence. Why should He waste words on "that fox"?* How could an adulterer, a coward, a slug-gish and cunning parasite, a murderer of the Prophets, com-prehend anything that He could say?

Antipas could make nothing of Him, but evidently saw and knew enough to convince him that the whole accusation was a conspiracy based on lies. In his petulant vexation that Jesus would say nothing to him, he allowed his myrmidons to mock the Prisoner, but sent Him back to Pilate practically acquitted.

3. The tumult, however, continued, and the guilty conscience and agitated career of Pilate made him anxious, if he could, while saving Jesus from death, to make some concession to this raging crowd of Jews hounded on by their religious leaders. He came out on the *Bena,* and again emphatically told the Chief Priests that both he and Herod saw clearly that they were try-ing to destroy an innocent man. Pilate—of whom it is a re-markable fact that the Evangelists speak far more moderately than Jewish writers like Philo and Josephus †—was, as Ter-tullian says, *" jam pro conscientia sua Christianus."* Neverthe-less he was willing to scourge Jesus; to make Him no longer dangerous by so agonising and shameful a humiliation, and then to set Him free.

4. This concession His enemies angrily rejected; and then, perhaps, he clutched at some suggestion that they might con-sent to set Jesus free in accordance with the annual act of grace by which he released a prisoner to them at the Passover. This was "the first step in that downward course of weakness which the world knows so well;—a course which, beginning with inde-

---

* Luke xiii. 32 ; Jos. *Antt.* xviii. 7.

† Philo and Josephus are very severe (Jos. *Antt.* xviii. 3, 4 ; *B. J.* ii. 9 ; Philo Leg. *ad Caiam.* § 38). Christian legends represent the ultimate suicide of Pilate as the result of his remorse. The Gospel of Nicodemus (ii. 13) goes so far as to speak of him as already " circumcised in heart."

cision and complaisance, passed through all the phases of alternate bluster, subserviency, persuasion, *suasion,* protest, compromise, superstitious dread, conscientious reluctance, cautious duplicity, and other moral cowardice, until this Roman remains photographed for ever as the perfect feature of the unjust judge, deciding

" Against his better knowledge, not deceived." *

The Jews, however, shouted in favour of his releasing a notorious criminal named Jesus Barabbas, a rebel and murderer, who had been guilty of the very crimes of which they were *falsely accusing* Jesus, and of crimes much more flagrant! Pilate, by his guilty and cowardly concessions, had only involved himself in more hopeless difficulties. He was still deeply unwilling to sacrifice an innocent man, who had inspired his callous mind with a sensation of awe such as he had never felt before. This awe was intensified by the message brought to him on the tribunal from his wife, Claudia Procula, that " he was to have nothing to do with that Just Man, since she had, that night, suffered many things in a dream because of Him." †
What *justice* required he had not a moment's doubt; but personal fear, and the consciousness that serious charges might be made against him by the Jews, hung over him, and tempted him to the unwilling sacrifice of all that yet remained to him of nobler principle. He had publicly proclaimed that Jesus was innocent, yet—Roman as he was—in dread of the yelling conspirators, he degraded himself to the iniquity of handing Him over to death as guilty.

At last the cry, " If thou let this man go, thou are not *Cæsar's* friend," decided him. He dared not face the deadly jealousies and awful cruelty of the gloomy Emperor Tiberius, a man who, surrounded by the unscrupulous informers whom he encouraged, was torn to pieces by mad and reckless suspicion.‡ Dread-

* Taylor Innes, *The Trial of Jesus Christ,* p. 93.
† The name of Pilate's wife is given in *Nicephorus* i. 30, and in the spurious Gospel of Nicodemus.
‡ The charge of *læsa majestas* was frightfully perilous. Tac. *Ann.* iii. 38 ; Suet. *Tib.* 61.

ing a delation of himself to this horrible tyrant, Pilate set Barabbas free, and ordered Jesus to be scourged. This scourging was a recognised preliminary to crucifixion, not an attempt to get Jesus spared out of pity; though after it had been inflicted, Pilate seized one more chance of getting the prisoner released, out of sheer compassion for an agony worse than death.*

5. From that awful scourging, Jesus came forth mangled, bleeding, agonised, wearing the crown of torturing thorns, and clad in the war cloak of faded scarlet in which the soldiers had mocked Him; but still so unsurpassable in His majesty that even this hardened Roman general could only exclaim, " *Behold the Man!* " But the unmoved Jews were still yelling " Crucify! " " Crucify Him yourselves," said Pilate, " for *I* find no fault in Him." " By our law," they shouted, " He ought to die, because He made Himself *a Son of God.*"

6. Here was a new and startling allegation! Pilate could not but make one final effort. He caused Jesus to be led into the Judgment Hall of the palace once more, and asked Him in awe and amazement, " *Whence art Thou?* " Jesus answered not, but when Pilate, driven to anger, reminded Him that the power of life and death was in his hands, Jesus gently told him that " he could have no power if it were not given him from above ; " —then, half acquitting his own judge, He added, " therefore he that betrayed Me to thee hath the greater sin." Was it possible that the multitude could still remain unaffected by the awful pathos of such moral and spiritual grandeur involved in such horrible misery? Pilate thought not. He led Him forth, and as he sat in his seat of judgment on the shining pavement, said, with awestruck accents:

" Behold your King! "

The answer was a fresh clamour of " Crucify! Crucify! " " Shall I crucify *your King?* " asked Pilate. Then came the fatal and apostate shout which terrified him from pity and from

---

* All the allusions in the classics (Hor. *Ep.* i. 16, 17 ; *Sat.* i. 3, 119 ; Juv. vi. 478 ; Cic. *Verr.* v. 54, 66 ; Val. Max. i. 7, etc., show the inconceivable horror of this cruel infliction, which frequently caused death (Plut. *Coriol.* 24, etc.).

justice, "*We have no king but Cæsar!*" At that cry the last barriers of the Procurator's conscience were swept away. In vain pretence of shifting the responsibility, he washed his hands as he sat on the tribunal before the people, and said, "*I am innocent of the blood of this Just Person! See ye to it.*" Would whole oceans have washed away his guilt? Would not his hands rather have "incarnadined the multitudinous seas?"

> "Ah nimium faciles qui tristia crimina cædis
> Fluminea tolli posse putatis aqua." *

They cried, "His blood be on us and on our children!" Then Pilate uttered the awful final words, "*Ibis ad crucem. I miles expedi crucem.*"

Pilate himself must have deeply felt the disgrace of being driven by personal cowardice into a flagrant and admitted violation of that sense of the sacredness of justice which was the strongest moral conviction in the mind of every genuine Roman. He had tried every device he could. He had said:

"Take ye Him, and judge Him " (John xviii. 31).

"*I find in Him no fault at all*" (xviii. 38).

"Will ye that I release unto you the King of the Jews?" (xviii. 39).

"Behold I bring Him forth unto you *that ye may know that I find in Him no fault*" (xix. 4).

"Behold the man!" (5).

"I find no fault in Him " (6).

"Behold your King!" (14).

"Shall I crucify your King?" (15).

"I am innocent of the blood of this Just Person. See ye to it" (Matt. xxvii. 24).

Yet, after all these declarations, a mere desire for personal safety—which proved to be perfectly useless!—made him condescend to the infamy of rending asunder every dictate of his own conscience, and of giving up to death One whose perfect innocence he had so repeatedly declared.

* Ovid. *Fast.* ii. 45.   Comp. Deut. xxi. 6, 7.

CHAPTER XXXVIII.

THE SUFFERINGS OF JESUS.

Ἐβασίλευσεν [ἀπὸ τοῦ ξύλον.].—Ps. xcvi. 10.

" Crudelissimum tæterrimuque supplicium."—Cic. *Verr*. v. 64.

"Nomen ipsum Crucis absit non modo a corpore civium Romanorum, sed etiam a cognitione, oculis, auribus."—Cic. *pro Rab*. 5.

" Quid dicam in crucem tolli ? Verbo satis digno tam nefaria res appellari nullo modo potest."—Cic. *Verr*. v. 66.

Τὸ πάθος χριστοῦ ἡμῶν ἀπάθειά ἐστιν, καὶ ὁ θάνατος αὐτοῦ ἡμῶν ἀθανασία.— ATHANAS., *De Incarn*.

IT is difficult adequately to realise the multitude and variety of the forms of spiritual distress and mental anguish, of scorn, and torture, to which the sinless Son of Man was continuously subjected from the time that He left the Mount of Olives to enter Jerusalem for the Last Supper.*

1. At the Last Supper He had the heavy sorrow of reading the heart of the traitor, and of uttering His last farewells— mingled with prophecies of persecution as the path to final triumph—to those whom He loved best on earth.

2. Then came the agony in the garden, which filled Him with speechless amazement and shuddering, until He had to fling Himself with His face to the earth in the tense absorption of

* I will not again re-enter on the highly disputed questions which do not bear directly on my subject. I still, however, remain unshaken in the conviction that St. John rightly represents our Lord as crucified on Friday, Nisan 14, the *day before the actual Passover*. It is impossible to believe that all the wild and hurried events of the trials and crucifixion took place on a feast day of special solemnity. To what I have said on an earlier page (p. 359, footnote) I will only add that Mr. Wright (*Some New Testament Problems*) concludes that, as to the date, " certainty is unattainable, but unless the ministry lasted about ten years, the most probable date of the Crucifixion is 9 a. m. to 3 p. m. on Friday, Nisan 14, A. D. 29, and Nisan 14 probably fell on March 18."

384

prayer, and His sweat was like great gouts of blood streaming to the ground.

3. Then the horror of Judas's over-acted traitor-kiss, the seizure, the binding, the leading away, the desertion of Him by all His disciples in His hour of need.

4. Then the long trials which, only broken by insult, lasted the whole night through; the sense of utter injustice; the proof that all those hierophants who should have been the very first to welcome Him with humble yet triumphant gladness, were fiercely bent on destroying Him by any means, however foul.

5. Then the insolent blow in the face from one of the servants.*

6. Then the hearing His chief Apostle deny Him with oaths and curses.

7. Then the night trial before Caiaphas and his most confidential adherents, with all its agitating incidents, its tumult of sneering voices, its dreadful adjuration, and the sentence on Him as "a Man of Death" by the "spiritual" court.

8. Then the accumulations of brutal insult as the crowd of vile underlings mocked Him,† and slapped and beat Him,‡ and spat in his face,§ and, bandaging His eyes,‖ bade Him name the wretches who had smitten Him.

9. Then the early morning trial before the whole Sanhedrin, with its continuance of agitating appeals, and the final proof that "He had come unto His own possessions, and His people received Him not."

10. Then, if we read the record rightly, another derision by the Priests and Sanhedrists.

11. Then the long and thrilling scenes of the trial before Pilate, as He stood in the centre of a crowd thirsting for His

---

* John xviii. 22. The word ῥάπισμα is used both for a blow with the fist and a blow with a rod.

† Luke xxii. 63, ἐνέπαιζον αὐτῷ δέροντες.

‡ Luke xxii. 63–65, δέροντες . . . ὁ παίσας ; Mark xiv. 65, κολαφίζειν ; Matt. xxvi. 67, ἐκολάφισαν . . . ἐράπισαν.

§ Matt. xxvi. 67, ἐνέπτυσαν εἰς τὸ πρόσωπον.

‖ Luke xxii. 64, περκαλύψαντες αὐτὸν ; Matt. xxv. 67.

blood, yelling for His crucifixion; heaping lies and insults upon Him; preferring to Him the robber and the murderer; defeating, by their ferocious pertinacity, the obvious desire of the Roman Governor to set Him free.

12. Then the leading through the city to Herod, and the vain attempt of that despicable prince to wring some answer or some sign from Him.

13. Then the coarse derision of Herod's myrmidons * as, in mock homage, they stripped Him of His own garments and arrayed Him in a shining robe, with every accumulation of disdainful insolence and cruelty.

14. Then the final sentence of crucifixion, pronounced by Pilate after vain appeals and efforts to overcome the furious animosity of His accusers.

15. Then the brutal mockery by the whole band of Roman soldiers as He stood helpless among them. These coarse legionaries were only too much rejoiced to pour on Him the contempt and detestation which they felt for all Jews,† and seized the opportunity to vent their callous savagery on One who, as they were taught to believe, had claimed to be a King. This King should have the insignia of royalty—a cast-off military *sagum* of scarlet;‡ a crown—only twisted of torturing thorns;§ a sceptre—a reed which they could every now and then snatch out of His tied hands, and beat Him with it as well as with rods; the mock homage of bended knees varied by execrable spitting,∥ and blows on the head, and slaps on the face with the open palm, and words of uttermost contempt.

16. Then He was mangled and lacerated almost to death by the horrible and excruciating *flagellum,* inflicted by executioners who had no sense of pity, with scourges loaded with balls of lead and sharp-pointed bones.¶

* Luke xxiii. 11, ἐξουθενήσας . . . ἐμπαίξας . . . περιβαλὼν ἐσθῆτα λαμπράν.

† See Jos. *B. J.* ii, 12, v. 11 ; *Antt.* xix. 9.

‡ Matt. xxvii. 28, χλαμύδα κοκκίνην.

§ Matt. xxvii. 29, στέφανον ἐξ ἀκανθῶν.

∥ Matt. xxvii. 30; Mark xv. 19. This was regarded by the Jews with special loathing (Num. xii. 14 ; Deut. xxv. 9 ; Is. l. 6).

¶ John xix. 1 ; Luke xxiii. 16 ; Matt. xxvii. 26. Hor. *Sat.* i, 3, 119 ; Apul. *Metam.* viii.

17. Then came the stripping bare of the robes, and the bending under the load of the cross—or rather, of its *patibulum*—the transverse beam of the cross, which He was too much exhausted to carry, while the herald went before Him proclaiming the supposed crime for which He was condemned.

18. Then the sight of the weeping and wailing daughters of Jerusalem.*

19. Then the driving of the lacerating, crushing nails through His feet, and through either hand, and the uplifting on the cross, that *" servile," " infame," " crudelissimum," " tæterrimum," " extremum," " supplicium."*

20. Then the sight of all the world's worst vileness flowing beneath His eyes in its noisy stream, as the Elders, in their heartlessness, wagged their heads at Him, and jeered, and blasphemed; † and the soldiers mocked, and the crowd howled their insults, and the two wretched robbers who shared with Him that hour of shame—though *they* were guilty and He was innocent—joined in the continuous pitiless reviling.‡

21. Then the sight of His mother in her unspeakable desolation.

22. Then the darkening by anguish of His human soul, which wrung from Him the cry, " My God, My God, why hast Thou forsaken Me? "

Yet, amid all these accumulations of anguish, only one word of physical pain was wrung from Him—the cry, *" I thirst "* §—and so deep was the impression caused by His majestic patience, as well as by the portents which followed, that the whole crowd was overawed and hushed, and returned to Jerusalem beating their breasts, and saying, " Truly, this was a righteous

---

* Luke xxiii. 27.

† To what awful depths of decadence these formalising hierarchs must have sunk before they could be capable of conduct so execrable may be illustrated by the fact that King Alexander Jannæus met with universal reprobation from the Jews when he adopted crucifixion as a mode of punishment (Jos. *B. J.* i. 4, 5).

‡ Mark xv. 29 ; Luke xxiii. 35 ; Matt. xxvii. 44.

§ He had refused to drink the stupefying potion offered to Him *before* His crucifixion (Matt. xxvii. 34 ; Mark xv. 23 ; Ps. lxix. 21).

man;" and the penitent robber implored Him to receive him into His Kingdom; and even the Pagan Roman centurion spoke of Him as " a Son of God."*

The uttermost depth of superhuman woe seems to be revealed by His cry, *"My God, My God, why hast Thou forsaken Me?"* But it has often been pressed to unwarrantable conclusions. The twenty-second Psalm was doubtless present to his mind *as a whole,* when He hung in the extremity of His lonely anguish; and it should never be forgotten that David's cry of despair is but the brief human prelude to the expression of uttermost trust, and to the outpouring of confident hope and triumphant praise. If in the " burning fiery furnace " of Nebuchadnezzar the Spirit of God was to the Three Children as " a moist whistling wind," we are not warranted in pressing the quotation by our Lord of one sad verse of a Psalm of which the gladness and trust no less than the sorrow must have been present to His mind, though He only uttered aloud the first verse of it. Nor must it be overlooked that, if one of the seven utterances from the Cross expressed spiritual anguish, and another the extreme of physical torment, all the other five were words of love, of forgiveness, and of triumph. The first was the prayer for His murderers; the second was the promise to the pardoned penitent; the third, the tender provision for the future of His mother: then came the " Why dost thou forsake me? " and " I thirst;" but they were followed by the one loud, triumphant word, " τετέλεσται," " It is over for ever! " and the ejaculation, " Father, into Thy hands I commend My Spirit," with which He bowed His head, and yielded up His human life.* " With a word," says Tertullian, " He voluntarily gave up His Spirit, anticipating the duty of the executioner." " He died," says St. Augustine, " because He willed

---

* In Luke xxiii. 47 it is " Certainly this was a righteous man." This in any case was the meaning of the centurion's exclamation. See Wisd. ii. 18.

† The words παρέδωκεν τὸ πνεῦμα (John xix. 30), ἀφῆκεν τὸ πνεῦμα (Matt. xxvii. 50), ἐξέπνευσεν (Mark xv. 37), seem to imply a *voluntary* yielding up of His life. See Bishop Westcott on John xix. 30.

it, when He willed, as He willed." The blood and water which burst from His riven side did, indeed, constitute a proof of death, but were a symbol of life and regeneration—of " the cleansing from sin and the quickening by the Spirit which are both consequent on the death of Christ."

CHAPTER XXXIX.

THE RIGHT VIEW OF CHRIST'S SUFFERINGS.

"The Fair Shepherd layeth down His life for the sheep."—John x. 11.

It must be admitted that the Church—not, indeed, the Early Christian Church, but the Church after some six or seven centuries had elapsed, and most of all amid the dense and ever-deepening superstitions and aberrations of the Middle Ages—has no Scriptural or primitive warrant for its deification of pain for its own sake. That was an outcome of Eastern Manichæism. "Suso," we are told, "used to lie in a miserable hole, on an old door for a bed, and in the depth of winter thought it a sin to approach the stove for warmth." He used to tear himself with iron tags for scourges; and "though filled with a feverish thirst, with the waters of the Lake Constance sparkling on all sides round his monastery, he would often pass the whole day without suffering a drop to moisten his lips." One of the sayings of "John of the Cross," was, "Whatever you find pleasant to soul or body, abandon. Whatsoever is painful, embrace it." Such examples and such precepts are founded in absolute error, and are totally alien from the teaching of Christ and His Apostles. They are a distortion of the true meaning of self-denial and self-conquest, and have often led to results the exact opposite of those which they were supposed to promote. Such examples do not, after all, represent a self-torture and self-maceration so severe as those which are inflicted on themselves by many a brainless idolator. They are alien importations into true Christianity. They are utterly unlike the example set by Christ. They represent an ordinance-ridden will-worship which becomes a direct intensification alike of bodily and mental temptations. "Have not the loosest of men," asks Dean Milman, "been often found with the roughest sackcloth swathing their limbs; the proudest with bare feet, and the cord around their loins; the most cruel among those who have most severely mortified their own bodies? Monks have ever been the most ready and remorseless executioners of persecution. Quench the habitual affections, in the long run you quench humanity." *

The anguish which Christ endured for our sakes was not self-sought. Though voluntarily endured as an inevitable portion of His great self-sacrifice, it was inflicted on Him by the wickedness of men, and could not have been avoided except at the impossible cost of swerving from the path of duty or righteousness. Under such conditions our Lord showed us by His example that any accumulation of anguish is to be preferred to the slightest abandonment of the cause of true holiness. But neither was any portion of his sufferings self-inflicted, nor (as we have seen) did it involve a lifetime of self-maceration.

The notion that mirth and pleasure are in themselves sinful is an idle superstition. The cross which we are to take up is not one of our own devising, but only the cross which God may see fit to lay upon us. Nor must we forget that all sorrow which is *not* self-sought and *not* self-inflicted has its own boundless and eternal consolations—as it had so abundantly for our Blessed Lord.

It is again a serious error to separate, or rather to isolate, the death of Christ from all His life, as though on His death alone, and not on His Incarnation and his whole life, depended the work of our salvation. "*Non hoc præcipuum amicorum munus est,*" admirably said the dying Germanicus, "*prosequi defunctum ignavo quæstu, sed quæ voluerit meminisse, quæ mandaverit exsequi.*" † True sorrow for our lost ones is

---

* " The ascetic theory of Christian virtue," says Dr. Bruce, " which so soon began to prevail in the Church, has been tested by time and proved to be a huge and mischievous mistake. The verdict of history is conclusive, and to return to an exploded error, as some are disposed to do, would be an utter folly " (*Training of the Twelve*, p. 249). See Isaac Taylor's *Ancient Christianity.*

† Tac. *Ann.* ii. 71.

best shown, not by idle wailings, but by active accomplishment of their wishes and continuance of their work.

Most of the erroneous notions which have been thrust into the forefront of the religion of erring Churches have been built on the isolation from their context of separate texts or phrases, which thus are robbed of their proper historic meaning. In favour of lives of ascetic self-torture, some have quoted the words of our Lord, "Whosoever shall seek to gain his life shall lose it, but whosoever shall lose his life shall preserve it," or "bring it to a new birth." How important this utterance was is proved by the fact that our Lord repeated it on four separate occasions, and that it is (alone of all his sayings) recorded by all four Evangelists. The words involve the duty of absolute self-sacrifice *when it is required in the cause of God;* the duty of bearing and of braving all that God sends to us when we are walking in the paths of His service. To interpret them of *self-inflicted* miseries and macerations is to wrest them from their context; to rob them of their real and deep meaning; to divorce them from the example personally set to us by Christ's own life; and to make them the basis of false systems. Whatever God sends or requires we must gladly bear; He will send all that is necessary to train and ennoble us: it is nothing but a faithless folly to invent needless miseries for ourselves.*

An isolated phrase, or emotional expression, unless it harmonise with the whole body of sacred teaching, is misused and perverted when it is treated as though it were a complete revelation. Now in the New Testament the death of Christ is never thrust into exclusive prominence. "It is Christ that died," says St. Paul, "*yea, rather,* that was raised from the dead, who is at the right hand of God, who also maketh intercession for us." "*Non Mors, sed voluntas placuit sponte morientis,*" said St. Bernard. "Christ's death," says Dr. Littledale, "in ancient Christian theology, did not pervade by any means so much space as it has done for several centuries past; but it was regarded as a single incident—of transcendent importance indeed, but still only a single incident—in the great

* Matt. x. 39, xvi. 25 ; Luke xvii. 33 ; John xii. 24, 25.

chain of events from the Incarnation to the Ascension. Suffering in itself is valueless and works no deliverance." The sufferings of Christ on the Cross, which could barely wring one cry of anguish from the Sufferer, were necessary because of man's vileness, selfishness, and sin, and were caused by the most awful object lesson which could have been given of the perversity of false religion. But they were a revelation not of defeat, but of victorious majesty. They indicate " the measure of our need, and of Christ's sympathy; the destruction of the selfishness of man, the consummation of the counsel of God." The Italian poet and ecclesiastic Tomaso Campanella (as translated by John Addington Symonds) writes—

> " If Christ was only six hours crucified,
>   After few years of toil and misery,
>   Which for mankind He suffered willingly,
>   While Heaven was won for ever when He died ;
>   Why should He still be shown on every side,
>   Painted and preached in nought but agony,
>   Whose pains were light, matched with His victory,
>   When the world's power to harm Him was defied ?
>   Why rather speak and write not of the realm
>   He rules in Heaven, and soon will bring below,
>   Unto the praise and glory of His name ?
>   Ah ! foolish crowd ! This world's thick vapours whelm
>   Your eyes, unworthy of that glorious show,
>   Blind to His splendour, bent upon His shame."

Campanella here wrote in strictest accordance with the views of primitive Christianity, and indeed of all the purest Christain thought for many centuries. All early Christian art is joyous. There is not a single Latin cross, much less a representation of the crucifixion, before the days of Constantine. The earliest known Latin cross is on the tomb of Galla Placidia at Ravenna, A. D. 451. The early Christians would have regarded a crucifix as an audacious profanation of the awful majesty of Him who now sitteth for ever, as Eternal God, on the throne of His glory. Even St. Gregory, when He sent to Queen Theodolinda an ampulla on which was painted the scene of Golgotha, had the two robbers represented nailed to their

crosses; but by the side of the cross of Christ kneel two angels, and *the cross is empty, while over it is the image of Christ in glory.** But in ancient art, for six centuries after Christ, painters did not venture to go so far even as this. In the Church of St. Apollinaris at Ravenna are painted consecutive scenes of the Life of Christ; but they end with Pilate washing his hands, and from that scene they pass—as they do on many sarcophagi—at once to the Resurrection. "It may well be doubted," says Bishop Westcott, whose authority as a theologian none will question, "whether the Crucifixion is, in any immediate shape, a proper subject for art. *The image of the dead Christ is foreign to Scripture. Even in the record of the Passion death is swallowed up in victory.* And the material representations of what St. John shows to have been life through death, perpetuate thoughts foreign to the Gospel." †
And again he writes, "We must not for one moment rest in the images of outward dissolution. We must keep together in closest union the Resurrection and the Passion; Easter Day and Good Friday, Life and Death. The Crucifix and the Dead Christ obscures our faith. Our thoughts rest not upon a dead, but upon a living Christ. The closed eye and the bowed head are not the true marks of Him who reigns from the Cross, who teaches us to see through every sign of weakness the fulfilment of His own words, '*I, if I be lifted up, will draw all men unto Myself.*' ‡ The Cross is a revelation not of humiliation but of majesty." One reading of Ps. xcvi. 10 was ἐβασίλευσεν ἀπὸ τοῦ ξύλου, *Regnavit a ligno.*§

---

* An early Christian gem in the British Museum represents a cross which has become a living Tree, with a dove resting upon it.

† *Victories of the Cross*, p. 96 ff.

‡ In support of the parallel revelation of glory and suffering he refers to John vi. 14 and 60–71 ; Matt. xvi. 13 ff., 21 ff., xvii. 24 ff., xx. 17–29, xxi.; Luke xix. 17 ff.; John xiii. 31, xvi. 33, xviii. 6 ff., xx. 9; Luke xxiv. 17 ff. See, too, *Religious Thought in the West*, p. 338. "It was felt that the realistic treatment of Christ's Person could not but endanger the living sense of the Majesty which the Church had learnt to realise." On the early Christian sarcophagi, as in many of the pictures drawn by Christians in the catacombs, Christ is ideally and symbolically represented, not as a livid and distorted sufferer, but as a radiant boy.

§ Just. Mart. *Dial c. Tryph.* § 73.

Utterly vain and futile is the wailing over the brief hours of physical sufferings which were but the episode of an Eternity of Glory. The Cross was Christ's throne. He speaks of His Crucifixion as His glorification. " The hour is come that the Son of Man should be glorified." In answer to His prayer, " Father, glorify Thy name," came a Voice from heaven, " I have both glorified it, and will glorify it again." And when Judas went out to betray Him, He said, " Now is the Son of Man glorified, and God is glorified in Him; and God shall glorify Him in Himself, and straightway shall He glorify Him." It was thus that He overcame the world and will draw *all men* unto Him.

Centuries ago so true a saint as St. Bernard—monk and ascetic as he was—warned men, though in vain, of " the error and the danger of extending the sufferings of Christ either in body or mind into the reign of His glory." Any contemplation of the Cross which inspires us to do all and bear all for His sake who died for us and rose again, is right; but the artificial heresy of " sobbing over the five wounds of the crucifix by way of Pity for the Eternal God is not in accordance with anything in Scripture." Those who lived nearest to the day of the Crucifixion, those who saw the Risen Lord with the marks of His wounds upon Him—did *not* indulge themselves by moaning in abject sorrow over His recent anguish. On the contrary—recognising that the revelation of suffering was coincident with the revelation of redemption, they were filled with a constant and superabounding joy. And why? Because " His loneliness is the breaking up of our solitude; His mourning our comfort; His thirst our supply; His weakness our strength. If we want power, we have the power of the Cross; if wisdom, we have the wisdom; if peace, we have the peace of His Cross. Thus is Christ crucified a treasure to His Church, full of all-sufficient provision both for its necessity and delight." *

* Bishop Reynolds, A. D. 1639. *Meditations on the Sacrament*, pp. 25-33. See on this subject Hausrath ii. 250 ff.; Wendt ii. 225, 233 ff. Schürer II. ii. 184-187.

CHAPTER XL.

THE ATONEMENT.

"My mystery is for Me, and for the sons of My house."—*Unwritten Saying* of Christ. CLEM. ALEX. *Strom.* v. 10, 64.

"Learn to say, I do not know."—*Rabbinic Saying*.

"'Cur' et 'quomodo' exitiales voculæ."—LUTHER.

MANY and serious are the misapprehensions, or purely one-sided views, respecting the whole doctrine of the Atonement.

(i) How false, for instance, and not only *un*-scriptural but *anti*-scriptural, is the teaching which represents the supposed *wrath of God the Father* as only averted by the *mercy of God the Son*—a view represented in such lines as those of Sir Henry Wotton—

> "One rosy drop from Jesus's heart
> Was worlds of seas *to quench God's ire*";

or of Dr. Watts—

> "Rich were the drops of Jesu's blood
> That calmed *God's frowning face;*
> That sprinkled o'er the burning throne,
> And turned the wrath to grace."

No epithet but "deplorable" can be given to the sort of theology which thus disintegrated the entire conception of the Trinity, and regarded the Father and the Son as actuated by antithetic impulses.

(ii.) How unwarranted, again, is such anthropomorphism as was habitually used till very recent times in the crude and ignorant language of many sermons. As Dr. Campbell rightly said, "The Scriptures do not represent the love of God to man as the *effect*, and the Atonement as the *cause*, but just the contrary; the love of God as the cause, and the Atonement as the

effect." *Men* have made themselves " enemies of God " (Rom.
v. 10), but the attitude of God to man even in his worst aber-
ration and lowest fall is always described as an attitude of forbearance and tenderest love.   It is not " Perish, as you deserve,
under the fury of My hatred "; but it is " Turn ye, why will ye
die? "   Nor is it said, as in the erroneous rendering of our Authorised Version, that God forgave us " for Christ's sake," but
—which is indefinitely more blessed—that " GOD IN CHRIST "
forgave us our sins.   " There was no wrath in God which was
not in Christ; and no mercy in Christ which is not in God."

(iii.) Again, what entirely false conceptions have been
mixed up with the notion of what is called " vicarious suffering."   How alien from true theology are the juristic and forensic theories introduced by St. Anselm, though he substituted
them for the preposterous, age-long perversion that God had
paid the ransom of Christ's sufferings to the Devil!   Anselm
only introduced a fresh error in representing that Christ suffered, as our substitute, *in order to reconcile God's justice with
His compassion*—as though they were conflicting elements in
the mind of God!   The Bible never and nowhere represents
the Death of Christ as effecting any change in the mind of God.
" *One* is the kindness of their mercy as the sentence of their
justice," said the Pope St. Leo the Great, " nor is there any
division in action where there is no diversity in will."   Its doctrine is one of free forgiveness, not of vicarious punishment,
nor does it once use the popular phrases of " vicarious," " substitution," " satisfaction," " expiation," or " imputed righteousness "; nor does it ever say that Christ saved us from the
penalty due to our sins; nor that His death was a penalty at all.
It is only by a wooden literalism; by turning rhetoric into logic;
by mistaking the impassioned utterances of emotion for the
formal statements of rigid reasoning; by extorting boundless
conclusions out of isolated metaphors which only touch the
subject at a single point; and by building inverted pyramids of
system on the narrow apex of single texts, that the whole meaning of the Atonement has been radically obscured.

(iv.) Fully admitting, and believing, all the mysteries which may lie under the word " propitiation," we yet see that, as regards God the Father, the sufferings of Christ, who was Himself Very God of Very God, are beyond our apprehension. If we pretend to *explain* them, we shall

" Find no end, in wandering mazes lost."

But when we think of the suffering and death of Christ, *in their relation to men,* we shall find them the source of hope, of joy, and of deliverance. Among many theories on the subject, some have regarded the sufferings of Christ as " simply incidental to His prophetic office." * Some theologians regard them as mainly expressive of Christ's *sympathy* as a revelation of divine self-sacrifice to win the hearts of men.† Some look on the death simply as the crown of a life of obedience, and unbroken fellowship with the Father, set forth as an example.‡ More common than these is the theory of " equivalent substitution," which is based on the futile desire to give logical distinctness to anthropomorphic metaphor. It should be enough to say, without any attempt " to soar up into the secrets of the Deity on the waxen wings of the senses," that Christ offered for us all one sacrifice for sins for ever, by the perfect example of self-surrender to the Divine will which He gave as the representative of our race; and that thus, in a way far beyond our power to explain, He became " the propitiation for our sins, and not for ours only, but also for the whole world." § " The doctrine of the Atonement," says Prof. Mozley, " parts company with the gross and irrational conception of mere naked material substitution of one term for another, and it takes its stand upon the power of love."

We must, then, be content to accept the death of Christ as a transcendent fact which we cannot categorise under systematically logical forms. It is set forth in varying metaphors which admit of varying interpretations, and which indicate its

* Socinus, Robertson, Ritschl. I borrow the brief summary from Bruce, *The Humiliation of Christ*, p. 350.

† Abelard, Bushnell.

‡ Some of the Fathers. Also Schleiermacher, Irving, Maurice.

§ 1 John ii. 2.

results as regards us men and our salvation, not the incomprehensible mystery of its exact place in the Divine councils. These metaphors are diverse, and cannot be rigidly harmonised with each other. They cannot be treated as "literal equivalents of spiritual truth." The author of the Epistle to the Hebrews writes much about sacrifices; but all that he thinks it reverent to say when he comes to speak of the death of Christ is that "it *became* God"—it was fitting that God—"in bringing many sons to glory should make the author of their salvation perfect through sufferings"; * and that, as every Jewish High Priest offered gifts and sacrifices, "it is necessary that this High Priest also have somewhat to offer." † But not once in the New Testament are we told that Christ saved us from the punishment due to iniquity, or that His death was "a punishment" at all. The metaphors of Is. liii. are applied by St. Matthew to His healings of the sick. "In the whole Jewish ritual," says Archdeacon Norris, "there is no trace of the idea that sacrifices were meant to reconcile the offender to God by the death of the Innocent in the place of the guilty." By the "blood" of Christ is meant always the essential life of Christ.‡ It would be well if theologians would bear in mind the warning of Bishop Butler that "all *conjectures*" about the manner of Christ's Atonement "must be, if not evidently absurd, at least uncertain."

In conclusion, then—passing over the monstrous errors of nearly a thousand years from Irenæus to St. Anselm, and from St. Anselm to the present day, when the Atonement has been represented as a forensic transaction between the Father and the Son—we must say that Scripture describes the Atonement, not in its inmost essence, which surpasses our powers of apprehension, but in *its effects. Ignorando cognoscitur.* "Scripture," says Bishop Butler, "has left this matter of the satisfaction of Christ mysterious, left somewhat in it unrevealed." Let it be enough for us that "God was in Christ, reconciling the world unto Himself" (2 Cor. v. 19); and that,

* Heb. ii. 10.   † Heb. viii. 3.
‡ Comp. Bishop Westcott on 1 John i. 7, and *Ep. to the Hebrews*, p. 287.

as regards its *results,* " God set forth Christ to be a propitiation " (Rom. iii. 25). The three great creeds of Christendom
carefully avoid all attempts to express the significance of the
Atonement by any rigid formulæ of explanation; they do not
build figurative illustrations into huge edifices of dogmatic theology.* They are content to indicate that " after a certain ad-
mirable manner "—but *how,* we are unable to define—the Life
and Death of Christ, as one great eternal whole, were " a full,
perfect, and sufficient redemption, propitiation, and satisfaction
for all the sins of the whole world "; and that " there is none
other satisfaction for sin but that alone." In this sense we
may say with Hooker,† " Let it be counted folly or fury, or
phrensy, or whatsoever, it is our wisdom and our comfort; we
care for no knowledge in the world but this, that man hath
sinned and God hath suffered; that God hath made Himself the
sin of men, and that men are made the righteousness of God."

* The variety of the expressions used to indicate the effects of Christ's death
(καταλλαγή, λύτρον, ἱλαστήριον, ἱλασμός) shows that the mode of our deliverance
is left undefined apart from its results. This will appear more plainly if any
one will search out the Old Testament for the uses of the term of which these
Greek words are the rendering—namely כִּפֶּר (Ex. xxi. 30, xxix. 36, xxxii.
30; Lev. i. 4, iv. 20; Num. xvi. 46, xxv. 13; 2 Chr. xxx. 18 ; Ezek. xlv.
15). כַּפֹּרֶת " the mercy seat " (Lev. xvii. 11).

† *Serm.* ii. 6. For a fuller and closer examination of the doctrine of the
Atonement, I must refer to my papers in " *The Atonement : a Clerical Symposium;* " and in *The Christian World* of November 16, 1899.

CHAPTER XLI.

THE RESURRECTION.

"Yet though we have known Christ after the flesh, yet now know we Him so no more."—2 Cor. v. 16.

> " Christ is risen ! Christ is risen !
> He hath left the cloudy prison,
> And the white-robed angels glimmer mid the cerements
> of His grave :
> He hath smiten with His thunder
> All the gates of brass asunder,
> He hath burst the iron fetters, irresistible to save ! "
> —F. W. F.

THE history of Christianity proves that it is far from being so easy as it might seem to keep " the due proportion " of the faith. If we would know Christ aright we must not isolate one part of His teaching to the exclusion of the rest, nor must we emphasise one part of His life and work in such a manner as to exclude the due significance of the whole. To do this is, as I have said, to make the same mistake as is committed by so many when they fix on a single text or even word of Scripture, and use it in such a way as to nullify its meaning as well as the meaning of all the rest of Scripture. The New Testament, I must once more urge, does not teach us to look at Christ's death *only,* but always to regard it in due connexion with His Incarnation, His revelation by His life, and words, and works, His Resurrection, His Ascension, His eternal exultation at the right hand of God. The one-sidedness of party-systems of theology has partly arisen from failure to catch the due shade of meaning in St. Paul's words, " For I determined not to know anything among you, save Jesus Christ, *and Him crucified.*"* The emphasis of the statement lies in the words

* I Cor. ii. 2 ; Phil. iii. 8.

"Jesus Christ": the words "and Him crucified" are added because the crucifixion was to the Jews a stumbling-block and to Gentiles foolishness, as it was to all "the perishing." It was necessary, therefore, to insist on the truth that the very Christ, in all "the glory of the only begotten of the Father," was none other than the man Christ Jesus, whom Priests and Romans had nailed to the Cross, so that the Crucified Teacher was one with the Risen Saviour, the power and wisdom of God.* St. Paul's own practice shows that, rightly as he gloried in the Cross of Christ, he did *not* make it the sum-total of his teaching, nor did he identify man's Atonement with the *death* of Christ only, but with all that He was, and all that He did.

Our Lord Himself taught the devoted, impassioned Magdalene, in the first great lesson which He uttered after His Resurrection, that the time for the ecstasies of *human* affection was over. He said to her, "Cling not to Me." If the Scriptures had been duly studied and understood, those words alone ought to have sufficed to condemn the emotional sensuousness—unscriptural, unprimitive, uncatholic—of going on hands and knees to kiss crucifixes, and adoring the five wounds. St. Paul expressed this lesson with almost startling plainness when he said, "From henceforth I know no man after the flesh. Yea, *though I have known Christ after the flesh, yet henceforth know I Him no more.*" In other words, the Christ of St. Paul was *no longer* an agonised victim, but an Eternal King, requiring our love and service, but exalted infinitely above all need of, or desire for, our *compassion*. "What do you mean by a *likeness* of Christ?" wrote Eusebius of Cæsarea to the Empress Constantia. "Not of course the image of Him as He *is,* truly and substantially; nor yet of His human nature as it has been glorified, of which the Transfiguration in its overpowering splendour offered some pledge or likeness. . . . Since we confess that our Saviour is God, and Lord, we prepare and purify our hearts to see Him. And if, before that Vision which shall be face to face, you value likenesses of the Saviour, what better artist can there be than the God-Word Himself?"

* 1 Cor. i. 24, ii. 8.

In point of fact, the Resurrection holds a place at least as prominent as the Crucifixion in the teaching of the Apostles and Evangelists. St. Matthew dwells on its glorious majesty; St. Mark on its reality; St. Luke on its spiritual necessity; St. John on its influence over men. They are careful never to let Christ's sufferings absorb the thoughts of Christians in such a way, or to such an extent, as to obscure the sense that, though for our sakes He passed through the brief moment of suffering and death, He desires *not our pity*, but our endless adoration, as the Divine King, seated on the throne of His Eternal Glory. Christ had taught them that " they who are accounted worthy to attain the world to come are sons of God, *being sons of the Resurrection.*" * He had said, " *I* am the Resurrection and the Life." † It was the condition of the Apostolate to have been a witness of the Resurrection.‡ The cause of the first persecution by the Priests and Sadducees was that the Apostles " proclaimed in Jesus the resurrection from the dead." § St. Paul woke the ridicule of the Stoics and Epicureans at Athens because he preached " *Jesus and the resurrection.*" || When he was seized and imprisoned at Jerusalem, it was " *concerning the resurrection of the dead* " that he was called in question, and because he had preached " that the Christ must suffer, and how that He first by the resurrection of the dead should proclaim light both to the people and the Gentiles." ¶ He began his Epistle to the Romans by the declaration " that Christ Jesus was declared to be the Son of God with power by the resurrection of the dead." ** In one of the most glorious chapters of all his Epistles, he based man's hope of resurrection exclusively on the resurrection of Christ.†† He tells the beloved Philippians that his own desire is " to know Him, and the power of His resurrection, and the fellowship of His sufferings, becoming conformed until His death, if by any means we may attain unto the resurrection of the

---

* Luke xx. 34–36. † John xi. 25.
‡ Acts i. 22. § Acts iv. 2.
|| Acts xii. 18. ¶ Acts xxiii. 6, xxiv. 21, xxvi. 23.
** Rom. i. 4. †† 1 Cor. xv.

dead." * When he says (Rom. viii. 34), " It is Christ Jesus
that died, *yea rather, that was raised from the dead, who is at
the right hand of God, who also maketh intercession for us,*"
it is almost as if he foresaw, and wished to correct, any partial
onesidedness in our conception of Christ. The whole Epistle
to the Ephesians had been rightly described as " the Epistle of
the Heavenlies," the Epistle of the Resurrection; and to the
Corinthians he said, " If Christ hath not been raised, your faith
is vain." † St. Peter's first utterance to the Elect of the Dispersion is to thank " the Father of our Lord Jesus Christ, who
beget us again unto a living hope by the resurrection of Jesus
Christ from the dead." ‡ The predominant thought of all the
early Christian teachers was *" Jesus, whom God raised up."*

It was the stupendous fact of the Resurrection of Christ by
His own Divine Power—a fact which the Jews regarded as
impossible—which changed the whole character of the Apostles,
and uplifted them from what they had been—timid, and dull,
and even half faithless—to what they became as the inspired
teachers and converters of the world; the heralds of the world's
last æon; the proclaimers and appointed founders of the kingdom which shall have no end. The Resurrection, as we have
seen, was " no mere *accessory* of their message, but the sum and
the centre of the message itself." They grasped, if millions of
Christians have failed to do so, the meaning of the angel message, *" Why seek ye the Living among the dead? He is not
here; He is risen, as He said."* They did not preach a dead
Christ, but rather a Risen Christ; not a lost Christ, but a Christ
ever Present; not one who was habitually to be regarded as a
tortured and agonising sufferer, but one who liveth for evermore, and imparts to us His life and His joy, so that in the
midst of death, we are still in life. They had been but as children, full of wavering misapprehension and timidity, because

---

* Phil. iii. 10, 11.

† See Acts ii. 24, iii. 15, 26, iv. 10, v. 30, x. 40, xiii. 30, 33, 34, 37, xvii. 31;
Rom. iv. 24, 25, vi. 4, 9, vii. 4, viii. 11 ; 1 Cor. vi. 14, xv. *passim ;* 2 Cor. iv.
14 ; Col. ii. 12, iii. 1 ; Gal. i. 1 ; Eph. i. 20 ; 1 Thess. i. 10 ; 1 Pet. i. 21.

‡ 1 Pet. i. 3.

" as yet they knew not the Scripture that He must rise again from the dead." * After the Resurrection they sprang into the full stature of men, because then first they began fully to apprehend all that Jesus was as " the only name under heaven, given among men whereby we must be saved." When Jesus finally parted from them at the Ascension they returned to Jerusalem " *with great joy.*"† All things had become new to them. They saw that the awful humiliation of apparent defeat was but the work of a self-sacrifice infinitely fruitful; that the death of Christ, immediately followed by His resurrection, was the inauguration of a new and the final æon in the world's history, in which God would not only be among them, but dwell in them, and walk in them. It was in this conviction that they went forth in Christ's name, conquering and to conquer.

Hence the Resurrection, together with the Incarnation, forms the most central event in the history of the world. It was the glorious consummation of all the past, the splendid inauguration of all that was most precious in all the future. And it should be noted that not only is it said that " God raised Christ from the dead " (Gal. i. 1), but also that Christ did not hesitate to attribute it also to His own divine power. " Destroy ye this Temple, and in three days I will raise it up."

St. Paul clearly saw, and decisively argued, that man can have *no* pledge of his immortality apart from the resurrection of Christ. If *Christ* has not risen, *we* shall not rise. Life becomes not worth living if it be but a term of affliction, and progressive decay, and constant sorrow, which ends with itself, and brings no hope whatever of a purer and happier existence beyond the grave. Life then becoms frail and futile, and there is no hope of redress. The terrible picture of the poet would then be no exaggeration—

> " Lo ! 'tis a gala night,
> Within the lonesome latter years !
> An angel throng, bewinged, bedight
> In veils, and drowned in tears,

* John xx. 9.   † Luke xxiv. 52.

Sit in a theatre, to see
　　A play of hopes and fears,
While the orchestra breathes fitfully
　　The music of the spheres.

" Mimes, in the form God on high,
　　Mutter and mumble low ;
And hither and thither fly—
　　Mere puppets they, who come and go
At bidding of vast formless things,
　　That shift the scenery to and fro,
Flapping from out their condor wings
　　Invisible woe !

" But see, amid the mimic rout,
　　A crawling shape intrude—
A blood-red thing that writhes from out
　　The scenic solitude !
It writhes ! it writhes !　With mortal pangs
　　The mimes become its food,
And the angels sob at vermin fangs
　　In human gore imbued.

" Out—out are the lights !--out all !
　　And over each quivering form
The curtain, a funeral pall,
　　Comes down with the rush of a storm !
And the angels, all pallid and wan,
　　Uprising, unveiling, affirm
That the play is the tragedy *Man*,
　　And its hero the Conqueror Worm."

If Christ never rose from the dead, this awful vision would
have elements of deep reality. If Christ be not risen from the
dead, and we are yet in our sins, our faith is vain, and they that
have fallen asleep in Christ have perished. All that is most
glorious, most beautiful, most inspiring, most holy in the
thought and progress of the world has risen, directly or indirectly, from faith in Christ. If He was crucified and did not
rise, the Apostles were false witnesses of God, and the world's
loftiest hopes were impossibly built upon a delusion, and all

that is best slips from us into dust and ashes, and Time becomes

> "A maniac scattering dust,
> And life a fury slinging flame."

Had it not been for the Resurrection, no defeat of all that is
divine in the life of man could have been more complete than
was involved in the Crucifixion; and therefore the evidences of
the Resurrection were, by God's mercy, made overwhelming.
There was not in all the world's history—there was not even
in the age-long history of the Jewish people—the slightest an-
ticipation of such a possibility as that One who had died, could
win the complete victory over death, and say to the world, " I
am He that liveth, and was dead, and behold I am alive for
evermore." Jesus had foretold to His disciples that He would
thus rise; but they did not receive or understand His prophecy.
It did not touch their " unbelief and hardness of heart." In
spite of such prophecies they had not the faintest expectation
that any such thing would take place. Nay, when the women
and Mary Magdalene reported that they had seen Him, they
regarded such statements as mere women's talk.* Not till they
had gone into the empty sepulchre did any gleam of hope enter
into the hearts of their leaders, Peter and John. When He
had appeared to all the Apostles except Thomas, Thomas still
refused to believe. Not till He had opened their eyes—not till
they had again seen, and heard, and their hands had handled
the Word of Life—not till " He showed Himself alive to them
by many infallible proofs, being seen of them and speaking of
the things pertaining to the kingdom of God " † did they begin
to apprehend that their Lord had broken the bonds of death,
" because He could not be holden of it." Then, indeed, they
were taught to see that the Resurrection, so far from standing
alone, was the crowning event of the history of all the past;
the opening of the history of all the future even to the consummation of the ages; the sole hope of the life of all the

---

* Λῆρος, " babble," Luke xxiv. 11. The word occurs here alone in the New
Testament.

† Acts i. 3.

world; and the sole explanation of all its mysteries. Absolutely
and finally convinced, they became the irresistible heralds of the
last Dispensation, and before thirty years had elapsed they
had everywhere proclaimed Jesus, and the mystery of His
death, and the Power of His resurrection as the Power of an
endless Life.

Could anything short of so immense a divine interposition as
the Resurrection, and the subsequent outpouring of the Spirit,
have accounted for the faith which overcame the world; the
faith by virtue of which the Jewish Dispensation, now that it
had waxed old, was swept away; the faith on which has been
founded for ever that Universal Church of Christ which is " the
blessed company of all faithful people; " the faith which gave
a wholly new glory and meaning to human life; the faith on
which was founded the perpetuity of the Christian sacraments,
and the observance of the Lord's Day; the faith which wrought
righteousness, subdued kingdoms, stopped the mouths of lions,
quenched the violence of fire; the faith which so transformed
the nature of man by the constraining love of Christ, that when
the Pagan mobs yelled *" Christianos ad leones"* the weakest
boy could answer with exultation *Christianus sum;* the faith
which was in no wise affected by the earthquakes which shook
the Roman Empire to the dust; the faith which converted and
swayed the wild hordes of northern barbarians, and inspired
them with the thoughts and aims which have achieved all that
is greatest in modern civilisation; that faith which even, most
marvellous of all, has survived the gross falsities which have
been taught, and the hideous crimes which have for centuries
been committed, in its name; which has succeeded in bursting
out of the foul dungeon in which it had been imprisoned by
priestly usurpers; which has shaken off the influence of centuries of mediæval impostures, ignorance, and corruption;
which has even outlined the infamies of the Inquisition, and
of the Moloch fires kindled in the name of Christianity by its
falsest representatives in spite of its plainest teachings, to
sicken into loathing the hearts of all who worshipped Christ in
sincerity and truth?

Hence we see that the recorded evidences of the Resurrection do not stand alone. St. Paul, within a few years of the death of Jesus on Calvary, tells us how He was seen of Cephas; of the Twelve; of about five hundred brethren at once, of whom the majority were living when he wrote; of James; of all the Apostles; and, last of all, of him also as of the abortive-born of the Apostolic band.* The Evangelists narrate to us how He appeared to the women at the Sepulchre, and to Mary Magdalene, and to the Ten Apostles, and to other disciples with them, to all of whom He gave His great Commission; and to the Eleven Apostles when Thomas was with them; and to the two disciples on their way to Emmaus; and to Peter, John, Andrew, Philip, and Bartholomew, on the old familiar shore of the sea of Galilee; and to the Eleven on the mountain in Galilee; and, possibly at the same time, to a multitude of more than five hundred disciples when He bade them go and make disciples of all the nations. Besides these eleven recorded appearances, He appeared doubtless on other occasions " by the space of forty days," and (apart from the visions seen by St. Stephen and St. Paul) He showed Himself last of all to the assembled disciples when He parted from them to continue His visible intercourse with them on earth no more.

This, surely, is distinct, decisive, and varied evidence; yet it acquires a thousandfold greater force from the fact that, so far from standing alone, it is charged with the deepest moral significance; that it is only the fraction of a vast whole; that it corresponds with all that we know of the nature and purposes of God; that it accords with our faith in all God's workings in the past which found their completion in the Incarnation; that, apart from it, all which has followed for well-nigh two thousand years would be inexplicable; that it is our sole positive pledge of the immortality which makes us instinctively feel that we were not born to die for ever; that it transfigured the whole nature of the Apostles, and alone rendered possible that work which *has* issued in the potential, and *will* issue in the final, regeneration of the world; that it has visibly affected all

* 1 Cor. xv. 5–8.

the subsequent destinies of the human race; that in it alone does the whole meaning of Christ's mission find its accomplishment and the secret and the explanation of its universal triumph.

It is evident that our thoughts are turned exclusively to the *reality,* not to the *modes* or details of this mighty consummation of our Lord's work. No eye witnessed the Resurrection. The earthquake, and the vision of a white-robed angel with countenance like lightning who had come and rolled away the stone, and sat upon it, had terrified the guards, and made them as dead men; but neither they, nor any believer, saw the Christ Himself rise out of the sepulchre. The angel told the women that He had already risen, and invited them to see the place where the Lord lay. Particulars and incidents of the actual miracle were wisely—let us say, rather, under the guidance of the Holy Spirit—left undescribed by the Evangelists. They did not admit of description. But the brief and reverent records show us that the mortal body of Christ was already changed, and was no longer subjected to the limitations of ordinary humanity. The Resurrection was something wholly different from other " raisings from the dead," like that of Lazarus. It was a Resurrection which, by Christ's inherent Godhead, finally overcame death, and him who, in one sense, has the power of death—that is the Devil.*

The Resurrection-body of the Lord had been in some way *transformed.* He was not immediately recognisable by Mary or by His disciples on the way to Emmaus, until by His voice or His action He made Himself known to them. When the assembled Apostles first saw Him they were terrified, and thought they saw a Spirit. Even when He appeared to the five hundred or more brethren on the mountain in Galilee, " some doubted." Nor was His body any longer subject to the ordinary laws of nature. He appeared and disappeared. He passes through the closed door and suddenly stands in the midst of them. The

---

* Heb. ii. 14 (comp. Rom. v. 12; John viii. 44). In Wisdom ii. 24, we read, " Through envy of the Devil came death unto the world." The Devil is identified with the Serpent of Paradise.

† Mark xvi. 12, ἐφανερώθη ἐν ἑτέρᾳ μορφῇ.

forty days of His earthly manifestations were, so to speak, an initial form of the ascended life. He was something more than He who, wont to stray,

> " A pilgrim in the world's highway,
> Oppressed by power and mocked by pride—
> The Nazarene, the Crucified."

" Cling not to Me," He said, " for I have not yet ascended to the Father; but go to My brethren and say to them, I am ascending to My Father and your Father, and to My God and your God." " *I am ascending* "($\grave{\alpha}\nu\alpha\beta\acute{\alpha}\iota\nu\omega$); the passing into the Father's presence, there to reign with Him, world without end, had already in one sense begun.

CHAPTER XLII.

THE Ascension was the natural and necessary completion of the Resurrection, but there are two different points of view from which it may be regarded.

That Christ "ascended into the heavens" is, of course, the belief of all Christians. Our Lord had asked, "What and if ye shall see the Son of Man ascending where He was before?"* Almost the earliest words of the Risen Christ were, "I have not yet ascended to the Father; I am ascending to My Father and your Father, and My God and your God." St. Paul, in the Epistle to the Ephesians, speaks of Him as "He that ascended far above all the heavens;"† and says "that He was received up in glory."‡ The Epistle to the Hebrews describes Him as "having passed through the heavens," and "having become loftier than the heavens."§ But this language is necessarily anthropomorphic, seeing that heaven is no more physically above our heads than it is beneath our feet. Heaven is a state, not a locality. It has

> "No limits, nor is circumscribed
> In one self place."

It is the abode of the Omnipresent God, who has neither body, parts, nor passions, but is everywhere, and filleth all things with all things. When we speak therefore of Christ's Ascension, we mean primarily that He withdrew Himself from physical manifestations to His servants on earth, in order to bestow on them that nearer, more intense, more spiritual presence—that indwelling which was more blessed and more expedient for them—which began with the promised gift at Pentecost. Since that time Christ is with us even to the end of the

*John vi. 62.   † Eph. iv. 10.
‡ 1 Tim. iii. 16.   § Heb. iv. 14, and vii. 26.

world.   God's temple on earth is no longer a material structure in Jerusalem, nor is it the human body of His Incarnate Son: it is the heart of all true believers.*   This is, henceforth, the earthly abode of Him who loves,

> " Before all temples, the upright heart and pure."

Besides *this* belief in the Ascension, it is regarded, by many, as the termination of Christ's ministry by the visible rising from earth upwards through the air in the presence of His disciples.   So the scene is often represented in Christian Art, and most notably in the famous picture of Raphael.   It is doubtful whether this view is correct, or whether the Ascension can be properly represented by Art.   That the *special mode* in which Christ left the earth was not meant to occupy a prominent place in our thoughts is proved by the fact that it is scarcely alluded to in the Gospels.   St. Matthew does not mention it.   In St. Mark it only occurs in the spurious addition made to the Gospel, whether by Aristion or another, and there it is only alluded to in a mixed quotation from 2 Kings ii. 11, " He was received into heaven; " and Psalm cx. 1, " and sat on the right hand of God: "—an allusion which does not bear at all on any visible rising through the air.   There is no narration of the event in St. John, but only the general references which I have quoted.   The sole authority for the material scene is St. Luke, and even in St. Luke the reference is vague and very brief.   He merely says that, after the last farewells of Jesus to His beloved followers, *" He stood apart from them."*   The words which follow, " and was borne up into heaven," are almost certainly spurious, as *they are not found in the best and earliest manuscripts.*

The only other reference is in the Acts of the Apostles, where we are told that, after His last words, " He was taken up, and while they were looking on, a *cloud received Him out of their sight.*"   If we interpret the first word ($\dot{\epsilon}\pi\dot{\eta}\rho\vartheta\eta$) in the general sense, and combine it with the " stood apart from them " of the Gospel, we might suppose that Christ simply vanished from the presence of His loved ones into an overshadowing and shin-

* I. Cor. iii. 16, vi. 19 ; 2 Cor. vi. 16 ; Eph. ii. 21, 22.

ing cloud. They all understood that it was the final parting, the end of earthly companionship; but as they stood with faces upturned towards the sky, which they regarded as the Throne of God, the Angel said to them, "Ye men of Galilee, why stand ye gazing up into heaven?" He whom "a cloud had received out of their sight" should return in the clouds of heaven, in the human form which he had for ever united to His Godhead.

All authority was given unto Him in heaven and on earth, and now they were to go and make disciples of all nations, baptising them into the name of the Father, and of the Son, and of the Holy Ghost; "teaching them to observe all things whatsoever He had commanded them;" and "lo, He would be with them all the days even unto the consummation of the age." Thenceforth grace was given "unto each one of us according to the measure of the gift of Christ; wherefore He saith—

> "When He ascended on high, He led captivity captive,
> And gave gifts unto men."

We have seen, then, that the *manner* of the Ascension is barely more than referred to, and only in general terms, by a single Evangelist. Similarly, in the Epistles the actual rising heavenwards is nowhere narrated, and the references are all to the heavenly super-exaltation.[*] But the *fact* of the Ascension of Christ "far above all heavens;"—the fact that having left the earthly life, He is seated for ever at the right hand of the Majesty on High;—underlies the whole Christian revelation. It is the basis of all our faith and all our hope.

> "The very God!—think, Abib!—dost thou think?
> So the All-Great were the All-Loving too—
> So, through the thunder comes a human voice,
> Saying, 'O heart I made, a heart beats here!
> Face, My hands fashioned, see it in Myself.
> Thou hast no power, nor may'st conceive of Mine;
> But Love I gave thee, with Myself to love,
> And thou must love Me, who have died for thee.'"[†]

[*] Eph. iv. 8–10; Heb. iv. 14, vii. 26; 1 Pet. iii. 22; 1 Tim. iii. 16. "In itself," says Prof. Dewar, "the Ascension is no more than a *point* of transition."

[†] Browning, *Men and Women* (Ep. of Karshish).

CHAPTER XLIII.

THE FINAL ISSUES.

"Securus judicat orbis terrarum."

"The World was only created for the Messiah."—SANHEDRIN. f. 98, 2.

"'Ο θαυμάσας βασιλεύσει καὶ ὁ βασιλεύσας ἀναπαήσεται.—Clem. Alex. *Strom.* ii. 9, 45.

"Amem Te plusquam me, nec me nisi propter Te."—IMITATIO CHRISTI.

"In Him was Yea."—2 Cor. i. 19.

"If this counsel or this work be of men it will be overthrown ; but if it is of God ye will not be able to overthrow it ; lest haply ye be found even to be fighting against God."—Acts v. 39.

How little did the Sadducean hierarchy and the Pharisaic externalists grasp the real significance of the deadly crime which they had committed! How little did they recognise that this deed of theirs, designed to maintain their party falsities, was the beginning of the awful end of the whole Jewish dispensation! Very shortly after the Death of Christ Caiaphas was deposed. Pilate was recalled, banished, and overwhelmed with disaster, dying at last by his own hand at Vienne in Gaul.* Antipas was deposed, and condemned and banished. The Emperor Tiberius died with a soul haunted by the demons of crime and misery. In the lifetime of many who had taken part in the awful tragedy, the House of Annas was destroyed, and his last son murdered. Jerusalem was besieged and went through spasms of inconceivable horror. It sank into a hell—a city of despairing madmen and raging cannibals.† The Temple was desecrated and burned into a blackened ruin ; the Jews were

---

* ποικίλαις περιπεσὼν συμφοραῖς, Euseb. *Chron.* p. 78 ; *H. E.* ii. 7.
† See Jos. *B. J.* v. 6, vi. 10 ; Renan, *L'Antéchrist*, p. 506.

crucified in such thousands that wood failed to provide crosses for them; the Holy City became a frightful desolation, unrecognisable by those who visited it; the Jewish system of religion was obliterated for ever.

" Vengeance ! thy fiery wing their race pursued,
  Thy thirsty poniard blushed with infant blood,
  Roused at thy call, and panting still for game,
  The bird of war, the Latian eagle came.

" Then Judah raged by ruffian discord led,
  Drunk with the steamy carnage of the dead ;
  She saw her sons by dubious slaughter fall,
  And war without, and death within the wall.
  Wide-wasting Plague, gaunt Famine, mad Despair,
  And dire debate, and clamorous strife were there.
  Love, strong as Death, retain'd his might no more,
  And the pale parent drank her children's gore.

  .   .   .   .

  Ah, fruitful now no more ! an empty coast,
  She mourn'd her sons enslav'd, her glories lost :
  In her wide streets the lonely raven bred,
  There barked the wolf, and dire hyænas fed."

Yes! from the hour when the Priests and Rabbis of a corrupted and hypocritic religion, consisting of outward forms and inward falsity, had achieved their crowning iniquity, began " the long, endless, hopeless history of Jewish decadence, and the historic and terrible corruption which, under the co-operation of tyrannous emperors, puppet kings, carnal patriots, and spiritually festering masses of the people, lasted for a generation, only to close with the frightful *coup de grâce* given by Titus's destruction of Jerusalem." The death of Christ was the close of an age-long Dispensation :—it was " the consummation of the age : "—the close of all the previous æons of the world's history ; the beginning of the last æon, and of the end of the world.

If ever God by the whole course of human history has set the seal to the truth of a Divine Revelation, it is in the progress of all the ages since Christ died. The history of Christianity has been a history of advancing victories. It has brought new life into a weary world. It has been as a regenerative force, not only to multitudes of men of the loftiest minds, but to Paganism in all its forms. " Old things have passed away; behold, they have become new." Christ has revealed such a knowledge of God as was wholly unknown to the earlier world. What word of His has failed? God has granted to mankind a new Life, and " that life " is—not in systems, or shibboleths, or churches, or priesthoods, but only " in His Son." " Neither is there salvation in any other; but in every nation he that feareth God and doeth righteousness is accepted of Him."

Even those who do not unreservedly accept the belief in Christ's Godhead, yet confess that " with reference to religion, He remains to us the highest we know and are able to conceive; " that " in the domain of the inner relations of Godhead and Humanity He has reached the extreme and unsurpassable stage of union; " that " the anxious inquiry after something higher in achievement and personal character must be relegated to silence as a Dream, and as a subtlety unworthy of a reasonable being; " that " the prejudices and the weakness of thousands of years fell into ruins before His masterwork; " that " the religious consciousness reached its acme and high personal greatness in the Founder of Christianity." * History has given decisive proofs, to repeat words cited earlier in this volume, that " Christianity is the crown of all the revelations of God, and that Jesus is the chosen of God, God's image, and best-beloved, and master-workman, and world-shaper in the history of mankind." †

How could the Almighty have given more decisively the Witness of History to Christ? How could He have shown more finally " that it was the good pleasure of the Father that in Him should all the fulness dwell," and " through Him to reconcile all things unto Himself, having made peace through the blood of His Cross; through Him I say, whether things upon the earth, or things in the heavens "? ‡ How could God more decisively have evinced to man that " He is our peace, who hath

* E. Zeller.   † Keim, vi. 426–436.   ‡ Col. i. 19, 20.

made both one, and brake down the middle wall of partition, having abolished in His flesh the enmity, even the law of commandments contained in ordinances"? * When we try to explain and formulate the exact *way* in which Christ's life and death procured our deliverance, we pass far beyond the region of human logic; yet it may be given to every one of us to know and feel, with a reality which passeth knowledge, that Christ has "blotted out the bond that was against us by its ordinances, which was contrary to us; and He hath taken it out of the way, nailing it to the Cross:" and that "having put off from Himself His body, He made a show of the principalities, and the powers, triumphing over them in it." †

Those verses represent, in the language of Scripture, the blessedness of personal salvation. The progressive consequences of the Life and Death of Christ over all the world are written plainly in "all the volumes vast" of Human History. Since His Resurrection, and as its direct consequence,

> "A new created world
> Springs up at God's command."

The conception of "Holiness," unknown to the ancient world of Paganism, became thenceforth a conception familiar to mankind. Read all the literature of the ancient heathen world, and though here and there you find a noble and righteous man, it would be difficult to find even one in the long ages of the story of Greece and Rome to whom you could apply the epithet "holy." *Now* we may trust that there is scarcely a village, scarcely a family, which has not been blessed by visible fulfilments of this divine ideal. In ancient days life was but a brief vision haunted by the grim spectre of death. The cry of despair rose from innumerable hearts. Man seemed to be but σκιᾶς ὄναρ, the dream of a shadow. The future life was but the dim guess of a few. Shakespeare asks—

> "Who would these fardels bear,
> To grunt and sweat under a weary life,
> But that the dread of something after death—

* Eph. ii. 14, 15.　　　† Col. ii. 15.

> That undiscovered country from whose bourn
> No traveller returns—puzzles the will,
> And makes us rather bear those ills we have
> Than fly to others that we know not of ! "

But that dread of death has an effect most salutary, for it teaches us that life is a thing too solemn and sacred to be desecrated by vile pleasures, or frittered away in frivolous pursuits. And when Life, in the realisation of its immortal dignity, is devoted to high and worthy ends, it reflects a light from heaven—a " light that never was on sea or land." It is transfigured by the thought that, as we have been planted in the likeness of Christ's death, so shall we be also in the likeness of His Resurrection. These convictions have made the humblest human life blessed and precious. The common conviction of antiquity was that life was not worth living, and many a sentiment of ancient philosophers might be summed up in the lines of the unhappy poet—

> " Know that, whatever thou hast been,
> 'Tis something better not to be."

But, in place of the natural apathy and utter hopelessness even of Stoicism, Christianity has taught us, day by day, to thank God for our creation and preservation, as well as for all the blessings of this life. And therefore Christ says (Luke xii. 29) to us all, even amid life's wildest storms, $M\dot{\eta}\ \mu\varepsilon\tau\varepsilon\omega\rho\iota\zeta\varepsilon\sigma\vartheta\varepsilon$, " Be not of doubtful mind "—be not like ships which toss in the stormy offing, instead of clinging to the anchor sure and steadfast which keeps them safe in the harbour's mouth.

The sinlessness of Jesus has been our example—an " underwriting"($\dot{\upsilon}\pi o\gamma\rho\alpha\mu\mu\acute{o}\nu$)* over which the best of the saints have striven faintly to trace their lives. He has been to the world, as is said in the Epistle to Diognetus, " a Nurturer, a Father, a Teacher, a Counsellor, a Physician, the mind, light, honour, strength, glory " of all who have received and trusted in Him. The Cross was to the Jews a stumbling-block, and to the Greeks foolishness; but " the foolishness of God is wiser than men, and the weakness of God is stronger than men." † The faith

---

* 1 Pet. ii. 21.   † 1 Cor. i. 25.

of Christ came of God, and therefore men cannot overthrow it.* No small part of the deadly hatred which Christians incurred was due to their hostility to the worst vices—the impurities and the cruelties—of Paganism.† They would have nothing to do with "the madness of the circus, the lewdness of the theatre, the heartlessness of the arena, or the vanity of the xystus": ‡ and because they would not be present at such spectacles, the heathen sneered and railed at them as "pallid, pitiful, stupid, wretched creatures;"§ "a lurking and light-shunning people, mute in public, and garrulous in corners;" "unlearned, rude, unpolished, rustic, barbarous, madmen, non-descripts—of trivial and sordid speech." ‖ Yet unaided by any, opposed by all, Christianity conquered the world. "We are but of yesterday," says Tertullian, "yet we have filled all that belongs to you, your cities, your islands, your fortresses, your free towns, your council chambers, your camps, tribes, decuries, the Palace, the very Senate; we leave to you your Temples only." ¶

To Christianity alone belongs the full conception of ἀγαπή, or *brotherly love*. In classical Greek the word *in that sense* does not exist, and "Charity" in the Christian sense has risen far above the narrow connotation of the Latin *caritas*. Humility, again, is a word which owes all its loveliness to Christianity; in Latin it is a term of contempt and means abjectness! The Greek word, ταπεινοφροσύνη, was regarded as a synonym of poor-spirited baseness. St. Peter, thinking how Christ girded himself with a towel, and washed the disciples' feet, bids Christians tie humble-mindedness round them with knots like a slave's apron.** *Humanitas* meant in Latin "human nature," or "refined culture;" in Christian language it means love to the whole brotherhood of man. Well may the author of the Epistle to Diognetus say, "What the soul is to the body, that Christianity is to the world."

Here, perhaps, I may be allowed to repeat words which I

* Acts v. 39.
‡ Tert. *Apol.* 38.
‖ Arnob. *c. Gentes* i. 28, 29, ii. 5, 58, 59.
** I Pet. v. 5.

† Aug. *De Civ. Dei.* ii. 20.
§ Minuc. Fel. *Oct.* 8, 12.
¶ Tert. *Apol.* 37.

have used before, and to say that the effects of the work of
Christ are, even to the unbeliever, indisputable and historical.
It expelled cruelty, it curbed passion, it branded suicide; it punished and suppressed an execrable, yet all but universal, infanticide; it drove the naked shamelessness of heathen impurities
into a congenial darkness. There was hardly a class whose
wrongs it did not remedy. It rescued the gladiator; it freed
the slave; it protected the captive; it nursed the sick; it shel-
tered the orphan; it elevated the woman, it shrouded as with a
halo of sacred innocence the tender years of the child. In every
region of life its ameliorating influence was felt. It changed
pity from "a vice of the mind" to a holy virtue. It elevated
poverty from a curse into a beatitude. It ennobled labour from
a vulgarity into a dignity and a duty. It sanctified marriage
from little more than a burdensome convention to little less than
a blessed sacrament. It revealed the angelic beauty of a purity
of which men had despaired, and of a meekness at which they
scoffed. It created the very conception of charity, and broad-
ened the limits of its obligation from the "slightly expanded
egotism" of the family to the broadest horizon of the race. It
evolved the Idea of Humanity as a common brotherhood, and
cleansed the life and elevated the soul of each individual man.
Mankind lay among the pots, and it clad them as it were with
the wings of a dove which is covered with silver wings and
her feathers like gold. Christianity inspired into its weakest
children a splendid heroism. "Call us *sarmenticii* and *semaxii*,"
exclaims Tertullian, "names derived from the wood wherewith
we are burned, and the stakes to which we are bound; this is
the garment of our victory, our embroidered robe, our triumphal
chariot." * "The nearer I am to the sword," said Ignatius,
"the nearer am I to God." † "We were condemned to the
wild beasts," said St. Perpetua, "and with hearts full of joy
returned to our prison." Whence came this rapture in the very
face of doom? It came from the constraining love of Christ.

At last, finding that they had to do with a host of Scævolas,
"the proudest of earthly powers, arrayed in the plenitude of

* Tert. *Apol.* 50. † Ignat. Ep. *ad Smyrn.*

material resources, humbled herself before a power founded on a mere sense of the Unseen." * The *Instans Tyrannus,* striving in vain to crush or undermine his humble opponents, was forced to exclaim—

> " When sudden—how think ye the end ?
> Did I say ' without friend ' ?
> Say rather from marge to the blue marge
> The whole heaven grew his targe,
> With the sun's self for visible boss,
> While an arm ran across
> Which the earth heaved beneath like a breast—
> When the wretch was safe pressed !
> Do you see ?   Just my vengence complete,
> The man sprang to his feet,
> Stood erect, caught at God's skirt, and prayed :—
> So I was afraid ! "

And having subdued and won the Empire, Christianity, by its nobleness and sympathy, subdued and won the wild horde of Northern barbarism.   Gibbon is a most unprejudiced witness, and he says, " The progress of Christianity has been marked by two glorious and decisive victories, over the learned and luxurious civilisation of the Roman Empire, and even the warlike barbarians of Scythia and Germany, who subverted the Empire and embraced the religion of the Romans." †   Attila the Hun was overawed by Pope Leo III. at Ponte Molino, and Genseric the Vandal at the gates of Rome.   Totila listened humbly to the rebukes and predictions of Benedict. The bishops of the Church won the title of *Defensores Civitatis,* and as Mr. J. S. Mill says, " treated with the conquerors in the name of the natives.   It was *their* adhesion which guaranteed the general obedience ; and after the conversion of the conquerors it was to their sacred character that the conquered were indebted for whatever mitigation they experienced of the fury of conquest." ‡   Thus did the Church preserve "the real property of the past amid the trembling destinies of the future." §   Christian

---

* Grammar of Assent, 472.   † Gibbon, iii. 258 (ed. Milman).
‡ *Dissertations.* ii. 263.
§ Ozanam, *Hist. of Civilisation in the Fifth Century*, i. 14 (comp. ii. 6).

missionaries converted and thereby civilised the world. Ulfila converted the Goths; St. Anskar the Scandinavians; St. Boniface the Germans; St. Patrick the Irish; St. Columba the Northern Britons; St. Aidan the Northumbrians; St. Remigius the Franks; St. Augustine, of Canterbury, the English. Two nations, England and Spain, owed their conversion to Gregory the Great. The heralds of the Cross went forth into every region conquering and to conquer. To prove how the tide of Christianity is ever advancing, it may suffice to say that if at the end of the third century the whole race of mankind had passed by in long procession, not more than one in one hundred and twenty would have been a Christian. Had they passed by fifty years ago, not more than one in five; but were they at this moment to pass one by one before our eyes, it is probable that one in three would have heard the name and accepted the faith of Christ. The Faith of Mankind has not been dimmed but rather brightened by the long progress of the centuries; and while we sing

> " Waft, waft, ye winds the story,
>   And you ye waters roll,
> Till like a sea of glory
>   It spreads from pole to pole :
> Till o'er our ransomed nature
>   The Lamb for sinners slain,
> Redeemer, King, Creator,"
>   Returns in bliss to reign,"

we may feel an ever-deepening confidence that now the time is not far distant when He who was lifted on the Cross will draw *all* men unto Him.

Perhaps the divinest gift of Christ to the Human Race has been that it has enabled every one of them—by the imitation of His example; by the gift of His grace; by the Holy Spirit; Who will make a temple of the mortal bodies of all who do not drive Him forth by self-chosen slavery to their own lowest desires and passions—to be true men, to be all that they may be and that God intended them to be.

Yes—and even if we accept the old sad Greek proverb that

"most men are bad "—let us not be blinded to the fact that Christ has immeasurably elevated the standard of human life in millions of individuals; that He has ameliorated the abjectness even of many who are bad; that he has bestowed on all alike the possibility of an infinitely blessed and ever-advancing holiness, and even to the fallen has extended the grace which extinguishes a fearful despair. The world is still infinitely far from perfect; but yet, to countless myriads more than in the Pagan world or the ancient Dispensation, God has granted the fulfilment of the promise, " Thou shalt tread upon the lion and the adder; the young lion and the dragon shalt thou trample under thy feet." The Christian Dispensation is, in comparison with all others which preceded it, "as sunlight to moonlight," and in spite of many causes for anxiety and discouragement, it still advances, and holds out to all human souls the means of ennoblement, the path of repentance, the hope full of immortality.

> " Askest thou in exultation
>   What the Cross of Christ has done ?
> Ask the splendours of creation
>   If they feel the noonday Sun ;
> Ask reviving vegetation,
>   Rushing forth on joyous wing,
> If it feels the inspiration
>   Of the breath-enchanting Spring."

Since Christ lived, and died, and rose again for us men and our salvation, no soul of man need lie in the dark depths of despair; and all of the multitude without number who love and fear His name, in every clime, may say to one another with humble exultation, " Beloved, now are we the sons of God, and it doth not yet appear what we shall be ; but we know that when He shall appear we shall be like Him, for we shall see Him as He is."

> " Haste then, and wheel away a shattered world,
>   Ye slow-revolving seasons ! We would see
> A world which does not dread or hate Christ's laws,
>   Where Violence shall never lift the sword,
>   Nor Cunning justify the proud man's wrong,
> Leaving the poor no remedy but tears ! "

" Terrena cœlestibus cedunt." * What Christ *has* done is a pledge of what He *will* do; and the fact that His name is now known and worshipped by at least one-third of all the Race of Man is a prophecy to us that ere long " the glory of the Lord shall cover the earth as the waters cover the sea." If there be not *this* hope for the human race, there is assuredly no other. And therefore we pray with all our hearts, " Oh, Lord, hasten Thy Kingdom! Put on Thy royal robes, oh, Prince of the Kings of all the world, for now Thy Church calleth Thee, and all nations sigh to be redeemed."

* Tert. *De Orat.* 2.

INDEX.

A

Abba Bar-Eshera, Rabbi, 273
Abiathar, Christ's reference to, 236
Abraham, Character of, 35
Akiba, Rabbi, 37–38
Alexandra, mother of Mariamne, 133
Ananeel, appointed High Priest, 150
Andrew, St., 317, 318, 319
Annas, the High Priest, 86, 368 ;
  Christ's trial before, 370–371
Aphorisms in Jewish literature, 216 ;
  Christ's use of, 216–218
Apocryphal Gospels, 52–53
Apollonius of Tyana, 30
Apostles, The, testimony of, to Christ's
  sinlessness, 58 ; their general char-
  acteristics, 314–317 ; division of
  into tetrads, 317–318 ; our ignorance
  of the majority of, 319–320 ; the
  secret of their mighty work, 320–
  322 ; Christ's commission to, 332–
  336 ; the power to forgive sins
  conferred on the disciples generally,
  and not only upon them, 334–336
Apostolic commission, The, see
  Apostles
Arnold, Matthew, Testimony of, to
  Christ, 43
Art, Witness of, to Christ, 8–9
Ascension, The, 412–414 ; manner or
  mode of, 413–414
Aspect, Christ's human, 121–122
Assonance, Christ's use of, in teaching, 220–221
Atonement, The, false and true views
  of, 396–400
Avoda Zara, The, and the Gentiles,
  259
" Avôth " and " Toldôth," 283, 286,
  287

B

Bacon, Francis, on Parables, 227
Baptism of Christ, 181

Baptist, John the, see John
Barabbas preferred to Jesus, 381
Bar-Cochba, overthrow of, 168
Bartholomew, St., 318, 320
Beatitudes, Christ's, 241
Bethany, 213, 352, 355
Bethany beyond Jordan, 200, 352
Bethsaida Julias, 132 ; site of, 205
Birth of Christ, 4–17 ; St. Matthew's
  narrative of the, 71
" Bread of Life, the," 63
Brethren of Christ, The, 71 ; who
  they were, 111 ; their relationship to
  Christ, 112–115 ; their opinion of
  Christ's mission, 116 ; character of,
  116–117
Brother, Christ the Elder, 254
Brotherhood of man, Christ and the,
  251–268
Buddha, The, and Buddhism, com-
  pared with Christ and Christianity,
  20–22

C

Cæsar, Julius, a friend of the Jews,
  135
Caiaphas, 368 ; the trial before, 371
Caligula, Golden statue of, 169
Cana, The miracle at, 117
Capernaum, Christ goes to, 201 ; site
  of, 205 ; description of, 206 ;
  Christ's home at, 213
Carpenter, Christ the, 92
Cato, Imperfections of, 29–30
Centurion, The Roman, a witness to
  Christ's sinlessness, 61
Ceremonial purifications of the Phari-
  sees, 274–277
Channing, Testimony of, to Christ, 43
Children, The teaching of, according
  to the Mosaic and Levitic Law, 75 ;
  Christ and, 266–268
Chorazin, site of, 204
Chosen One, The, a title of Christ,
  251

427

Christ, Supernatural birth of, 4–17; witness of history to, 6; great rulers as witnesses to, 6–7; poets as witnesses to, 7–8; philosophers as witnesses to, 8; witness of art to, 8–9; witness of science to, 9–10; witness to of men eminent for their goodness, 10–13; unique supremacy of, 18–40; sinlessness of, 19; superiority of to other founders of religions, 19–25; to ancient philosophers, 25–32; to patriarchs and saints, 34–39; testimony of sceptics and free enquirers to, 41–45; a Perfect Man, 54; testimony to the sinlessness of, 55–62; claims of, 63–69; human education of, 70–79; first Passover of, 80–91; unrecorded years of, 92–106; home of, at Nazareth, 107–109; a descendant of David, 110; brethren of, 111–116; mother of, 117–121; human aspect of, 121–122; lessons involved in His years of obscure labor, 123–125; not an Essene, 146; and the Herodians, 151; and the Pharisees, 154; baptised by John the Baptist, 181–183; temptation of, 186–199; scenes of His ministry, 200–209; His methods of teaching, 210–214; form of His teaching, 215–234; His illustrations drawn from familiar occurrences, 216; aphorisms of, 217; His use of " exceptionless principles," 218–219; His use of assonances and plays upon words, 220–221; poetry and parallelism of, 221–223; parables of, 224–234; the substance of His teaching, 235–240; uniqueness of His teaching, 241–250; His scorn of the idolatry of symbols, 242; essence of His teaching, 242–243; His parable of the prodigal son, 246–248; His summing up of the Ten Commandments in two, 248; the titles He gave Himself, 251–255; and the Samaritans, 256–258; and the Gentiles, 258–259; and the " common people," 259–261; and the publicans, 261–264; His attitude towards women and children, 264–267; His condemnation of Pharisaic religionism, 269–281; and the Sabbath, 282–292; and the " Scribes of the Pharisees," 289; and the Pharisees, 289–291; His miracles, 293–300; His gladness and sorrow, 301–313; His pity, 307–308; His wonder or surprise, 308; His grief and anger, 309; His indignation, 309; His self-restraint, 310; His groaning, 310; His tears, 311; His wailing, 311–313; and the Apostles, 314–315, 316; His mission to establish a kingdom, 333; order of events in His life, 337–354; length of His ministry, 337–340; beginning of His ministry, 341; its first period, 341–343; its second period, 343–348; its third period, 348–353; its fourth period, 353–354; His closing days, 355–359; at the Last Supper, 360–363; in Gethsemane, 364–365; His trial before Annas, 370–371; His trial before Caiaphas, 371–373; His trial before the Sanhedrin, 373–375; His trial before Pilate, 376–383; His scourging, 382; His sufferings, 384–389; how they should be regarded, 390–395; His Resurrection, 401–411; His Ascension, 412–414; His death the close of an age-long Dispensation, 416–417; His sinlessness our example, 419; the effects of His work, 420–425

Christianity, its history a history of victory, 416–419; its full conception of brotherly love, 420; its humility, ib.; its " humanity," 420; its effects, 420–425

" Church," term only once used by Christ, 333

Cicero on perfect wisdom, 27

Claims and promises of Christ, the, 63–69

Claudia Procula and Jesus, 60

Claudius expels the Jews from Rome, 135

" Clean and unclean," according to the Pharisees, 276–277

Closing days of Christ's life, The, 355–359

Condition of the world at the time of Christ's appearance, 125–143

Confucius and his religion, compared with Christ and Christianity, 22–23

Congreve, Dr., Testimony of, to Christ, 43

Cordus, Cremutius, Suicide of, 128

Covenant, Christ a son of the, 74

PASSAGES OF SCRIPTURE QUOTED OR REFERRED TO.

THE OLD TESTAMENT.

435

THE NEW TESTAMENT.